PREHISTORY AND PROTOHISTORY OF THE ARABIAN PENINSULA
VOLUME TWO

BAHRAIN

BY

DR. MUHAMMED ABDUL NAYEEM
DEPT. OF ARCHAEOLOGY & MUSEOLOGY,
KING SAUD UNIVERSITY, RIYADH

WITH A FOREWORD BY
PROF. DR. ABDUL RAHMAN T. AL-ANSARY
DEAN : COLLEGE OF ARTS & PROFESSOR
DEPARTMENT OF ARCHAEOLOGY & MUSEOLOGY,
KING SAUD UNIVERSITY, RIYADH

HYDERABAD PUBLISHERS, HYDERABAD (INDIA)
1992

TO MY BELOVED PARENTS IN MEMORIUM

Hyderabad Publishers, 10-2-5/8/1, A.C. Guards, Hyderabad - 500 004. (India)
Text Composed by M/s DISHA, 11-4-636/A, A.C. Guards, Hyderabad - 500 004. Ph : 228495.
Printed at : M/s PRAGATI ART PRINTERS, Hyderabad - 500 004. India.

ISBN : 81-85492-026

CONTENTS

V

FOREWORD

Dilmun emerged once more from the mist of oblivion to history in 1850, after a lapse of about three millenniums, when M.Leake first published an inscription discovered on the Cythera island mentioning Tilmun (Dilmun). J.Oppert, a French Orientalist identified Dilmun from a cuneiform text in January 1880. But the world attention was drawn only in April 1880 when Sir Henry Rawlinson identified it in his note appended to Captain Durand's report about the discovery of black stone in Bahrain with cuneiform inscription. Since then, more than a century, Dilmun has continuously occupied the mind of archaeologists as well as Assyriologists. Scholars have been trying to identify Dilmun, to trace its origin, to discover its culture and the important role it played in the international trade passing through the Arabian Gulf during the third-first millennium B.C.

The fame of the presence in Bahrain of several thousands of tumuli, unique in the world, attracted archaeologists from all over the world to explore this virgin field. Thus surveys, excavations, research and writing about Dilmun/Bahrain were undertaken from time to time by the archaeologists from nearly a dozen countries of the world: Australia, Denmark, England, France, India, Japan, Jordan, Pakistan, U.S.A. and Bahrain.

Captain E.L. Durand's visit in 1878 to Bahrain to survey the antiquities was the first step in Bahrain's archaeology. His report is not only the first document but one of the most important about Bahrain's archaeology. To this report Sir Henry Rawlinson appended a note analysing the cuneiform inscription which Durand had discovered at Bahrain. Durand's discovery of immense number of tumuli on Bahrain attracted several others to visit Bahrain. Mr. & Mrs.Theodare Bent (1890) and M.A. Jouannin (1903) came in search of antiquities. Subsequently, Captain F.B.Prideaux (1906-1908), E.Mackay (1925) and P.B.Cornwall (1940) excavated several tumuli in Bahrain. By this time Bahrain acquired reputation in the scientific circles as "International Burial Ground". However, there was another group of archaeologist who did not believe in Bahrain as a sepulchral island. Thus to investigate and find traces of settlements on Bahrain the Prehistoric Museum in Aarhus (Denmark) despatched in 1953-54 a team of archaeologist led by P.V.Glob and T.G.Bibby. The Danish team's excavations in Bahrain made startling discoveries. Their brief reports published in *Kuml* (1954-70) and Bibby's popular book *Looking for Dilmun* revolutionised Bahrain's prehistory in particular and the Arabian Gulf in general. This created great interest among archaeologists and teams from several countries undertook excavations. They were joined by the local Bahraini teams. Several sites through the length and breath of the tiny island were the centre of excavations. Bahrain's Antiquities Department also undertook excavations. Abdul Kader al Takriti worked on several sites during 1970's followed by Shaikha Haya al Khalifa in 1980's. Currently excavations are being conducted under the Direction of Dr.Khadhim Rajab. The foreign teams comprised: Michael Rice (1970-71); McNicoll and Michael Roaf (1973-75); Moawiyah Ibrahim (1977-79); Monik Kervran *etal* (1977-79); Petocz and Hart (1980); Serge Cleuziou etal (1980); Philip J. Habgood (1982); M.A. Konishi etal, (1987-88), Pierre Lombard etal (1989-92); H.E.H.Crawford, Robert Killick and Jane Moon etal (1990-92). Excavations by the two teams, last mentioned, are still in progress.

Some of the excavation reports are published by Bahrain's Directorate of Archaeology and Museums, Ministry of Information; and a few are published in periodicals. However most of the reports are regretably unpublished. As such, much important data about ancient Bahrain and its civilization is still in dark and unknown to the scholarly world, thus leaving a cultural hiatus.

The need for a comprehensive archaeological book on Bahrain with overall perspective and combining the investigation and researches carried out during the past century by scores of persons has long been realised. An attempt in this direction was taken by the Ministry of Information, Government of Bahrain by holding a Bahrain Historical Conference in 1983 and subsequently publishing its proceedings; *Bahrain through the Ages-the Archaeology* (edited by Shaikha Haya Ali al Khalifa and Michael Rice) in 1986. It comprises lectures delivered by 46 eminent scholars at the conference on different aspects.

In the present volume Dr.Abdul Nayeem has succeeded skillfully in bringing together under one cover both the published and unpublished data and has creditably presented a cohesive and most comprehensive up-to-date account of Bahrain, substantiated by scores of illustrations (unpublished and published). Indeed it is a great achievement by Dr.Abdul Nayeem to handle various aspects single handed which exhibits his versatile scholarship. An exemplary effort by all means which should not only be appreciated but must be encouraged in the better interest of Arabian archaeology.

In the twelve chapters of the book, Dr.Abdul Nayeem covers a vast span of time from the Early Pleistocene to the Later Holocene (upto 400 B.C.) and includes all the aspects relevent to most ancient Bahrain and the Dilmun civilization. Dilmun and Dilmun in Bahrain in chapter two discusses various cuneiform texts in order to trace the origin, identification and territorial extent of Dilmun. After discussing several Sumerian myths about Dilmun being holy, pure, paradise etc., he asserts that Sumerian myths may be attested.

The chronological chart with detailed list of principal archaeological sites are useful for reference. As in the preceeding volume in this series, here also Dr.Abdul Nayeem provides for the first time an Atlas of stone-age tools with scores of illustrations running into 30 pages. It seems that the entire stone-age material (except a few exhibits) was lying in the stores of the Bahrain National Museum and Dr.Abdul Nayeem gets the credit of bringing to light unknown material for the first time. From the Atlas it appears that he has taken great pains to trace and study the material and give it a proper shape. The Atlas which elucidates and illustrates the evolution of stone-age cultures of Bahrain is not only the essence of the book but in itself a major contribution.

Likewise every chapter of the book not only synthesizes archaeological and historical data, both new and existing, but brings to light new material and provides most interesting and useful reading. The study of seals is yet another important contribution. Hitherto Dilmun seals were known by different nomenclature. In this book he has given a new classification and new interpretation to the study of Dilmun seals which were discovered not only in Bahrain but abroad also. Incidently, I may mention that during the excavations (conducted under my direction) at the site of al-Fau, in Saudi Arabia, a steatite Dilmun seal was discovered from a prehistoric tomb during the thirteen season (1988). On the obverse it has a tall naked hero standing in the centre flanked by antelopes, two on either side. The figure of the man is schematic. On the reverse the high botton boss has four dotted circles, two on either side of the three grooves. It is preserved in the Museum of the Department of Archaeology, College of Arts, King Saud University, Riyadh.

Based on several cuneiform inscriptions and archaeological evidences, the chapters on Religion and the people, the Dilmunites, are once again very interesting with sound critical discussions. Of the inscriptions cited, one of them is about Inzak and Agarum. In this regard, I may mention that though Agarum has been identified as Hajar / al - Hofuf of later period, I would suggest that Agarum was one of the tribes of eastern Arabia. Likewise, Lakhanum also seems to be a tribe and probably Lakhmids of later times orignated from it.

On the whole the book provides immense volume of information with many rare photographs hitherto unpublished and introduces new dimensions in the prehistory and archaeology of Bahrain. It is a most welcome addition to our knowledge, not only of Bahrain but of entire Arabian Gulf and eastern Saudi Arabia. It is designed equally for the specialist as well as a general reader. It is a must for those interested in Arabian archaeology. The second volume shows alround improvement over the first volume in research, writing, illustrations and quality of printing.

Dr. ABDUL RAHMAN T.AL-ANSARY

Dean: College of Arts, King Saud University and

Professor of Pre-Islamic History and Archaeology of Arabia,

Department of Archaeology & Museology, Riyadh

PREFACE

The original plan to publish volume two in this series covering all the Gulf states had been modified on the advice of some authorities of the Gulf states. During my visits to Gulf states the concerned officials of the Antiquities Departments and some at the ministry expressed their desire that I should write and publish separate volumes relating to the individual states-Bahrain, Kuwait, Qatar, United Arab Emirates, and Oman. In compliance to this request and in view of large volume of archaeological material now available as a result of extensive excavations being carried out in the Gulf countries, it was considered prudent to re-plan the series and enlarge the text and material. I am glad to present this volume on Bahrain, the second in the series of the prehistory and protohistory of the Arabian peninsula and the first among the Gulf states. Other Gulf states will be covered in the future volumes, hopefully if God willing.

I hope I have succeeded, to the best of my ability, in my objective to bring together in a single volume the outstanding archaeological discoveries made in Bahrain for more than a century. It is an attempt, based upon findings of archaeology, to trace the early foundations and evolution of human culture from the Pleistocene times when man settled in Bahrain and ending around 400 B.C. In doing so, I have tried to integrate in a brief coherent synthesis, all the material available, both published and unpublished. Owing to the book's nature, I had to depend entirely upon the work of scores of persons. I crave the indulgence of the learned authors, listed in the acknowledgements and bibliography, for making free use of their material, textual as well as illustrative. To them I am highly indebted. The topics discussed in a dozen chapters are detailed in the table of contents and it is redundent to repeat them here.

I am grateful and beholden to Professor Dr. ABDUL RAHMAN T. AL ANSARY for his help, guidance and encouragement. He was always kind, pleasing and ever obliging with his most exemplary manners. Without Dr. al Ansary's help it would have been well neigh impossible for me to under-take this project. Further, he was kind enough to grace this volume with his Foreward and erudite comments and to introduce it to the learned readers.

I fervently hope that the readers would find this work useful and interesting.

Muhammed Abdul Nayeem

ACKNOWLEDGEMENTS

My largest debt is to *Shaikha Nayla A. al Khalifa*, Director of Museums and Heritage, State of Bahrain, for very kindly providing me numerous photographs of the antiquities and sites, and permitting me to photograph the exhibits of the Bahrain National Museum (Manama); allowing me to study and photograph the stone-age tools preserved in the stores of the Museum at al-Maharaqa; and above all graciously permitting me to publish all the material. Without Shaikha Nayla's kind gesture not only this book but Bahrain's ancient history would have remained incomplete. She was ever obliging and kind during my numerous visits to Bahrain. I am deeply obliged to her.

I am a greateful to *Mr. Khalil Al Thawdi*, under Secretary for Tourism and Archaeology, State of Bahrain for his kind permission which enabled me to work at the Bahrain National Museum and take photographs. p73

Greateful thanks are due to *Dr. Kadhim E. Rajab*, Director, Directorate of Tourism and Archaeology, State of Bahrain, for very kindly arranging my visits to archaeological sites and for allowing me to take photographs. I have benefitted much from his discussions.

Mr. Ahmed A.Al-Sheroogi, Director, Media and Public Relations, Ministry of Information, helped me in several ways during my visit to Bahrain.

I am thankful to *Shaikha Haya Ali Al Khalifa*, former Director of Archaeology and Museum, and later on Under Secretary, for her kind help and very useful discussions about Bahrain's archaeology.

Mr. Khalid al Sindi, Curator, Bahrain National Museum was of great help in locating the relevent photographs required by me and for so kindly providing them. He was immensely helpful to me during my several visits to the National Museum and was instrumental in tracing the stone-age tools lying in the stores. But for his help I would not have been able to complete the Atlas and Bahrain's stone-age culture would have remained in dark. He also provided me information about the provenance of several seals.

At the Department of Archaeology and Museology, College of Arts, King Saud University (Riyadh), I am thankful to the following persons for their kind help in various capacities: *Dr. Ahmed 'Umar Zalaiy* (Chairman of the Department); and *Dr. Sa'ad Abdul Aziz al Rashid*. With *Dr. Yousuf Mukhtar El Amin* and *Dr. Asem Naif al Bourgouti* I had very useful discussions and I have benefited much from their learned advice. Others who helped are: *Dr. Abdul Karim Gamdhi, Mr. Ibrahim Nasir al Ibrehi, Mr.Fowad Amair, Mr.Jamal Sa'ad 'Umar, El-Saddig Satti Hamad, Mr.Abdel Rahim M. Khabir*, and *Mr.Abd El Rahim Haj El Amin.*

I express my grateful thanks to *Dr.Harriet E. Crawford, Dr. Robert Killick* and *Dr. Jane Moon*, Directors of London-Bahrain Archaeological Expedition 1990-92, for very kindly providing me with unpublished field reports of excavations at Sar settlement; for allowing me to visit the site and take photographs and for providing some photos.

I am highly obliged to *Dr. Essa Amin*, President of the Bahrain Historical and Archaeological Society for kindly allowing me to use the library as a member of the Society and to take photocopies of important reports. At Society's library Mr.Venu was of much help to me.

To my friend *Mr.Ali Akbar Bushiri* of Bahrain for so kindly taking me round to the archaeological sites several times, during my visits to Bahrain and for very useful discussions about Bahrain's archaeology and the problem involved. He was kind enough to place at my disposal his specialised library. I am grateful to him for his cooperation and hospitality.

Mr.Abdul Rahman al Musameh, Museologist of the Bahrain National Museum was kind and very helpful to me during my visits to the Museum. I am thankful to him for his guidence.

Thanks are due to *Mr. Abdul Aziz Sowailah*, Superintendent of Bahrain's Antiquities Department for taking me round to the sites and allowing me to take photos.

I am very much thankful to the following archaeologists and authors for useful information/discussions/personal communications/sending their published or unpublised material: Dr. Flemming Hojlund, Dr. Michael Roaf, Dr. Pierre Lombard, Dr. Jesper Eidem, Dr. Jean-Francois Salles, Dr. Yves Calvet, Dr. Howard-Carter, Dr. Michael Rice, Dr. Joan Oates, Dr. David Oates, Dr. Gherardo Gnoli, Dr. Ernie Haerinck, Dr. Philip J. Hobgood, Dr. Judith Littleton. I Owe a debt of gratitude to Dr. Loraine Copeland for useful suggestions and discussions on the controvertial aspects of Stone Age tools of the Gulf states.

I am grateful to *Dr. Muhammed A. Zulfa*, Vice-Dean College of Arts, King Saud University for helping me.

I am highly obliged to Professor *V.N. Misra*, Director of the Deccan College, Pune (India) and *Dr. K. Paddayya* of the Deccan college for their kind help, cooperation and useful information during my visit to their post-Graduate and Research Institute, pune.

Mr. Salah Turkey, Map production Expert, Department of Geography, King Saud University (Riyadh) kindly made some of the maps in this volume.

Thanks are due to *M/S. Lillian Cloud*, public relations, the Bahrain Petroleum Company, Bahrain for the supply of important literature.

Thanks are due to *Ms. Shafiqa* at the Directorate of Tourism and Archaeology, Bharain.

At Hyderabad I am thankful to *Dr.Taj Ahmed Khan* and *Mr. Minhaj Ahmed Khan*. Also at Hyderabad, I am thankful to the following for facilitating printing and publication: *Mr. Satyam*, (M/S Satyam Process); *Mr. P. Narendra Rao* and *Mr.M.G. Neelakanteshwara Rao.* (of M/S Pragathi Art Printers), *Mrs. and Mr. Manoj K Saraogi* (of M/S. Disha Graphics).

The script was typed and retyped on Computer by *Mr.Mohd Ziauddin Nawaz Khan* at Riyadh and *Mr. Ganesh* (of M/S Disha Graphics) at Hyderabad. I appreciate their diligence and patience.

Lastly, I owe a debt of gratitude to my wife *Dr. Fouzia Nayeem*, three sons *Dr. K.M.A. Nadeem, Dr.M.A. Vaseem, M.A. Muqeem*, and my daughter-in-law *Dr.Seema Nadeem*, who have borne with me patiently the stress and strain in the research, writing and printing of this book and during my several visits to the Gulf States. The last mentioned, *Dr. Seema* patiently and intilengently corrected the proofs late in the nights when free from her infant son M.A. Naseer.

Muhammed Abdul Nayeem

XI

CREDITS FOR ILLUSTRATIONS

I wish to express my thanks to the authorities of the following Museums for the illustrations: Bahrain National Museum (Courtesy: Shaikh Nayla al Khalifa); Department of Western Asiatic Antiquities, the British Museum, London (Courtesy, Trustees of the British Museum); Forhistorisk Museum, Moesgard, Denmark (Courtesy: Dr. Flemming Hojlund and Dr. Karen Friefelt); and Babylonian Collection, Sterling Memorial Library, Yale University, New Haven (Courtesy: Dr.Ulla Kasten).

Thanks are due to the following persons for their kind permission to reproduce illustrations from their learned publications and or unpublished field reports: Dr. Harriet E.Crawford; Dr. Robert Killick; Dr. Jane Moon; Dr. Poul Kjaerum; Dr. Peder Mortensen; Dr. Jesper Eidem Dr. Karen Frifelt; Dr. Julian E. Reade; Dr. Betrice de Cardi; Dr. Pierre Amiet; Dr. Pierre Lombard; Dr. Jean Francois Salles; Dr.John C. Doornkamp; Dr. Geogry L. Possehl; Dr. Curtis P. Larsen; Dr. C.Vita-Finzi; Dr. Elizabeth During Caspers; Dr. R. Englund; Dr. Juris Zarins; Dr. C.E. Larsen; Dr Anthony Lowe; and Mr. De John Lawrence.

Thanks are due to the following institutions for the permission to reproduce from their publications: Jysk Arkaeologisk Selskab (Jutland Archaeological Society, (Denmark); The University of Chicago Press, Chicago, American School of Oriental Research, N. Caroline, Journal of Cuneiform Studies; Middle East Digest (MEED), London Immel publishing London, for the reproduction of two seals (one on the Jacket cover and Fig.33a in Chapter VI), from Peter Vine: Immel's New Guide to Bahrain (1988).

Illustrations have been also reproduced from the following publications:
1. Geoffey T. Bibby *Looking for Dilmun* (1969/1974).
2. Michael Rice (ed.): *The Temple Complex at Barbar, Bahrain* (1983).
3. Michael Rice (ed.): *Dilmun Discovered* (1983).
4. Shaikh Haya Ali al Khalifa & Michael Rice (ed.): *Bahrain Through the Ages - the Archaeology.* (1986).
5. Shaikha Nayla Al Khalifa: *Bahrain National Museum Guide.* (1992).
6. Daniel T. Potts (ed.): *Dilmun-New Studies in the Archaeology And Early History of Bahrain* (1983).
7. *KUML.* Annual of the Jutland Archaeological Society. (1954-1970).
8. Pierre Lombard & Monik Kervran: *Bahrain National Museum* - Archaeological Collections Vol.I. (A selection of Pre-Islamic Antiquities) (1989).
9. *Antiquities of Bahrain* (Bahrain Historical and Archaeological Society). (n.d).
10. Peter Vine: *Immel's New Guide to Bahrain.*
11. Jacquetta Hawkins: *Atlas of Archaeology*
12. Abdul Aziz Sowailah: *Bahrain Archaeological & Tourist Attraction Guide* (n.d.).
13. Moawiyah Ibrahim: *Excavations of the Arab Expedition at Sar el-Jisr Bahrain* (1982).
14. Rafique Mughal: *The Dilmun Burial Complex at Sar* (1983).
15. M.A. Konishi, T.Gotoh and Y. Akashi: *Excavations in Bahrain and Qatar.* (1989).
16. K.M. Srivastava: *Madinat Hamad Burial Mounds* (1991).
17. *Sumer.*
18. *Proceedings of the Seminar for Arabian Studies.*

Muhammed Abdul Nayeem

LIST OF FIGURES, MAPS AND TABLES

TABLES

CHAPTER I

THE PHYSICAL ENVIRONMENT

The physical environment of Bahrain island (partly DILMUN of ancient times - see Chapter II *infra* for its origin, identification, etc.) played most important strategic role during the prehistoric times in linking Arabia and Bahrain with the east and the west and in evolving a culture and civilization of its own. The environment also influenced greatly the existence and daily life of the prehistoric and protohistoric people of Bahrain. Hence for the proper understanding of the prehistory of Bahrain, knowledge of its geographical and geological features is essential. The Bahrain islands acquired the present form after a very long time passing through several Geological Eras; and each Era having left its own characteristic features. Bahrain became island about 6000-7000 years ago when it was set apart from the eastern Arabian mainland. (Kassler, 1973; Doornkamp et al., 1980). Thus, environment is an integral part of Bahrain's archaeology. Hence, it is deemed necessary to give here a brief outline of the geography, geology and palaeo-climate of Bahrain. Elaborate and complete details of these aspects are beyond the scope of this book.

(A)   GEOGRAPHY

The group of islands (Map 1) known as the Bahrain (Arabic dual form of *Bahr*, i.e., two seas), lies along the western coast of the Arabian Gulf, approximately latitude 26°N., longitude 50° 30'E., about mid-way, in a large bay cutting deeply into the land, in the Gulf of Salwa which separates the promontory of Qatar from the coast of eastern Saudi Arabia.

Geographically, Bahrain is located in the core of an extensive zone of aridity which extends from the Sahara north-eastwards across Arabia and Afghanistan to the Gobi Desert. In the north, across the Arabian Gulf, lie the Zagros Mountains and the extensive area of continental sedimentation, including that of Great Nafud, Dahna and Rub al Khali deserts of Arabia. (Doornkamp et al., 1980:1). It consists of an archipelago of 33 small low-lying islands (Map 1). Of these, seven principal islands are Bahrain, the largest about 48.3 kilometers (27 miles) long and about 16.1 kilometres (10 miles) wide, al Muharraq, Umm Na'san, Sitrah, Nabi Salih, Jidda, and Hawar islands. The greater part of Bahrain island is flat and low, but the surface rises gradually from all sides towards the centre to form a plateau about 100-200 feet high. In the middle of the plateau is an oval-shaped depression, about 13 miles long from the north to the south and by 4 miles from east to the west, containing in its centre the solitary hill of Jebel Dukhan ('the mountain of mist') which is 400 feet high, the highest point on the island. The descent inwards from the plateau to the depression is at many places too steep. While the northern end is nearly a vertical drop of 20 feet followed by a steep slope of 30 feet. The plateau is stony and of low cliffs, about 15 feet high, to the north. Below it is a sandy plain extending in all directions to the coast and draining from the west to the east. Jebel Dukhan is of a dark hue. However, the rocks are of light yellow or light pink, indeed almost white in colour. The rest of the island is of coral formation.

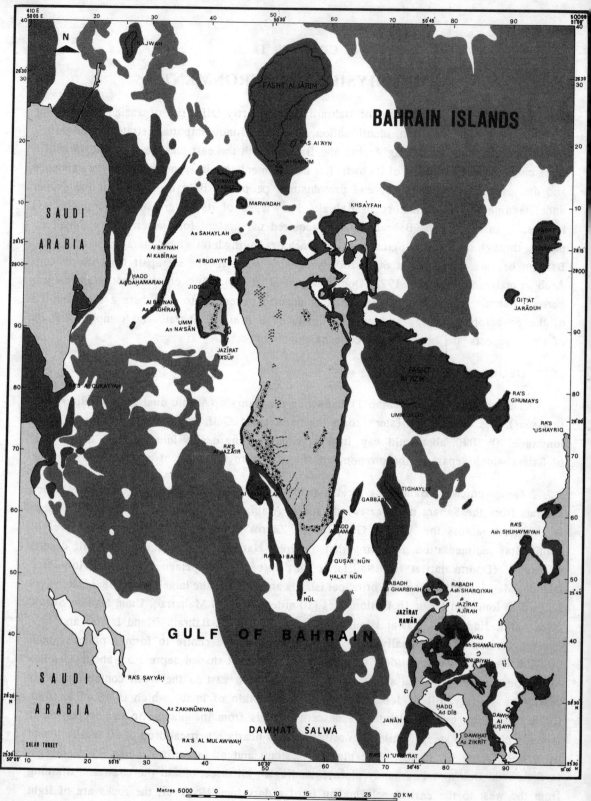

BAHRAIN ISLANDS

NAJWAH

FASHT AL JÄRIM

RA'S AL 'AYN

AL QADÜM

KHAWR
FASHT

MARWADAH

KHSA'YFAH

As SAHAYLAH

FASHT
AZ ZUBR

AL BAYNAH
AL KABÏRAH

AL BUDAYY

SAUDI
ARABIA

HADD
Ad DAHAMARAH

JIDD

QIT'AT
JARÄDUH

AL BAYNAH
As SAGHÏRAH

UMM
An NA'SÄN

JAZÏRAT
YÄSÜF

FASHT
AL 'AZM

RA'S AL QURAYYAH

RA'S
GHUMAYS

UMM JALID

RA'S
'USHAYRIQ

RA'S
AL JAZÄ'IR

TIGHAYLIB

GABBÄR

RA'S
Ash SHUHAYMIYAH

AL UMM LÄH

HADD
Ad DAMM

RA'S AL BARR

QUSAR NÜN

HALAT NÜN

RABADH
Al GHARBIYAH

RABADH
Ash SHARQIYAH

AL HÜL

JAZÏRAT
AJÏRAH

JAZÏRAT
HAWÄR

WÄD
Ash SHAMÄLIYAH

ANUBIYAH

GULF OF BAHRAIN

SAUDI

ARABIA

RA'S SAYYÄH

Az ZAKHNÜNIYAH

JANÄN

HADD
Ad DÏB

DAWHAT
AI HUSAYN

DAWHAT
Az ZIKRÏT

DAWHAT SALWÄ

SALAH TURKEY

RA'S AL MULAWWAH

RA'S AL 'UWAYRAT

Metres 5000   0   5   10   15   20   25   30 KM

Fig. 1 Map of Bahrain Islands

CORAL

SEA DEPTH LAYER
0 — 10 M.
10 — 20 M.
20 — 50 M.

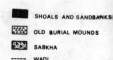

SHOALS AND SANDBANKS

OLD BURIAL MOUNDS

SABKHA

WADI

Around Jebel Dukhan is a depression started by low cliffs. The second island in point of size is Muharraq, north of Bahrain, and separated from it by a strait one mile broad, it is of horse shoe form, seldom more than half a mile broad, and is about five miles in length and one mile wide. These two islands enfold two harbours. The remaining islands are rocky. The most striking feature of the Bahrain group of islands is the lowness and levelness of the land and the shallowness of the sea surrounding it. The whole Gulf of Bahrain from Ras Raqan to Ras Tanurah, a distance of 73 miles is a mass of reefs and shoals, except, for one channel running north and south off the eastern coast of Muharraq island. The shallowness of the sea between Bahrain and the Arabian mainland has contributed much to the geographical and mercantile importance of the Bahrain during the prehistoric and proto-historic times. (Bent, 1889; Lorimer, 1908:212,234; Willis, 1967:E1).

The remaining principal islands are Sitrah four miles long, Nabih Salih, north of Sitrah, famous for its prolific fresh water, Jidda, a small rocky islet off the west coast of Bahrain, Umm Na'san, a large low-lying island to the south-west of Jidda, and Hawar group of 16 islands, a few miles south of Bahrain. The largest of this group is 11 miles long and a mile wide. (Belgrave; 1975:14).

The geomorphological sculpturing of the main domal structure has resulted in a topographic pattern characteristic of unroofed upfolds. The relatively simple pattern of concentric geological outcrops is reflected in the topographic form. The latter is dominated by infacing escarpments. The relief of Bahrain island is only 122.4 metres and more than half of the surface is below 20 metres, and is composed mainly of low angle slopes. Doornkamp et al (1980 :45) identify five major physiographic regions, which occur as concentric units of variable width. These regions, shown in the map 2 are; the central plateau and jebels, interior basin, multiple escarpment zone, upper Dammam back-slope, and coastal lowlands.

The central plateau or the Ar-Rumanum plateau has upstanding residual hills and has developed almost entirely on resistant rocks which occur in the centre of the island and in the core of the denuded dome. Number of steepsided and flat topped residual hills or jebels surmount the general surface level at about 40-60 m. The jebels rise upto 122.4 m. at Jebel Dukhan, and to its north the plateau surface is most complete. A characteristic feature is that the extensive areas of exposed indurated bedrock have been sculptured and polished by sand blasting. The interior basin is the asymmetrical ring of lowland surrounding the central plateau and it varies in width from 2 km. in the west to 8 km. in the south. Its surface elevation declines outwards from the centre from 70m. to 20 m. The surface form of this region is very variable and includes wind-faceted bedrock surfaces near the central plateau, gypcrusted erosion surfaces, marginal sedimentary basins and playa basins. A number of outward inclined surfaces, small escarpments and residual hills are the characteristic form of this region. The largest playa which occupies the south-east sector of the interior basin and contains dissected remnants of playa deposits including evaporites, is the most interesting and important feature of its kind on the island. The multiple escarpment zone surrounds and overlooks the Interior Basin and it is almost a continuous belt of low multiple infacing escarpments. Most of the beds are scarp formers, and shows considerable variation, ranging from a single bold escarpment to multiple steps and benches forming a belt up to half-kilometer wide. A small, nearly circular, totally enclosed depression occurs in the north-western sector of this zone and this feature, called the north-west playa Basin is rimmed by multiple escarpments. The main (upper Dammam) black slope is an extensive, gently inclined surface declining away from the crest of the uppermost escarpment. Its topographic slope cuts across the bedding so that higher and younger beds in the stratigraphic sequence and encountered as the coast is approached. This is indicator of erosional feature in origin and not dipslope. Thus it is suitable to term it 'backslope'. Bahrain's landforms are greatly influenced by the structure. Firstly, the gross form of the backslope area, being broad and gently sloping in the north (5km) and south (7km) but rather narrower in the last (1.5-2.5 km) and very narrow (1 km) in the west. This reflects the general asymmetrical shape of the main Bahrain dome. Secondly, the simplicity of this pattern is somewhat modified by the impact of secondary structures. The region presents a rather monotonous landscape, the only local relief being provided by shallowly incised valleys created by the drainage lines which are active during heavy storms. The episodic courses end at the foot of the backslope in small playa-like areas, as at 'Ali, or get lost in the sands, in the west. The northern part of the Bahrain islands consists of subdued landforms with elevations of less than 10m. above mean sea level. The northern coast, where signs of erosion are apparent, has a thin spread of dune sand and beach material overlying either quaternary beach rock or tertiary limestone. Many of these areas have been levelled and used for cultivation. Scattered outcrops of almost horizontal limestones occupy a small proportion of the total area of the northern Bahrain. Areas of sand dunes are prevalent in the north-west of Bahrain. Land with a very low elevation extends inland and a feature of this low-lying land is the development of gypsum soil with ground water levels only 60-70 cms below the surface. Sand frequently occurs as a soil parent material and this is significant for agriculture because of its free drainage and low salt water. Large areas of northern plain are composed of unconsolidated sandy clay loams. On the south-west coast accumulations of beach ridge deposits have gradually grown, forming extensive areas of low-lying sabkha adjacent to the coast and remarkable elongated pits. Both the south-west and southern sabkhas grow southwards as the beach ridge complexes of sand and numerous shells comprising the greatest proportion of the beach material. (Doornkamp et al., 1980 : 2-20)

(B)   GEOLOGY

Bahrain is situated in the Arabian Gulf which is a basin of Late Pliocene to Pleistocene age with tectonically-influenced morphology. The relief is more subdued on the Arabian side because of lesser disturbance and folding, faulting and salt diapirim are superimposed upon mainly meridional "Arabian faults" (Bowen and Jux, 1987:221).

The principal outcropping rocks of Bahrain are of early and middle Eocene age, with

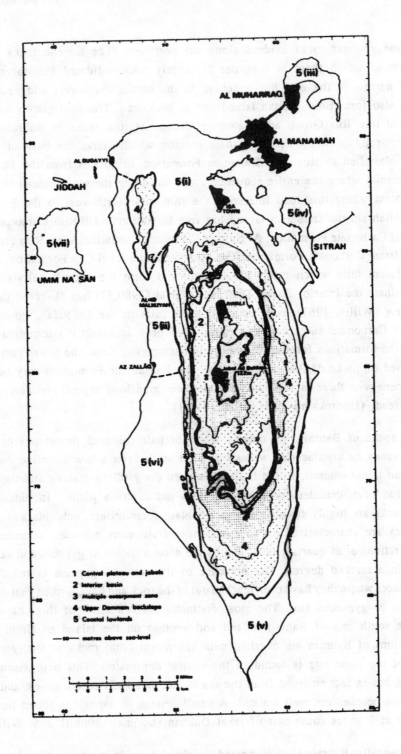

Fig.2   Relief and Physiographical sub-divisions of Bahrain.
(After J.C.Doornkamp etal., 1980, courtesy : Geo Abstracts Ltd. U.K.)

Miocene and younger rocks evident along the periphery. The Eocene rocks form an oval outcrop around which there is a border of largely unconsolidated Pleistocene and recent sediments, narrow in the east but widening in the north, south-west and south. The latter two series also form Umm Na'san island and al Muharraq. The stratigraphy of Eocene may be classified into Rus Group and Dammam Group. All the rocks in Bahrain that outcrop in the Interior Basin below the first shale horizon which marks the base of the Dammam Group are classified as Rus. The Dammam Formation, originates from the Dammam Dome in Saudi Arabia, where the entire sequence crops out along the old Dhahran to Al'Alah road from the point where this road intersects the rhin rock north-west to the Eocene-Miocene contact. In Bahrain the Dammam Group has five formations : Dil'Rifa Carbonate Formation, Forminiferal Carbonate Formation, Al Buhayr Carbonate Formation, West Rifa Flint Formation, and Jebel Hisan' Carbonate Formation. The Miocene is the jebel Cap Formation. Jebel Dukhan and its adjacent hills which reach 122.4 metre and form the highest parts of the Bahrain island, dominate the Interior Basin. Doornkamp et al (1980:37) has observed that the earlier accounts (e.g. Willis, 1967) have assigned these hills to the Dil'Rifah, Foraminiferal and Al Buhayr Carbonate and that these rocks have been incorrectly interpreted as erosional outliers of the formations forming the Multiple Escarpment Zone. the lower part of the jebels are composed of rocks of Awali Formation. The Ras al'Aqr Formation may be assigned to the Pleistocene with three facies, caprock limestone, mudflood deposit and calcisiltites, which are widespread. (Doornkamp et al, 1980: 21-41).

The rocks of Bahrain are chiefly white or pale-coloured limestones of eocene age, sometimes sandy or argillaceous, and so diposed as to form a low anticline dome of which jebel Dukhan is the summit. In the hollow between the girdling plateau and the central peak the rock has been denuded by marine agency and forms a plain. In places the eocene limestone rocks are highly fossiliferous and contain foraminifera, echinids and mollusca. As a whole they are characterised by an abundance of siliceous material, occuring as flint, as cherty concretions or as quarts geods, and by the dissemination of gypsum and salt throughout the series in a marked degree. The presence of the salt and gypsum is most conspicuous in certain places where they have been leached out of the rock and have formed vast accumulations of saliferous or gypseous soil. The most distinctly marked areas of this character are one towards the south end of Bahrain island and another on the island of Umm Na'san. The coastal portions of Bahrain are overlaid with sub-recent coral rocks or shelly concrete, and sandstone of the same age is found in the central depression. This depression, as well as littoral flats, has in fact emerged from the sea in comparatively recent times, and the remains of the old sea-beaches are well marked. A small deposit of asphalt is found penetrating the ocene rocks of 3 miles south-east of jebel Dukhan (Lorimer, 1908:II 235; Willis, 1967:E).

Geologically, Bahrain is an elongated anticlinal dome in structure, of sedimentary rocks-which was created by the folding and uplift of Tertiary Age limestones and shales but with a central erosional depression. Geology of Bahrain is shown in Map 3, which indicates the approximate shoreline of the last interglacial, the lowlands around the coast, escarpment around

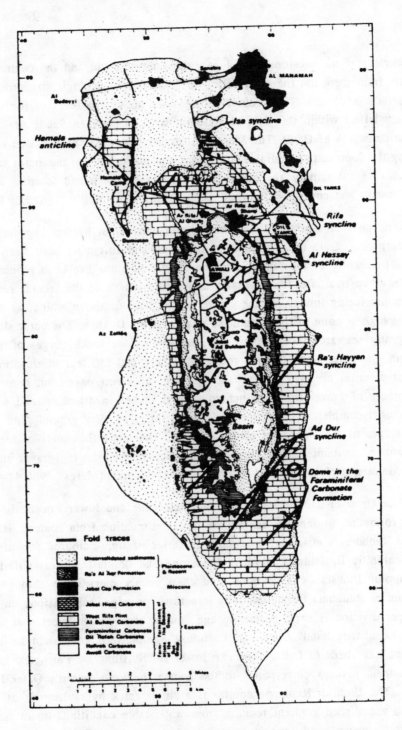

Fig.3   Generalised Geological outcrop and some of the structures.
(After J.C.Doornkamp etal., 1980, courtesy : Goe Abstracts Ltd., U.K.).

the central region, limestone backslopes, the interior basin and the central mountains. The geologic framework has the sedimentary rock formations geologic structure, water resources, and surface landforms. The geologic dome rises above the level of the Arabian Gulf and forms an island within the Gulf of Bahrain, situated between Saudi Arabia's eastern coast and the peninsula of Qatar. The Map 4 illustrates east-west cross-section through the island showing the dominant structural relationships and the attitude of the major sedimentary strata. Sediments of quarternary age cover the periphery of the island forming a relatively broad coastal plain, and cover the floor of the interior basin (Willis, 1967:E3; Larsen, 1983b:3).

The physical setting of most of Bahrain consists of barren, unpromising desert land. The alternating strata of hard Eocene limestone and soft marl have been downed upward towards the centre of the island, and the middle portions has been reduced by erosion so as to leave an oval, flat-floored basin almost the length of the island, surrounded by step escarpments facing inward. In the centre is the plateau, above which, as mentioned above, rises the highest point of the island, the peak of jebel Dukhan. The outer slopes of the dome slope gently seaward, except where cut into steep-sided rocky gorges of Wadi torrents. In the north, the outer slope forms a rocky table land 100-150 feet in elevation. The principal surfacial material on most of the island is reg, or desert pavement, consisting of angular small pieces of gravel from an inch to several inches in diameter, and so closely spaced as to almost completely cover the underlying sandy or silty ground. The reg covers most of the slopes of the dome and central plateau. The many thousands of the prehistoric and protohistoric tumuli of Bahrain were made by scraping up the reg gravel into mounds. Sand is the common surface material of the peripheral zone. (Meigs, 1966:44-46).

The Umm er-Radhuma formation of Paleocene and lower Eocene is the oldest near-surface formation present in Bahrain. It is a continuation from eastern Saudi Arabia. The Umm er-Radhuma consists of a repetitious series of light-coloured foraminiferal aphanitic and calcarenitic limestone, dolmitric limestone and dolomite. Local silicification of thin, benchcapping limestones is common, and chert occurs sporadically throughout the section. The Umm er Radhuma Formation falls into three principal subdivisions on faunal grounds. The upper division is early eocene in age and it carries such species as Sakesaria cotteri Davies, Lockhartia humti Ovez var, Pustulosa Smout. It is equivalent to lower Eocene of Qatar and Lake beds of India. The two lower subdivisions are Paleocene in age, the break between them perhaps corresponds to the contact between Smout's Qatar Paleocene zones 4 and 5. The Umm er Radhuma aquifer is a single thick hydraulic unit of regional extent. It has an established gradient ranging from water-table conditions on or near the out-crop to flowing artesian conditions in Bahrain and the Arabian Gulf. Water from the Umm er Radhuma ranges in quality from excellent at or near the outcrop to poor. The quality of water and the cast-dipping hydraulic gradient is influenced by the local structural features in the coast areas. A decrease in permeability on the flanks of the features tends to divert regional flow and to restrict flushing by fresher meteoric water. (Powers et al, 1966: D 84-87)

Likewise the Rus Formation of the Dammam dome, eastern Saudi Arabia extends into Bahrain. The rocks of the Rus outcrop are light-coloured soft, chalky limestone and marl, while the rocks of the Dammam Formation are characteristically light-coloured limestone, marl and shale. Rus Formation is underlain and overlain by the rocks of proven early Eocene age. As a dominantly evaporite sequence, the Rus has few porous beds. Limestones at the base and top of the interval are porous and probably water bearing. Some shows of low-gravity oil have been found in offshore wells. The Dammam Formation base is at the contact of Calcerenite or limestone of the Rus Formation with the overlying brown shale and light-gray marl of the basal Dammam. The Dammam Formation is divisible into five members, two of which possess distinctive and laterally persistent basal marl units. These members are — Alat (limestone, marl), Khobar (dolomite, marl), Alveolina limestone, Saila Shale, and Midra Shale. The uppermost Alat member found in Bahrain is generally known as Alat limestone, and the marl. The top of the Alat is light-coloured, chalky above. Two carbonate members of the Dammam Formation — the Khobar and Alat - are acquifers, in Bahrain. As in pre-Dammam acquifers, both hydraulic and salinity gradients are evident. Artesian conditions occur near the outcrop band. Khobar water is used extensively in communities and agricultural area of Saudi Arabia's eastern region and in Bahrain. (Powers et al., 1960 D87-93). In Bahrain, the Rus Formation is the oldest which outcrops, is located in the central part of the flat anticlinal island and reaches a total thickness of 65m. Made up of chalky and cherty dolomitic limestones, it includes anhydroite beds and quartz geodes of which some contain petroleum. The Rus Formation as an acquifer, yields a limited amount of fresh water derived from rainfall, this floating on top of the usually saline water of the Formation to comprise a cap upto 4.5 m thick. Further Bahrain is characterized by the Karstic hydrology developed as a result of the Pleistogene invasions or the retreats of the sea (Bowen and Jux, 1987 : 208, 220).

The Arabian Peninsula is divided into two structural provinces, the Arabian Shield and the Arabian Shelf. The latter is divided into several subprovinces - an Interior Homocline everywhere marginal to the Shield, an Interior Platform bordering the Homocline, and several basins, adjacent to the platform, that have collected thicker sedimentary deposits (Chapman, 1978:13). The nearly fault structural Interior Platform is sharply set off from the homocline by an abrupt break in slope — a hinge line between the two structural provinces. The opposite edge of the platform is less well defined, trending south-east from Kuwait into Arabian Gulf, Bahrain, far out around Qatar and reaching east as far as the coast of Iran and passing inland. The deep structure of the sedimentary rocks of the platform indicate that the beds are unusally flat in a geological sense and irregularities are limited to low, gentle structural undulations that lack any strong orientation. The north-south trending anticline are the examples of folds and the folds of Abqaiq and Qatif extend into Bahrain. The origin of the major anticlines is still obscure; but it seems that they are related to some sort of horst like uplift at great depth. This hypothesis is supported by the gravity data. However, the Dammam dome and the Bahraini dome departs completely from some expression of north-south trend or

10

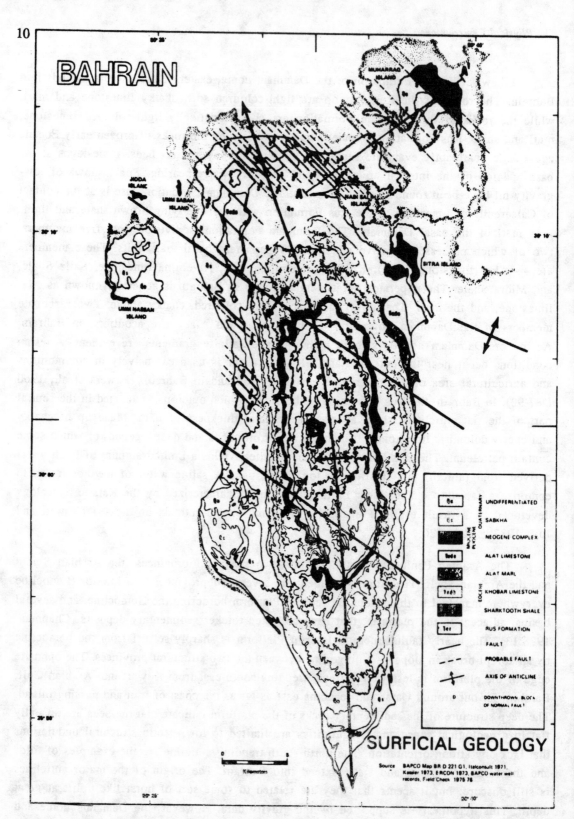

BAHRAIN

SURFICIAL GEOLOGY

Qu	QUATERNARY	UNDIFFERENTIATED
Qs		SABKHA
	MIOCENE PLIOCENE	NEOGENE COMPLEX
Teda		ALAT LIMESTONE
		ALAT MARL
Tedb	EOCENE	KHOBAR LIMESTONE
		SHARKTOOTH SHALE
Ter		RUS FORMATION
		FAULT
		PROBABLE FAULT
		AXIS OF ANTICLINE
D		DOWNTHROWN BLOCK OF NORMAL FAULT

Source BAPCO Map BR D 221 G1, Italconsult 1971,
Kessler 1973, ERCON 1973, BAPCO water well
records, Field Check 1975 76

Fig.4   Surficial Geology of Bahrain.
(After C.E.Larsen, 1983, Courtesy : The University of Chicago, USA)

elongation. This is because of complex crestal faulting, strong negative gravity anomaly and oval shape. (Powers et al, 1966:D105, Chapman, 1978:14). While the Arabian Gulf which is a tectonic basin of late Pliocene to Pleistocene age, its morphology is greatly influenced by the tectonic style, observes, Kassler (1973:11f). The much more subdued relief of the Arabian side of the Gulf, where Bahrain is situated, is the result of gentler tectonic movements; Plio-Pleistocene folding, faulting and salt diapirism, super imposed on older, predominantly north-south trending growth structures (Arabian folds). The area between Qatar and Jabrin Ridge is a transverse shoal between two syncline areas and seems to reflect uplift along the northward prolongation of the Qatar anticlinal axis. Sparker reflections from probable Miocene levels in the Gulf of Salwa, west of Qatar, suggest folding on axes oblique to the marked north-south trend of nearby growth structures at Dukhan and Awali in Bahrain. The whole Salwa-Bahrain-Qatar area is a structural complex of north-south Arabian trend structures deformed slightly by north-west and south-east crossfolds of the Zagros trend. The quarternary uplift along these trends is strongly suspected of having had some Pliocene folding. The "shell" sparker profiles of the eastern Gulf of Salwa or the Gulf of Bahrain provide evidence of a fault and fracture system affecting Miocene and possible Pliocene rocks. The trend is north-west to north-north west, as in the case of major portion of Saudi Arabia's eastern coastline, which may itself be partly controlled by faulting. (Kassler, 1973:11-19).

The mouth of the Gulf of Bahrain is marked by a series of small anticlines and synclines superimposed on a larger broad anticline referred to as the Bahrain ridge. This is shown in Map 3 along with other geological feature of Quaternary, Miocene-Pliocene and Eocene. (Larsen, 1983a:122).

The photogeological study of drainage pattern of Qatar suggests that they are partly radial around a number of low domes. The southernmost dome corresponds to a residual negative gravity anamoly is perhaps a salt feature. While the northern group lies on the trend of the Bahrain/Pearl Bank Ridges and is probably related to Zagros trend cross-folding, and salt movements might have had some influence. The subsidence of the Gulf of Salwa west of Qatar is a Quaternary feature. (Kassler, 1975, 21).

SEA LEVEL VARIATIONS

Based on the report of G.R. Varney, Kassler (1973:21) suggests that the Bahrain Ridge has been rising in the last few thousand years. Partial confirmation of this suggestion comes from the recognition within the Gulf of Salwa of Holocene marine platforms at -5 fm, and -10 fm. With the present configuration of the Bahrain Ridge, the rising Holocene sea could not have entered the Gulf of Salwa before it reached -4 fm. (about 6000 years ago). The platform at -10 fm. would be about 8000 years old. However, he suggests still earlier marine conditions by the recent dating of an eolitic sand from there at 11000 ± 400 years old. The Bahrain ridge is a young structural uplift. But the Holocene blockage of the Gulf of Salwa

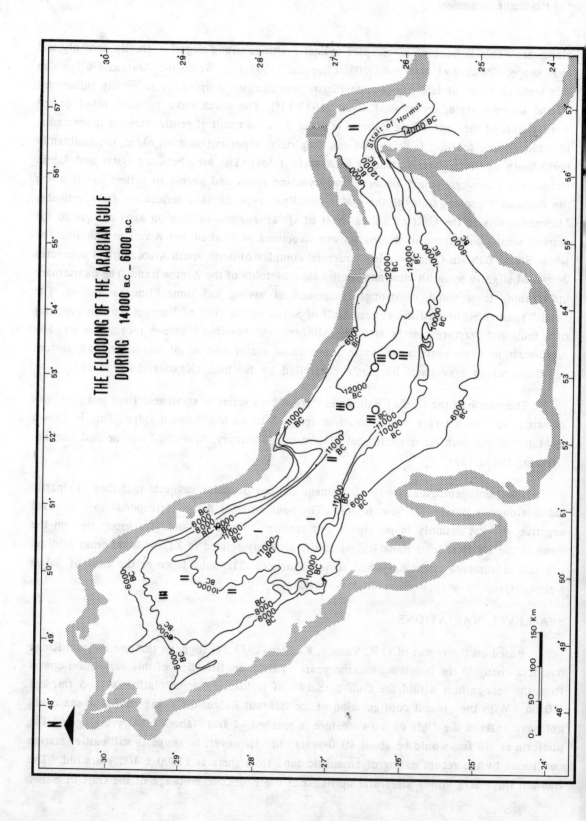

THE FLOODING OF THE ARABIAN GULF
DURING 14000 B.C. – 6000 B.C.

might have been completed partially by the uplift and partially by the sedimentation. The Bahrain Ridge is the area of active coral reef growth. (Kassler, 1973 : 11-23).

The sea level of Bahrain between 125,000 and 80,000 years B.P., that is, during the period of the last interglacial, was perhaps about 4 to 5 metre higher than the present level. The anticline tructure of Eocene limestones which constituted the central region of the Bahrain's mainland alone emerged from the sea. While the coastal plain around the central region was submerged except the Sar-Hamalah rocky highland. Beach sediments were found at the foot of a former subdued cliff. During the last glacial regression the continental erosion truncated the conglomerates. The bottom of a wadi between Awali and Zallaq reveals Eocene limestones. While sandy deposits, horizontally bedded and several centimetres thick have been found at Malakiyah. Marine sediments have been found around Dumistan. Around Mamlahat al Mamtalah, cross bedded conglomerates have been found. Several field evidence are in support of the idea that a former shoreline of Bahrain was located at about + 5 metre in the western plain, dating to the last interglacial period. It is further suggested that similar higher level by one or more older quaternary transgressions. (Sanlaville and Paskoff, 1986 : 15f). Radio carbon datings and field studies reveal that the sea-level in Bahrain at the end of post-glacial transgression approached thc present position and reached +2 metres. At Karranah, west of Qal'at al Bahrain, there are evidence of a post-glacial sea level 0.80 to 1 metre higher than the present one. But absolute dates cannot be ascertained. (Sanlavilee and Paskoff, 1986, Doornkamp et al, 1980).

During late Pleistocene from 18,000 to 13,000 B.C. (Oxygen isotope storage 2) the climate throughout the south west Asia was cool and arid. The mean annual temperature dropped about 6o°C. below the Holocene maximum (West, 1977 : 240; Butzer, 1975 : 402).

The maximum of cold of the Ice Age Wurm lasted from about 14000 to 13000 B.C. Consequent to enormous extension of the glacial regions on the Earth so much water was withdrawn from the sea that at time sea level fell about 110 metres below the present. Since the Arabian Gulf, says Nutzel (1975:101f), has no depths exceeding 10 metres, the present Gulf region must have been a dry depression during the Wurm period. Due to postglacial melting process the sea level began to rise again until it attained its present level in the fifth millennium B.C., and then the Gulf subsequently reached its present form. The investigations conducted in 1964-65 by the German research ship "Meteor" confirm that the Arabian Gulf had been arid about 14000 B.C. and the Pleistocene estuary of the ancient Euphrates - Tigris river emptied directly into the Gulf of Oman. During the Last Ice Age the length of the river had increased about 800 kilometres to the south-east. It reached the shelf edge in the Gulf of Oman which today lies 100 metres below sea level. Here, the river apparently formed on elongated estuary. Then the melting process began and therewith the rise of the sea level began. Consequently, the Gulf advanced at the rate of 100 metres a year, perhaps by jerks. This corresponds to a displacement of the shoreline of about 500 km. in four to five thousand years. The sea level variations are quite visible owing to the

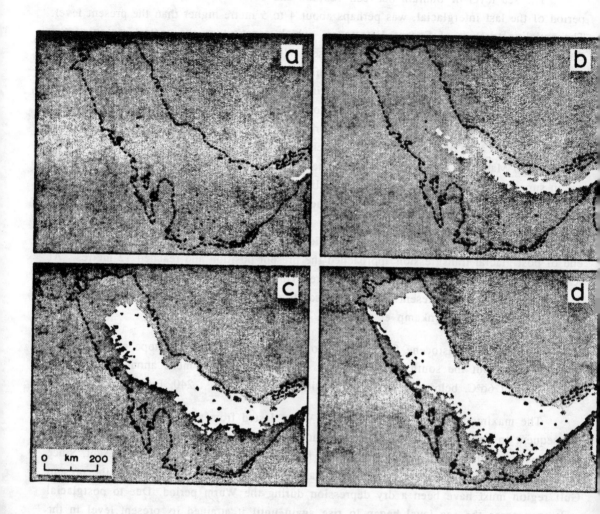

Fig.6 Approximate position of coastline in the Gulf.
       (a) 15,000 B.P. (b) 12,000 B.P. (c) 10,000 B.P. and (d) 8,000 B.P.
       (After C.Vita Finzi, 1978. Courtesy Oxford University Press, U.K.).

minimal and almost constant slope of the Gulf. The postglacial rise of the sea level was interrupted by several transgressions stagnatious as such it was not uniform or continuous. This stagnation was the result of world-wide rush of temporary cold which in turn slowed the melting process. Consequently, shore lines were formed during the period of stagnation, which number three at an average depth of 62, 50 and 30 metres below the present sea level. Map 5 shows the flooding process of the Arabian Gulf on the basis of the positions of the shorelines at the time of the transgression stagnations. (Nutzel, 1975:101-104).

The approximate positions of coastline in the Arabian Gulf during 15,000 to 8,000 years ago is indicated in Map 6. It seems that between about 70,000 and 44,000 years ago, the floor of the Arabian Gulf was dry land. (Vita-Finzi, 1978:23). The development of coastal plain of Bahrain has resulted largely from the submergence of a desert landscape in the late Holocene followed by a subsequent emergence. Evidence from the western and southern coasts of Bahrain indicates that the Holocene transgression led to the advance of the sea over a cover of a aeolian sands onto the Lower flanks of the backslope. This resulted in the development of a cerithid-rich beach complex. Although erosion has removed much of this feature, part of the well-developed beach deposit has been found overlying truncated dune sands at Ras Hayyan at levels of 4-5 metres ADD (dated as 6,940-6,330 B.P.). Further, remnants of a similar but undated deposit with heights of between 4-5 metres have been found at the southern sabkha. The rather bewildering morphology of the south-west sabkha is the result of the drawing of the irregular sand dune topography, which flanked the western backslope of Bahrain, by the rising of seas of the Holocene transgression. Drowning of the desert landscape in the latter part of the Holocene isolated Bahrain from the Arabian peninsula and prevented the continued transportation of aeolian sand to the area from Arabia. This inundation resulted in the planation of earlier dune sands which surrounded the rocky core of the island and also of earlier Quaternary limestones. Evidence of this transgression has been found to prevent day heights of approximately +5 metres above Admiralty Datum (about 2-3m, average high water mark) at the following places: Al Aqr, Sitrah, Ras Hayyun, south of Ra's Hayyan, south-west Sabkha, Az Zallaq, Qal'tal Bugayshi, al Qurayyah, and Jamirah. The sea appears to have been at the higher height, mentioned above, at about 6,300-7,000 years B.P. During this period almost the whole of the coastal plain was submerged and the contemporary shoreline lay along the foot of the backslope. Surrounding the rocky core of the island. Then there followed a relative fall of about 2.5-3 metres in about 6,500 years, in the level of the sea to that of the present. This might have been due to a reporching of the Bahrain area. Possibly there was a fall of the sea below the present level after the relatively high level recorded at Ras Hayyan and elsewhere, and this was followed by a re-submergence. This fall led to the re-emergence of much of its extent, with a layer of cerithid-rich calcareous quartzose sand. (Doornkamp et al, 1980: 315-327). The coastline variations in Bahrain are shown in Fig. 8 along with archaeological chronology (after, Larsen and Sanlaville, 1986).

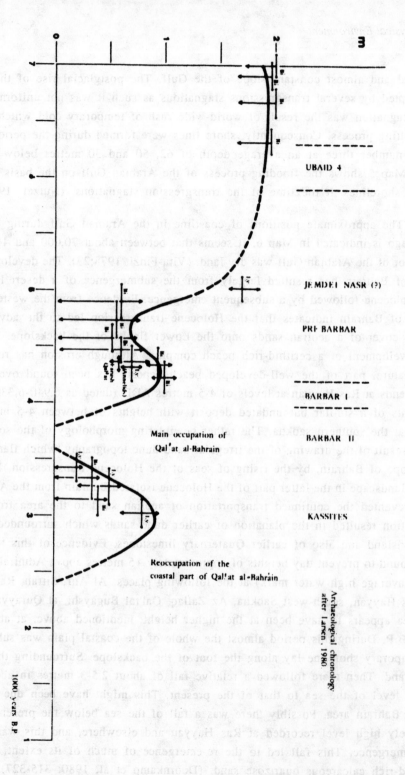

Fig.8 Archaeological Chronology and variations of the coastline in Bahrain between 7,000 and 2,000 years B.P. (After P.Sanlaville and R.Panskoff, 1986).

Radio carbon dating has revealed that in Bahrain the shoreline ran approximately 2m. higher between 7,000 and 5,000 years B.P., than the present one. San Laville and Paskoff (1983:17-24) conclude that the sea level of Bahrain was higher by about 2m. during 7000-5000 B.P.) then it fell and during this period the Ubaid sites of southwest sabkha were inhabited, then around 4,300 B.P. it was about +1 m and the shoreline was offshore when compared to the present position, then during the second half of the second millennium B.C., the sea level rose and between 3,430 and 3,030 B.C. it reached +1 m. The sea level variation had an important impact on harbour activities of trade and land cultivation in the coastal plain through water table variations.

ARCHAEOLOGICAL EVIDENCE OF SEA LEVEL VARIATIONS

Archaeological evidence corroborate geological evidence of sea level variations. The Palaeolithic and Neolithic sites discovered by the Danes are all inland from the present day coast, apparently along the 10m. Contour line or thereabouts. Glob (454:114) mentions that one of the flint sites, his No. 27, lies on an ancient coast line. This particular site produced Palaeolithic as well as Neolithic flint tools. As such, we may conclude that the shore line may have been as much as 10m. higher than the present day beach during the Stone Age.

Bibby's excavations (1969) at Qal'at al-Bahrain revealed that, in layer 29, at 1.5-1.9 metre above present average sea level, there were cemented marine sands, called farush-limestone conglomerate and it dated back to 2,400-2,300 B.P. These marine sands says Sanlaville and Paskoff (1986:19) are evidence of a beach which is contemporaneous with human occupation of the site of Qal'at al-Bahrain. Marine sands are found upto +0.60 metre above the present average level of the tides. These marine sands are evidence of a beach which was contemporary with the Qal'at al-Bahrain. (Sanlaville and Paskoff, 1986:19). That site of al-Markh was at one time higher than the present level is also deduced from the fact that large quantities of flint were found on the surface and in the top sand, contrasting with the generally small numbers of flints in the stratified deposits. The surface and tops and flints apparently represent the indestructable residue deposited in and on the uppermost surviving stratum from higher deposits which have been stripped off the site by the wind. The maximum height of the site during the period of its occupation, fourth millennium B.C., by the stone age people has been roughly estimated by McNicoll on the basis of the flint count from the top sand and stratified deposits and it works out for square K19 to approximately 0.80m. Assuming that the deposition of flints took place at a reasonably constant rate, the ratio of last deposits to surviving deposits works out to be in the order 12:5, that is, a depth of 1.92m. Thus the total depth of the occupation by the Stone Age people at square K19 was rather more than 2,.70 m while the depth of occupation at the square G17 was 1.20m. (McNicoll, 4, Ms.), Sketch of the environs of al Markh with possible coastline in 3,800 B.C. is shown in Map 7, after Roaf (1976:148). It seems that around 3,800 B.C. the site of al Markh was a small island of the west coast of the main island of Bahrain. at a later date the channel between these islands silted forming a sabkha and making a single island. As the sea level rose at the end of the last ice age, the sand-dunes were drowned and around 4000 B.C. only a small island remained (Roaf , 1976:158 f). Archeaological excavations at al Markh have revealed that since during the last Ice Age the sea-level was more than 100 m. below the present level, Bahrain was connected to the Arabian main land until 6000 B.C. As such any settlement on Bahrain before it was an island must have been on the sea shore. (Roaf, 1976:159).

The Bahrain islands are famous for remarkable set of springs, beautifully clear and but slightly brackish, some of which are submarine. In the northern part of Bahrain, north of Khor-al-Khob, the springs are warm, copious and nearly fresh and, the best known in that district are those of 'Adari, Qassari, and Abu Zaidan. The most worthy springs in the sea are that of Abu Mahur close to Muharraq and the Kaukab on Fasht Khor Fasht. The best water in the islands is from the Hanaini wells, at the north end of the central depression of Bahrain, and form the Khalid and Umm Ghuwaifah wells on the plateau adjoining. The springs of Bahrain, like those of Hofuf and Qatif oasis (in Saudi Arabia) are fed by the drainage of part of Najd (Saudi Arabia). (Lorimer, 1908, II 235 f). Bahrain's water supply is furnished from three deep acquifiers, known collectively as the Eocene Acquifier system. These acquifiers are: the Umm er-Radhuma, Alat and Khobar. (Larsen, 1985:12).

Finally, we may conclude that there were quaternary changes in sea level of Bahrain in two phases, firstly, prior to c 100,000 years B.P., and secondly during post c. 100,000 B.P. During the first phase, the area underlying the Gulf of Salwa subsided along north-west-south-east oriented faults and, the sea level appears to have fallen to approximately to its present level so that the Palaeogene core of Bahrain island would have become increasingly subjected to subaerial sculpturing processes. Subsequently, during the second phase, the sea level is considered to have been generally low and oscillating due to the dominance of glacio-eustatic controls, and to have fallen to a minimum level of about 120 metres by 20,000 B.P. This phase of low-sea level had a significant impact on the evolution of the relief of Bahrain for the surrounding sea-floors of the Gulf of Salwa and the Hasa Terrace were exposed to subaerial processes, until resubmerged in about 7,000 B.P. by the later stages of the Flandrian transgression. During this time (100,000 - 7,000 B.P.) Bahrain became part of the Arabian mainland, a low dome rising above the desert plain with drainage lines radiating southward to the low internal basins of the present Gulf of Salwa, and northward via structurally controlled incising channels towards the extended Tigris - Euphrates some 200 km away to the north. Between 20,000 B.P. and 7,000 B.P. sea level rose rapidly in the Gulf due to the post-glacial eustatic Flandrian transgression. This transgression eventually led to the flooding of the Hassa Terrace by about 7,000 B.P., so that Bahrain once again became island. This event had great geomorphological significance as it resulted in the creation of a suitable environment for colonization as part of the Dilmun by 5,000 B.P. the highest point reached by this transgression on Bahrain island is evident from the cliff lines, beach deposits and shell ridges standing at +4.5m to +5.0m. The most important result of the low phases of sea level which lasted from about 100,000 - 6,5000 B.P. and may well have occurred earlier in the Pleistocene, was the passage of sands across the emergent sea flow from Arabia to Bahrain and Qatar. (Doornkamp et al, 1980:411-420).

(C)   PALAEO-CLIMATE

Bahrain shares the general climatic characteristics of the Arabian mainland, littoral. As such, the palaeo-climatic conditions during quaternary period in Bahrain were almost the same as that of the Arabian Peninsula. (See Volume I in this series). Moisture climate is implied during the period, as in Arabia lake-beds and spring-deposits seems to show that one or more moist spells occurred in Mid-Holocene times. (Butzer, 1978:10).

Bahrain is more humid than the Arabian mainland littoral. From May to October the temperature usually rises above 90°F during the day and from June to September even the lowest temperature at night is usually above 80°F. Relative humidity in summer remains high even during the hottest time of the day, averaging 69 percent in the evening and 67 percent early morning. The high termperatures and humidity of summer are accompanied by almost cloudless skies, and the total absence of rainfall. The average rainfall is not sufficient to support dense perennial vegetation.

The palaeo-climatic conditions in Saudi Arabia and Bahrain has been summarized chrono-logically as follows, based on Larsen (1983a : 169f), Nutzel (1975:101-108), and Butzer (1978:11).

27,000 - 15,000 B.C. - A major moist interval prevailed over in South Arabia and Bahrain playa lakes' growth was pronounced with grasslands.

15,000 - 13,000 B.C. - Around this period Bahrain and the whole Arabian Gulf was an arid depression due to the maximum cold of the Wurm.

13,00 - 68,00 B.C. - End of the moist phase marked by dessication and eolian deposits. Minor lake development at the western edge of Rub al-Kahli is indicative of subdued moisture peak during 13,000 - 9,500 B.C. This was followed by renewed aridity.

6,800 - 4,000 B.C. - Moisture phase resulted in the growth of lakes in Bahrain and in Arabia. With a flooding rate up to 120 metres annually, Bahrain and the Gulf obtained its present form in the fifth millennium B.C.

4,000 - 3,000 B.C. - Moisture phase was interrupted by the aridity around 4000 B.C. Because of the climatic optimum (postglacial Wurm age) which took place around 3500 B.C. With the annual temperature of 2-3 degrees above today's Bahrain Gulf level was raised above its present level. Lakes became choked with eolian silts. However, lake levels again rose around 3000 B.C.

3,000 - 2,000 B.C. - Lakes surpassed the level of the preceding peak; resulting in the occupation of lake shone by the villages dating from Early Dynastic period to Dilmun I phases of the third millennium B.C. But with the dessication at the end of the third millennium B.C., the lakes fell.

1500 - 800 B.C. - Development of paleosols on eolian sand and subdue moisture peak behind the dunes. Subsequently the palesols buried by the eolian sands.

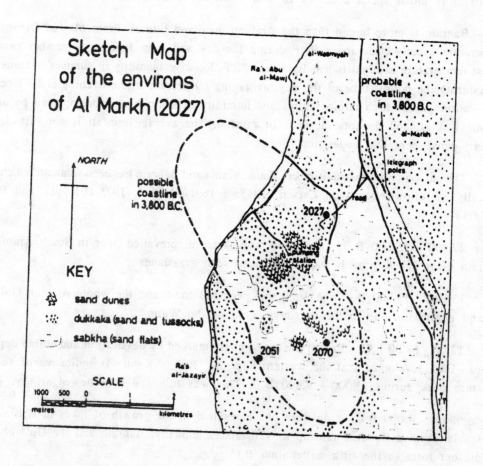

Fig.7   Environs of al Markh - possible coastline in, 3,800 B.C.
(After M.Roaf, 1976).

CHAPTER II

CONSTITUENT ELEMENTS

(A)   DILMUN AND DILMUN IN BAHRAIN

(1)   ORIGIN, IDENTIFICATION AND TERRITORIAL EXTENT

During the prehistoric and protohistoric times Bahrain was not famous or called by the same name. It was known by different names during different periods. One of them was Dilmun. The origin of Dilmun has been discussed briefly in Volume I of this series (pp 160-162) alongwith a map (p. 163) showing Dilmun's territorial extent within the Arabian Peninsula. However, in order to render this account of Bahrain's prehistory and protohistory intelligible, a detailed reassessment of cuneiform texts of Mesopotamia and Ebla is made here alongwith different opinions of the contemporary authors on this controversial topic.

The word Dilmun or Tilmun is mentioned in several categories of cuneiform texts throughout the long history of Sumer, Akkad, Babylonia and Assyria. The word came to light in 1850 A.D. with the publication in France of the first inscription found at Botta, Khorsabad, in Mesopotamia relating to the Assyrian King Sargon (724 - 705 B.C.). Thus Dilmun re-entered history (Bibby, 1969:41 f). The inscription mentions the places which Sargon conquered - "all of Chaldea, as much as there was; Bit-Iakin on the shore of the Bitter Sea as far as the border of Dilmun; - all of these I brought under my sway, over them I set my officers and governors, the yoke of my sovereignty I placed upon them." (Luckenbill, 1968 : 26). This is also attested by a clay tablet with an outline map of the world and a text relating to the conquests of Sargon of Akkad, including Dilmun, illustrated in Fig. 1.

In 1861 Sir Henry Rawlinson published in London volumes on cuneiform tablets from the British Museum collection, in a series entitled "The Cuneiform Inscriptions of the Western Asia". Dilmun has been mentioned in two tablets in each of the second, third and fourth volumes of the series. One of the tablet mentioned simply a list of gods, with the regions under their protection appended. In the list occurred the line : "The God Enzak; the God Nabu of Dilmun." Another tablet described the career of King Sargon of Akkad, and states that he reached the "Lower Sea", which is the Arabian Gulf, and conquered Dilmun. It may be mentioned here that the Sumerians and Babylonians used commonly three expressions the Lower Sea, the Bitter Sea, or the Sea of the Rising Sun, to describe the Arabian Gulf (Bibby, 1969:41-43:78). Subsequently, many references to Dilmun, its land, holiness, its kings, its commerce, items of trade, its religious pantheon etc., have been discovered in the records. The earliest reference comes from the corpus of archaic Uruk texts of Lexical tests and economic documents dated <u>ca.</u> 3200-3000 B.C. Euglund (1983:35f) illustrates the unusual development of Dilmun sign upto the Late Early Dynasty and is reproduced here.

Fig.1   A Cuneiform Clay Tablet mentioning Dilmun with an outline map of the
world relating to the conquests of Sargon of Akkad, including Dilmun.
(Courtesy : Trustees of the British Museum)

Uruk IV

Uruk III

Archaic Ur

Fara

Abu Salabikh

Ebla

Fig.2   Development of the Dilmun sign—upto late Early Dynasty Period.
(After R.Euglund, 1983).

Dilmun is attested in the Jamdat Nasr texts dated to c. 3000 B.C. (Potts, 1983:15). Dilmun as toponym is mentioned in the economic and Lexical texts of Fara and Kish texts of personal names, dated to 2600 B.C. (Potts, 1983:18:1990:87). Dilmun boats are mentioned in the inscriptions of Urnashe of Lagash which are dated to c. 2500 B.C. (Alster, 1983:50). Alongwith Magan and Meluhha, Sargon of Akkad mentions Dilmun, dated to 2500 B.C. (Alster, 1983:50). The Lugalanda and Honkagina inscriptions dated to c. 2400 B.C. mention mountain of Dilmun. (Cornwall, 1944,16;Potts:1983:18). The legend of Sargon dated to 2360 B.C. mentions Dilmun. Telmun appears in the Sumerian-Akkadian vocabularies. There occurs u-ur-si-ib as pronunciation of URU+ (HA) meaning Telmun. This recurs with the graphic variant URD+UD. The series malku-saru (I 219) has GUG.GI.RIN.NA = Tel-mun identifying this famous red stone, of which Gudea speaks repeatedly, as imported from Meluhha with the island. The latter inscription is dated 2200 B.C.   (Oppenheim, 1954:6f). Assyrian King Tukulti-Urta I's inscription commemorating the founding of the suburb of Assur called Kar-Tukulti-Urta dated c. 1250 B.C. mention "King of Dilmun and Meluhha" implying probably that Tukulti-Urta I is King of these places. (Luckenbill, 1975: I, 59).

The Khorsabad texts of Assyrian rulers has numerous references to Dilmun and its

King. These are cited here. Inscriptions pertaining to the period of Sargon (724-705 B.C.) numbering 13 are as follows :

(1)   "— Uperi, King of Dilmun, who lives (Lit. whose camp is situated), like a fish, 30 beru ("double-hours") away in the midst of the sea of the rising sun, heard of my lordly might and brought his gifts". (Luckenbill, 1968: I,21).

(2)   "— the subjugation of Uperi, King of Dilmun, whose abode is situated in the midst of the sea (sic.) — in the midst of his land, distress - his ambassador, offering submission (lit., servitude) and bring tribute (and) gifts, he sent to me to the sea (of the east)," (Luckenbill, 1975: II, 22);

(3)   "— Bit-Iakin on the shore of the bitter sea as far as the border of Dilmun, —" (Lukenbill, 1968: II, 26).

(4)   "Uperi, King of Dilmun, who lives (lit. whose camp is situated) like a fish 30 beru ("Double-hours") away in the midst of Assur, Nabu (and) Marduk, and sent his gifts". (Luckenbill, 1968: II, 36).

(5)   "Uperi, King of Dilmun, whose camp is situated a journey of 30 beru in the midst of the sea, like fish, heard of the might of Assur and brought his gifts". (Luckenbill, 1968: II, 41).

(6)   "Bik-Iakin which is on the shore of the Bitter Sea, upto the Dilmun border, I brought under one rule and added them to the territory of Assyria". (Luckenbill, 1968: II, 41).

(7)   "Uperi, King of Dilmun, who had his abode a journey of 30 beru in the midst of the sea of the rising sun, like a fish, heard (about it), and sent his gifts—" (Luckenbill, 1968: II 46).

(8)   "— the land of Bit-Iakin on the shore of the Bitter Sea as far as Dilmun's border —" (Luckenbill, 1968: II, 48).

(9)   "— Bit-Iakin on the shore (on both shores) of the Bitter Sea, as far as Dilmun's border —" (Luckenbill: 1968: II, 49)

(10)   "— Bit-Iakin on the shore of the Bitter sea, as far as Dilmun's border, —" (Luckenbill, 1968: II, 50).

(11)   "— Uperi, King of Dilmun, who had his abode a journey of 30 beru (double-hours") in the midst of the sea, like a fish, heard of the might of my sovereignity, and brought his gifts, who in the power and might of the great gods his lords, has carried warfare (lit. weapons (to a successful issue) and has cut down all of his foes; who beginning with Iatnana, which is in the midst of the sea of the setting sun, to the border of Egypt   —" (Luckenbill, 1968: II, 52).

(12)   "— Bit-Iakin which is on the shore of the Bitter Sea, as far as Dilmun's border — all these I brought under my way — ". (Luckenbill, 1968: II, 54).

(13)   "(Uperi), King of Dilmun, who lives (lit., whose camp is situated) 'like a fish' 30 beru (double-hours) away 'in the midst' of the sea of the rising sun, heard of (the might) of Assur, Nabu land) Marduk and sent his gifts." (Luckenbill, 1968: II, 102).

(14)   Sennacharib's (705-681 B.C.), inscription of the Temple of the New Year's Feast (bit-

akiti) reads, "After I had destroyed Babylon, had smashed the gods thereof, and had struck down its people with the sword, — that the ground of that city might be carried off, I removed its ground and had it carried to the Euphrates (and on) to the sea. Its earth (lit., dust) reached (was carried) unto Dilmun. The Dilmunites saw it, and the terror of the fear of Assur fell upon them and they brought their treasures, with their treasures they sent artisans, mustered from their land, carriers of the headpad, a copper chariot, copper tools, vessels of the workmanships of their land, — at the destruction of Babylon". (Luckenbill , 1924, 137f, 1968, II 185).

The inscriptions of Esarhaddon (680-669 B.C.) relating to Dilmun are :

(15)   "— the lands of — mash and Dilmun, whose place is as far off, and no—" (Luckenbill, 1968: II, 223).

(16)   "— (King) of the Kings of Dilmun, Magan (and), Meluhha, King of the four regions of the world—" (Luckenbill, 1968: II, 257).

(17)   An inscription of Assurbanipal (668-626 B.C.) of cylinder text mentions that Assurbanipal "— who established the yoke of his rule over Tyre, which is in the midst of the Upper Sea, and Dilmun, which is in the midst of the Lower Sea, and they drew his yoke —" (Luckenbill, 1968, II, 374).

(18)   The inscriptions of Sargon II transliterated and translated by Lit (1929:66f) has slightly different version wherein the four paras in continuation reads :

"— — Uperi, King of Dilmun."

"Who at a distance of thirty (double hours) in the midst of the sea where the sun is rising had (his) dwelling, heard of the power of my lordships etc."

"who at a distance of thirty (double) hours in the midst of the sea where the sun is rising like a fish had (his) dwelling, heard of the power of my lordship", and "and brought his gifts —".

In the above passage, as we see, the lines of para 2 "who at a distance - - rising sun", is repeated in para (3) in continuation, and the words "like a fish" are added to it obviously with a specific reason.

One of the evidences for the identification of Dilmun is the black stone (see Chapter IX, *infra* for illustration) with cuneiform inscription discovered in Bahrain in 1878 by Captain Durand. Latter's report was published in 1880 by the Royal Asiatic Society along with comments of Sir Henry Rawlinson. The inscription on the stone reads: e-gal-ri-mu-um eri din-za ak Lu a-aga-rum—" meaning, palace (of) Rimum, servant of (the god) Inzak, man (of the tribe of) Agarum". Rawlinson, on the basis of this inscription, claimed that Bahrain was identical with Dilmun, and it is dated by Cornwall to the second-half of the second millennium B.C., as according to him this lapidary script is archaistic Old Bablylonian with forms the Lu in particular. (Durand, 1880 :189 :27; Cornwall, 1952:141;Rice: 1983:11)

The cuneiform characters Niduk-ki, a term which persisted for a long time as an alternative to Dilumn of the Sumerian and Babylonian texts was identified first by Sir Henry Rawlinson in 1861 with Bahrain. Rawlinson states that throughout the Assyrian tablets from the earlier to the latest, there is constant allusion to an island. Niduk-ki in Akkadian, and Tilvun or Tilmun in Assyrian; and this name is associated with two others, Milukh and Magan. The meaning of the Akkadian name Niduk-ki seems to be either 'possessing altars' or 'possesing a God', for the letter has been used as a monogram, has both significations, and one suitable to the holy character of the island. Tilvun and Tilmun seems to mean 'the blessed hill' or 'the blessed isle'. (Rawlinson, 1880:47-51; Rice, 1983:38; Bibby, 1969, 29). Since Rawlinson's first identification of Dilmun scholars have been trying for more than a century to find geographical location of Dilmun and interpret the cuneiform texts of Mesopotamia relating to it. Assyriologists and archaeologists have different opinions. Writing about the identification and location of Dilmun, Langdon states that "on the whole the identification with a strip of land from about the eastern coast of the Persian gulf including the islands off the coast perhaps as per as the strait of Hormus and the Arabian Sea will satisfy all the known references concerning Dilmun". (Langdon, 1915, 10). This statement is just a theory without any substantial evidence.

In 1928 Burrow corroborated Rawlinson and suggested that the cuneiform characters Ni-tuk (with Ki added as an unarticulated determinative to demonstrate that the word is the name of a country) can also spell Dilmun. He further pointed out that Ni-tuk in Sumerian can also be pronunciated as Dugud. He thus wrote, "Tilmun is the name of an island, and of a continental coast-land of the Persian Gulf, probably on the Arabian side. Bahrain, insular and continental, is far suitable". Borrow uses the term Bahrain in inclusive sense to mean a group of islands and parts of main land of eastern Arabian coastland. (Burrows, 1928:170, Rice, 1983:166). Dougherty (1932:51,115) equates Dilmun with Bahrain. Kramer (1944:19fn) tries to prove that Burrow's interpretation of Ni Tuk or Ni Ur4 are a result of superficial and factitious etymologizing and suggested that it should not be taken seriously.

Following the publication of the Sumerian "deluge" tablet by Arno Poebel in 1914, which mentions Dilmun, "In the mountain of crossing, the mountain of Dilmun, the place where the sun rises", (Langdon translates this as "they caused to dwell in the inaccessible mountain; mountain of Dilmun"), scholars started to trace the location of Dilmun. Scholars were divided in their opinion. One group favoured to define it as a land bordering the eastern shore of the Arabian Gulf and extending, to put it very roughly, from somewhere south of Elam to the strait of Hormuz. While the second group preferred to identify Dilmun with the island of Bahrain. (Kramer, 1941:18, and 1961:97f, Langdon, 1967: 208). Kramer, in 1944 tried to find a solution to Dilmun and begins with examining the "deluge" myth. After Ziusudr had been granted life everlasting an eternal soul, the text continues with the line "Kur-bala Kur-dilmun-na Ki-dutue-a-se mu-un-ti-es. Meaning, "they (An and Enlil) caused him (Ziusudra) to dwell in the land of the (sun's) crossing, in Dilmun, the place where the sun rises". Kramer argues that since this line expressly describes Dilmun as the "land where the sun rises", it should be sought quite obviously east of Sumer and evidently in western Iran. Further, since Dilmun is regularly coupled with Magan and Meluhha and that in the Assyrian historical inscriptions it is described as situated immediately below Bit-iakin, the place is to be sought south of Sumer, and as much Kramer infers that it is the more southernly part of western Iran, that is, somewhere south of Elam, where Dilmun is to be sought and that it is not to be identified with the island of Bahrain. In order to prove his point of view Kramer cites several passages from Sumerian literature (Kramer, 1944:18-28).

Cornwall in 1944 in his thesis (unpublished) evaluates Sumerian and other classical evidences and concludes that "Dilmun = Tylos = Bahrain". (Cornwall, 1944:6-14). Subsequently he slightly modified his opinion in 1946 and came out totally contradicting the views of Kramer and tried to prove that Dilmun was the island of Bahrain - and also, at least during some periods, a stretch of territory on the nearby Arabian mainland. Cornwall, discern's two definitions/illusions to Dilmun in the cuneiform sources that Dilmun is a definite geographical locality as gleaned from the historical, commercial, epistolatary, dedicatory sources and astrological inscriptions, and a fabulous land of spirit world depicted in the Sumerian literary compositions. Obviously the allusion in both cases is to one and the same Dilmun. Cornwall (1946:3-10) enumerates several inscriptions in support of his contention that Dilmun is Bahrain. He cites the inscriptions of Sargon of Assyria which states that Uperi, King of Dilmun, "lives like a fish 30 beru away in the midst of the sea of the rising sun", and the inscription from the time of Asshurbanipal declares that Dilmun" is in the midst of the Lower Sea" and states that the "sea of the rising sun" was an Assyrian name for the Arabian/Persian Gulf. Other names were "Lower Sea" and "Bitter Sea". The distance of 320 beru to Dilmun implies, says Cornwall, the reckoning must refer to the number of hours required to reach Dilmun by sea from the initial point, and quotes Albright (1918-19,183) as follows : "It would be a very slow bark that could not make 5 miles an hour or 10 miles a beru. That is, at this modest speed of 30 beru would be 300 miles, nearly the distance from Bahrain to the mouth of the Euphrates in Sargon's reign". This is corroborated by a later evidence of Arrian, who states that Tylos (the classical name for Bahrain) "was said to be distant from the mouth of the Euphrates about a day and a night's voyage for a ship running before the breeze". As such, Cornwall concludes that, the Assyrian estimate appear to suit Dilmun = Bahrain with no strain whatsoever.

Out of the eighteen inscriptions cited above we find that six inscriptions (Nos. 1,4,5,7,11 and 13) mention Uperi as King of Dilmun, who lives like a fish 30 beru (double hours) away in the midst of the sea. Two inscriptions (Nos. 5 and 7) state that the Dilmun is situated at a journey of 30 beru. This term is defined differently as a distance and as an hour. According to Smith (1928:89), one beru is equal to 6.66 miles. That is Dilmun was situated at a distance of 199.8 miles. While as per Delaparte (1923:249), a beru is equal to 10.690 kilometres. According to a third source Luckenbill, (1968, 50), one beru = "double hour" = 1,800 GAR = 8.553 km. And 30 beru equals 256.6 km. While Albright (1918-19:19) estimates 30 beru equal to 300 miles, as the distance between the mouth of Euphrates and Bahrain in Sargon I's time.

The Babylonians, according to Langdon, reckoned a day as 12 hours, or double hours of 120 minutes each. A double hour, or two hours was a beru, and this was divided into 30 us (units) of 4 minutes. (Langdon, 1935, 56). In case of Dilmun the inscription "a journey of 30 beru -" implies that Dilmun was situated at a distance of 60 hours' journey from the place of reckoning. And this distance was possibly 256.6 kms. or 199.6 miles or 600 miles, whichever is true as per the different methods of calculations.

In 1952, Cornwall again came up with more evidences - an inscription of the reign of Esarhaddon and Nippur letters, attesting emphatically his earlier contention that Dilmun could not possibly have been on the eastern side of the Persian Gulf, and that the identification with Bahrain's islands and part of the Saudi Arabian province of Hasa may be accepted without reservations. These two letters Ni 615 and 641 in the museum of the Ancient Orient at Istanbul, are dated to the period of Burnaburiyas (c. 1370 B.C.). The letters written by one Ili-ippasra to Ililiya, who is former's superior and obviously a high official at Nippur in Babylonia. Cornwall infers that Ililiva was Ellit Kidimi, the governor (guenna) of Nippur during the reign of Burnaburiyas and first years of Kurigalzu IV. That the letters emanated from Dilmun is evident from the internal evidence - mention of men holding position and authority in Dilmun, carrying of dates by Ahlamu etc., and the greeting formula of both the letters which mention Enzag, worshipped in Dilmun. (Cornwall, 1952 137-142). (For the text and translation of these letters see Chapter IX, *Infra*).

Langdon (1964:194) though mentions Cornwall's ideas for the location of Dilmun but seems to be inclined favourably to Kramer's inferences and locates Dilmun on the eastern shores of the Arabian/Persian Gulf. However, Langdon concludes that "whatever may have been geographical definition in historical times, Dilmun must have included Eridu at the mouth of the Euphrates in mythology, and Dilmun was the Sumerian land and garden of Paradise". Langdon's idea of Dilmun inclusive of Eridu arises from his own doubtful interpretation with interrogation mark for the word Eridu for Dilmun in the poem of Enki and his wife (Damkuria) reposed in Dilmun. The last two lines of the poem - Ninsikilla saying to her father Enki, translates as : "Dilmun, the city thou hast founded, thou hast founded to which thou hast assigned a fate...". The same lines Kramer (1955:38) translates as follows :

"Dilmun, the city thou has given, the city (thou has given thy...),

Has not... of the river.

Dilmun, the city thou has given, the city (thou hast given, thy...)".

Langdon's use of the word Eridu for Dilmun seems to be incorrect on the grounds that the whole poem is devoted to Dilmun and does not mention any other city, Sumerian or otherwise. Throughout the poem Dilmun alone is mentioned. Bibby discussed at length the cuneiform inscriptions bearing on the historical fact of Dilmun's existence and its historical association with Mesopotamia and concludes that : "we must agree that Rawlinson's identification of Dilmun with Bahrain is the guess that best fits the facts, though we must keep in mind that Dilmun was more than just Bahrain, it was also a still unidentified area of the Arabian coast". (Bibby, 1969 : 46f, 184). On the basis of a large number of archaeological finds from Tarut, Golding (1974:26) identifies earliest Dilmun with Taurt island, the capital of the eastern province' during the Early Dynastic Period, first half of the third millennium B.C. That is, a Tarut-centered - Dilmun is implied. Golding is corroborated by the latter investigators, Piesinger (1983) and Larsen (1983). (See below for their inferences).

Thaper's (1975:1-42) "tentative hypothesis", as she puts, regarding Dilmun's identification with western India is unsound with no basis or evidence and as such untenable. Caspers et al (1978:113-144) identify Dilmun with the islands of Bahrain, Failaka, Tarut and some parts of east Arabian littoral and comes out heavily on Thaper's interpretation and use of the three places names. Caspers is corroborated by Potts (1978:47). Howard-Carter (1981 : 210-273) while re-evaluating the tangible evidence for the earlier Dilmun makes a differentiation between the earliest Dilmun and later Dilmun of the late third millennium B.C. on the basis of evidence from Sumerian mythology, archaeology of Mesopotamia and the Arabian Gulf and most recent and revealing geological data from the Arabian Gulf and suggests strongly that the earliest Dilmun was most likely located in the region of Qurna, lying to the east of the Sumerian cities at the mouth of the two rivers, the Tigris and the Euphrates. Her contentions are that the name Dilmun identified as the islands of Bahrain and Failaka, together with the adjacent sections of east Arabia became associated with a trading area in the Gulf during the late third millennium B.C., no objects from Mesopotamia were found in either Bahrain or Failaka which could be dated earlier than 2200 B.C.; and Qurna meets the characteristic description given in the Sumerian mythology for Dilmun. Lamberg-Karlovsky (1982:45) classified the cuneiform references about Dilmun, recovered from Mesopotamia, into two categories: (a) commercial, dedicatory, and astrological inscriptions, and (b) Sumerian literary compositions; and suggested that from the former there can be little doubt that Dilmun was a specific geographical entity involved in international trade and that ancient Dilmun is correctly identified as modern Bahrain while the second category of sources referred to Dilmun as a fabulous land, as a land of paradise and as an antechamber to the spirit world, due to the presence of several thousands of tumuli-tombs in Bahrain. The strong Mesopotamian presence found at ar-Rafi'ah, prompted Piesinger (1983:830) to suggest that Tarut was once earliest "capital" and religious centre of the ancient Dilmun.

According to Alster (1983:39-74) cuneiform textual evidence of the Assyrian kings indicates that Dilmun was an island, the presence of dates of Bahrain supports the identification of Dilmun with Bahrain, and this identification fits the archaeological remains (p. 44). Thus, he concludes that Dilmun was Bahrain, and there is no ambiguous evidence that there was a continental Dilmun and further he says that this identification is valid for all periods of Mesopotamian history (p. 52). This opinion is contradicted by Howard-Carter (1987:69) who says that Alster has not really produced sufficient evidence (new or old) to support that statement, and in any case inadmisible on archaeological grounds. Since other evidences have shown that Dilmun was also continental, as such Alster's opinion cannot be accepted.

Ebla cuneiform texts from Tell Mardidh dated to third millennium B.C., also mentions at several places "gin-dilmun", implying "Dilmun-shekal" (Pettinato, 1981; 169-172). In the Ebla texts the shekel, always written with the Sumerian term 'gin', is generally suffixed with "Dilmun". This suffix, says Pettinato, may be parsed either as a noun or as an adjective. Then, in the first case, "Dilmun" implies a unit of weight originating from Dilmun comprising Bahrain and eastern Arabian littoral. While in the second case it implies "noble shekel" or a measure of standardized weight. (Pettinato, 1981: 182). Subsequently, Pettinato (1983:75-82) brought to light the lexical list of geographical terms and literary texts mentioning Dilmun with or without the determinative "IC"; and concludes that Dilmun is a "geographical entity". Thus, in view of the above, we may consider that "Dilmun" suffix as a noun and shekels as Dilmun weight originating from Dilmun, a geographical entity. Further, this assumption is also proved from the Ebla texts listing commercial articles suffixed or prefixed by the word "Dilmun", Pettinato (1983:77-80) cites the following: "gis dilmun" (Dilmun date-palm), "bappir-dilmun" (Dilmun beer-bread), "nagga-dilmun" (Dilmun-tin); "Urudu-dilmun" (Dilmum-copper), "dilmun-balag" (Dilmun harp) etc., and that the list of professions of Ebla also mentions Dilmun suffixed or prefixed to the trade name. From the above list of articles it is evident that Dilmun in the Ebla texts is recorded in the sence of a noun, implying a geographical entity for the articles originating from Dilmun; and not in the sense of an adjective meaning "noble". It does not make sense if we consider it as an adjective and say "noble date-palm", "noble-beer-bread", "noble-tin", "noble-copper" etc. Here it implies items or articles coming from Dilmun. Further, the mention of terms "alik Telmun" (merchants or traders of Dilmun) in Ur texts and repeated mention of travels to Telmun in a group of tablets from the archieves of temple of the goddess Ningal clearly imply that Dilmun as a geographical entity was implied (Oppenheim, 1954:79).

In 1983 Potts came out with "Dilmun: where and when?" and tried to identify Dilmun's name usage with time. Potts, on the basis of archaeological finds, suggests that: (1) during the Early Dynastic Period, and perhaps also in the Jamdat Nasr and Late Uruk era, the Mesopotamian references to Dilmun apply to eastern Arabia, and not to Bahrain; (2) during the latest phase of the Early Dynastic Period (III), the Akkadian era, and subsequently the Ur III and Isin-Larsa periods, the situation changed considerably and Bahrain became centre of a Dilmun that also encompassed parts of eastern Arabia; and (3) towards the end of the Third Dynasty of Ur, a Dilmunite programme of colonization appears to have been initiated and Failaka was colonized around 2000 B.C. and incorporated into Dilmun. (Potts, 1983: 15-19). Potts conclusions implies that the evolution of Dilmun was in three phases and during each period it's geographical entity was not the same. This is attested by Piesinger's (not referred by Potts) archaeological finds from eastern Arabia. Piesinger (1983:830) on the basis of her excavations at ar-Ra'fiah suggests that Tarut was the "capital" and religious centre of the ancient Dilmun during early third millennium B.C. Piesinger is supported by Larsen (also not referred by Potts) whose archaeological analysis of stratified ceramic collections from Bahrain indicates that the major Dilmun occupation did not occur in Bahrain till the Ur III and Isin-Larsa dynasties of Mesopotamia (2100-1800 B.C.). Larsen (1983b, 17) suggests that at the end of the third millennium B.C. the administrative centre of Dilmun was apparently shifted to Bahrain.

Zarins (1986:236) while discussing the Mar-Tu people and the land of Dilmun illustrates the techno-complex limits in south west Asia in relation to Mesopotamia, Dilmun

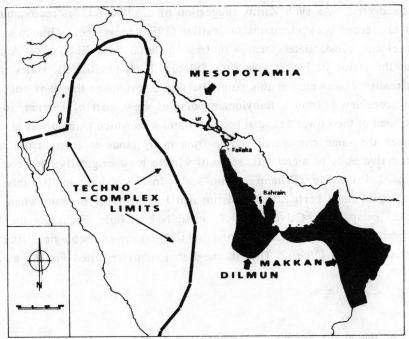

Fig.3   Territorial Extent of Dilmun in the Gulf and Eastern Arabia. (After J.Zarins, 1986).

and Makkan and indicates the territorial extent of Dilmun and Makkan. The map is reproduced here (Fig. 3). Zarins does not discuss the territorial extent of Dilmun nor mentions its basis. However, the territorial extent shown by Zarins is in accordance with the conclusions drawn above and it seems to be of the final phase of evolution of Dilmun when it encompassed north-eastern Arabia from Failaka islands to Qatar and mainland of eastern Arabia. Potts is corroborated by Howard-Carter (1987:54-115) who makes a detail reassessment of "Dilmun: at Sea or not at Sea? and finally concludes that the geographical entity Dilmun was not located in the same place at all times for which we have evidence. Hence Calvet (1989:5) while accepting the generally accepted definition of Dilmun: Failaka, Bahrain, province of Hasa etc, extends the northern limits of Dilmun to Kuwait upto the mainland and the island of Umm an-Namel, off Shuwaikh, on the basis of archaeological excavations at this latter place by Fahed al-Wohaibi.

Hence in view of the above discussions, until such time we discover Dilmun archives enlightening us about its origin and extent etc., the generally accepted definition of Dilmun which includes Failaka island, Bahrain islands, Tarut island, certain portions of the mainland of eastern Arabia (as in Zarin's map) is adopted here. Dilmun as a historical entity, probably, states Zarins (1986:247), on the basis of Mar-Tu migration, goes back to at least c. 6000 B.C. with the onset of the southern 'Ubaid cultures' involvement in the east Arabian littoral. Even though the earliest reference so far discovered, about Dilmun in cuneiform texts are dated to c. 3200 B.C., it does not mean that Dilmun was not existing much earlier than the texts discovered. As such Zarins suggestion of c. 6000 B.C. is reasonable. Potts (1990:85-89) in his recent book maintains his earlier (1983) ideas about Dilmun's identity (mentioned above) and substantiates them with fresh material from Ebla texts. And while discussing about the status of Failaka vis-a-vis Dilmun, Potts (1990:292), states that this question cannot really be answered at this point. He thinks and states that it is not unlikely that Failaka was considered, from a Babylonian point of view, part of Dilmun, in that it : (a) stood at the head of the Lower Sea, that body of water with which Dilmun was associated; (b) exhibited much the same mixture of people from many lands as Bahrain did; and (c) probably had an active body of merchants, some of whome must originally have come from Bahrain, who used distinctive Dilmun stamp seal. In this situation like this, Potts concludes, there would have been little to distinguish Failaka from Bahrain when viewed from a Babylonian perspective. Calvet (1991:7, unpublished) while discussing the Dilmun culture and its border with Mesopotamia in the light of recent archaeological finds attest the view expressed by Potts (1990). That is, the Babylonians regarded Failaka as part of Dilmun.

CONCLUSION

In view, of the above arguments, textual and archaeological evidences, we may conclude that the name Dilmun mentioned in the cuneiform texts of Mesopotamia and Ebla was a geographical entity, varied in time and space. Firstly, during the third millennium B.C. it comprised the east Arabian mainland and its littoral with its centre at Tarut island, secondly, during the second millennium B.C. the centre shifted to Bahrain island, thirdly, with the incorporation of Failaka island it comprised the east Arabian mainland and its littoral Bahrain island the centre and the Failaka islands, and fourthly, this region was generally referred as Dilmun, with its headquarters changing from time to time according to the exigencies of time and necessity. Thus finally, Dilmun was *not* Bahrain. Bahrain was part of Dilmun. In this volume, as the study is restricted to the present state of Bahrain, the word Dilmun is used in this restricted sense and not in the broader sense or Greater Dilmun, involving its entire geographical extent as in the Map 3. That is, the word Dilmun henceforth in the following chapters of this volume implies partly in the restricted sense to the geographical entity of the present state of Bahrain and hence 'Dilmun in Bahrain'. It does *not* mean Dilmun is Bahrain alone. To avoid confusion I have tried to use the term "Dilmun in Bahrain" and "Bahrain" synonymously.

(2)   MYTH ABOUT DILMUN — HOLY, PURE, PARADISE ETC.

In the Mesopotamian sources Dilmun is not only mentioned as an important trading centre but also as a famous place of prosperity and happiness, and as a place of eternal life. Consequently contemporary authors have tried to designate and locate it as Garden of Eden paradise. Kramer (1964:44) designate Dilmun as "the Sumerian Paradise Land". Recently, Alster (1983:44ff) made a critical examination of this "alleged paradise" myth and does not approve of it, while Michael Rice has published a book entitled "Search for the Paradise Land" and tries to argue that Dilmun was "the Paradise Land" and the "Original Holy Land" (1985:115ff). Zarins and Hamblin (1987:127ff) believes that the Garden of Eden vanished under the waters of the Arabian Gulf. But with the Flandrian Transgression (See *supra* chapter I), the Gulf began to fill with water and actually reached its modern day level about 4000 B.C., and swallowed Eden and all the settlements along the coastline. Though the original Eden had gone, but a new one called Dilmun, believes Zarins, enters the epic and poems in the third millennium B.C. This hypothesis of Zarins has yet to be proved.

In the cuneiform literature Dilmun is generally famous as a trading centre. However, two texts - the Sumerian myth of "Enki and Ninhursag" and the "Flood story" gives the scope for considering Dilmun as holy, pure, clean, paradise etc. It is proposed to briefly mention here about the contents of these two texts relating to the Dilmun myth, without going into detail discussions which several contemporary authors have attempted.

A tablet from Nippur about Enki and Ninhursag describes Dilmun land as "pure", "clean", and "bright", a land which knows neither sickness nor death, had been lacking originally in fresh, life-giving water.

Thus, Ninsikilla, the tutelary goddess of Dilmun pleaded Enki, who is both her husband and father, for filling up Dilmun with sweet water. The later complied with the request and ordered the sun-god Utu to fill Dilmun with sweet water from earth's water-sources. Dilmun thus became a divine garden with fields producing grain etc. In this paradise of gods, Ninhursag, "the mother of the land", the great mother goddess of the Sumerians, utilizes the semen of Enki leading to the sprouting of eight different plants. Then Enki commits a sin by eating these eight plants. This brings the wrath of Ninhursag, the goddess who was so largely responsible for their first coming into existence, who uttered a curse against Enki, saying that until he dies she will not look upon him with the "eye of life". She then immediately disappeared. Consequently, Enki fell ill and his health began deteriorating quickly. At this point the fox comes to the rescue and on the advise of Enlil, the leader of the Sumerian pantheon, brings Ninhursag back to the gods in Dilmun. Ninhursag then cures the ailing Enki and each time an organ is cured, a diety is born. The last of the deities named Ensahg was destined to be "the lord of Dilmun". Finally Enki was brought back to life and health. (Kramer, 1955:37f; 1964:46). The first part of the Dilmun myth, reproduced from Alster (1983:63f), is as follows :

1.   The city is pure, give it you a share! the land Dilmun is pure!

2.   Sumer is pure, give it a share! the land Dilmun is pure!

3.   The land Dilmun is pure, the land Dilmun is clean.

4.   The land Dilmun is clean, Dilmun is bright.

5.   When he alone had lain down in Dilmun,

6.   the place where Enki had lain down with his wife,

7.   that place is clean, that place is bright!

8.   When he alone had lain down in Dilmun.

9.   the place where Enki had lain down with Ninsikilla,

10.   that place is clean, that place is bright.

11.   In Dilmun the crow screams not,

12.   the *dar* bird cries not *dar-dar*,

13.   the lion kills not,

14.   the wolf snatches not the lamb,

15.   the dog knows not to eat kid

16.   the swine knows not the early barley

17.   the widow, after having spread malt on the roof (to dry),

18.   the birds of heaven eat not that malt

19.   the dove drops not its head (to pick up seed),

20.   the eye-sick one says not "I am eye-sick"

21.   the one suffering from headache says not "I am headache-sick"

22.   its old woman says not "I am an old woman",

23.   its old man says not "I am an old man",

24.   the young girl places not water for her bath in the city.

25.   the ferry-man says not "It's midnight",

26.   the herald circles not round himself,

27.   the singer sings not *elulam*,.

28.   at the outside of the city no shout resounds

29.   Ninsikilla spoke to her father Enki:

30.   "You have given me a city, you have given me a city, in you giving it

31. You have given me Dilmun, the city, you have given me a city, in your giving it

32. My father, you have given me a city, you have given me a city, in your giving it

33. my city is not provided with water in its rivers.

34. You have given me a city, you have given me a city, in your giving it,

35. my city is not provided with water in its rivers.

36. Wells of bitter water let no barley sprout in the fields, meadows, and furrows.

37. My city is not the "house of the banks and quays of the country:"

38. Let Dilmun be the "house of the banks and quays of the country!"

39. Her father Enki gave her the following answer:

40. "Now, under the sun of this day,

41. as the sun stands on heaven,

42. from the ... of of Ezen,

43. from the ... of Nanna,

44. from the "mouth of water flowing on the river bank", sweet water shall flow for you from the ground!

45. From your ... water shall come up,

46. Your city shall have water of abundance to drink for your sake.

47. Dilmun shall have water of abundance to drink for your sake.

48. Your well of bitter water shall be a well of fresh water!

49. Your city shall become the "house of the banks and quays of the country"!

50. Dilmun shall be the "house of the banks and quays of the country"!

51. Now, under the sun of that day,

52. as the sun stood on heaven,

53. from the ... of Ezen,

54. from the ... of Nanna,

55. from the "mouth of water flowing on the river bank", sweet water came up, from the ground.

56. From her ... water came up.

57. In her city they had an abundance of water to drink.

58. Dilmun had an abundance of water to drink.

59. Her bitter wells indeed became wells of fresh water!

60. Barley sprouted on the fields, meadows, and furrows.

61. Her city indeed became the "house of the banks and quays of the country."

62. Dilmun indeed became the "house of the banks and quays of the country"!

63. Now, under the sun of this day, so it is indeed!

ti dingir-gin$_x$ mu-un-na-si-mu
zi-da-rí dingir-gin$_x$ mu-un-<na>-ab-e$_{11}$-dè
u$_4$-ba zi-ud-sud$_x$-rá lugal-àm
mu-níg-gilim-ma numun-lú-lu$_7$ uru-ag
kur-bal kur-dilmun-na ki-^{d}utu-è-sè mu-un-ti-es

Life like a god they (the gods An and Enlil) gave him,
Breath eternal like a god they brought down to him.
Then, Ziusudra, the king,
The preserver of the "name" of vegetation and the seed of mankind,
In the land of crossing, the land Dilmun, the place where the sun rises,
                                                they caused to dwell.

Copy of the last lines of the "Flood" tablet with transliteration and translation

From the above mentioned myth it is clear that the Sumerians considered Dilmun as pure, clean, bright, and peaceful where the crows scream is not heard, a place free from fear and as lion does not kill, wolf does not snatch the lamb, and so on. It is the place where Sumerian gods Enki, Ninhursag, Enlil, etc., lived.

The last lines of the "deluge" or "flood" tablet from Nippur mention Dilmun and Ziusudra, the counterpart of biblical Noah, who is described as a pious, god-fearing king. The myth states that when the divine decision was taken to bring flood and destroy mankind, Ziusudra stations himself by a wall, where he hears the voice of a diety, probably Enki, informing him of the decision taken by the assembly of gods to send a deluge and "destroy the seed of mankind". (After this the text is missing). Then it continues, when the flood was ravaging and devastating, the sun-god, Utu, comes up forth lighting and warming up the earth, and Ziusudra prostrates himself before him and offers him sacrifices of oxen and sheep. The last extent lines of the myth describe the deification of Ziusudra, after he had prostrated himself before An and Enlil, he was given "life like a god" and transported to Dilmun, the divine paradise-land "the place where the sun rises (Kramer, 1955:42ff, 1964:47f). It seems that the passage that follows is fragmentry and judging from the preserved lines, states Kramer (1964:48), it contained the goddess

Ninsikilla's prayer to Enki to supply Dilmun with water.

The passage cited above reveals that Dilmun, was especially famous for its cleanliness and purity and it was the water-god who played a leading role in the religion of Sumer as well as Dilmun. The cleanliness and purity of Dilmun is also attested by another myth entitled "Enki and the world order". Six lines concern Dilmun, but it seems that only two lines are intelligible. They read : "He (the god Enki cleaned and purified Dilmun, placed the goddess Ninsikilla in charge of it". Again the meaning of the Sumerian compound word Ninsikilla placed in charge of Dilmun literally means "the pure queen further attest the popularity of Dilmun's cleanliness and purity. (Kramer, 1964:48f).

In view of the cuneiform texts, mentioned above, about Dilmun's myth it is quite clear that the Sumerians characterized the land of Dilmun as holy, pure, clean, bright, peaceful, free from all evils etc., and a safer place for the god Ziusudra to migrate and live when the divine decision was taken to deluge and destroy the mankind. This implies that Dilmun was considered by the Sumerians to be an extraordinary land, safer than Sumer and others, where Ziusudra could live peacefully without being affected by the flood of destruction. And this extraordinary characterized land of Dilmun, different from all other lands can only be the paradise of the myths. The attributes of Dilmun mentioned in the myths qualify it to be called the paradise, as originally understood as a happy, peaceful land or state. Alster's (1983:55) interpretation of the term paradise from a different point of view to explain an ideal ruler, the Sumerian king, who was responsible for creating a happy and well-organized society etc., is not applicable here in context to Dilmun, which has all the attributes, as mentioned in the myths to be designated as a paradise.

The attributes of a paradise in the myths are about Dilmun (which includes Bahrain) and not Bahrain alone as suggested by Michael Rice (1985:116ff) who has captioned the sixth chapter as "Bahrain : The Paradise Land".

(B)   CLASSIFICATION OF PERIODS AND CHRONOLOGY

Man lived in Arabia since time immemorial. Archaeological evidence point to his existence in Arabia since early Pleistocene and Lower Palaeolithic times. (See Volume I in this series). And since during the period (100,000 - 7,000 B.P.) Bahrain was part of Arabia's mainland, (Doornkamp et al, 1980 : 325,414), there can be no doubt that man lived here during the early Pleistocene and Lower Palaeolithic times. This is attested by the typical handaxe tools of Lower Palaeolithic period (100,000 - 50,000 B.C.) found in Bahrain. The Danish expedition discovered Middle Palaeolitic tools at several sites in southern and central Bahrain which Glob (1954:112f) compared them to Soan culture of Indus (now Pakistan) dated to ca. 50,000 B.C. So we may tentatively consider Bahrain's prehistory to begin from ca. 75,000 B.C. when man was savaged, unspecialised and specialised hunter-gatherer and a nomad. This period we may consider upto ca. 8000 B.P. i.e., the beginning of the Neolithic period. The period of New Stone Age in Bahrain is characterised by the traits of civilization, such as domestication of plants and animals, fish-curing, agriculture, use and manufacture of pottery, trading etc. Based on the archaeological evidence from Bahrain with regard to the shape and method of manufacture of stone implements, the prehistory and protohistory of Bahrain may be classified into traditional system called the three Age Systems - the Stone Age, the Bronze Age and the Iron Age. Within the purview of prehistory of Bahrain, the Old Stone Age culture can be classified into Lower Palaeolithic, Middle Palaeolithic, Upper Palaeolithic and Epi-Palaeolithic. The last being transitional between the Palaeolithic and the Neolithic. The protohistory of Bahrain may be classified into the Bronze Age and Iron Age cultures. Since we are able to document Bahrain from the cuneiform records found both at Bahrain and in Mesopotamia, and since Dilmun is attested in the corpus of archaic Uruk texts dated roughly between 3200-3000 B.C. (Euglund, 1983:35), we may tentatively assign a date of 3000 B.C. for the beginning of Bahrain's protohistory and ending around 400 B.C. Around this later date Aramic language seems to have been in use, as was in the Arabian Peninsula. This is attested from an Aramic inscription found on a potsherd. (Boucharlet and Salles, 1989:88). In view of the archaeological evidences of Stone Age tools recovered from Bahrain and other artefacts and considering the relative chronologies of the geological periods and cultures described in Volume I in this series (p. 15), we may tentatively classify Bahrain's prehistoric and protohistoric chronology as follows :

1)   The Palaeolithic period from the earliest time to ca. 10,000 B.C.

2)   The Epi-Palaeolithic ca. 10,000 B.C. to ca. 6,000 B.C.

3)   The Neolithic period ca. 6,000 B.C. to ca. 3,000 B.C.

4)   The Bronze Age ca. 3,000 B.C. to ca. 1,200 B.C.

5)   The Iron Age ca. 1,200 B.C. to ca. 400 B.C.

Larsen (1983:30) states that the picture of the late prehistoric and early protohistoric period is still largely incomplete and he dates the initial occupation from c. 5,000 B.C. to 4,750 B.C. by a population utilizing the Group D flint tool. This is not the case, as will be evident from the following Chapter II that the occupation may be dated to Lower Palaeolithic period.. The time and duration of the Palaeolithic culture in Bahrain falls into Quarternary and may be placed between Lower Pleistocene and Upper Pleistocene of the Geological Ages. The Pleistocene began about 2.4 million years ago and ended 10,000 years ago. The Pleistocene is by fluctuations of temperature which effected flora and fauna.

During the last interglacial period between 125,000 and 80,000 years B.P. sea level of Bahrain was about 4 to 5 metres above the present one. Sea-level at the end of the post-glacial transgression approached its present position and reached +2 metres in Bahrain (Doornkamp, 1980 : Sanlaville, 1986:17). The Upper Palaeolithic culture of Bahrain seems to have continued for some time during the Holocene and post-glacial period of the recent epoch. The Epi-Palaeolithic culture is intermediary of post-glacial times with different types of tools - microliths, apparently seems to have appeared around ca. 12,000 B.C. during the Holocene and continued until ca. 6000 B.C., when the Neolithic or the new Stone Age Culture with its polished and grooved tools appeared and flourished until ca. 4,000 B.C. It was succeeded by the Bronze Age (ca. 3000 B.C. - 1200 B.C.) and Iron Age (ca. 12000 B.C. - 400 B.C.). The use of stone tools seems to have continued during the Bronze Age and the Iron Age. The Neolithic period of Bahrain is characterised by two phases : pre-pottery Neolithic and pottery Neolithic. During the first phase no pottery was used; while during the second phase pottery was used for domestic purpose. The earliest prehistoric pottery recorded from Bahrain is 'Ubaid pottery'. It is attributed by Joan Oates (1978: 44, 1986:85) to 'Ubaid 4 at the earliest and dated to ca. 3,800 B.C. However, she concludes that there was contact between 'Ubaid 3 and continued during 'Ubaid 4 period. That is, during this earlier period, the Neolithic phase, there is a possibility of use of 'Ubaid' pottery in Bahrain. However, so far, earlier type has not been recorded.

The Bronze Age of Bahrain, similar to that of Saudi Arabia, begins about 3000 B.C. as evident from the Bronze Age mounds of Bahrain dated to the third millennium B.C. and ends about 1200 B.C. The most characteristic features of Bahrain's Bronze Age is the flourishing of the Dilmun civilization which had established international cultural and economic relations. The earliest reference to Dilmun in the Mesopotamian sources is in the corpus of archaic Uruk texts, dated around 3200 B.C. (Euglund, 1983:35; Nissen, 1986:336). That is during the fourth millennium B.C. Dilmun and its civilization existed, that too, with foreign cultural and trade relations. Bibby (1969 : 376) dates origin of city to ca. 3000 B.C. on the basis of archaeological excavations at Qal'at al Bahrain. Further, we have evidences of Mesopotamia's culture relations with eastern Arabia as early as sixth millennium B.C. (Masry, 1974:197 ff). It must have existed before it developed with foreign contacts. As such, the period before ca. 3000 B.C. may be termed the Earliest Dilmun period. In fact, in Bahrain there was culture before the generally believed 'Early Dilmun' period which Bibby (1969:356) discovered below the *farush* (limestone conglomerate) or the bedrock, below level 28. Here the pottery shreds found were layered sherds. The Danes found at that time. Bibby says that this is a new and quite unexpected culture, "earlier than the cultures which we had, perhaps prematurely, called Early Dilmun". Thus, we may designate this as the earliest Dilmun culture and assign its period as the Earliest Dilmun period ca. 3000 B.C. During this period we find 'Ubaid' culture sites in eastern Saudi Arabia and as well as in Bahrain. 'Ubaid pottery has been recorded from Bahrain. Thus implying that civilization existed in Bahrain before the Early Dilmun period or 3000 B.C.

Based on archaeological excavations at Qal'at al Bahrain, Bibby (1986:109ff) tries to trace the origin of Dilmun civilization to 2600 B.C., the traditional date for Gilgamesh and the first settlement at Qal'at al Bahrain to 2800 B.C. (Bibby, 1969:362). But, around this date, we find, as evident from the artefacts recovered, the Dilmun civilization in the developed form. As such, we may allow a margin of a few centuries for the evolution of the civilization and push the beginning to ca 3,000 B.C. Bibby (1969:378) also suggests date of ca. 3000 B.C. for the beginning of city I and early Dilmun period. From this date we may term it as the Early Dilmun period. The subsequent periods at Qal'at al Bahrain may be divided, based on archaeological evidence, into Middle Dilmun period (from ca. 1700 - 1200 B.C.). and Late Dilmun period (ca. 1200-400 B.C.) Thus, we may classify Bahrain's four evolutionary phases of Dilmun civilization as follows :

1)	The Earliest Dilmun Period	-	——	- ca. 3000 B.C.
2)	The Early Dilmun Period	- ca. 3,000	- ca. 1700 B.C.	
3)	The Middle Dilmun Period	- ca. 1700	- ca. 1200 B.C.	
4)	The Late Dilmun Period	- ca. 1200	- ca. 400 B.C.	

The relative chronologies of Geological periods, archaeological cultures and sub-culture of the Dilmun civilization are given in Table 1 in volume I (Saudi Arabia) in this series.

The chronology of Bahrain's prehistory and protohistory is mainly based, besides flint tools, on the excavations carried out at Qal'at al Bahrain, Diraz, Sar, Barbar temples and various burial mounds. Diraz and Sar though contribute to the chronology, but they do not provide regular sequence of level of occupation as does Qal'at al Bahrain. The main cultural elements of Bahrain's chronology, besides Dilmun, are 'Ubaidian, Jamdat Nasr and Umm an Nar. These elements have been traced during the excavations and in the surface collections made up of the archaeological finds from Mesopotamia, Saudi Arabia, Makkan (Oman), Indus Valley, United Arab Emirates, Iran, Qatar, Syria, Palestine, Jordan, Egypt, etc. Ceramics and seals are the main and important chronological indications and tie which are helpful in dating.

The Danish excavations at Qal'at al Bahrain yield a long sequence of successive settlment pattern. However initially (1954-1957), Bibby (1957:158-163) distinguished the level of occupation by the type of pottery recovered from each level and likewise he assigned periods. Thus, after the excavations of the 100-meter section, he made the chronological order, beginning from the bottom level and suggested the tentative dating as follows :

a)	the "chain-ridge" period	-	possibly Early Dynastic III b, 2459-2304 B.C.
b)	the "Barbar" period	-	probably Akkad Dynasty, 2303-2108 B.C.
c)	the "Caramel-ware" period	-	possibly some short time wtihin the range of the Early Babylonian Kassite periods, 1894-1165 B.C.
d)	the "glazed-bowl" period	-	probably Achaemenid -Selucid period about 500 -0 B.C.
e)	the "Islamic-palace" period	-	probably about 900-1000 A.D.
f)	the "Portuguese" period	-	about 1500-1650 A.D.

An important marker in the Umm an Nar type of sherd Eibby found below City I (*farush* levels) at Qal'at al Bahrain very similar to the one found at Umm an Nar settlement in Abu Dhabi. (Bibby 1969:360). The Umm an Nar culture is dated to entire third millennium B.C. by Frifelt (1975:359 ff). However, Tosi (1976:81 ff) dates it between 2200-1800 B.C.; while Potts (1990:93) considers ca. 2500 to ca. 2000 B.C. as Umm an Nar period. Larsen (1983:222) dates the lowest levels in the north wall excavations to 2300-2200 B.C. or 2400 B.C. That is, to Akkadian period or the later phases of the Early Dynastic period of Mesopotamia.

Further excavations necessitated revision in the periodisation. Thus, in 1969 Bibby (1969:378) revised the above classification, based on the ceramics recovered from different occupational levels (Sondages A-C), and designated the periods by Cities I- VII, and also dated them, as follows : City I (levels 19-16), City II (levels 15-11); City III (levels 10-7) also, City IV (?), City V (levels 11-5) and City VI (levels 4-1). These cities were dated by Bibby (1969:378; 1977, 352) as follows :

City II	-	ca. 2350 B.C.	- ca.	1800 B.C.
City III	-	ca. 1800 B.C.	- ca.	1200 B.C.
City IV	-	ca. 1050 B.C.	- ca.	600 B.C.
City V	-	ca. 500 B.C.	- ca.	000 B.C.

However, at this stage, the upper date of the Dilmun period of the City I at Qal'at al Bahrain was thought to be inconclusive because, the remains were not fully investigated. The early levels were just debris from the main settlement, the pottery sherds being wave-rounded and were found in beach sand. Later on, Larsen (1981) studied the ceramics in detail. The ceramic forms have Akkadian or perhaps late Early Dynastic parallels. (Bibby, 1969:373, Lowe 1984:8 Ms.; Larsen 1983: 212, 278). Again in 1986 Bibby (1986: 108-115) reclassified the periods within the city wall as follows : City I (levels 28-22); City II (levels 21-8); Hellenistic period (levels 7-4) and Islamic phase (levels 3-1). Bibby does not classify the *farush* levels (31-29). However, we may imply that these levels represent pre-city phase. The vertical distribution of significant artifacts within the city wall, Qal'at al Bahrain is shown in Fig. 4, after Bibby (1986:110).

In accordance with the levels of occupation at Qal'at al Bahrain the general periods of Dilmun cities may be classified into periods as follows :

Dilmun I	- pre-City phase
Dilmun II	- City I phase
Dilmun III	- City II phase
Dilmun IV	- City III phase
Dilmun V	- City IV Phase
VI	- City V phase
VII	- City VI phase

42

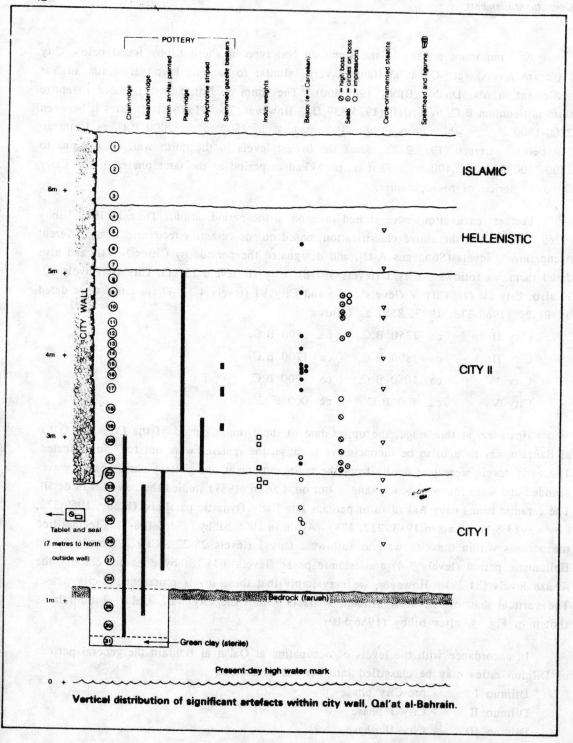

Fig.4 Vertical distribution of significant artifacts within City Wall at Qal'at al
Bahrain (After G.Bibby, 1986)

The first five Dilmun periods corresponding to the pre-city phase and cities I-IV fall within the purview of prehistory and protohistory of Bahrain, the subject of this volume. While the periods V to VII, which corresponds to the Hellenistic and Islamic periods of history in Bahrain are out of the purview of this volume.

Subsequent to Bibby's and Glob's excavations and investigations, Larsen (1983:214f) on the basis of ceramic analysis, equates Bibby's City I to Barbar I and City II to Barbar II and assigns them levels 25-22 and 21-17 respectively. And for pre-Barbar he assigns levels 30-36, which we may consider pre-City I phase. Later on, Hojlund studied the pottery assemblage and concluded that Bibby's City II may be sub-divided into six periods and City III into two periods and there was occupational continuity on the Qal'at from City II to City III, i.e., from the third millennium B.C. till at least about 1500 B.C., and probably throughout the second millennium B.C. The City II has been sub-divided as II A, II B, II C, II D and II F, while II E is the missing link. The City III has been divided into III A and III B. The chronology of the 'Ubaid and Dilmun periods and cities of Qal'at along with that of Barbar Temples and burial mounds is given in Table - I in correlation to the Mesopotamian periods. The chronological periods of cities I-IV of Qal'at al Bahrain in correlation to the Mesopotamian periods are : City I is dated to ED : III b (2400-2300 B.C.); the City 2A to 2B to Akkadian (2200 B.C.); City 2B, Ur III (2100 B.C.), City 2C Ur III (2000 B.C.); City 2D, Isin-Larsa period (ca. 1900 B.C.); City 2F Old Babylonian (1850 B.C.); City 3A to Old Babylonian (1750 B.C.) and City IV to Kassite (1600-1000) (Mortensen, 1986 b : 183 ; Hojlund, 1986 : 224).

Diraz was excavated by al-Tikriti who found the traces of architecture of houses and the artifacts recovered were found to be contemporary with Barbar assemblage. He thus dated Diraz settlement between 2500-2000 B.C. (al-Tikriti, 1975 : 16 ff).

The Sar settlement was first excavated by the Department of Antiquities in collaboration with Jordanian team during 1983-1985. Subsequently, during 1990-91, the British expedition of Robert Killick, Jane Moon, Harriet Crawford et al, excavated major portion of the Sar settlement adjoining the site excavated earlier by the Arab team. Based on the ceramics recovered from the settlement the British have dated the site to ca. 1900 B.C. corresponding to the Qal'at al Barain City II c-d. The origin of the settlement post-date City I at Qal'at (Killick, Crawford, Moon et al., 1991:133).

The Barbar Temple complex chronology extends over a period of six to seven centuries. Bibby (1969:378) assigned date of ca. 2250 B.C. to Temple I, on the basis of the Umm an Nar sherd; ca. 2100 B.C. to Temple II; and ca. 1800 B.C. to Temple III. Bibby is corroborated by Glob (1954:152) who excavated Barbar temple and suggested a third millennium date on the basis of the finds, with Mesopotamian parallels, of the first two years of excavations.

The dates given by Bibby and Glob were generally accepted. Subsequent excavations and research by several individuals and teams necessitated reconsideration of this date. Mortensen (1986:178 ff) makes an overall assessment of the chronology of the Barbar Temple which is discussed here. In 1970 dating was made on the basis of individual phases of the temple complex. Mortensen suggested an Early Dynastic I date for Temple I on the basis of a polychrome Jamdat Nasr sherd of a jar found in a layer north of the first temple and the deposit of conical clay goblets recovered from the foundation of the earliest temple. The second temple or the first oval temple at Barbar was dated to the middle to the third millennium. While the stamp seals of third temple were dated to 2000 B.C. Caspers (1971b:217-224 and 1974), Potts (1978:37) - and Larsen (1983:38f) suggested an Ur III-Isin-Larsa date for the three temples basing primarily on an examination of a ceramic sequence from Qal'at having Mesopotamian parallels, and or a correlation between the sequence of Qal'at and the Barbar temples. Mortensen makes a preliminary re-examination of the ceramic sequence in seven phases and other evidence in combination with Andersen's stratigraphy of the temples in phases. But one of the problem is that pottery from Temple II and III deposits are mixed with sherds from earlier phases.

A fairly long chronology for Barbar is suggested on the assumption that the temples cover a period of roughly six to seven hundred years. The date of building of the Temple I is uncertain though it is believed to have been built by the middle of the Akkadian period. However, it may be mentioned that the early temples at Barbar seem to reflect archaic traditions expressed in the architecture as well as in the pottery and in the tradition of scattering votive goblets over a large area in the interior of the temple terrace. Akkadian or early Ur III date is suggested for the Temple IIa on the basis of the foundation deposits. And Ur III - Isin-Larsa date is suggested for Temple IIb on the basis of two radio-carbon date 2035 B.C. and 2070 B.C. ± 10 years. There is uncertainity about the dates of the NE - Temple and third temple which might have been founded in the middle of the Isin-Larsa period and probably during third and early second millennium B.C. That is, throughout the Old Babylonian period and beginning of the Kassite period in the Arabian Gulf. (Mortensen, 1986:185; Hojlund, 1986:224). Hojlund's (1986:224) study confirms the earlier observations by Bibby (1969) and Larsen (1983:214) that there is a close resemblance between the pottery from the Barbar temples and City II at Qal'at al Bahrain. Hojlund has correlated the Barbar temples more exactly with the sequence at Qal'at al Bahrain. This enables us to draw a correlation with the chronology of the two sites. The presence of both chain ridged and ridged wares, characteristic of Temple I, is only paralled at city II A. The materials from Barbar II A is closely related to the II B. Phase at Qal'at and the late sample from Barbar III seems to be similar to late city II or III. Whereas the pottery from NE-Temple at Barbar typically seems to fit in approximately at the end of Temple II B - before city II F at Qal'at. The chronological correlation between Barbar Temple and Qal'at is as follows.

TABLE 1

CHRONOLOGICAL CHART OF THE DILMUN PERIODS IN BAHRAIN

Date B.C.	Mesopotamia Period	Period	Bahrain					
			Dilmun Settlements			Burials	Temples	
			Cities at Qal'at	Diraz	Sar		Barbar	Others
4500	'Ubaid 4	'Ubaid 4						
4000		Earliest Dilmun	Origins Evolutionary phase (pre-city phase)					
3000	Jamdat Nasr-Late Urk	Jamdat Nasr Umm an-Nar Early Dilmun	City I			al-Hajjar		
2800						New City site		
2600	ED III A							
2500	ED III B			Houses				Diraz
2400								Umm Es Sujur Temple
2300	Akkadian					Rifa'a		
2200			City IIA			Buri	Temple I (A-B)	
2100	Ur III		City IIB			Sar al-Jisr Barbar Hamad Town Hamala N.	Temple IIA	
2000	Isin-Larsa		City IIC		Houses	Ali	Temple II B N.E.	Sar
1900			City IID					
1800	Old Babylonian		City IIE (Missing)				Temple	
1700		Middle					Temple	
1600	Kassite	Dilmun	City IIIA			Al-Maqsha	III A	
1500	Babylonian		City IIIB				Temple	
1200							III (Late)	
1000								
600	New Babylonian	Late	City IV			Janussan Mound III B		
400								

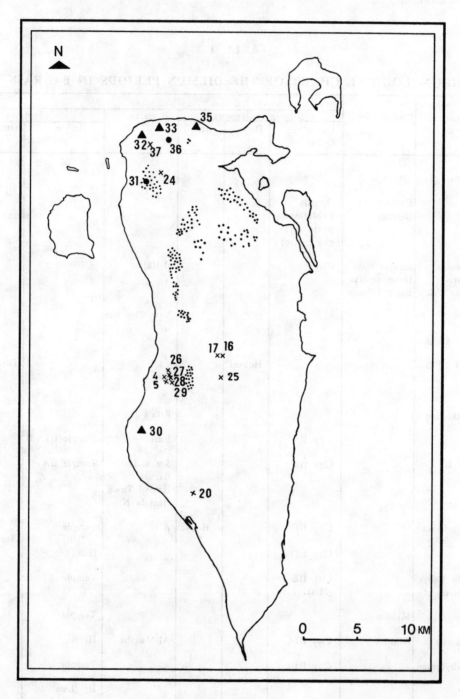

Fig.5   Flint and Tumuli sites - Danish Expedition, 1954. (After P.V.Glob, KUML, 1954)

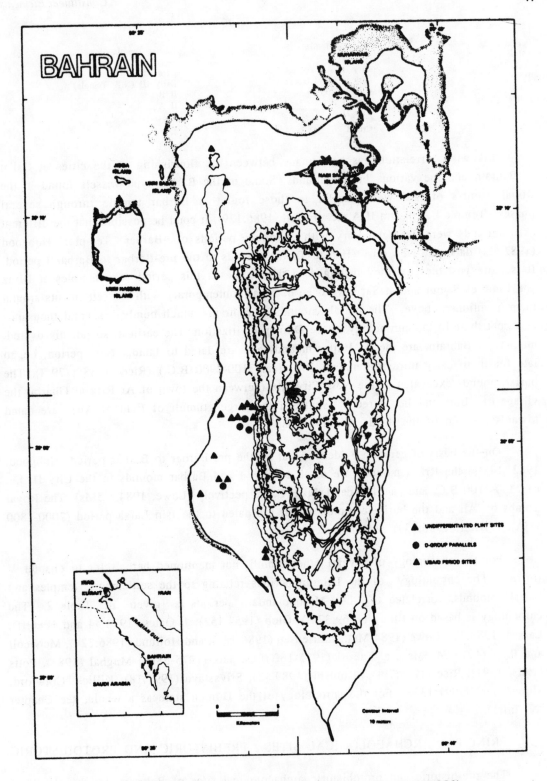

Fig.6   Neolithic and Proto-historic Sites (After C.E.Larsen, 1983)

Period B.C.	Qal'at al Bahrain	Barbar Temple
1500	City III B	—
1600	City III A	
1900	City II E (Missing)	Late III
2000	City II C	Early III (N.E. Temple)
2100	City II B	II B
2200	City II A	II A
	City II A	I
—	City I	—

Likewise correlation has been made between the flourishing of the cities at Qal'at al Bahrain and the various burial mounds. Some of the Barbar type vessels found in the Royal Tomb's of 'Ali were similar to those found at Barbar temple through several phases : Temple I A, B and II A etc. (Frifelt, 1986:129). It coud be possible that the different 'Ali mounds were contemporary with various periods of Barbar Temple. Hobgood (1982:Ms) dates the New City (Hamad Town) mounds to the pre-Barbar to Barbar I period. It is quite possible that they belonged to the people of this period. The temples at Diraz and Umm es-Sejour and at Sar have been dated as contemporary with the settlements around them, mentioned above. The burial mounds of Bahrain which number several thousands also contribute to the chronology of the Dilmun civilization. The earliest, so far, discovered, mounds in Bahrain, are the Al Hajjar mounds and are dated to Jamdat Nasr period, i.e. to late fourth to early third millennium B.C. (ca. 3100-2900 B.C.) (Rice, 1988 : 79 f). The burial mounds excavated at the New City site (between the town of Ar Rifa al Gharbi, the village of Buri and lie directly south of the large tumuli of field of Ali) are dated towards the end of the third millennium B.C.

On the basis of ceramic evidence, that is, the pre-Barbar to Barbar period (Hobgood, 1982, 14Ms) the Rifa'a mounds are dated to City I and Barbar mounds to the City II, i.e. ca 2300-2100 B.C. and ca 2100-ca. 1800 B.C., respectively (Lowe, 1984 : 5Ms). The Royal Tombs of 'Ali and the burial complex at Sar are dated to the Isin Larsa period (2000-1800 B.C.). (Frifelt, 1986:134).

For the chronology of several other tumuli, not mentioned here, refer to chapter V (*infra*). The chronology of the Dilmun periods relating to the settlements, temples and burial mounds, correlated to the Mesopotamian periods is given in Table 2. The chronology is based on Bibby (1969:378f); Glob (1954:152); J. Oates (1978:44 and 1986:ff), Larsen (1983:42); Lowe (1984:Ms); Mortensen (1986:183), and Hojlund (1986;224), McNicoll and Roaf (1973-74 Ms.), al-Takriti (1975-16ff), Caspers (1975-58ff); Mughal (1983), Potts (1983, 1991), Rice (1988;79f), Konishi (1989:12); Srivastava (1991:18); Killick, Crawford, Moon, et al (1991:133). For the chronology of the Dilmun state as a whole, see Chapter IX (infra).

(C)   PRINCIPAL ARCHAEOLOGICAL SITES : PREHISTORIC AND PROTOHISTORIC

The pre-historic and protohistoric archaeological sites of Bahrain may be classified into five categories as follows : (1) Old Stone Age sites; (2) New Stone Age sites; (3) 'Ubaid

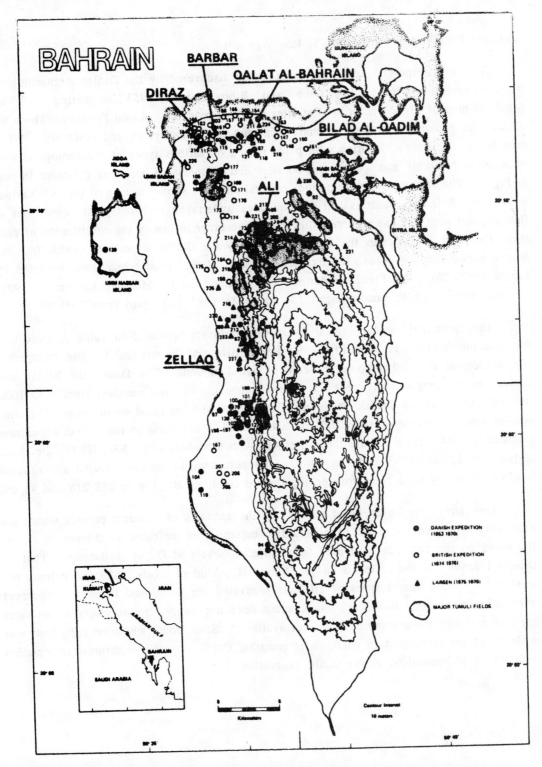

Fig.7   Archaeological sites indicating Danish Expedition (1953-70); British Expedition (1974-76); and Larsen's survey (1975-76). (After C.E.Larsen, 1983).

sites; (4) Bronze Age sties; and (5) Iron Age sites.

The most important flint and tumuli sites discovered by the Danish Archaeological Bahrain-Expedition, led by P.V. Glob and Bibby, during 1953 numbering 1-37 are shown in map of Fig.5. (List of flint sites kindly provided by Karen Freifelt). These are of four categories; flint sites, tumuli-excavated and unexcavated and other sites. While map of Fig. 7 shows location with place names of various types of archaeological sites in Bahrain. Neolithic and 'Ubaid period sites and protohistoric sites are indicated in map of Fig. 6. The Dilmun (Barbar) period cultural sites are shown in map of Fig. 8. Various teams of different countries and persons have undertaken archaeological expeditions to Bahrain, and each one has recorded sites. Thus, in order to justify the contribution of each team, the, map 7 indicates the sites recorded by the Danish expedition (1953-70), the British expedition (1974-76) led by McNicoll and Michel Roaf, and those recorded by Larsen (1975-76). The French undertook excavations led by Monique Kervran in 1977-79, and later on by P. Lombard and J.F. Salles in 1982 and again from 1989-92.

The principal archaeological sites of Bahrain are tabulated in Table 2, indicating the serial number (col. 1), name of the site (col.2), nature of the site (col.3) - site, occupation site, settlement site and tomb in the case of burial mounds. The Danes, the British and Larsen have assigned different set of site numbers. The site numbers from 1 to 1000 in col.4, are as per the Danish Catalogue (Glob, 1954) and indicated on the map. The sites bearing numbers beginning from 2001 to 2049 in Col. 5 are those of the British expedition (McNicoll, 1974 : Ms.); while those prefixed with alphabets (e.g., SSI, JG-1) are those assigned by Larsen (1983:295ff) in Col.6. Sites pertaining to the same period and situated in close proximity have been grouped together in col.4; as 207,208 or 212-216 and so on.

The sites have been dated (col. 7) by the artefacts of different periods which the excavators recovered and dated. The period in column 7 is indicated as Dilmun, I, II and III, based on the ceramics recovered from different levels at Qal'at al Bahrain. That is, Dilmun I denotes period of levels 26-30; Dilmun II, period of levels 22-25 and Dilmun III, levels1-7. The different types of artefacts recovered are mentioned in col.8, wherever information available. However, blank space does not imply non-recovery of artefacts but may be taken for granted as data not available. Sites from where no collection was made at all are mentioned in col.9 under remarks. Col.9, furnishes additional information with regard to soundings, empty tomb, excavation, etc.

51

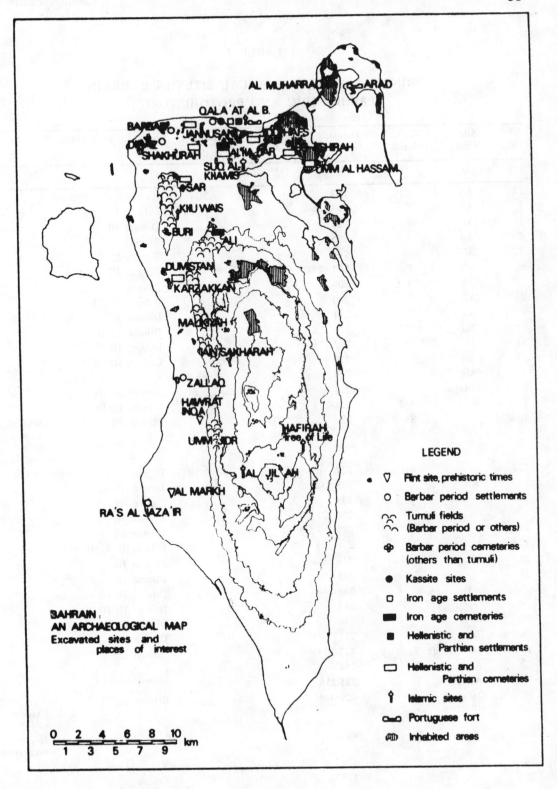

Fig.8　Archaeological Map showing excavated sites from pre-historic to Islamic times. (After J.F.Salles, 1984 and P.Lombard 1989).

TABLE 2

PRINCIPAL ARCHAEOLOGICAL SITES IN BAHRAIN
(PREHISTORIC AND PROTOHISTORIC)

Site No.	Site Name	Nature of site	Danish Site No.	British site No;.	Larsen Site No.	Period	Artefacts	Remarks
(1)	(2)	(3)	(4)	(5)	(6)	(7)	(8)	(9)
1	'Ali	T	202	-	-	Kassite	Pottery	
2.	'Ali	T	203	-	-	Dilmun II	-	
3.	'Ali	T	204	-	-	Dilmun III		
4.	'Ali	T	205	-	-	'Ubaid		
5.	'Ali	T	206	-	-	Dilmun II, III		
6.	'Ali	T	207, 208	-	-	Dilmun III		
7.	'Ali	A-T	209	-	-	Dilmun		
8.	'Ali	"	210	-	-	Dilmun II, III		
9.	'Ali	"	211	-	-	Dilmun II		
10.	'Ali	"	212-216	-	-	Dilmun II, III		
11.	'Ali	"	217,218	-	-	Dilmun III		
12.	'Ali	"	219	-	-	Dilmun II, III		
13.	'Ali	"	220	-	-	-	-	
14.	alHajjar	T	221	-	-	Dilmun II, III		
15.	'Ali	A-T	222-225	-	-	Dilmun II, III		
16.	"	S	226	2073	-	Dilmun III		With Neo-Babylo-nian burials
17.	"	B-T	227	-	-	Dilmun III		
18.	'Ali	"	228-232	-	-	Dilmun II, III		
19.	"	"	233	-	-	dilmun III		
20.	"	"	234-236	-	-	Dilmun II, III		
21.	"	"	237	-	-	Dilmun III		
22.	"	"	238-243	-	-	Dilmun II & III		
23.	"	"	244	-	-	Dilmun III		
24.	"	"	245	-	-	Dilmun III		
25.			246-248	-	-	Dilmun II, III		
26.	"	"	249	-	-	Dilmun II, III		
27.	"	"	250	-	-	Dilmun II, III		
28.	Umm Jidr	T	251	-	-	Dilmun III	-	-
29.	Dar Chulaib	T	252-253	-	-	Dilmun III		
30.	'Ali	T	254	-	-	-		-
31.	'Ali	T	255,256	-	-	-		-
32.	Qal'at alBahrain	S	420-424			Dilmun II, III		West wall Exca-vation
33.	"	S	425	-	-	"		Southwall excavation
34.	"	S	426			"		"
35.	"	S	428	-	-	Kassite		"
36.	"	S	431,518			Neo-Babylonia Collection		Sounding

Site No. (1)	Site Name (2)	Nature of site (3)	Danish Site No. (4)	British site No;. (5)	Larsen Site No. (6)	Period (7)	Artefacts (8)	Remarks (9)
37.	al Hajjar	T	441	-	-	-	-	-
38.	S.W. Coastal plain	S	442,508 508-511	-	-	Stone Age	Flints	-
39.	Buri	T	443	-	-	-	-	-
40.	Diraz	S	484					Temple
41.	S.W.Coastal	Sett	486 (979)				Flints	Settlement
42.	"	"	487			Dilmun II,III	Flints	Settlement
43.	Zallaq Road	S	488		SS-2	Dilmun III		
44.	Sar Village	S	490	2004				
45.	al Maqsha	S-T	495	-	-	Bronze Age Dilmun II, III		
46.	W. Coastal plain	S	497			"		
47.	Jebel Dukhan	S	498,507			Stone Age	Flints	
48.	Jid Ali	S	500			Stone Age	Flints	
49.	Mattala	S	502,503	2066		Stone Age	Flints	
50.	al Wasmiyah	S	505	2053	WS-1	Dilmun-III	Flints	-
51.	Sar	S	506	-	-	Stone Age	Flints-Pottery	
52.	Ras al'Jazayir	S	512	2015		Dilmun III	-	Shell Midden
53.	Sar	T	513			Dilmun III	-	-
54.	Diraz	S	516			Dilmun III	-	-
55.	Barbar Temple	S	517	-	-	Dilmun II,III	Pottery	Temple
56.	Qal'at	S	519	-	-	Neo-Assyrian	-	Palace
57.	"	S	520	-	-	Dilmun II (Akkadian)		N. Wall
58.	"	S	521	-	-	-	Surface Collection	-
59.	al Hajjar	T	522-524	-	-	Kassite	-	-
60.	Hamad Town	T	-	-	-	Kassite & earlier, end of 3rd Mill. B.C.	Pottery	
61.	"	T	-			Dilmun II, III	Pottery	
62.	"	T	-			Dilmun II	-	
63.	"	T	-	-		-	-	
64.	Diraz-east	S	525	2042(7)		'Ubaid	Pottery Flints	
65.	N.W.Coastal Plain	S	526			Dilmun II,III	-	
66.	S.W.Coastal Plain	S	548	-	-	-	Flints	
67.	S.W.Coast (Near SP)	S	549	-	-	Dilmun III	Flints Ceramics	
68.	N.W.Coast plain	S	550	-	-	"	Pottery	-

Site No. (1)	Site Name (2)	Nature of site (3)	Danish Site No. (4)	British site No;. (5)	Larsen Site No. (6)	Period (7)	Artefacts (8)	Remarks (9)
69.	N.Coast plain (along Budaiya Rd.)	T	551	-	-	-	Diorite fragments	-
70.	Hafira (Tree of Life)	S	473		-	-	Flints	-
71.	S.W.Coastal plain	S	574	-	-	Dilmun III	Flints &	-
72.	"	S	575	-	-	-	pottery Flints	-
73.	"	S	684		-	Dilmun III	Sickle blades Pottery	-
74.	"	S	685	-	-	-	Flints-DGr.	
75.	"	S	972	-	-	Dilmun II,III	Flints	-
76.	"	S	973	-	-	-	Flints	-
77.	"	S	974-977	-	-	Dilmun III	Flints & pottery	-
78.	"	S	978	-	-	1st Mill B.C.	Steatite	
79.	N. Coast plain (along Budaiya Rd)	T	980	-	-	Dilmun III	Pottery	-
80.	Zallaq	S	981	-	-	-	-	
81.	Zeera's Mound	S	982	-	-			
82.	Buri	T	-	-	-	Dilmun II end 3rd Mill B.C.		
83.	Buri	T	983	-	-	Dilmun III	-	-
84.	Mast-T158 N coast plain)	T	985	-	-	1st Milli. B.C.-	-	-
85.	Qal'at	O.S.	519-521	2001		Dilmun I	Pottery	-
86.	Jid Hafs (South)	T	-	2003			-	
87.	Bilad al Qadim	S	-	2006		Dilmun II,III		
88.	Barbar Village	S	-	2020	-	Dilmun III	-	-
89.	" (S.W.)	S	-	2021	-	Dilmun II,III	-	-
90.	al Markh	S	-	2027	-	Stone Age Late 'Ubaid	Flints, pottery	
91.	Makaba	S	-	2028	-	-	-	
92.	Khuwais (North2)	S	-	2031		Dilmun III	-	
93.	Sar (West)	T	-	2038		Dilmun II,III	-	
94.	Diraz (East)	T	-	2042+		Dilmun III	-	With intrusive Kassite burials
95.	Hawar islands	S	-	2043-46	-	-	Flints	-

Site No.	Site Name	Nature of site	Danish Site No.	British site No;.	Larsen Site No.	Period	Artefacts	Remarks
(1)	(2)	(3)	(4)	(5)	(6)	(7)	(8)	(9)
96.	Ain Umm Ijaiyi	S	-	2047	-	Ubaid	Flints Pottery	-
97.	Al Wasimiyah	S	505	2053	-	Dilmun III	-	-
98.	S.W.Coast Plain	S		2054	-	Dilmun III	Pottery	-
99.	S.W.Coast Plain	S		2061		Dilmun II,III	-	
100.	Al Maqsha	T		2067		Kassite	-	
101.	Barbar Village	S		2068	-	Kassite	Flints, DGr.	-
102.	S.W.Coast Plain	O.S		2070		Ubaid		
103.	S.W.Coast Plain	S		2071		Dilmun		
104.	"	S		2072		Post-Ubaid		
105.	Barbar area	S		2019	JG-1	Neolithic, Dilmun III		
106.	Buri	O.S.		-	Bu-1	Dilmun III	-	
107.	Barbar (South)	S			TG-1	Dilmun III		
108.	Khadra	S			KH-1	Neo-Babylonian	-	-
109.	Rifa'a (west)	S		-	RW-1	Stone Age, flints	-	-
110.	'Ain Sakhara	S	492	-	AS-1	Dilmun III	-	with spring

* S=Site   T=Tomb   O.S. = Occupation site   A,B = Group   Sett = Settlement

CHAPTER III

THE STONE AGE

(A) CLASSIFICATION OF STONE-AGE TOOLS

Bahrain was inhabited since the Pleistocene times is evident from the archaeological finds of Stone Age tools first discovered in 1952 by Peter Cornwall in a small cave at Jebel Dukhan. (Field, 1961:76). Later on, Bibby and Glob made their first reconnaissance in 1953 and found numerous Stone Age sites and flint tools (see maps). They have observed that the Stone Age sites in Bahrain ran along the ten-metre contour, suggesting that sea lay that much higher at the date of the flint sites, which could be, as estimated by them, anything from 20,000 to 40,000 years ago. They found the implements lying on the surface just as they had been dropped thirty or forty millennia before. These tools were mainly scrapers and rather crude cutting tools. These tools were used by the hunters to prepare skin and to work in bone and have been dated by Bibby and Glob to Middle Palaeolithic cultures. (Bibby 1969:48f, 63:320). The middle Palaeolithic culture of the Arabian Peninsula is dated between 50,000 to 30,000 years B.C., and flint tools of this period have been found throughout the main land of Arabia. (See Volume I in this series). Subsequently the Danes found large variety of tools belonging to the Old Stone Age, the New Stone Age and Chalcolithic period.

The chronological classification of Bahrain's Stone Age tools can be made, in accordance with the system adopted earlier in Volume I (p. 35) in this series, as follows : tools of the Lower Palaeolithic Culture; tools of the Middle Palaeolithic Culture; tools of the Upper Palaeolithic Culture; tools of the Epi-Palaeolithic Culture; tools of the Neolithic Culture; tools of the Chalcolithic Culture

This classification is based on the archaeological evidence with regard to the shape and method of manufacture of stone implements within the purview of prehistory of Bahrain. The Early Stone Age Culture can be classified into Lower Palaeolithic, Middle Palaeolithic, Upper Palaeolithic and Mesolithic/Epi-Palaeolithic. The last being the transitional between the Palaeolithic and the Neolithic. The proto-history of Bahrain covers the Chalcolithic period, comprising the Bronze and Iron Ages. Since there is no context or stratified sites (McNicoll and Michael Roaf of the British team recovered flints in 1973, from statified trenches, but there is no detailed report) in Bahrain, this classification is not based on stratified evidence nor on evidence pertaining to the various forms of dating. Lacking these two criteria, I have based my study almost entirely on the technological and typological criteria.   First, in technological criteria, various techniques used for manufacturing flakes, blades, and various techniques of secondary working, like retouch, blunting preparation of notch edges, etc.

Secondly, typological criteria, analysis is based on the classification of assemblies into various types as used generally for the classification of Old World's Palaeolithic and Neolithic tools. Thirdly, the nomenclature assigned here is also tentative and not to be considered rigidly in the form of water tight compartment. However, keeping in view that chopper, chopping tools etc., of Lower Palaeolithic culture reappeared again in quantity, after long hiatus, in the Epi-Palaeolitic / proto-Neolithic period in south west Asia (Solecki, 1985:103ff) and also in Bahrain.

The Danes found the worked flints where the wind had uncovered the ancient ground surface, which in majority of the sites in the coastal areas was covered by yard-stick sand deposits or by high cliffs. There are therefore, observes Glob (1954:112), no possibilities of stratigraphical distinction between the various flint cultures which are represented. Thus in the absence of stratified sites, it is quite possible that the period which I have assigned to a particular type/class of tools, might have as well in use during other period (s) - both earlier, and later. So, until we have more elaborate details and stratified sites, there can be no rigidity in the classification and use of the Stone Age tools of Bahrain. It is also possible that the tools classified here into different periods might have been in use simultaneously. However, it may be mentioned that it is not proposed to make here a specialised study of the tools of Bahrain; as it is not the purpose of the book. Here an attempt is made to list and illustrate for the first time all the tool types of Bahrain in order to high-light the existance of large variety of Stone Age tools in Bahrain.

In view of the above, I have cautiously classified, after sorting out from several mixed collections preserved in the stores of Bahrain's National Musuem, the Stone Age tools into Six Groups with affinities to various cultures. The tools are illustrated in the ATLAS of the Stone Age tools at the end of this Section, from page 70 onwards.

GROUP ONE (LOWER PALAEOLITHIC AFFINITIES)

The Danish Archaeological Bahrain - Expedition under the leadership of P.V. Glob made several surveys and discovered many Stone Age sites in the south western desert at, two points in the north west of the island, and three sites on the near and the highest point of the island, Jebel Dukhan. In all they recorded 12 surface sites (Map 5), 300 implements and about 3000 flakes. Most of these sites were dominated by massive flint retouched cores with rough shaping or jagged edges. (Glob 1954:94,113). Subsequently, the Danes, during the course of their annual expeditions from 1954 to 1970 collected a large number of Stone Age tools from various flint sites in Bahrain. However, so far, only 45 tools have been published by Glob (1954) pertaining to the middle Palaeolithic and later periods. Glob did not publish any Lower Palaeolithic tools. And since Glob's publication in 1954 no one paid attention to study these tools and I have tried to classify and illustrate them here with brief citation. Exact site provenance of majority of these tools is unknown. They are in plastic bags without tags and without any details. But according to the Museum authorities they are from Jebel Dukhan. (Khalid al Sindi, personal communication) and other sites mentioned by the Danes and shown on the map (5).

The earliest of these tools are the core tools. Pebble-tool culture has not been, so far, recorded from Bahrain. A mid-Acheulean type of hand-axe(Fig I/1a) with most of the cortex remaining on the reverse side is bifacially worked, it measures 9.5x5.5 cms and is sharply pointed. An ovate handaxe is illustrated in Fig. I/1b. Two shaped blanks for making hand-axes are shown in Fig. I/2 a, b. Four hand-axes of small sizes are illustrated in Fig. I/3a-d. A bifacially worked tool on nodule, probably a hand axe, but unfinished is illustrated in Fig. I/5e. Three oval shaped handaxes on nodules and flaked on both the sides are illustrated in Fig. I/5 a-c. While one specimen in the figure, on the bottom right side is a core (5d). Miniature hand axes are illustrated in Fig. I/4a,b. These small size handaxes are of evolved type. A few core tools, discoidal in shape, (Fig. I/6 a,b) have been found in the collection. Their sizes are 7.5x7 cms, and 7.2x5.2 cms, respectively. A core scraper is shown in Fig. I/6c. A hand axe is shown in Fig.I/6d. A few varieties of the chopping tools are illustrated in Fig.I/7a-d.

Several sites, such as, Wasmiya (50° 29' 47"E., 261°'39"N.), Jebel Dukhan (50o32'41"E., 26°1'6N), and a site immediately south of Sar (50°219'15"E., 26°11'26"N) have been found by the Danish team to be of Palaeolithic scraper culture. (Glob's list, courtesy Frifelt, personal communication). Tools recovered from these sites are mentioned below. A core scraper (Fig. I/8) measures 7 x 6 cms. A large variety of scrapers of varying sizes and shapes were found to be in use in Bahrain and that this culture was dominant. The sharp edges and points of some suggests that they were also used as cutters or piercers. The scraper culture was not only dominant but popular also. A blade core is illustrated in Fig. I/9. An example of knife on a flat nodule, chipped on one surface of the working edge is shown in Fig. I/10a,b. The tool of Fig. I/10c was probably used as a knife. A specimen of miniature cleaver like flake, unfinished, is illustrated in Fig. I/11.

GROUP TWO (MIDDLE PALAEOLITHIC AFFINITIES)

Cornwall in 1952 discovered a small cave on Jebel Dukhan and thus wrote in a letter to Henry Field that : "putting my hand in a narrow cleft of the sandstone mass outside the Jebel Dukhan cave, I pulled out an artifact which typologically could be called a chopper of the middle Palaeolithic. It seems highly probable - on several counts that it remained there, undisturbed, since the Pleistocene" (Field, 1967:76). Subsequently the Danish team found several middle Palaeolithic tools from various sites in Bahrain.

Most of the flint tools discovered by Glob and his team during the survey of 1954 were of clear dark-brown or opaque light - brown colour. They exhibit same cultural characteristics and consists of cores, flakes, chips, regular blades etc. Their characteristic features reveal that they belong to the middle Palaeolithic flake culture, asserts Glob (1954:112) and Field (1956:107). The Danes have found that during the middle Palaeolithic period the scraper culture was pre-dominant in Bahrain, especially at the following sites ; Jebel Dukhan, Wasmiya and a site south of Sar. (Glob's list, courtesy Frifelt, personnal communication). Some of these tools, which are cores both plain and retouched and flakes, with rough shaping or jagged, are of grey colour and number over 200. Some selected specimens are illustrated here.

The tradition of smaller hand axes of the late Lower Palaeolithic period seems to have continued during the middle Palaeolithic period in Bahrain. This is evident from several miniature hand axes found in the collection and illustrated in Figs. II/1 a, b, c, and II/2abc. The latter are bifacially worked. The handaxe of 1c is also bifacial and pointed. Three similar handaxes exhibiting Levallois technique have been found and are illustrated in Fig. II/3abc. They are exhibited in the Bahrain National Museum.

Several specimens of flaked cores, worked bifacially have been found. These are illustrated in Figs. II/4 a, b, c, and II/5abc.

In Bahrain's two retouched cores (Fig.II/14,15) Glob (1954:94, 113) finds closest parallels in the Indian (now Pakistan) Soan (Sohan) culture. The earliest the late Soan is dated to the last Ice Age. But Bahrain's flints have close resemblance to the later phase of Soan Culture. (Krishnaswamy, 1947:Fig. 6 No. 4-11; Shankalia, 1954: Fig. 7 : Wheeler, 1959:41, Fig. 5). This late Soan culture of Punjab is of Levallosian character and is dated to Wurm I and II, 80,000 by Bordes (1968:135). Shankalia (1974:15) though discussed and classified the Soan Culture in the chronological table under Early Palaeolithic period of Middle Pleistocene dated to 5,00,000 B.P., but at another place of the work (1974:22) he has suggested Middle Palaeolithic or the early part of the Upper Plesistocene dated to 50,000 B.P. to 20,000 B.P. for the late Soan A Culture. The general date of the Middle Palaeolithic of India is between c. 50,000 B.P. to 20,000 B. P. And the Middle Palaeolithic of the Pleistocene deposits of the Middle Soan valley in dated to c. 40,000 years. (Allchin, 1982:15). Stratigraphically and typologically, the late Soan industry of Terrace 2 is of two phases. Tools of phase A from the basal level is particularly characterised by rough oval pebbles with untouched but along one side and flaking along the opposite side, though sometimes from the two surfaces alternates, producing a wavy edge, straight or convex. Phase B is more outstandingly a flake-tool industry comparable with the Late Levalloisian of Europe. In the early stages of Soan industry the flakes are crude. While the late Soan has not only simple forms but other flakes manifesting development in technique, with more regular primary flaking and often with faceted platforms. (Wheeler, 1959:39f; Piggot, 1962:30f; Fairservis, 1971:46). Tool of Fig.II/13 also is a similar retouched core.

Two more tools (Fig. II/7,8) of Bahrain from a site immediately south of Sar (Glob's No. 24) are similar to those found in the late Soan culture. (Glob, 1954:113). The first one is a flake knife or point and has very little flaking; and the other is a borer or perforator and has no flaking along the edges. Like Glob, Caton-Thompson (1952:189-218) also found resemblence of South Arabia's (Hadramauth's) Palaeolothic tools to that of late Soan industry.

Two massive flakes with coarse edge flaking (Fig. II/16,17) have been found from a site about a mile south of Jebel Dukhan, which are reminiscent of Levalloisian technique. They are comparable to similar specimens from Mount Carmel (Garrod and Bate, 1937. Pl. XXV Og, XXXVI). From the same site, a triangular flake like a three pointed star (Fig. IV/1) has been recovered by Glob which belongs to the Middle Palaeolithic culture of Bahrain (Glob, 1954:112). It is a notched tool used as a spoke shave. A variety of flake implements have been recorded from site immediately south of Sar. These are : a flake with scraper edge (Fig. II/11); a centre burin (Fig. II/6); a unique blade with surface flaking on both sides (Fig. II/9); a massive flake of triangular form worked with toothed scraping edge (Fig. II/12). Similar flake chiped to a point Fig.II/10. A borer or perforator (Fig. II/19) is bent at the point and is worked at the distal end. A core (Fig. II/18) has been retouched to form an scraping edge. From the same site there is a circular flake scraper (Fig. V/1) with working on all sides and uniformly retouched edge on the opposite end to the bulb of percussion. From the collection in the stores of the Bahrain National Museum we have typical knives (Fig. III/6, 7) worked bifacially on a nodle. A specimen of borer-cum-scraper is illustrated in Fig. III/10. Allround scrappers on Levellois flakes are illustrated in Fig. III/1, 2. Another is shown in Fig. III/8. A burin on a thick blank/nodule, in crude form is illustrated in III/12. Two core-scrapers illustrated here (Fig. V/2-3) with side working and retouches are exhibited in Bahrain's National Museum. Retouched flake-scrapers are shown in Fig.III/3,4. A point made on a flake is in Fig.III/5.

A variety of middle Palaeolithic tools discovered during the Danish expedition of Bahrain from numerous sites are preserved in the stores of Bahrain's National Museum at al Muhrraqah. Some of them are described here. An example of twisted triangular point is shown in Fig. IV/2. Two crescent - like flakes are with partial side working (Fig. VI/2,3). Tools of Fig. VI/1 and Fig. VII/3, are points with incipient tang. Could be a notch. While illustration of Fig. VI/1 b, c, are bifacially worked points. Apparently leaf shaped tool of Fig. VI/4 may be a bifacially worked ovate point. While Fig. VII/2 is a retouched flake. Circular flake scrapers (Fig. VIII/1,2) with flakes removed leaving partly cortex in the centre and having side working have been recorded from Bahrain. The illustration of Fig. VIII/ 3 is of a straight convex scraper with flakes removed allround leaving cortex in the centre. A denticulate blade with side working is illustrated in Fig. IX/1. Flakes, retouched on one side are illustrated in Fig. IX/2,3. A few varieties of ovate type scrapers (Fig. X/1-3) have been found. Flake scrapers (Fig. X/4,5) bifacial and used as multiple tools are also recorded. As seen from these, flakes have been removed and cortex is remaining. A few specimens of hanaxes, probably used during the middle Palaeolithic period are illustrated here in Fig. XI/1-4. The last one (No. 4) has a twisted end. Belonging to the same period of the same dark brown flint are three chopping tools (Fig. XII/1-3).

GROUP THREE (UPPER PALAEOLITHIC AFFINITIES)

Bahrain's inventory of Upper Palaeolithic tools is not as rich as its predecessor. It is quite possible that the tools of the earlier period might have been in use for a prolonged period. Also these tools might have been in use simultaneously along with the characteristic blade tools of Upper Palaeolithic Culture. This feature has been noticed in Arabia's mainland also. (See Vol. I in this series, p. 49). Advancement in stone tool technology with the introduction of microliths is the characteristic of Bahrain's Upper Palaeolithic Culture. New type of tools that seems to have appeared during this period are : shouldered points of Solutrean type; microlith burins, scraper, micro-blades, both plain and denticulated, end-scrapers, microlith knives, arrow-heads resembling Aterian, etc. The microlith tools were evidently set in a shaft or handle to form a tool or a weapon such as barbed arrows or fish-spears. There is a marked difference, as will be evident from the following page, between the microliths of the Upper Palaeolithic period than those of its succeeding Epi-Palaeolithic period. The only specimen of shouldered and tanged point found from Bahrain's collection (Fig. XII/1) is a single-shouldered bifacial point made by the pressure flaking techniques with rough working on the vertical as well as shouldered side. Back edge of the stem is smooth unworked. This specimen from Bahrain is similar in typology to that found in the Solutrean industries of Upper Palaeolithic of France. (cf. Fig. 12, p. 188 Wymer, 1982, Bordes, 1971, p. 160). This type of tool has not been recorded in Saudi Arabia's collection. Two triangular micro-blades, one plain (Fig. XII/2) and another denticulate (Fig. XII/3) have been recorded. Two backed knife-points are recorded. (Fig. XII/4,5). A specimen of burin/point is illustrated in fig. XII/6. An end scraper is illustrated as Fig. XII/7. A bifacial borer is illustrated as Fig. XII/a. A strangulated blade is in Fig. XII/8b.

A few specimens of bifacially flaked miniature points are illustrated in Fig. III/1 (top row). In the lower row are allround scrapers, the second from left being broken. A different variety of bifacially flaked points are illustrated in Fig. XIII/2. A specimen of unfinished, but bifacially worked, point is in Fig. XIII/3 (above). While below is an elongated hammer stone. Bifacial points are illustrated in Fig. XIV/1-4. Two large crescent shaped scrapers are illustrated in Fig. XIV/5, 6.

GROUP FOUR (EPI-PALAEOLITHIC / MESOLITHIC AFFINITIES)

Epi-Palaeolithic/Mesolithic in Bahrain is a transitional phase from the Old Stage Age to the New Stone Age. In the Arabian mainland it begins from about 10,000 B.C. with the Holocene and seems to have lasted until about 6000 B.C. As in other places of west Asia it is characterised by microlith flint as well as obsidian tools. Bahrain's Mesolithic inventory is not richer in variety of tools. Three specimens of notched foliates have been recorded. One of them (Fig. XV/1) is with rounded base and tip broken. While the other (Fig. XV/3) is slightly different with smaller base and narrower with pointed tip. The third (Fig. XV/1) has notches at the base.

Two specimens of notched arrowheads (Fig. XVI/1, 2) have been recorded. Several triangular microlith points. (Fig. XVII) have been recorded. They are almost of the same uniform design, with their base sloping on one side and one of them is an isoceles triangle. These microliths were evidently hafted by the prehistoric people of Bahrain into a shaft and used for hunting the game. The microliths of Bahrain has close resemblance to those of the Mesolithic industry of the Natufian of Palestine recorded by Garrod (1932:262f) and Kirkbridge (1966:49) for the Beidha Mesolithic Natufian flint industry. Several varieties of these points are recorded in Bahrain. (Fig. XVII). Some of them are symmetrical, asymmetrical, triangular, and the base hollow or concave. They are in different sizes.

Crude blades from an unknown site are recorded. (Fig. XVIII/1, 2). A variety of points, piercer-cum-cutting tools, in different shapes and sizes, are recorded in the collection from an unknown site. (Fig. XVIII/3).

GROUP FIVE (NEOLITHIC AFFINITIES)

Neolithic flint tools are wide spread in Bahrain (see Map 6) and are found in abundance. From a little site about 1.6 miles east of Wasmiya (50°30'4"E. 26°1'37"N.) along the coast line (site No. 27=509 of Danish list), covering an area of approximately 30 square yards, a collection of arrowheads along with fragments of semi-fabricated arrow heads, and chips was made by Glob (1954:113; Glob's list, courtesy Frifelt), who asserts that the site belongs to a flint smith and might have existed for a day or for a few hours only. On the site was also found several hundreds of extremely small falkes from the surface flaking of arrowheads. This raw flint is of the same dark brown variety as found in the Palaeolithic tools discovered at the site. However, two specimens are an exception. These were of transparent grey flint and of a dull reddish flint. The collection contains cores, flakes, chips, rejects or incomplete implements and tools used in the manufacture of Neolithic tools. The collection represents the stages in the making of the arrowheads from raw material to the finished product. They are illustrated here. Fig. XIX/1, is that of a flake, which was struck off roughly and shows a commenced retouch on one of the sides. Fig XIX/2 is that of a more finished preparatory piece. Fig. XIX/2 is that of a blank for making arrowhead. On one preparatory blank the flat flaking was completed, but during the final stage of this flaking or while chipping the barbs out the bottom of the blank was accidentally broken off and the piece discarded. Finally we have the completed arrowheads, Fig. XXI. The chipping tool (Fig. XIX/3) discovered with the collection is a little spherical flint pebble used by the flint smith. This is attested by the traces of striking on both the sides of the tool. This was the only chipping tool found on the site by Glob. (1954:114). It must have been utilised for striking flakes and for initial rough shaping of the implements. These illustrations elucidate vividly the work of the flint smith. However, the animal bone or the tool used for the final flaking of the arrowheads was not found on the site. Obviously it must have perished. The Danes found from a site 29 (=511 of Danish Catalogue) a tanged arrowhead (Fix. XX/7) which was fashioned from a pointed blade with the tang flaked from the front.

Glob (1954:113) assigns this piece a Late Palaeolithic date, or later. However, I would rather prefer to classify it under the latter, Neolithic period along with the entire group of arrowheads. This is also in accordance with general developments of culture in the Arabian mainland. It is obvious from this artifact that the technique of making arrowhead from a pointed blade by flaking tang from the front continued to be adopted in the Neolithic period as well.

McNicoll and Michael Roaf led British expedition to Bahrain during 1973-74 and 1975 and made surface surveys and excavations on several sites. During the first season they made soundings at the following three sites : al-Markh, Janussan north and Diraz east. These sites were numbered by McNicoll as, 2027, 2011 and 2023 respectively. From al Markh which lies about 1400 m. from the south-west coast of Bahrain and six kilometers south of the town of Zallaq, McNicoll recovered a large quantity of flint from the surface and from a few stratified sites. The flint collection comprises : cores, flakes, blades/bladelets, scrapers, unclassified tools and unworked pieces. The quantity of flints of different categories recovered from different surface and stratified sites is detailed in the tables (1-4) based on the preliminary count made by Mary Forst, Gary Pierson and Stephen Collier of the McNicoll team. Besides these flints, the British team also found projectile points during their initial reconnaissance. (McNicoll, 1975, Ms).

At al Markh (For the environs see map in chapter I, *supra*), large quantities of flints were found on the surface and in the topsand. But comparatively smaller number was found in the stratified deposits. This may imply that the site was at that time higher than at present. Apparently the surface and topsand flints are the deposits of the uppermost surviving stratum and other layers of sand over them was stripped off by the wind. Different heights of the sites during the period of its occupation by the flint-users has been roughly estimated by McNicoll.

AL-MARKH FLINT COLLECTION

TABLE 1 : SURFACE FLINT GRID AREA

	K17	G17	H19	K19	L20	M20
Cores	18	121	74	99	11	27
Flakes	649	570	781	511	788	633
Blades/Bladelets	51	27	59	57	46	18
Scrapers	31	30	8	29	18	3
Unclassified tools	140	154	261	415	94	146
Unworked	1452	916	2045	1685	2123	1334
Total	2341	1718	3228	2796	3080	2161

TABLE 2: TRENCH K19 STRATIFIED FLINT

Deposits	1*	1.2	1.2a	1.3	1.3*	1.4	1.5	1.6	1.7	1.8	1.9	1.10	1.10*	1.11	1.12	1.13	1.13a
Flakes	511	237	3	43	33	-	8	50	5	4	-	8	6	15	17	3	1
Blades	57	15	-	15	3	-	1	12	1	2	-	1	2	-	-	-	-
Scrapers	20	1	-	2	2	-	2	1	-	2	-	2	1	-	-	-	-
Unclassified Tools	415	35	5	8	4	1	1	12	2	2	9	3	13	6	4	-	'
Cores	99	34	-	11	4	-	1	33	2	2	1	4	-	2	2	4	-
Unworked	1685	472	3	24	39	-	2	33	22	22	5	5	2	6	13	13	4

* Deposit 1.1 covered an area of 10x5m. All the succeeding deposits were taken from an area 5x2.50m.

(After McNicoll, 1975, Unpublished Report)

TABLET 3 : TRENCH G17 : STRATIFIED FLINT

Deposit	21.1	21.2	21.3	21.3a	21.3b	21.4	21.5	21.6
Flakes	14	37	121	5	3	5	21	2
Blades		1	8	-	-	-	5	
Scrapers								
Unclassified								
Tools	9	16	31	-	1	2	11	1
Cores	6	6	11	-	1	-	1	
Unmarked	43	53	199	14	6	3	42	-

TABLE 4 : TRENCH D19 : STRATIFIED FLINT

Deposit	1.1
Flakes	138
Blades	2
Scrapers	-
Unclassified tools	32
Cores	13
Unmarked	128

(After McNicoll, 1975, Unpublished Report)

For instance; in area K19 surface examination produced a total of 2796 flints. One-eight of this quantity (i.e., 349 flints) came from the surface trench of 5x2.5m. Flints from the topsand numbered 895. The stratified flints from a depth of about 0.8m. numbered 489. The ratio of surface/topsand to stratified flint works out to 12:5. This is the ratio of lost deposits to surviving deposits by assuming that the process of deposition of flints was at a reasonably constant rate. However, at another site G17 the mound seems to be less crowded. Here surface flints from an area of 10 M^2 numbered 1718. One-sixteenth of this number came from an area equivalent to the surface of 2.50 M^2 trench. While only 72 flints were recovered from the topsand. The stratified flints numbered 607 from a depth of 0.90 m., of the occupation deposits. The ratio of surface/topsand to stratified flints is 1:3. The lost deposits was 0.30m. and the total depth of occupation was 1.20m (McNicoll, 1975 Ms).

As mentioned above, the Danish expedition not only found Palaeolithic tools but also Neolithic from Wasmiya (Glob's No. 27) which is inland from the coast, apparently along the 10 m. contour line approximately suggestion that the shore line might have been 10m. higher during the Stone Age than the present time. The evidence from al Markh also confirms that the sea level during Bahrain's Stone Age period was much higher, may be 3-4 m. (McNicoll, 1975 Ms.) The British excavation led by Michael Roaf at al Markh in 1975, 1400 m from the west coast of Bahrain and about 6 kms., south of the village of Zallaq produced 6896 pieces of flint consisting mainly various forms of scrapers. Francis Healy who studied Roaf's flint collection says that it is a distinct tool collection, consisting of : tile flint, barbed and tanged arrowhead, bifacially worked; a fragmentary bifacially flaked ovoid or foliate projectile head, three tile flint knives, and a small awl or borer. These flints are comparable with finds from sites both with and without 'Ubaid pottery in the eastern region of Saudi Arabia (See Vol.I) and from sites of Kapel's C and D groups in Qatar. Besides these flints from excavated site, surface finds from al Markh include arrowheads showing a variety of shapes, technique and materials. This site of al Markh (Fig.A) is dated to about 3,800 B.C., on the basis of a painted sherd found there which according to Joan Oates, is similar to those of Ur-'Ubaid 3 of Mesopotamia. (Roaf, 1974:449f; 1976:151).

The Neolithic flint tools collected by the Danes, the British, the Australian, the Bahrainis and other amaetures are preserved in the stores of Bahrain's National Museum. Some of these implements from this general collection are illustrated here at Figs XIX to XXVII. Precise details of their provenance and the name of the person(s) or team who discovered the individual piece(s) cannot be provided as the record is not available, at least to the author. However, they are said to have come mainly from al Markh and Wasmiya. The collection consists of following tool types (both complete as well as incomplete): Unfinished arrowheads, shaped blanks with side working (Fig. XX/1-5, Fig. XXII); complete arrowhead, Fig XXI and a few pieces in Fig. XXII, shaped flake (Fig. XX/5); proto-arrowheads, an attempt to make pseudo types (Fig. XX/8 a,b). They resemble the arrowhead from Naqdan collection of Rub al-Khali, illustrated by Edens (1989:18); foliate points of three types and of different sizes, (Fig. XXIII); an spear. (Fig. XXIII). It is exactly same as that found at Thumama, 90 km. north west of Riyadh, Saudi Arabia. (See Vol.I.p 66 and Fig XXXVI, p. 252). The Thumama lithic industry exhibits fine workmanship and characterised by elongated spears with round and sharp distal ends and made of flint and chert. (Abu Daruk etal 1984:109f).

Bahrain's bifacial elongated tanged shouldered arrowheads are reminscent of similar types found in the Neolithic Naqdan collection from Rub al Khali, Saudi Arabia. (Edens;1981 L 18, fig. 1); but with elongated stem. In the figure they are crudely worked at the sides, while some pieces show attempt to work uniformly.

Bahrain's Neolithic collection comprises : tanged and barbed triangular arrow-head, notched on the left side. Tanged and barbed triangular arrowhead, elongated tang but tip broken. A broad retouched flake with broken tang, brown flint. A broader tanged bifacial arrowhead, altogether different from the rest of collection. Dark brown flint. Hallow based arrow head (Fig. XXII b) in the second row, but broken of light blue flint. Bifacial foliates (Fig. XXIV) of various types and sizes. The first one is a blank or flake in the shape of a broad foliate for making foliate points but partly broken. One specimen is of a tanged foliate. Arrowheads of different varieties, in shape, technique and material. (Fig. XXII). One barbed and tanged arrowhead, is of pale brown flint, made on a flake. Flat bifacial flaking, is incomplete, retouched and is parallel to the edges. Slightly denticulate. It measures 3.3 cms. in length, 2 cms. in width and 0.4 cms thick. It is from al Markh (site No. 2027). (Roaf 1976:156f). Barbed and tanged arrowhead (1b) darkbrown flint. Flat bifacial flaking on a flake, parallel along the edges, tip broken. Barbed and tanged arrowhead of darkbrown flat bifacial flanking, sharply pointed. Barbed and tanged elongated, arrowhead of dull reddish flint are also found. In some specimens the tang is slightly worked and ends at a sharp point. An elongated unfinished arrowhead of dark brown flint has a tang too small compared to the size of the main head. Two fine, broad triangular or kite shaped arrowhead (Fig. XXII, third row). Two incomplete/broken arrowheads of bluish-grey flints are also found. They differ in shape and size from each other. Different types of arrowheads in different shapes partially complete/broken are illustrates in Fig. XXII, in order to show the variety of tools from Bahrain. An awl (Fig. XXIII/at the bottom) worked to point as micro-Mousterian, is from site No. 28 of Glob (1956:11) and 510 of Danish catalogues, i.e., south western coastal plain. This is the third flint site of Wasmiya located at longitude 50°30'7", and latitude 26°1'4". From the same site sickle blades (see below) dated to early Neolithic period have been found.

Two samples of Rastro-Carinate scrapers (Fig. XXIII/first two in the third row) have been recorded from Bahrain. They resemble the one from Saudi Arabia. (See Vol.I in this series). The Danish expedition under Glob (1954:112-114) discovered a series of toothed sickle blades in Bahrain at sites No. 24 and 29 of Glob Nos. Thus indicating that the people of Bahrain during Neolithic period not only lived on hunting but also adopted to agriculture. Cultivation of corn was practised is evident from the discovery of sickle blades. The sickle blades (Fig. XXV) which the Danes discovered were all fashioned of brown flint with the exception of one which is of a light grey, transparent flint. These are illustrated here from the collection preserved in the stores of Bahrain's National Museum. However, from the inventory No. 510 registered on some of the blades, it is evident that the blades used by the Bahrain's prehistoric people were of different shapes and sizes and not one particular type of uniform dimensions were used. All varieties coming from a single site shows that individual person or a group used its own type of blade designed according to their own exegencies or needs. Alternatively, each variety might have been used at different times. These blades are formed from narrow blades, of which one is a typical keeled blade. The first blade struck off a core after it had been flaked into shape for striking. Several of these blades were used together, set in a row to form a cutting edge in a sickle of some other material, bone, wood, or earthern ware. A bright and sparkling surface on the toothed edge shows where the sickle edge has been worn by the silica contained in the harvested corn stalks. Similar types of sickle teethed blades have been found in Mesopotamia and Egypt (Glob 1954:114) which are dated to ca. eight millennium B.C. (Clark, 1980:22).

Sickle blades on flakes with and without polish and on backed flake with polish were discovered in the Oasis of al Hasa, in the eastern Saudi Arabia, and in close proximity to Bahrain. They are the result of the pressure flaking on one side only of a normal trapezoidal-section flake. There seems to be a cultural link, observes Raikes (1967:28-38), between the al Hasa sickle blades and the biface toothed blades of Pirak of Indus Valley Civilization.

A large number of bifacial foliates of varying sizes have been found in the stores of Bahrain's National Museum. They are illustrated here. (Fig. XX). Their lengths and widths at the middle points are :4x2.8 cms., 3.9x2.7 cms., 3.6x2cms 4.4x2.2 cms., 4.5x2.2cms., 3.6x2 cms., 3.6x2 cms.

A large number of obsidian tools are present in the Bahrain collection, which comprises of arrowheads of various sizes, blades, knives, burins, trihedral rods, borers, flakes, etc. These are illustrated in Fig. XXI.

GROUP SIX (CHALCOLITHIC AFFINITIES)

The traditional Chalcolithic material of the Levant (Helms/Duckworth, 1976:31-35; Kalpan;1969;2ff) made especially by tabular flint side-and-end scrapers, awls, and micro-awls, choppers, plain and retouched blades and flakes, notched pieces etc., are found in Bahrain's collection. Some of these are illustrated here. A large variety of tabular cutting tools in numerous sizes have been recorded from Bahrain. (Fig. XXX) and are preserved in the stores of the Bahrain National Museum. Different shapes and sizes indicate that they were used for different types of cutting and for different material. They resemble the tabular cutting tools found in Qatar (Ras Abaruk, al Da'asa) in very close proximity to Bahrain. (Smith, in de Cardi 1978). All the tabular flint tools from Bahrain seems to have been used as sickles for reeping corn. The sickle edge of each one of them is worn by the silica contained in the harvested cornstalks.

Three variants of notched points/piercers (Fig. XXIII/1-3) are found in the Bahrain collection. Two of them are bifacially flaked; while the third is retouched along the edges leaving the cortex. A bifacially worked foliate with double-notch is found in the collection of Bahrain of unknown function. It measures 6x2.3 cms. Scrapers of different shapes and of different material are recorded from a site. The triangular one has no working and broken; and seems to be a discard. The oval one has been retouched more on one side. The half pieces appears to be of a broken oval scraper, retouched and used. A sandstone pounder (Fig. XXIX) has been recorded from Bahrain. It is similar to those found in the neighbourhood at al-Da'asa in Qatar, (Smith in de Cardi, 1978). There are three cutters and choppers in the collection. They measure 11.3 x 6.3 cms. A large triangular shaped cutter-cum-scraper (Fig. XXX) measures 10.7x7.4 cms. Another one is of smaller size. An axe is of size 7x7 cms (extreme points). A large sized tool, probably a saddle quern is found in the collection with retouches on the lower edge. The collection consists of four triangular shaped sand stone tools and one irregular rectangular.

RESUME

From the foregoing details and illustrations of Stone Age tools from Bahrain there is no doubt that it was inhabited by the prehistoric man. Bahrain provides an excellent example of continuous occupation from prehistoric times to recent times. The large variety of tools of different periods suggests that different Stone Age cultures developed in Bahrain as in the case of the Arabian mainland and other neighbouring countries. Bahrain's tools have parallels with those from Saudi Arabia and other south west Asian countries. The earliest choppers, chopping tools of Olduvai type and Acheulean handaxes have not been recorded so far, from Bahrain. Different varieties of raw material for making stone tools was abundant in Bahrain and was easily available to the Stone Age man. Most of the sites are located on higher terrace adjacent to the Jebel Dukhan. The raw material is usually embeded with lime. That the tools were made in Bahrain and not brought from far away is evident from the chipping site of flint smith from where fragments of semi fabricated tools were recovered along with complete peices and hammer stone meant for shaping the tools. But since Bahrain formed part of Arabian mainland during prehistoric times the possibility of migration and remigration of both men and culture to Bahrain from Arabian mainland and visa versa does exist. All the tools of Bahrain have parallels with the tools of Arabian mainland, Levant etc. For comparison see Atlas of Stone Age Tools in Volume I in this series.

(B) ATLAS OF STONE AGE TOOLS OF BAHRAIN

GROUP ONE (LOWER PALAEOLITHIC AFFINITIES)

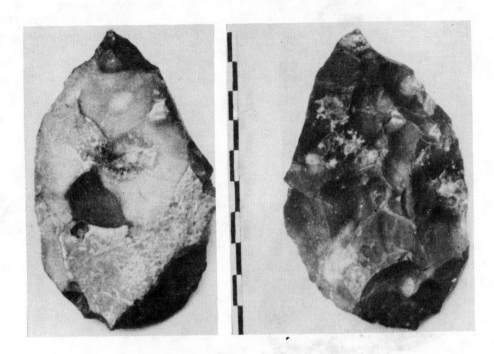

Fig.I/1a   A mid-Acheulean type of Hand-Axe

Fig. I/1b   An ovate Hand-Axe

Fig.I/ 2a,b

Shaped blanks for making Hand-axes

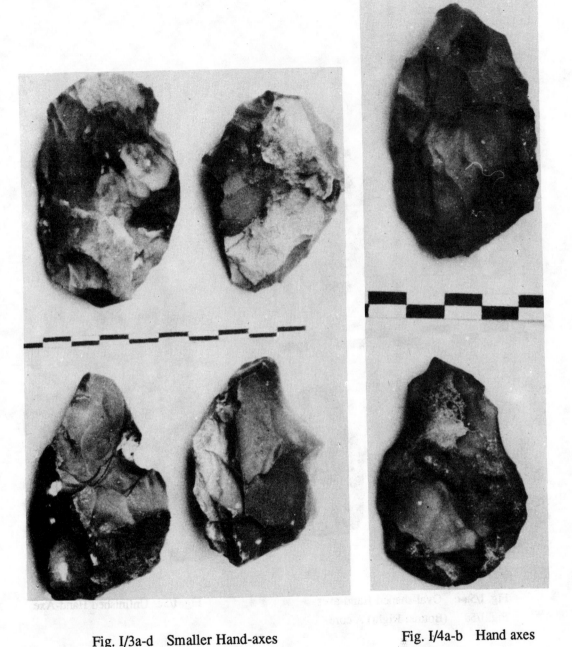

Fig. I/3a-d Smaller Hand-axes

Fig. I/4a-b Hand axes

74

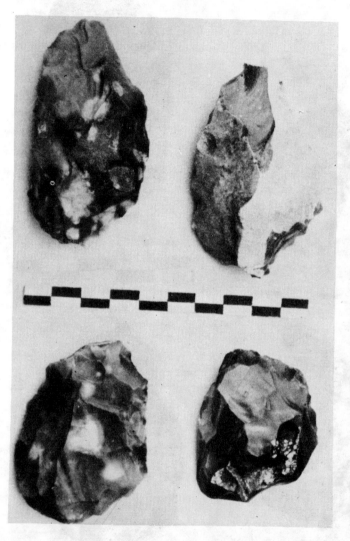

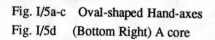

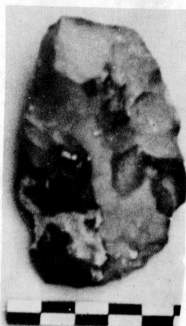

Fig. I/5a-c Oval-shaped Hand-axes

Fig. I/5d (Bottom Right) A core

Fig. I/5e Unfinished Hand-Axe

Fig. I/6a-b Core tools - discoidal (Top row)
Fig. I/6c   A core scraper (Bottom left)
Fig. I/6d   A Hand-axe (Bottom right)

Fig. I/7a-d   Chopping Tools

Fig. I/8   A core scraper   Fig. I/9   A blade core

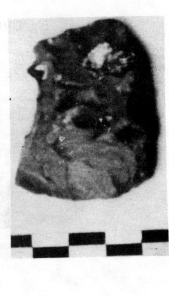

Fig. I/10c   A knife   Fig. I/11 A cleaver shaped tool

Fig. I/10a,b   Knives

GROUP TWO (MIDDLE PALAEOLITHIC AFFINITIES)

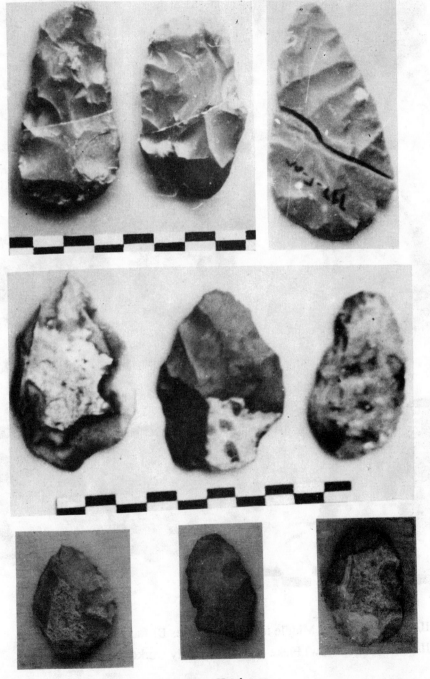

Miniature Hand axes

Fig. II/1a,b,c (Top row) Fig. II/2a,b,c (Middle row) Fig. 3abc (Bottom row)

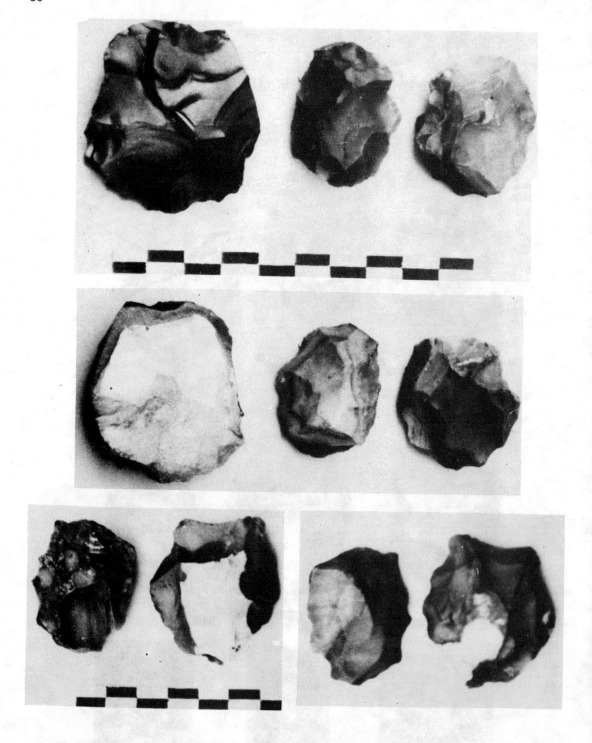

Fig. II/4a,b,c (Top and Middle row) Flake cores Bi-facially worked

Fig. II/5 a,b (Bottom row) Flake cores Bi-facially worked

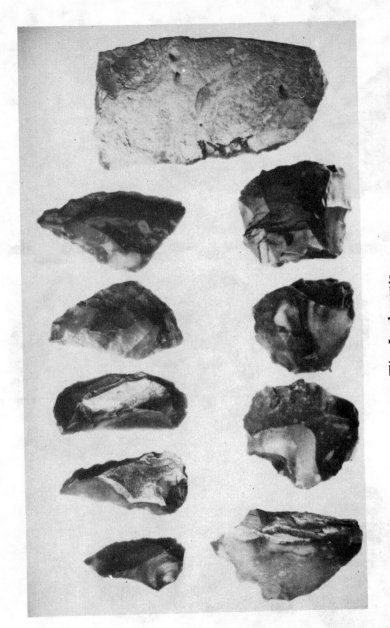

Flint Implements

(Top Row L. to R.) Fig. Nos. II/6, II/7, II/8, II/9, II/10.

(Bottom Row L. to R.) Fig. Nos. II/12, II/13, II/14, II/15, II/11

82

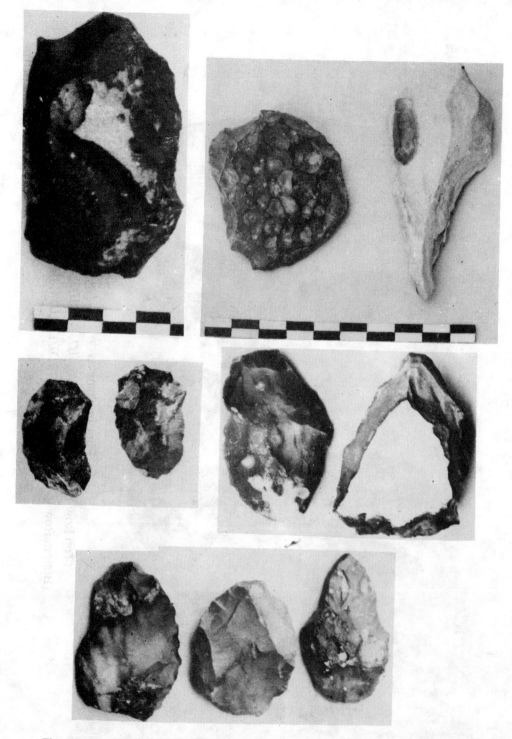

Fig. II/5 (Top) (L. to R.) Flaked core; Fig. II/18 Retouched core with scraping edge
Fig. II/19 A borer or perforator
Fig. II/16,17 (Centre) (L.-R.).Massive Flakes; Fig. III/1,2Scrapers on Levellois Flakes
Fig. III/3-5 (Bottom) Retouched Flakes, a point made on a flake (last one).

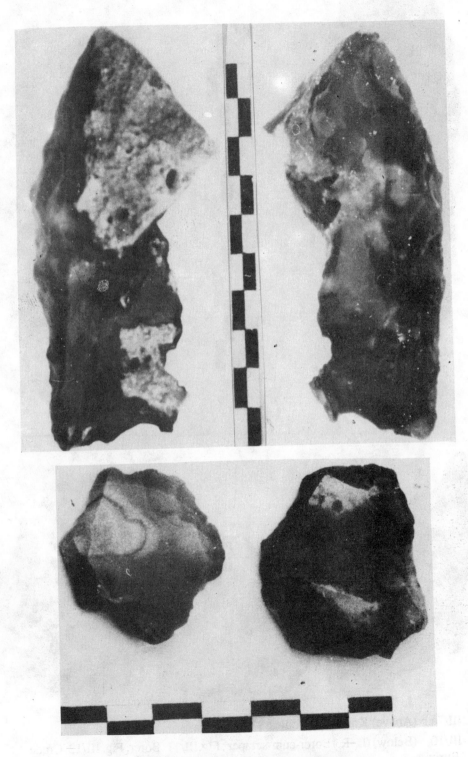

Fig. III/6 (Above) Bifacially flaked knife
Fig. III/8,9 (Below) Allround scrapers

84

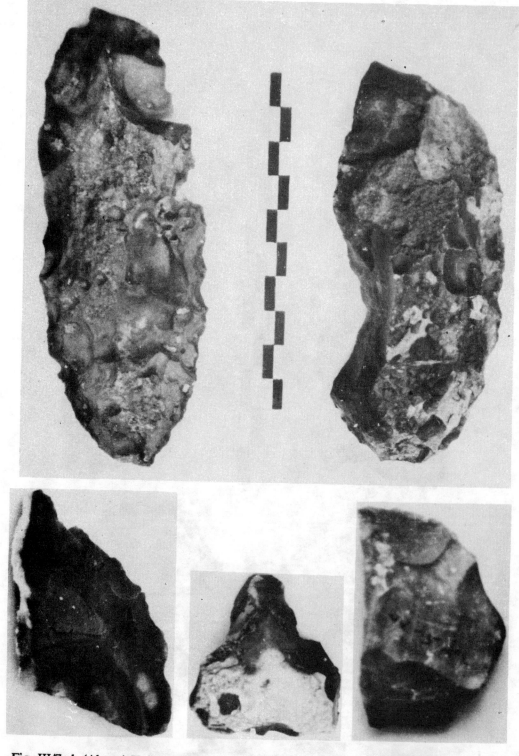

Fig. III/7a,b (Above) Knives on Nodles

Fig. III/10 (Below) (L.-R.) Borer-cum-scraper; Fig.III/11 Borer; Fig. III/12 Crude Burin

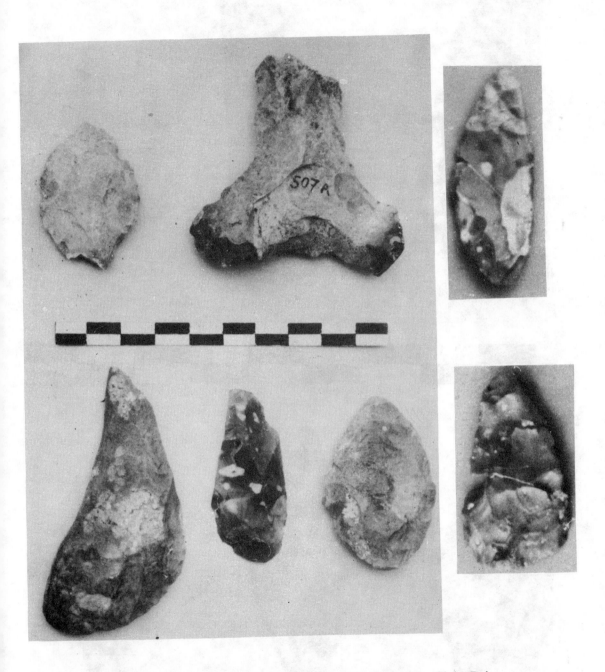

(Above) (L.-R.)   Fig. IV/2   A flake scraper   Fig. IV/1 Triangular Flake Point.
Fig. VI/1b.   A point. (Below) (L.-R.)   Fig. IV/3 Twisted Triangular point.
Fig.IV/1a Point   Fig.V/1   Circular scraper.

86

(Above) (L.-R.)   Fig.VI/2,3 Crescent shaped flakes.   Fig. VI/4 Leaf shape flake.
(Below) (L.-R.) Fig.VII/1. Ovate point. Fig.VII/2. Retouched Flake. Fig. VII/3. A
point

87

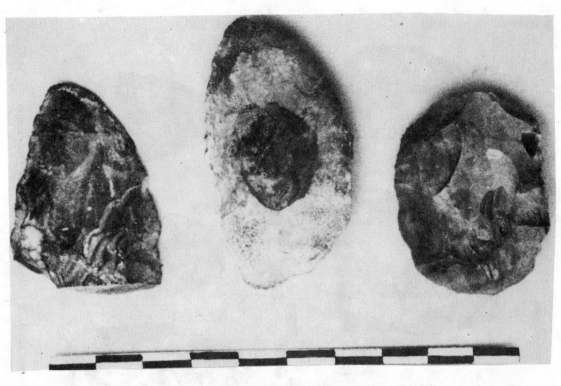

(Above) Fig. VIII/1-3. Flake scrapers.

(Below) **Fig. VIII/4** A Crude hammer stone with battering marks.

88

(Above) (L.-R.) Fig. IX/1 A Denticulate Blade; IX/2,3 Retouched Flakes. Fig.X/1 Ovate scraper
(Below) (L.-R.) Fig. XI/2-5. Hand axes

GROUP THREE (UPPER PALAEOLITIC AFFINITIES)

(Above) (L.-R.) Fig. XII/1. A shouldered Tanged point.   Fig.XII/2,3 Triangular
Micro blades. Fig. XII/6 A burin/point

(Below) (L.-R.) Fig.XII/4,5 Blade Knives.   Fig. XII/7 Oblique Blanded blade.

Fig. XII/8. A strangulated blade

Fig. XIII/1a-d. Bifacially flaked Mini-points

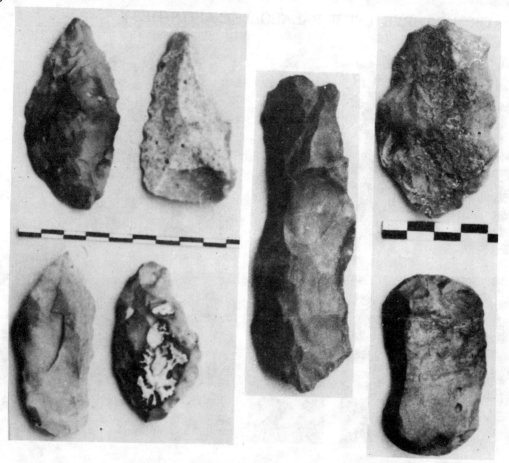

(Left) Fig. XII/2a-d. Bifacially worked points. (Centre) Fig. XII/4. Blade. (Right) Fig. XIII/3. Unfinished point (Above) Hammer Stone (Below). Fig. XIV/1-4. Bifacial points

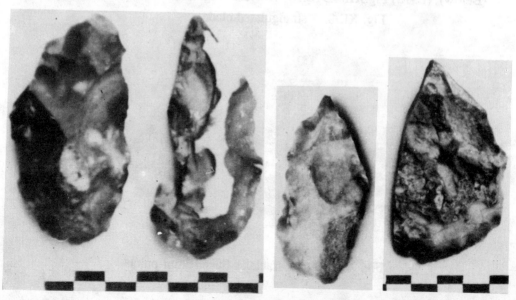

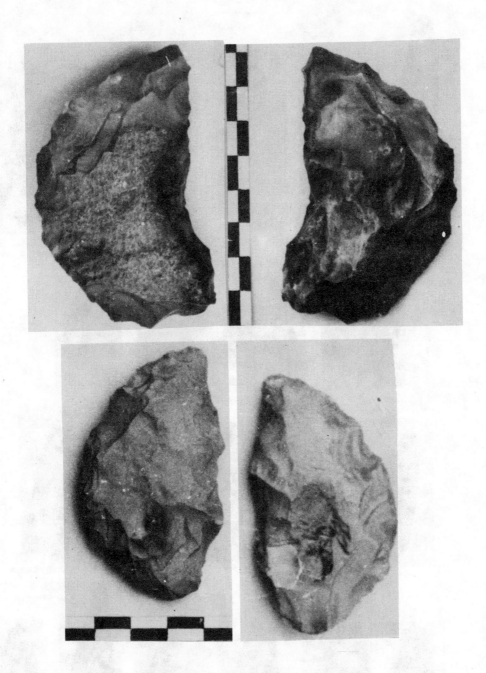

Fig. XIV/5,6 Crescents

GROUP FOUR (EPI - PALAEOLITHIC AFFINITIES)

(1st Row) Fig. XVI/1-4 Notched Foliates

(2nd - 4th Row) Fig. XVII Microlith points

Fig. XVIII/1,2 Crude blades

Fig. XVIII/3 Tanged and simple points

GROUP FIVE (NEOLITHIC AFFINITIES)

(1st Row, L.-R.) Fig. XIX/1. A struck retouched flake. Fig. XIX/2 A preparatory piece. Fig. XIX/3 A hammer stone. (2nd Row) Fig. XX/1-5 Unfinished arrowheads. (3rd row) Fig.XX/7 A tanged arrow head. XX/6 Unfinished arrowhead XX/8a,b Pseudo Types. Fig. XX/8c Shaped flake

Fig. XXI   A selection Arrowheads.

Fig. XXII Different varieties of Arrow heads

Fig. XXIII   Foliates of various types, Spears, Rastro-Carinate Scrapers and Awl.

98

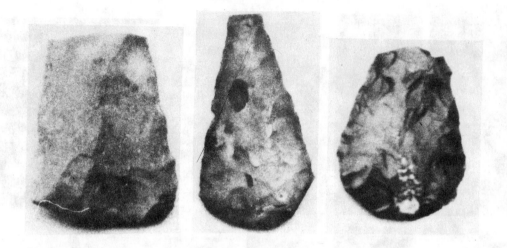

Fig. XXIV/1-3   Shaped blanks for making foliates

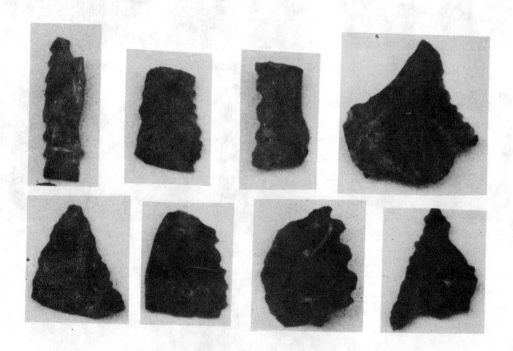

Fig. XXV   Sickle blades of different shapes and sizes.

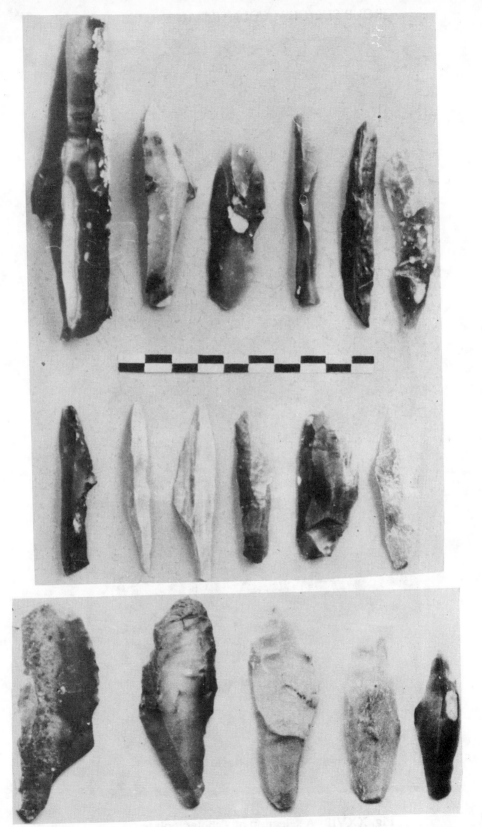

Fig. XXVI   A selection of Obsidian tools

Fig. XXVII A selection of Tabular tools

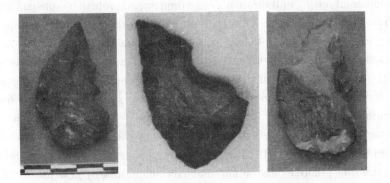

Fig. XVIII   Notched Points/Piercers

Fig. XXIX - XXXII   Sand stone pounders, large cutting tool, an axe and a fabricator

(C)   SUBSISTENCE STRATEGIES AND SETTLEMENTS

The environmental setting of Bahrain played a fundamental role in its subsistence strategies and economy. The subsistence pattern in Bahrain during the prehistoric and protohistoric periods or during Pleistocene and Holocene was not different from that of the Arabia when Bahrain was attached to the mainland until its separation as an island around 6000 B.C. (See Chapter VII in Volume I in this series). During our period of study the subsistence strategies, in Bahrain, evolved in four stages. Firstly, subsistence based on intensive exploitation, hunting and gathering, and littoral biomass. Secondly, with the change in environmental conditions, from cool, dry climate during the late Pleistocene, increase of rainfall, developed a more sedentary life and vegetation. Thus resulting in the intensification of hunting and gathering practices and simultaneously adaptation of new means of obtaining food, including sea-food. With the beginning of Holocene around 8000 B.C., which coincided with the beginning of the Neolithic in the Levant/South West Asia, the environment changed, creating better conditions favourable for agriculture and thus resulting in the Neolithic Revolution. The practice of agriculture in Bahrain during the Neolithic and later periods is evident from the New Stone Age tools found in abundance and illustrated above. During the initial stage of food production, forms of food production were developed within each specialised foraging system, organised around the domestic animals of Bahrain along two distinctive techno complexes, pastoral and maritime. It is possible that through maritime contacts, domesticates from outside were also introduced into Bahrain. Thirdly, Developed Farming Economy, according to Tosi (1986:17) which was derived from the social integration of the three specialized forms of subsistence economy, oasis farming, navigation, and camel herding were practiced, Fourthly, with the emergence of Bahrain as an important entrepot for the maritime trade between the east and the west and vice-versa, the subsistence strategy took a new dimension with a momentous economic development from the revenue derived from imports and exports. Consequently, civilized urban society and cities developed in Bahrain, whose remains still survive to this day.

The   inhabitants of the Palaeolithic Bahrain seems to have relied largely on the exploitation of inshore resources comprising small to medium-sized fish along with the gathering of molluscs, mostly venerids and pearl oyster, as readily available in addition to their diet. They might have relied largely on nets and traps perhaps laid out across the channel separating al Markh from the main island. (de Cardi, 1986:90). That the Stone Age hunter-gatherer's of al Markh depended on sea for their food resource is evidenced from the fish bones found in bulk of the skeleton remains. This is also attested by the discovery of projectile points, used for hunting of mammals and scrapers and blades suitable for cutting and scaling fish and probably for opening shells. That shells were gathered for food is evident from McNicoll expedition 1973-75 to al-Markh were shells found were predominantly oyster (pinctade and murex) and were concentrated mainly in the burnt deposit and were severly burnt. But this interpretation for shell gathering contradicts with that suggested by Nielson for the third millennium site of Ras al-Jasayir. (McNicoll, 1975 : 5 unpublished report). The latter deposits from al Markh 1 and 2 contained the bones of much larger fish together with dugong, mammal and goat, and it has been suggested that breakages resulting from the heavier work of scaling and getting the catch and butchering the animals explains the greater quantity of flint tool discarded. (de Cardi, 1986:90).

Several shallow pits and a fish-midden of about 10 meters in diametre were found at al-Markh. This is indicative of probably fish-curing activity at a larger scale than the domestic needs. (de Cardi, 1986:89).

Recent excavations by the British team during 1990-91 at the Sar settlement site reveals that fish was the regular sea-food of the Sar population as fish bones were found in abundance at Sar. At one place they found heep of the remains of fish and shell-fish. (Killick, Moon, Crawford, 1991, Unpublished Field Report). That Bahraini's main seafood was shell-fish, is evidenced by the very large number of shells scattered on the ground all over the Sar site. Similar scatter is found at Qal'at al Bahrain. They are found in heaps and dump adjacent to the remains of the Dilmun Cities. The Danes expedition in 1954 found two sites (Nos. 4 and 2) in the area south of the Zallaq-Awali road from where they recovered flint sickle blades, indicating early agricultural activity. (Glob, 1954 b). The Nippur letters (Cornwall, 1952; Oppenheim, 1954) dated to the reign of Burnaburiah II (ca. 1370 B.C.) suggest the practice of agriculture by the nomadic tribes of Dilmun. The lithic assemblage comprising of scrapers, points and cutters, querns, domestic implements like pounder, hammer and rubbing-stones, etc., indicate that grain was either cultivated or collected.

The animal bones invariably found with the human skeleton in the scores of graves in Bahrain (Bibby, 1969; Ibrahim, 1982; Mughal, 1983; Srivastava, 1991), reveal that the Bahraini's mainly consumed non-vegetarian diet during the third-first millennium B.C. Date was the staple food. There is evidence of date cultivation and date trade in the second millennium B.C. (Mc Nicoll, 11). Date-stones were discovered at Sar settlement by the British team. (Jane Moon, personnel communication). The material, teeth and jaws, recovered from scores of graves dating from third through first millennium B.C. reveal that the Bahraini's suffered with caries lesions and other dental diseases. Their cause being excessive consumption of dates and carbohydrates. Dilmun was famous for its cultivation of fine sweet dates. The dates were used for making juice, syrup etc. Beside dates, figs, raisins, baked cakes and bread were all consumed. This is also attested by the large number of baking ovens discovered in the Sar settlement (See *infra* chapter IV). (Hojgaard, 1983: 11f; 1986:64ff).

Prehistoric occupational sites are extremely rare in Bahrain though we have in Bahrain houses and cities of late prehistoric and protohistoric period. McNicoll's expedition 1973-75 to al Markh (low sandy desert, about 1400 m, from the sea, see map), could not find any traces of permanent structures and the random scatter of fireplaces in squares G17 and K19 they found were attributed to a seasonal occupation. However, ceramic evidence, the surviving stratified deposits date the occupation to fourth millennium B.C. But since only one single recognizable sherd of second millennium B.C. was painted, it is presumed that the site was visited. There is, so far, no evidence for occupation after the fourth millennium. (McNicoll, 4). The occupational sites of prehistoric and protolistoric Bahrain are indicated in Map 8 (chapter II *supra*). The only structural features found at al-Markh were a number of shallow pits and a fish-midden of about ten meters in diametre. This size surely indicates some sort of activity and most porbably fish-curing was carried out on a larger scale, more than the domestic requirement. When the pits in the sand were dug, it was found that a few were lined with either shells and flints in as by layers which alternated with sand. A similar alteration of debris layers and sand was observed in the build up of the midden. This leads to the conclusion that the site was probably used on seasonal basis. The first phase of occupation has been dated to ca. 3800 B.C. on the basis of the pottery found and assigned at the earliest to 'Ubaid 4 and may be later. (J.Oates, 1978:44; de Cardi 1986:89f). The 'Ubaid occupation took place only along the south west coast and the flint assemblages recovered, may reflect the entire 'Ubaid range.

Larsen (1983:76) suggests that the evidence for pastoralism and fishing along the south west coast of Bahrain may represent area of peripheral to cultivation zones farther to the north. Roaf's (1976:144ff) excavations at al Markh reveals that there were two phases of occupation at al Markh with major differences in their subsistance bases. (See Fig.D). He suggests that during the first phase the economy was based on fishing and gathering shell fish; while during the second phase the population relied both on fishing and on the capture of dear and herding of goats. The site was impoverished and no permanent structures were found in the six trenches that were excavated. The earlier phase or the lower layers were a number of shallow pits, of approximately 60 cms., in diametre and between 10 cms., in depth, Roaf believes that these were probably used as fire places and it was a seasonal settlement. Pits before excavation are seen in Fig. B. In one of the trenches (J19-see Fig.C) measuring 6x6 m. the excavators found two phases of occupation. The later or upper phase of light sand contained flint chips, fish bones and shells. The earlier or lower phase had light and dark sand and the latter was full of fish bones. A hard packed patchy surface separated the two levels of the two phases. (See Fig.D). The material found in the two occupational phases of trench J19 has been tabulated by Roaf (1974:499), and is reproduced here.

From the above table it is inferred that there was a marked change in the subsistence pattern during the two phases. Product of the sea was the main subsistance during the earlier phase, and fishing of medium size fish was made. During second phases besides sea the subsistance depended on goats. They caught dugongs and large carnivorous fish. In the later phase much more, about five times, flints per cubic metre were found. This site, on the basis of 'Ubaid pottery found here, has been dated to ca.3800 to after 3,000 B.C. (Roaf, 1974:499ff). This pastoral pattern of sheep and goat herding and a coastal maritime strategy is known only for al Markh and its environs. Obviously, the same subsistance might have

FINDS FROM TRENCH J19, AL MARKH, BAHRAIN

	Volume excavated	Fish bone	Mammal bone	Edible shells	Flint chips	Pottery sherds
Later Phase	c.12m³	Common large fish	common goat, dugong and hare	pearl Oyester and Murex Kusterianus	6,225	8
Earlier Phase	c.10m³	Very common, medium fish	Very rare	A large Venerid and pearl, oyester	713	143

been practiced in other parts of Bahrain; as well as some others. Thus, Larsen (1983:76) suggests that, as in the case of 'Ubaid sites of eastern Arabia, in Bahrain also, the 'Ubaid settlements must have been more or less permanent, but occurred only in widely scattered locations.

In the mountains in the centre of the island, the Danes found a large number of shelters, projecting ledges of rock, beneath which Stone Age hunters established their dwellings. However, such settlements have not been found so far. The Danes also found along the coast of flint smith workshop of Neolithic period. (Glob, 1954:112ff). In Table 2 (Chapter II, *supra*) are listed all the archaeological sites (prehistoric and protohistoric). At these sites (except the sites of burial mounds or subterranean graves) some sort of occupation or settlement might have existed during the ancient times. The sites where major settlement or occupation had existed for considerable period of time and where structural remain still survive are described and illustrated in Chapter IV (*infra*) under "Cities, Towns and Houses". The temple sites were also settlements sites. In fact the temple was the nucleus of inhabitants or the urban society. Excavation has revealed traces of al 'Ubaid settlement in the later phase at Al Markh, dated to fourth millennium B.C,; and which does not use pottery. (Roaf, 1976:160). The general characteristics of the al 'Ubaid settlement, in the Dilmun area, according to Tosi (1974:153) are mobility of settlement as a result of flunctuation in hydrological conditions; extensive exploitation of sea resources for domestic consumption as well as for regional interchange; and despite the mobility of settlement the index of stability is probably much higher than in the delayed Epi-Palaeolithic. Al 'Ubaid is a partial variation of the latter period, both with respect to the position of the settlement (partial location change) and the economic exploitation of resources.

However, the range of food resources, states Tosi, was quite extensive; hunting of small and large animals, gathering of herbs and roots; gathering of sea shell-food, and fishing. Finds, such as, fish bone, sea-shell of snail, etc from the Sar settlement, excavated recently by the British (Killick, Crawford, Moon etal 1991, 134) indicate that sea food was the staple diet of the people even thorough the site is not directly situated on the shore. The use of grains is indicated by the number of large mortars, grain-qurerns, hand pounders and grinders found during excavations of Sar settlement. (Killick, Crawford, Moon, 1991, Field Report Unpublished). Mortars from Sar settlement and other sites are illustrated here (Fig.E) from the Bahrain National Museum. Use of bread in attested by the large number of ovens found in the settlement. Use of cereals etc., are suggested by the large number of cooking pots. (Killick, Crawford, Moon et al, 1991:132). Larsen's (1983:90ff) detailed study of life and land use on the Bahrain island reveals that: there were episodic changes in the area extent of land occupied; land was abandoned; continuous settlement along the north coast of the island where the most copious artesian springs are located; population and agricultural areas spread outward from the artesian centre; the peak settlement occured during the late 'Ubaid interval, the Barbar/Dilmun period, the first millennium B.C. During Neo-Assyurian through early Parthian period of settlement covered only one third the area of earlier period, and archaeological evidence show continuous occupation of Bahrain from Old Stone Age till today. However, Bibby (1957:162) suggests that for some time by the Kassite period in second millennium B.C., Qal'at al Bahrain was not inhabited. But he does not find any break in the cultural sequence of the pottery. Again there is no historical record of Dilmun between ca. 1240 and 709 B.C. This makes Kervran et al (1987:77ff) to infer that there is a gap in occupation of Bahrain between the 13th and the 8th Century B.C. Consequently, they have come out with a hypothesis for the understanding of the ocupational enigma of this period of gap. They have proposed that due to the lowering of the sea level towards the beginning of the second millennium B.C., the site of Qal'at al Bahrain was abandoned from the end of Kassite period until the Neo-Assyrian period. This gap is situated between City IV or between the Middle Dilmun and Late Dilmun, periods in the chronology proposed by Bibby (1969:352). However, the pottery recovered from the sondages carried out by the Danish and French at Qal'at suggest that the site was abandoned for a short time and was re-occupied by the people who continued to produce Kassite pottery. (Kervran, Mortensen, Hiebert, 1987 : 77-93).

107

Fig. A Areial view of al Markh looking east. Showing trench J19 of the British excavation in the foreground with the dumps. Beyond the site are *subkha* and *dukka*. Far beyond is Jebel Dukhan. (Photo courtesy M. Roaf, U.K.)

Fig. B East section of the trench J19 at al Markh. The highest lavel marks the division
between the early and the late phase. (Photo courtesy, M. Roaf, U.K.)

Fig. C Al Markh, trench J21/22, showing pits before excavation by the British. (Photo courtesy M. Roaf, U.K.)

Fig. D Al Markh, trench J19 A.D. North section. The highest white label indicates the division between the early and late phase. The lowest label marks the earliest level above the natural sand. (Photo courtesy M. Roaf, U.K.)

Fig. E. Mortars, querns etc. from Sar. (Courtesy : Bahrain National Museum)

PART III

THE DILMUN CIVILIZATION

THE BRONZE AND IRON AGES

The archaeological excavations conducted in Bahrain during the past several decades have brought to light new facts about Arabian Gulf's prehistory and protohistory. The most remarkable character in this feature is the discovery of the Dilmun civilization that flourished during the Bronze Age beginning from early third millennium B.C. with international relations with the contemporary civilizations, both western as well as eastern. The archaeological finds not only establish the flourishing of Dilmun civilization, but contribute to the understanding of its origin and development through third and second millennium B.C., and continuation into the later period, the Iron Age. It was Bahrain's or Dilmun's strategic location almost mid-way between the Arabian Gulf on the international trade route between Mesopotamia and Indus Valley that contributed tremendously to the origin and growth of Dilmun civilization and its sustenence for nearly two millennium. Though the people in Bahrain were living with their own local or indigenous culture but their commercial contacts with Mesopotamia, and other countries of the Levant and Indus Valley resulted in interaction of different cultures. This resulted in the blending of cultures in Bahrain and giving rise to a new indigenous Dilmun civilization with its own characteristics. This is evident from the archaeological discoveries of structural remains, and a wide variety of antiquities recovered from the excavations during the past five decades or more.

In view of the vast number of archaeological material that has been unearthed from various sites, it is considered suitable and convenient to describe the antiquities thematically or topically classified into different categories *viz.*, seals, pottery, soft stone vessels, metal objects and jewellery, standard, sculpture, glass objects, beads and lapis lazuli, coffins and ivory objects, etc. These antiquities are described in chapters VI-VIII. This type of description helps us to understand the development of culture and contribution of each aspect to the overall evaluation of the Dilmun civilization as a whole. However, it is essential to know first the archaeological remains from where the artifacts were recovered. Hence, the description of the archaeological finds in preceded by the description of the occupational sites and the structural remains. These remains may be classified into the following four categories - settlements; cities, towns, and houses; temples, tumuli and subterranean burials. The first two categories are grouped under Architecture in Chapter IV; and the latter in Chapter V. The other major aspects of the Dilmun civilization: the State, the Religion and Foreign Trade are described in Chapters IX, X and XI, respectively.

CHAPTER IV

ARCHITECTURE

(A) CITIES, TOWNS AND HOUSES

SETTLEMENTS

Excavations have revealed so far, only a few settlement sites in Bahrain, of the Bronze and Iron Ages. That too little is known about them before the mid-third millennium B.C. Some seventeen sites have been recorded with evidence of occupation during the late third and early second millennium B.C. (Map 5). From these sites the finds recovered range from al'Ubaid, and Akkadian periods to the more common type of Early Dilmun (Barbar I and Barbar II) assemblages at Qal'at al Bahrain. Larsen (1983:78) suggests that the total range of occupation for these sites (Danish No. 486 and 7) could be from 2300 to 1800 B.C.; however most of the sites belong to the Early Dilmun period ca. 2200 to 1800 B.C. Of these, seven of them may be of first period while the remaining sixteen may be assigned to the later period. The Early Dilmun period occupation sites and tombs present dense array of settlement. The early Dilmun period sites are spread over a distance of about 30 km. south along the west coast of Bahrain and occupy some of the earlier sites of 'Ubaid period. After Early Dilmun period, we have only two Kassite period occupation sites - Qal'at al Bahrain and Barbar village (British site No. 2068). These sites are located less than one km. inland from the north west while the Kassite burials are situated 10 km. inland. Several, at least six settlements and rural burials of first millennium B.C. belonging to Neo-Assyrian and later periods are identified with the help of pottery from different levels at Qal'at al Bahrain. The settlement (Danish site No. 226 near the village of 'Ali) of first millennium B.C. seems to be that of Neo-Assyrian through Achaemenid period. (Larsen, 1983; 78-81). But when the excavations by the British (London-Bahrain Archaeological Expedition), now in progress from 1990, at Sar, when completed, will prove to be the biggest Dilmun settlement. The factors that contributed to the occupation of a site was the nearness to the water sources, and higher level of ground above sea-level. It is observed that in Bahrain the prehistoric and protohistoric settlements are frequently located above the level feasible for flow, irrigation, as for instance site No. 2055, Dumistan, or ground unsuitable for agriculture. It seems that during the third millennium B.C. the settlements and grave-mounds were situated so as to interfere as little as possible with irrigable ground. Some such relationship, observes McNicoll, probably existed between settlements, cultivated land and groups of graves in other areas in the third millenneum B.C. In that case, we might reasonably expect third millennium B.C. settlements to have existed near 'Ali, Jubailant, Isa Town, Sar and the west coast mound fields. (McNicoll, 1975, 12, Unpublished Report). But the situation is not the same during the later period. For instance, Janussan north is situated on potentially cultivable ground. The line of Janussan mounds is the same. The so-called Alpha mound along the Budeiya road, the classical period graves outside Barbar village, the graves of al-Hajjar, all these

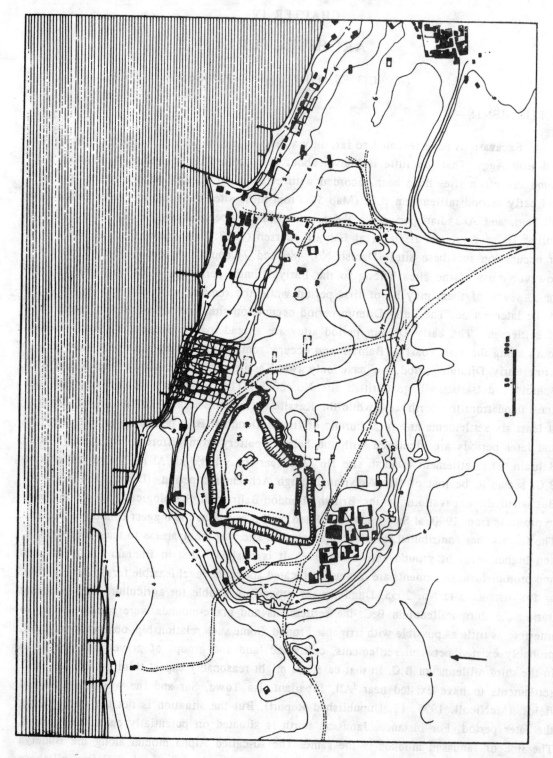

Fig. 1 Site of Qal'at al Bahrain. (After Monik Kervran, 1982).

occupy potentially cultivable land. Consequently, we may conclude that after the Barbar period there was a less pressing need to utilize agriculture land. (McNicoll, 1975 : 12f. Ms).

The excavation conducted by the Danes (from 1954-1970) at Qal'at al Bahrain traces the course of the fortification wall of the Early Dilmun period around the greater part of the perimeter of the tell. However, substantial remains of the settlements - streets and houses are found only within the northern run of the wall, close to the sea. It is here that occupational levels earlier than the construction of the city wall, were found. These remains represent the earliest traces of civilization in Bahrain. (Bibby, 1986:108). The Sar site excavated by Ibrahim (1982:2) is close to the sea, about 700 meters. While the Sar site excavated by Mughal (1983:3) which looks like a settlement mound is situated two km. south of the present-day Sar village on the eastern edge of Sar ridge which rises more than ten meters above the sea level or five meters from the plain level on its east. The Sar settlement site currently excavated by the British team is also located close to the sea nearly three km. Archaeological excavations have brought to light, so far, seven cities at Qal'at al Bahrain, a well planned town at Sar, and a village of houses at Diraz. Probably future excavation may bring to light new settlements.

(1)   DILMUN CITIES AT QAL'AT AL BAHRAIN

The "tell" or the mound at Qal 'at al Bahrain (Fig.1)whose excavations by the Danish team brought to light existence of third millennium B.C. settlement of cities situated in the centre of the northern coast of Bahrain island at the head of a shallow bay. It has acquired the name from the fort (*QALA´*) which crowns the tell.The fort is of much later period and does not belong to the Dilmun period. It is a large mound of about 400 yards from north to south and twice that distance from east to west. It was about 15 meters in height. Excavations have revealed that the tell was composed entirely of the ruins and debris of the considerable city which has at various periods occupied the site. And the modest height of the tell was due to the stone by which the city was built. That the tell was formed by centuries of human settlements is evident from the numerous potsherds found on the surface of the mound and in its steep edges on the side bordering the sea, where the breakers at high tide have cut into the side. Further out, below the high-water mark, was found by the Danes, embedded in the sand, the ashlar foundations of a building. One end of the building was washed away by the sea, while the other end extended under the black occupation earth of the tell. The exposed foundations stretched 16 meters in length and 8 meters in width. The Danes excavated the site at the highest point of the ground. The tell here was 10.19 meters high, and the bottom of the adjoining moat was 0.45 meters above high-water mark. The tell revealed ten occupation levels. Here at the earliest phase, few sherds of painted pottery with patterns in black· or red on a yellow ground were found. This, Bibby says, are virtually identical with that of Umm an Nar and Tepe Yahya VA and IVB, which are dated to ca. 2800 B.C. (Glob, 1955:193; Bibby, 1969:136-140).

Seven major building phases have been revealed at Qal'at. These are : City I, unwalled; City II walled; City III possesses a rebuilt wall; City IV has large stone buildings; City V extends beyond the original wall; City VI is of tenth century Islamic date; and City VII comprises the Portuguese castle of sixteenth century date. Though Bibby mentions City VIII but is not of importance. (Bibby, 1969 : 148-152;1974:187). The location of the cities in Qal'at are shown in Fig. 2, along with the approximate course of the wall of the third millennium B.C. on the three sides, north, west and south of the tell and the location of sonding trenches made by the Danes. This classification of the cities by Bibby is based on the levels of occupation which he distinguished by the type of pottery he recovered from each level and likewise he assigned cities. Thus, after the excavations of the Hundred Meter Section, Bibby (1957:162) first assigned periods and later on (1986:110) cities, as follows according to the pottery;

The "chain-ridge" levels : City I

The "red-ridge" levels : City II

The "caramel-ware" levels : City III

The "glazed-bowl" levels : City IV

To this we may add thick straw tempered ware for the pre-City I levels. Of the seven cities, at Qal'at; the first four fall within the Dilmun period covering the Bronze and Iron Ages. While the cities V - VII pertaining the Hellenistic and Islamic periods, respectively, are out of the purview of this book and hence not considered here.

CITY I

The origin of City I may be traced to the pre-City I phase. The earliest occupational levels at Qal'at, before that of City I, has been traced by Bibby (1966:92) at the bed rock (*farush*) level. During 1965 season, the Danish team re-established the baulk, involving the removal of the walls edging the Seleucid road and cutting through the solid foundation of the road itself. Excavation was then made in the east and west sections layer by layer. To the east of the baulk, about one-and-half meter above the bedrock the Danes discovered a thick levelling layer, and below it the house-walls which were built of somewhat larger stones than those above the layer though the material was the same, the sea-bed limestone coglumerate known as *farush* where the house-walls above the layer coincided with those below they were almost separated by a thin clay layer, while at four points the city wall was built above the surviving courses of house-walls of this period. Below the levelling layer were characteristic dark occupation levels, with numerous chain ridge sherds. The lower levels were completely without stone walling, and the last half meter above bedrock had beach sand, potsherds and copper pieces. The horizontal layers of bed-rock had embedded potsherds and even persisted further down to 30 cms, below the bed rock. Below this the bed-rock ended in a thin layer of coarse gravel followed by sterile green sand. (see chart of Fig. 4 in Chapter II, *supra*)

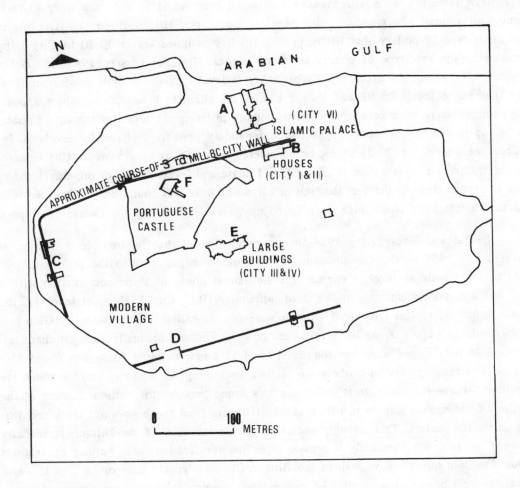

Fig. 2   Location of Cities I - VI at Qal'at al Bahrain and showing approximate course
of the third millennium B.C. City Wall (B-D) : B-North City Wall; C-West
City Wall; D-South City wall; E-Buildings of Kassite and Assyrian Periods
(Cities III - IV); A-Islamic Palace; and F-Portuguese Fort. (Based on maps in
Hawkin's Atlas, 1974; and "Antiquities of Banrain").

Bibby (1966:92; 1986:108ff). We may make a distinction between the occupational levels of pre-City I and City I on the basis of large quantity of a completely new type of a fairly thick straw tempered ware with massive out-turned rims found at bed rock (*farush*) level along with a small admixture of chain-ridge ware of City I (Bibby, 1966:92). It is due to this latter type of pottery that Bibby (1986:110) has assigned levels 30-20 to City I, by overlooking the new type of pottery he found earlier. However Larsen (1983:215) makes distinction between pre-Barbar and Barbar (City I) levels. Larsen assigns pre-Barbar (Pre-city I) phase to levels 26-30, and Barbar I (City I) phase to levels 20-30. There appears to be some disagreement between these two authors in fixing the levels of the City I phase. Supposing that Bibby overlooked to mention separately pre-City I phase, for levels 30-28, his remaining levels i.e. 20-28 should be considered authentic, as excavator, for City I phase. However, Larsen assigns levels 21-25 for City I phase and levels 26-30 for pre-City I phase. This is contradictory to the fact that the new type of ware was found only at the bed-rock and the characteristic chain-ridge ware found up to level 20, as per the excavator's report.

Several soundings during 1954-56 and excavation of the Hundred-Meter Section at Qal'at during 1956 by the Danish team, at the northern edge, close to the sea brought to light the first building level, a corner of a substantial house of stone construction with a wall and a threshold entrance of the third millennium B.C. City I. Here, at level 11, the Danes found the typical red-ridged Dilmun ware (the so-called 'Barbar' ware by Glob and Bibby) in large quantities. As the levels went down the pottery gradually changed character. By level 16 only ridged ware was found. At level 17 a new building phase was found with a stone wall running parallel to the main section, containing the doorway besides which lay a hallowed hinge-stone. A great difference was found between the cultural content of the portion of the section dug to bed-rock at 63-71 meters from the high-water mark and that dug at 99-104 meters. This strongly indicated the demarcation of the Dilmun period city between the two; but eventually it proved to be the fortification wall. Further excavations brought to light the defensive wall of the Dilmun City (designated later on as City II), with a massive work of gypsum-concrete, 3.5 metres thick, running obliquely across the excavations from east south to west north west. The City I was unwalled and existed before the city wall was built.

Having excavated for more than a decade the Danish were not certain of the origin and date of City I. (Bibby, 1969:148). Subsequently, while tracing the origin of Dilmun Civilization, Bibby (1986 : 144) expressed that we should not exaggerate City I, perhaps to call it a city at all is a misnomer. As, he continues, that there is no evidence for more than a small collection of stone houses along the shore, perhaps, nothing bigger than the little fishing village of Umm an-Nar itself, a settlement of local people, but with very strong connections with what we may call Makan (Magan), perhaps even incorporating a trading-port of Magan merchants looking for outlets for their copper to the north, as a large number of corroded scraps of copper was found in the sands of City I, suggesting that copper was abundant.

(Bibby, 1986; 114). Bibby, in 1969, could not fix up the date for City I. However, later on, in 1986, he suggested that the beginning of City I depends on the date of Umm an Nar sherd found in basal City I levels, which is still a subject of disagreement. But, he suggests, a time in late Early Dynasty III, perhaps 2400 or 2500 B.C. would seem to fit the facts, and the early pottery has a very E.D.III 'feel' to it. And, finally, he pushes the beginning of civilization in Bahrain back to 2600 B.C., the traditional date of Gilgamish. (Bibby, 1986:114f).

CITY II

The origin of City II is City I. As mentioned above, below City II was City I and the difference in their level of occupation, the upper most corner of a stone building is that of City II. The difference between City I and City II was a change in fashion of pottery. City II had lasted for considerable time period, long enough to fill up five levels in the tell, to build and rebuild and rebuild again. (Bibby, 1969:148).

The excavations of 'the Hundred Meter Section' in 1957 brought to light the City Wall (Fig. 3, 4,5) and City II in the section of 95-99 metre. City II was reached after digging through several levels of later periods. Digging deeper below the Seleucid levels, into early Dilmun, with its neatly stratified layers of Dilmun (Barbar) pottery the red-ridged pottery by which City II is distinguished. Bibby states, that they found an orderly planned municipality. Here all the walls ran due north-south or due east-west and a street run due north-towards the City and to a gate in the wall. This gate in the City's perimeter opened out to the uninhabited foreshore. Its location was a metre further east away from the Seleucid gate. Though the two gates overlapped, but did not coincide. Both gaps in the wall were about ten feet wide, though constricted by the hinges of the gates to a little under eight feet. There were also a pair of hinge-stones of polished black diorite, about 20 inches across with cups to accommodate the hinge-parts hollowed into their tops. The lower gate also, had been blocked, before it was abandoned, with a wall of rough stones built across it. However, when further deeper digging was made, a thined and earliest gate was found below the line of the repairs to the wall in the middle of the Dilmun period. This gate also overlapped, but did not coincide with the one above, its gate posts stood a meter away to the west. This was not blocked. The gate in the City wall suggests that much of the commercial and municipal activity of the City took place immediately within the gates. Inside the gate and City, there was a small open square. In its centre was a well, and besides it an oval cement-built through. This may be a halting-place for pack-animals. On either side of the square were two houses, each of two rooms. In one of them nine stamp seals were found. In another are three seals and five stone weights were found. This discovery of seals and weights in the houses suggest that the two houses on either side of the square must have been municipal office, where loads were weighed, and either the loads themselves or the clay documents accompanying them were stamped with the seals by the officials who inspected the in-coming and out going goods. Probably, the houses were of the customs and port authority of Dilmun. Further digging

Fig. 3   Western portion of the city wall around City II at Qal'at al Bahrain. (After P.V. Glob, 1960. Courtesy Jutland Archaeological Society).

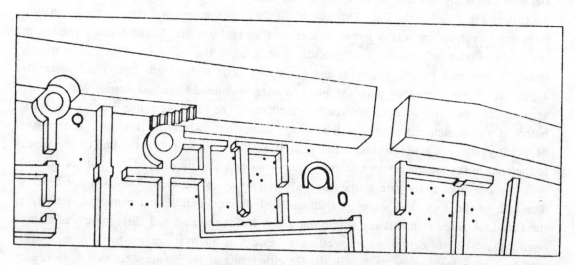

Fig. 6. Isometric view of the City II area within the North Wall at Qal'at.

At the bottom the Cul-de-sac, and at top the City gate, with between them, the guard room with its well and staircase to the ramports. Finding places of seals (.) and weights (O) are marked, showing their preponderance in the rooms on either side of the gate. (After G. Bibby, 1969).

brought to light earliest period of the wall, five feet above the bed-rock. Here the City I had existed before the City Wall was built. The pottery changed to chain-ridge ware. And here the house walls ran-on under the City Wall. Between these walls and the City Wall lay once more the burnt level which showed that the unfortified city had been destroyed by fire. Here one socketed copper spear-head was found. Further digging deep to level between 28 and 29 exposed the *farush* or the bed-rock (Glob, 1957:157; Bibby; 1969:351-356).

An Isometric view of the City II area within the north wall is shown in Fig. 6. It was a cul-de-sac street which ran north to the wall, with substantial stone houses on either side and a well and sunk basin at the end of the street. In the lower-half of the illustration is the cul-de-sac, and the upper-half shows the city gate, with between them, the guard room with its well and staircase to the ramports. It also indicates the location where seals, and stone weights, were found in the rooms. The City II shows signs of municipal planning. It was well-built, of stone, with mathematically laid-out streets and house aligned by the cardinal points of the compass, observes Bibby (1957:162). He further asserts that this planning of City II resembles the gridiron plans of contemporary Mohanjo-Daro and Harappa of India (now in Pakistan). This is attested by the Indus weights found here in the room of City II. The planning of City II contrasts, says Bibby (1969:351f), with the winding alleys and haphazard houses of Ur.

The plan and elevation of the inner face of gate in the City Wall shows where the Seleucid road, with its drain-system, met the city wall there the Danes found a pair of limestone hing-holes for a gate (port 3A) similar to those found in the bath-rooms, and beneath it lay the city gates of the earlier periods. In the upper most Dilmun levels not very much deeper appeared two bluish-black diorite hinge post-stones (stolpesten-port 2B) against the inner (southern) face of the inner wall, and beneath these came further gateways (port 1, port 2A). In the western section there was a well, partly stone-plundered. Besides it was a trough of the cement-hard local gypsum, with another similar through immediately below it in the previous building phase. The Danes have distinguished several building phases in the houses excavated here on either side of the road. The house-walls above the upper layer/level, coincided with those below and were separated by a thin clay layer, while at four points the city wall was built above the surviving courses of house-walls of this period. In association with these walls four pottery vessels without bottoms were found in the last section, three of them half way under the City Wall, they may be bread-ovens. This evidence suggests that the stone fortification wall of the city was not built at the same time as the first stone building, but relatively shortly after wards. (Bibby, 1969 : 91f). The section through the north wall of the city tell of Qal'at al Bahrain, at the point where the well at the end of the cul-de-sac cuts into the wall on its inner side, showing levels of Cities I, II, III, VI and VII. The area of the city according to Bibby (1969:91), within the city wall is almost forty acres or about 250x600 metres or about 15 hectares according to Hojlund (1989:45). Hojlund (Personal Communication) finds two phases in the construction of the City Wall

Fig. 4a (Above) Inner side of the City Wall (Phase I), built during City II period.
Fig. 4b. (Below) Outer side of the City Wall (Phase II), City II.

(Figs. 4,5). The phase I of the wall was built during period III or IV of City II. Hojlund (1986:224) has divided City II into six phases or periods, (A to F), of which one II E is missing link.

Bibby (1986:113f) while discussing the origins of the Dilmun Civilization in the light of the assemblage from City I and II of the Qal'at al-Bahrain, observes that there appears to be a definite discontinuity between City I and City II, in that the people who built the city wall used a different type of painted pottery, introduced seals and carnelian, and so on, and yet the innovations and disappearance were only superficial changes in a basic identity of pattern. For example, the 'hole-mouth' jars of City II, which comprised about half of the total pottery, was identical with those of City I, while the general shape of the chain-ridge ware was a clear precursor of the plain-ridge ware of City II. It is not, Bibby concludes that, apparently, the culture that changes, it is the out-side influences upon the culture. Thus, we find at the close of City I and with the beginning of City II Harappan influence which played the chief role as evident from discovery at Qal'at al-Bahrain of Harappan weight, carnelian beads and seals with Harappan script. But when we come to City I we find that the most obvious foreign influence is that of Umm an Nar. But city I was not an Umm an-Nar settlement. Umm an-Nar appears rather a very strange intrusion in an indigenous culture. But on the basis of the pottery from two sites north of Hofuf oasis in Saudi Arabia, which Bibby found as a very plausible forerunner of the hole-mouth jars suggests that the origin of Dilmun Culture should be traced to the main land of eastern Arabia. (Bibby, 1986: 113f). Bibby (1969:148) dates City II to c. 2300 B.C. City II is dated on the basis of the Isin-Larsa type tablet, found in the basal City II levels, bearing Amorite names and associated with the seals of Arabian Gulf style, which are dated by Buchanan to c. 1923 B.C. (Eden, 1968:196).

In the southern most sondage, Bibby found streets and buildings of City II, at the same level as, farther north, he found thick levels of City V remains. However there was a difference of 2000 years between City II and City V. A wall surrounded City II. (Bibby 1969:148-153). The five levels of City II which Bibby found enabled Hojlund (1986:217ff) to divide its occupation into six periods on the basis of pottery assemblages. The first period, City II A is characterised by plain jar rims found in layer 21 in Bibby's trench south of the North Wall. City II B found at layer 18, had triangular rims with a convex upper surface, a painted lip and a tall, splaying neck. City IIC pottery is very typical and had still thicker hole-mouth rims with a concave bevelled front, sometimes with two shallow grooves. (City IID pottery found in layers 10-15 had some low-necked jars with thick triangular rims. City IIE is missing as there is a gap. City IIF is characterised by elongated and smoothed triangular rims. The City II seems to have ended abruptly about 100 yards from high-water mark and seems to be without any fortification. Evidently this 100 yards of foreshore was the harbour of the City for the ships trafficking in Gulf, both from the north and the south. The archaeological finds from the beach sand and behind the later wall, such as, seals, beads, pieces of pottery

Fig. 5a (Above) Inner side of the City Wall (Phase I and II).
Fig. 5b. (Below) Northern or outer side of the City wall with gate through phase II.

and stone ware indicate that the foreshore was a busy place of trade between the east and the west. The last of the unfortified levels of the City ends in conflagration in a thick blackened storage jars with carbonised content. Apparently the City was destroyed by fire. This possibly happened in 1180±110 B.C., as per the radio-carbon dating. However, there was no discontinuity in the cultural sequence; as the excavators found the very same artifacts and pottery being used by the people both before and after the fire. The city was rebuilt on the same plan, but with the addition of a massive stone rampart built around it. From there, successive habitation levels within the City Wall are evidence of settled and continuous occupation, and gradually raise the ground level within the walls. It is not known as to how and when the period of occupation came to an end. Evidence suggests that by the Kassite period, during the second millennium B.C., this area of the city was no longer occupied. This abrupt decline in size and importance of the city and its occupation, Bibby attributes to the cessation of trade with India after the Aryan conquest of the Indus Valley. Even as late as the seventh century B.C., this area of the city was still not inhabited. However, the recovery of bath-tub coffins of the burials of the period suggests that there was a settlement at that period elsewhere on the large extensive tell. Subsequently, probably during the fifth century B.C., a new building phase commenced in this area. Within the ruined walls of the then two-thousand-year-old city. There are no traces of any building on the higher ground. However, the hundred yards of the foreshore was covered with scattered buildings of later period. (Bibby, 1957: 152-163; 1969:342-346; 1974:321-328; Larsen, 1983-203; Edens:1986:196).

CITY III

The structures at Qal'at al Bahrain on the so-called "Caramel-ware" people which existed between levels 7 to 10 eventually proved to be of City III. This City has been suggested by Bibby as that of Kassite occupation due to the presence in these levels of caramel ware of the Kassites of the Mesopotamia. During 1962 excavations, the Danes cut completely through the west wall of the City, and found Kassite sherds embedded in the upper, rebuilt portion of the wall within the wall, in the 99-104 meter section, to its full depth, were four meters of occupation earth, full of quantities of Kassite pottery. So, Bibby called it a Kassite wall, and says that it looked as though the Kassite City has extended over larger area than the city which had preceded it. After several annual excavations the Kassite building emerged. To the east of the "throne-room", the rooms of the "palace" building were removed during the excavations by Hans Berg and Karen Frifelt. Below these, they found, portions of two buildings of the Kassite period or the "Caramel ware" period with a narrow alley between them. Portions of drains were found covered by stone and cement slabs. Thus indicating well planned city with drainage facility. However, the drains were interrupted by the foundations of the Kassite buildings. This suggests that the drains were of earlier period or were older than the Kassite buildings. The southern Kassite building had consisted of a central court running east to west and might have been roofed, with rooms on both sides. (Fig. 8). There were three rooms at the south of the court, which were destroyed by fire. The Kassite building measuring about 22.5m x 17.5m, had four rooms on either side of the corridor of about 5m.

126

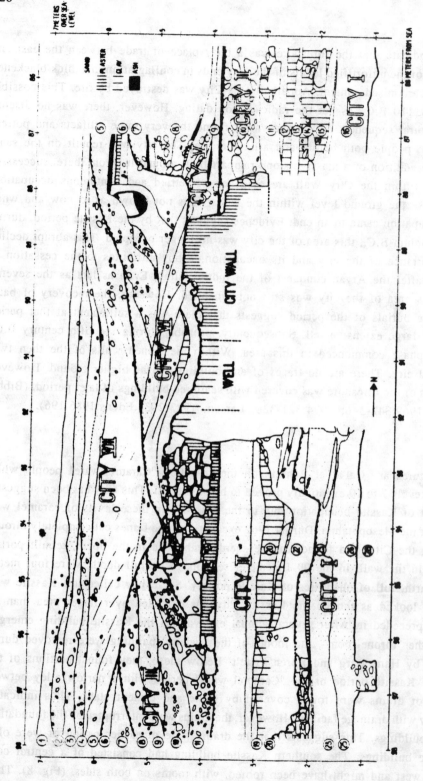

Fig. 7 Section through the North Wall II at Qal'at al Bahrain at the point where the well at the end of the Cul-de-sac cuts into the wall on the inner side. (After G. Bibby, 1969).

width (Fig 8). These dimensions are without considering the possibility of more rooms on either side of the building. The possibility does exist, as indicated by the two incomplete walls, on the north-east side and far western side. Here were found potshreds, remains of bronze and iron, and the impress of wood. Below the cement floor of the "palace" building and above the burnt layer, was found a pottery vessel containing silver and remains of woven cloth. This hoard is dated to 650-550 B.C., on the basis of the signet ring bearing Egyptian hieroglyphs. There were two rooms on the north of the Kassite building. The western-most of these rooms had a floor raised above the general level and approached by two steps extending to the full width of the room. Within the central room, first above the burnt level was found a thick layer of bitumen mixed with potsherd and the impress of wood, and a heap of burnt date-stones. First above this burnt level was found a fragment of a Cuneiform tablet (the first clay tablet to be found in Bahrain). (Bibby, 1964:102; 1969:344ff). This fragmentary Cuneiform tablet, recently illustrated by Andre (1989:171), is of local course unfired beige clay of which one face is inscribed, the reverse bearing only name incomplete letters or signs. It is dated to the middle-Babylonian period. The plan of City III overlapped with City IV was published by Bibby (1969:34) and is shown here in Fig. 8a. The shaded portion represents the City III or the 'Kassite ware house'; while the plain portion that of City IV. The plan of the two Cities III and IV have been redrawn and shown in Fig. 8. However when one visits the site at Qal'at al Bahrain the situation is altogether different. One will not find the structures of the two cities separately. The complex now existing is partly of City III and partly of City IV. The structural remains of the two cities as per the plans, do not exist in tauto. The reason being that in the course of the Danish excavations during the 1950's and 1960's, in order to reach lower levels of City III, some structures of City IV were removed by the excavators. Likewise some structures of City III were removed to preserve those of City IV. However, before demolishing them, Bibby states (1964:106) plan of the structures were drawn and dimensions were recorded by the excavators.

The illustration of Fig. 9 shows an aerial view of the structures of City III and IV as now existing todate. In the foreground are the walls of the street-leading of the main-gate of City IV at the left far-end. As seen in the figure, on the right of the right street-wall the area is now plain. In fact there should have been rooms of the "palace" as in Fig. 8. These room walls were removed by the Danes during excavations. A wall protrudes at the bottom from the superimposed wall of lesser width in the area on the left side of the left street-wall is seen in Fig. 9a. In the central portion of the Fig. 9 are the structures of City III. The two rooms of City III are more clear in Figs. 9b, 9c, showing south-north view. In the latter illustration a plaster base is seen on the extreme right. On the outer face of the room wall of City III, in the centre of the figure are seen two features. One appears to be either a portion of the rectangular column attached with the wall. Or part of the wall which might have been removed during excavations. The other is a small pedestal-like feature on the left attached to the wall. In the left room, attached to the horizontal

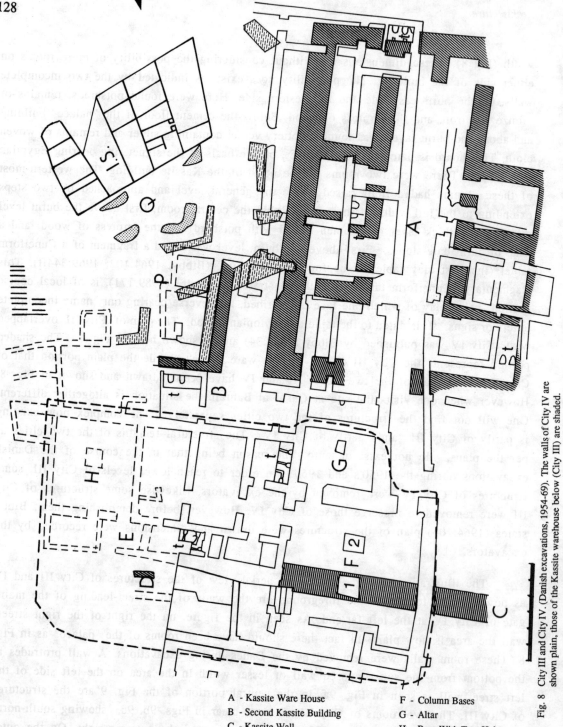

Fig. 8 City III and City IV. (Danish excavations, 1954-69). The walls of City IV are shown plain, those of the Kassite warehouse below (City III) are shaded.

KEY

KASSITE REMAINS (MIDDLE DILMUN)

A - Kassite Ware House
B - Second Kassite Building
C - Kassite Wall
D - Kassite Wall
E - Deep Sounding

F - Column Bases
G - Altar
H - Base With Two Holes
I - Base
J - Column

(A-C : Danish Excavations 1954-70;D - E : French Deep Sounding 1989-91)

Palace And Building (Late Dilmun) - (Danish Excavations)

Temple (Middle And Late Dilumn) - French Excavations - North of the line.

Walls of Palace - Late Dilmun (French Excavation)

Hellenistic Walls (French Excavation)

Islamic Levels (15th - 13th Century A.D.) - (French Excavation).

wall of the City IV is the parallel wall of City IV but of a lesser height. In the foreground on either side of the door-way are incomplete walls of City III. On the extreme left are lying adjacent the wall two querns, one circular and one rectangular. The walls of City III (Fig. 9d) are a meter-thick with foundations of massive cement-set blocks of stone. In the same room of this wall, adjacent the wall two querns, one circular and one rectangular. The walls of City III are a meter-thick with foundations of massive cement-set blocks of stone. In the same room of this wall, adjacent to its opposite wall is a circular oven (Fig. 9d). And opposite to it a rectangular depression, could be possibly unfilled sondage trench left by the Danes. In the adjoining room is a rectangular plastered platform (Fig. 9e) with a raised head at one end and has a plastered base (remains of the floor, left over around the platform. Its purpose is not known. From the same site from where Cuneiform tablet was recovered were also found two bronze spearheads and a bronze hoe-blade. A sample from the burnt date-stones recovered from the Kassite rooms are dated 1180 ± 110 B.C. by the C14 analysis. The burnt wooden beams of the roof of the Kassite store house destroyed by fire are illustrated in Fig. 10 (Friefelt, 1964:102f;1965:145; Bibby 1969:137-140, 318 ft.)

Occupational continuity on Qal'at al Bahrain from City II to City III is established from the pottery recovered and studied by Hojlund (1986:217-224). Hojlund divides the City III into two phases covering the periods from 1600 B.C. and 1500 B.C. respectively. The City IIIA and City IIIB are comparable to Cities IIIB and IIIC respectively of Failaka settlement.Thus, the important fixpoint for the establishment of an absolute chronology for the Cities II and III relative sequences, say Hojlund (1986:222), is the beginning of the Failaka settlements which has been dated by Poul Kjaerum to around 2000 B.C., on the basis of cylinder and stamp seals.City IIA and B should consequently be put in the Ur II and the Akkadian period Hojlund says that how far back City IIA can be pushed is rather uncertain and that room has been made for the Akkadian dating of City I. (Hojlund, 1986:222).

CITY IV

On the tell of Qal'at al Bahrain Iron Age archeological levels were discovered in the stratigraphical soundings 518 carried in the inner courtyard of the Portuguese fort and in the large excavation 519 south of the fort. Huge building complex, which was first considered to be the 'palace' of Dilmun's king Uperi was unearthed. The building complex was later on designated by the Danes as City IV. Bibby's plan of City IV which emerged after several years of exacavations is shown in Fig.8b. However, as mentioned above, in relation with City III plan, all the structures, as shown in the plan of City IV, do not actually exist now. Some of them, especially on the eastern half of the plan have been removed by the excavators in order to reach lower levels of City III, because structure of City IV rested directly on that of City III and in some cases even incorporated them. The Danes began excavations in 1954 at the highest point of the ground , where the tell was 10.19 meters high, at the bottom of the adjoining moat was 0.45 meters above high-water-mark. At a depth of 7 meters, they discovered the floor levels of a monumental building, when a corner of this building

Fig. 9. An aerial view of City III and City IV and later temples at the ... left ...

was uncovered.Here the walls stood to a height of about 5 meters. The walls are 1.10 metres thick and consisted of massive ashlar masonry.One of the walls had 14 courses and the other 17, the block at foundation level were two metres long. The walls were originally coated with a thick layer of plaster. The floor was of gypsum plaster; but it seems to have been relaid several times. The second floor level was 0.45m. and the third about 0.82m. above the original floor. These three floors are visible in Fig.8. (Glob, 1954;167-169;Bibby, 1957:152f;1969:).

The plan of City IV (Fig. 8) shows existence of several separate and contemporary building or units. Lombard (1986;226) remarks that the impressive structures, discovered and designated as City IV by the Danes are still difficult to interpret.This huge complex was at first considered by the Danes to be palace of Dilmun's king Uperi. To be safe, Lombard suggests to avoid the subjective term palace which implies a political and economic functions, not really evident from the structures. Excavations of warehouse destruction layer, which is 1.50m. thick and lay directly on three successive floor, did not reveal any occupation material, except the snake-bowls. Thus, Lombard concludes that the term City IV covers a somewhat complex and confuse layer. While Salles (1984:155) has suggested two phases of City IV: Phase A represented by the buildings layer and a later phase B represented by the intrusive burials. Lombard accepts Salles proposal, which he says does not give anydate to the first phase, and concludes that no definite date can be provided for City IV.

Little can be said, rightly remarks David Oates (1986: 432) about the building of City IV exposed in the 'palace' area until we have detailed Danish report on the excavations they had carried out nearly three decades ago.   Bibby's plan of City IV (Fig. 8) shows existence of four separate units, clearly contemporary since they are inter locked with each other. Unit A and B are more palatial and are designated by the Danes as 'palaces'. The functions of unit B are apparently religious; but that of Unit A is not clear. We may examine the utility of these two building units of the five rooms of unit A. We may presume that they functioned as: reception room; private room; two lobbies with openings on either sides; and a toilet. And a sixth room of unknown function. The same layout, says David Oates (1986-433) is found at the arsenal palace known at Fort Shalmaneser in the south east corner of Nimrud, the first capital city of the late Assyrian Empire, and dated to clearly ninth century B.C. As in Mesopotamian plans, the City IV plan also has the main reception room facing north to avoid the direct rays of the sun, and an entrance from an outer court, or courtyard of the gate, where generally public business was carried out. Oates observes that in view of the striking similarities of lay out, the City IV palace was planned probably on the same style as that of Nimrud. Though the entrances to both the units open off a street about two meters wide, leading to the doorway of unit B at its eastern end inspite of its fine ashler construction and massive stone, still, it does not seem probable that this nor the entrance of Unit A on the north side of the 'street' was the main entrance to the two building units.

The plan of Unit B does not seem to resemble any Mesopotamian buildings.As such

132

Fig. 9a,b City III and City IV Remains.

in Oates' opinion it is the result of local requirement. It seems to have served religious function. The room may be presumed to have served as: shrine, lobby, may be double storey with a massive pillars, a stairway, ante-chambers, and a courtyard. Though Oates (1986:425 f) identifies and discusses the internal organization of buildings of City IV, but he does not provide any plan. Bibby's (1969) combined plan for the two cities, City III and City IV and is illustrated here in Fig. 8, for the two cities.

The main entrance gate/door along with its side wall of City IV is shown in Fig. 11,11a. The building technique adopted is significant. In contruction massive square-cut building stones (Fig.11b) of local lime stones were used with the coating of gypsum plaster. On entering through the main gate, there is a big hall (Fig.11c) which Bibby had designated it as the great court. There are two pillar bases in the middle of the hall seen in the illustration.At the far end, besides the main entrance is the small room, which Bibby called it chapel with its altar. Opposite to the main entrance is a small side room, with a raised floor level. There is thick plastering on the three sides of this room. The differences in levels of the main gate, the main hall or the court and the small side room and the thick plastered flooring of the court is also clearly seen in the illustration.

In one of the room a square lime stone block (Fig. 13) is lying. It has two rectangular holes in the centre. Most probably these holes were meant for holding some statuttutes in them. In another room two rectangular lime stone blocks are found placed on a slightly raised platform. (Fig. 12a,b). Top of these block have several irregular marks. It is believed that before or after worshipping at the altar, the people used to sacrifice animals here on these block and the marks are believed to be the result of striking by a sharp knife or blade. The markings on the top of the blocks are shown in Fig. 12c. Close to these blocks, in the same room is found a rectangular plastered base (Fig. 12a). Its purpose is not known. However, it is believed that probably it was meant for placing a deity or something else.

In another adjoining room is an almost full size square/rectangular pillar (Fig. 14) of about 12 feet height with edges tapering downwards and then broadening from above 2 feet above the ground to the floor. It may be of lime stone blocks but appears to be monolith. It is plastered all over. As it stands in the middle of the room it was obviously meant for supporting the roof. Strangely this column is not shown in the plans of both Bibby (1969) and that of Potts (1990) nor any mention of it is made in their texts.

In one of the rooms there is a plastered feature like a bench having a raised platform with a back-rest of equal width.May be it has some religious function and significance. An interesting feature in the buildings of City IV is the so-called 'water closet' by Glob and Bibby (1979:205), complete with tank and running water. From the nature of the construction, as seen in Fig. 15 a-b, they do not seem to be lavatories in true sense. They are baths with a channel sloping outwards for the flow of water into the room and not flowing inwards into the basin. The sides of the basin are parallel, slightly tapering or rounding at the channel

Fig. 9c (Above) City III and City IV Remains.

Fig. 9d (Below) Oven in one of the rooms of City IV.

point to facilitate flow of water. There are eight such baths in the two units of the building. Construction of back seats of these basin with a niche, may be for candle or lamp is seen in Fig. 15. along with a window at the extreme end. This bath has three basins, one pair and one opposite as seen in Fig. 15a. Another bath (Fig. 15b) has a small hole in the floor opposite the basins. Obviously it is an out-let to drain out the water. Thus, implying the existing of double water system for fresh water and consumed water. Another type of construction has stone rests on two ends of the basin and one in between the two. May be there was a partition. Another bath has three basins, on the same platform two in alignment and one faced in opposite direction. The channels for the two basins in straight towards the floor; while in the case of the third are the channel has been bent at right angles to divert the flow. In one case no channels have been provided for the flow of water.

The construction of these basins and the water channel suggests that these were not lavatories in the real sense but were meant for washing or cleaning oneself and for ablutions before proceeding to the temple located inside the 'palace'. David Oates (1986:434) and Potts (1990:318) are of similar opinion.Some of the domestic features in the room are: storage pottery jar (Fig. 16,16a), plastered basins (Fig. 16c); probably hearths (Fig. 16d,e); two stone querns (Fig.9c) in the fore-ground in two shapes, rectangular and circular. There are probably three wells, as seen in Fig. 17.

Regarding the dating of these buildings, since they are built over the City III warehouse, whose date of destruction is 1180 ± 110 B.C. i.e., 14th century B.C., they are considered to be later than the Kassite period. The stratigraphy reveals that this place was later re-used as a kind of rubbish dump during the Seleucid-Parthian period (City V of the Danes). Lombard consideres this lengthy chronological interval backed by the intrusive burials which are earlier than the Hellenistic City V. The bath-tub coffins have been dated by Glob (1956:173) from the seventh century B.C. Excavation of the warehouse destruction layer, which is 1.50m.thick and lay directly on three successive floors, did not reveal any occupation material, except the snake bowls.The phase of Kassite domination came to a violent end, which David Oates (1986:428) presumes at or before the fall of the Kassite dynasty in the early twelveth century B.C. and after that there seems to be no intervening building level until City IV structure in which some of the 'palace' walls rest directly on their Kassite predecessors and in some cases even incorporates them. These buildings seems to have been abadoned for about five centuries with their walls standing and subsequently replaced by structures which the excavators have assigned to ca. seventh century B.C. In the light of the evidences available, David Oates suggest (1986:434), that the end of City IV was as a result of Persian conquest of Babylonia, which must have dealth a severe blow to Dilmun's laboriously maintained trading connections and perhaps opened the way for rivals on the Gulf's eastern shores. This does not seems to be totally true.It is quite understandable that it might have resulted in the break of Mesopotamian -Dilmun relations and collapse of trade and comerce. But it does not mean that the City IV and its inhabitants ceased to exist as a result of Persian conquest. They

Fig. 9e   (Above) Probably base of an altar City IV.

Fig. 10   (Below) Burnt Roof Beams City IV. (Courtesy Bahrain National Museum).

might not have flourished as before but would have survived in a poor state depending upon local resources. Reade (1986:325) is also of similar opinion. She observes that the people in the Gulf were living and working with their indigenous traditions and culture, even at periods when Mesopotamia itself was not prosperous, and when contacts were minimal.

From the excavations (519) of City IV an unusual discovery of clay bath-tub coffins (Fig. 16) was made by the Danes. Glob (1956:173) dated it to the seventh century B.C. on the basis of Canoid stamp-seals in chalcedony which were associated with two of these burials. This date, Lombard (1986:227) suggests, is rather early in many respects and proposes a slightly later date. Another undisturbed coffin yielded several bronze implements which help in dating. For instance, a well known bronze strainer which cannot be earlier than the fifth century B.C. The earthen sarcophagi found in City IV is exactly the same found in Mesopotamia, Levant and Syria during different periods. However, this burial custom of coffin is highly unusual in Dilmun. Only a few such graves have been found at Karzakan, in Bahrain and one such cemetery was excavated south of Dhahran (Saudi Arabia). Lombard (1986:227) observes that this very scarce find of coffins is indicative of a practise alien to the land of Dilmun and to the inhabitants of Iron Age and suggests that this burial custom is the result of a limited foreign population settled in Bahrain in the mid-first millennium B.C.

Excavation 519 in City IV dated to the Assyrian period ca. 700 B.C . brought to light typical bowls in which the snake-burials were found. They are shallow bowls of two types and deeper type of vessels with a narrow rim. The upper bowl formed the lid to the lower bowl. Three more of the vessels contained a few loose snake-bones, and the remaining two contained only sand. Bibby found in over half the bowls loose among the coiled snake-bones, a single bead, in most cases a tiny turquoise. It seems that in Dilmun, far more than in Cleopatra's Egypt, the snake and the pearl were regarded as the symbols of freedom from sickness, old age, and death. The practice is a clear proof of the legend of Gilgamesh was still living and formed an integral part of the religion of Bahrain at the time when the palace was built and inhabited. (Bibby, 1969:164f; Lombard, 1986:229f),

The French Archaeological Mission to Bahrian consisting of Pierre Lombard, Monik Kervran and others undertook excavation at Qal'at al Bahrain from the point where the Danish left in 1970. Three seasons (1989-92) of French excavations have contributed substantiallly for the advancement of archaeology of Bahrian. The French excavation at City III and City IV have unearthed new building structures. They have discovered walls of late Dilmun "Palace" of Kassite (City III) period. Several new rooms including new hall with a full size column (Fig. 14), an extension of the large building of City IV were discovered by the French team. The French sounding, in City IV building, down to the foundation revealed remains of much older structure. (Fig. 18), which are much older than previously supposed (City IV). Lombard is of the opinion that this site or building was in use before City IV date, at least from the Kassite period (City III), if not earlier. (City II). He infers that the place was continuously occupied, repaired and reused until the Achaemenian times. (ca. sixth/fifth century B.C. =

Fig. 11a   Main Entrance to City IV.

Fig. 11   Street and Wall
leading to main entrance to City IV.

Fig. 11b   (Above) Masonry of City IV wall.
Fig. 11c   (Below) Main hall with column bases City IV

140

Fig. 12a, b   Column bases of the main hall of entrance, City IV.

Fig. 12c.   Top of the base (of 12a, b) with markings.

Fig. 13   Stone base with rectangular holes in a room of City IV.

Fig. 14.   Column in the centre of one of the halls excavated by the French (1989-92).

142

Fig. 15 a, b Wash-rooms City IV.

Fig. 16

(Left) Coffin with skaletal remains and funerary gifts found in one of the City IV rooms. (Courtesy, Bahrain National Museum).

Fig. 18 Walls of earlier period below the foundationof City IV.

144

Fig. 16, a-c Portions of storage jars, pits and plaster bases in the rooms of City IV.

Fig. 17 a, b Wells in City IV.

Fig. 16 d, e Wall plaster and flooring in rooms of City IV.

146

PLAN OF SÃR SETTLEMENT

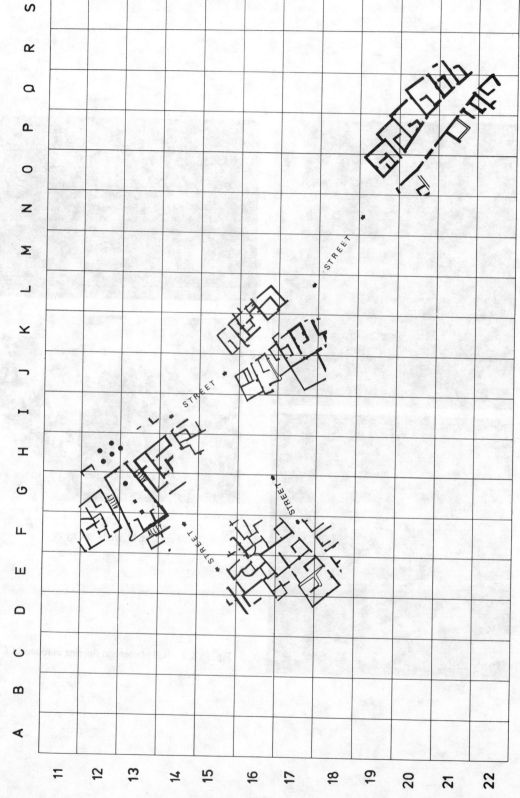

Fig. 19. Plan of Sãr settlment. (Based on the plans of R. Killick, J. Moon and H. Crawford, Directors of the London - Bahrain Archaeological Expedition, Field Reports, 1990 - 92 Ms.)

end of City IV), when it was also abandoned and used as a rubbish and burial place. The excavations and new finds of the French at City III and City IV are shown in Fig. 8, as dintinct from the earlier excavations of the Danes. The plan is based on the outline on two photographs and notes of Lombard. (Personal communication, forthcoming, 1993).

As a result of three seasons of excavations at Qal'at al Bahrain, Lombard has hypothesized that the palatial building of city IV, ("Palace" of the Danes), shown by an outline in Fig.8 a, b is a "temple". This conclusion is based on the unusual features and antiquities found in this area. The features which have been already described and illustrated above, suggest that the building was used for religious purpose and not totally as residence. Lombard dates this "temple" to middle and late Dilmun period. (Lombard, personal communication). In view of the peculiar features (Figs. 12 - 15) in the building, and the antiquities (Snake bowls, offerings, coffins etc.) recovered from the area, I think Lombard's (1993) hypothesis is tenable, unless we have evidence to the contrary. In the light of this new idea the established notion about City IV's building needs reconsideration.

(2) SAR TOWN

During 1977 the Arab expedition excavated the burial mounds at Sar al Jisr (or Sar) site; and its director Moawiyah Ibrahim in his report (1982) stated that they were still eager to find a settlement site in the close vicinity which would be connected with the burial field. He suggested that the only site which might relate to the mounds is a rise along the western edge of wadi Sar, almost half-way between Sar village and the burial complex. Here large quantities of third and early second millennium B.C. pottery sherds were found lying on the surface of the tell. The pottery included ridged Dilmun ware, painted and redslipped wares, hole mouth jars and cooking pots, all typical of the Dilmun culture. Further, here they found exposed portions of the walls which were covered with plaster, fire places and heaps of local small shells. These are still spread over a wide area of the settlement. Ibrahim observed that here they cannot exclude the possibility of a Kassite occupation. Much earlier in 1954 also, at Sar, Glob in a sounding, ten feet deep, found remains of buildings and pottery of Islamic date (Bibby, 1969:67). Thus finding the site of great potential, the antiquities department of Bahrain in collaboration with the Jordanian team undertook excavations of the Sar settlement site under the direction of Shaikha Haya Ali al Khalifa during 1983-85. They excavated at three places and made numerous soundings. They were successful in the venture by the discovery of an important temple and houses in the nearby settlement. (For the details about the temple with illustrations see *infra* Sect. B in this chapter). Here buildings/ houses of Sar settlement, which is proving to be a well planned town is described. The plan of the Sar town as it has emerged after two seasons of British excavations (1990-92) is shown in Fig 19. As seen in this plan on the three adjacent sides of the temple (in the centre), i.e., on the northern, western and southern sides, (the entrance side of the temple being the eastern side), there are buildings, seperated by narrow lanes. Actually the location of the temple is not exactly to the north; but towars north-west . Thus, the buildings and the lanes are actually situated on the north-west, west-south and south-east of the temple. The lanes on the three sides run parallel to the external walls of the temple. In Fig.20a,b (a-front view, b-back view), the north-west lane and the adjoining building to its right (a) and left (b) are seen in Fig.20c the south-east lane and the adjoining building to its right are seen.In Fig.20d the west-south lane (partially filled with debris) and the structure adjoining it are seen. These buildings, along with the temple were excavated by the Bahrain - Jordanian team during 1983-85. The buildings on the three sides of the temple considered as three units are shown in the schematic plan Fig. 19a. The rectangular building on the north west side seems to have been approached by three or four doorways. Two doorways in the foreground are visible in the illustration (fig.20e) on the west south-end; while a possible entrance(s) on the north-west side is covered by the debris. Since there are two internal doorways on this side, it is quite obvious that there were external approach door also. Apparently there seem to have been at least six rooms in the rectangular building, with a kitchen in the extreme south corner. Here on the right side an oven is located (Fig.20f, at the far end). also seen in the illustration (in the foreground) is the round internal wall of the room. In this kitchen or the room, on the left side, are two doorways leading to a double room and to a single room. The latter has an external doorway from the north south-end. In this single room, as seen in Fig.20g, on the opposite wall, on its right hand at an height of more than a metre, a broken mouth of a jar has been inserted as a reuse to serve the purpose of the door socket.

As we enter from the west-south doorway, what appears to be along "L" shaped room was probably a common corridor connecting the internal rooms, as it has an opening or doorway between the small rectangular room right opposite the entrance and the main unit, leading into a rectangular space, which in turn has another opening on its eastern side. Thus the main unit of the building is approached internally from the back side, while it has external doorway at the south-end . The oven suggests that the building was used for residential purpose, probably by the persons/officials working at the temple. Further, the kitchen has direct approach from outside through a doorway at its west-south side and connected to internal rooms through another doorway at its east-north side and south-east side.

The building on the south-east side of the temple is also separated by an alley running through the entire south-east wall of the temple. A portion of this unit is seen in Fig.20h. Also seen in the illustration are two ovens, besides two walls, (Fig.20i). In the corner of the room there is a small semi-circular platform or base, in two levels (Fig.20j). Probably it was meant for a storage jar or to serve as a table for any purpose. These features indicate that the building was used for residential or domestic purpose. In one of the rooms of this building unit comprising two units, the British excavators in their second seasons (1991) have found a large copper hoe (see Fig. in Chapter VIII) weighing over two kilograms. (Crawford etal, 1991:10 Ms.). The third building unit, behind the temple, on the west end of the temple, is a smaller unit compared to the other units. It comprises of three/four smaller rooms (Fig.20k) and is also separated from the temple by an alley.

Fig. 20 a, b. Buildings adjoining the Sar Temple. (Front and Rear).

150

Fig. 20 c (Above) South-east lane and adjoining buildings of the Temple.
Fig. 20 d (Below) West-south lane and structures.

The general practice during the ancient times was that the priest and other persons attending the temple usually resided in the quarters close to the temple. But the number of such persons might not have been so great as to require three large building units on the three sides of the temple. May be the smaller one on the west-south would have been sufficient for the priest or administrator of the temple. It is quite clear from the integral organization of these buildings that they were potential houses, especially those on the north and south of the temple, and used for domestic purpose by very high ranking person. Possibly the chief of the settlement or the Sar town. The administrative office and stores of the temple, seem to have been located in the rooms within the temple premises, at the rear or the western end of the temple.

However, the planning and construction of these three buildings or houses differ from those of the settlement situated at a very close proximity and separated by a street only. May be these houses adjoining the temple, were of earlier phase, built before the houses of the settlement were planned. Still, they were well planned with narrow lanes on the three sides and the main street on one side. The difference in plan of the houses adjoining the temple and the nearby settlement suggest two building phases. However, the time difference between the two phases may not be much. The artifacts recovered from the temple and the adjoining buildings, such as seals, pottery, metal works are dated to the early Dilmun period, i.e. late third and early second millennium B.C. (Killick etal, 1991, *passim*).

The houses excavated by the Bahraini-Jordanian team at two places, one close to the temple on its south-east side, just on the other side of the street and at the far end of the site, have been found to be similar in architecture and plan in a row with stones. At one of the sites they have excavated two houses, almost complete, with wall rising more than a metre. It is observed that one house has four interconnected rooms with a courtyard. Possibly this served as a table for keeping things one is carrying on entering the house. The shallow basin was probably filled with water for washing hands and face as from outside. At another nearby site they found several plastered rooms. (Killick etal, 1991).

The Bahraini-Jordanian team did not undertake full scale excavation of the Sar settlement site. But their initial work and success encouraged the British to undertake further excavations at the same site.Thus, the incomplete work after a lapse of five years was taken up in 1990 by the British team directed by Harriet Crawford, Robert Killick and Jane Moon and sponsored by the Institute of Archaeology, University of London.

The first season, during 1990, of the London-Bahrain archaelogical expedition was a great success with remarkable discoveries. During the short period of ten weeks the British were able to excavate substantial area of the town and were able to identify the main streets, public buildings, areas of town houses, and specialized craft working quarters. The combined results of the Bahraini-Jordanian and the British excavations, observes Killick, Crawford, Moon etel (1990:107-137) that the Sar settlement is a one-period settlement dated, on the

152

Fig. 20e. Two door-ways in the rear of the north-west building.

Fig. 20f. Front view of north-west building with an internal curved wall at the extreme end in the right corner is an ovan.

Fig. 20g. (Above) Re-use of a broken jar as door socket in the wall.

Fig. 20 h. (Below) Portion of the south-east building adjoining the temple. Ovens are
seen adjacent to the walls.

basis of the ceramic parallels, to c.1900 B.C., corresponding to Qal'at al Bahrain City II c-d, and Failaka period I. The beginning of the settlement has been suggested by the excavators to post-date City I at Qal'at, as at Sar, they did not find a single sherd of the distinctive City I chain-ridged pottery. They could not fix the length of occupation at Sar; but suggest that the end must pre-date at least City III, if it does not fall within the City II sequence. (Killick etel, 1990:107-137). The British excavated and cleared six houses at three different sites within the Sar settlement. They have assigned arbitrarily house number as 1 to 3, 50 to 53, and 100-101, for the three sites situated at short distance from each other. Probably the British hope to excavate in future the space left in between these houses and possibly they hope to link-up the whole settlement. However, in numbering the houses the British have not assigned any number to the houses situated adjacent to the temple. This may be for obvious reasons that they did not excavate them and that, they consider these houses as administrative buildings. But since we find ovens and other domestic fixtures inside these buildings it is quite clear that they were used for domestic purposes. Probably they were also used partly to house administrative offices of the temple as well as the settlement.

Of the three sets of houses, three houses (Fig.24 b) were excavated in the immediate vicinity of the temple complex, only the street separating them. These three houses have a common plan, each having an inner rectangular room and an outer "L" shaped room. The walls were built by using rough limestone and were finished with an ashly plaster rendering. However, it has been observed that all rooms were not uniformly furnished. The degree of finishing varied.Some of the rooms were finished smoothly using harder gypsum-based plaster. The entrance to the three houses was from the common street. Except house 2, the other two(houses 1,3) did not had a doorway in the rear. And this house 2 alone, did not had any domestic installations, as found in the other two houses 1 to 3. An oven (bottom portion) measuring 30 cms in diameter with clay lining is found in the corner of the outer room of house 1, as seen in Fig.21. Also seen in the illustration is an oval-shaped plastered basin, at the south-west corner of the inner room. Obviously the houses were roofed for protection from sun and rain. This is evident from the buttresses found on some of the walls. Most interesting finds from house 1 are five circular stamp seals of Dilmun type. They are similar to those found from other sites in Bahrain. Another interesting find, which indicates fishing as one of the profession of the Sar inhabitants, is the net-sinker of stone with a pock marked line through the middle. Net sinkers are common in the Gulf states. Similar specimens have been found from the sites excavated in Ajman and Ras Al-Khaimah. Two such specimens from Ajman have been recently published by Haerinck (1991:88). Other recoveries include fragment of a steatite bowl, s shell bead, jar stoppers, a stone button, an oval-shaped "weight", worked stones, enlarge stone weight/pounders. The stone weights are similar to those found at Qal'at al Bahrain. An intact socketed copper spear head from house 2 is another interesting find. It is similar to those found in Bahrain and in other Gulf states and dated to early second millennium B.C. That all houses were not used for residential purposes only but for other purposes as well is evident from the range of installation and pits found in the

Fig. 20 i   (Above) Oven of Fig. 20 h.
fig. 20 j   (Below) Semi-circular platform. (Of Fig. 20h).

house 3, area 10, (see Fig. 24b). Also in the rectangular room immediately to the left of the entrance, there is a circular plaster basin, as seen in Fig.21b, in the corner opposite to the room doorway. The British suggest that the area 10 had a special function and that the pits belong to different phases. These pits have been extensively re-plastered with up to eight coats of gypsum. In the same area, at the north-east corner was also found base of a storage pot sunk into the floor. Animal skull and bones, probably of a gazelle, were found in a pit of a later phase. Further, in the same area, in the south-west corner, two basins are located. These features suggest that the room of area 10 of house 3 was used for some commercial purpose, while the other areas of the same house must have been used for domestic purpose. (Killick, Crawford, Moon etal, 1991:117-121).

In the second group of houses (50-53) two buildings covering an area of 125 Sqm, were excavated earlier by the Bahraini-Jordanian team, but the work was incomplete. So the British undertook in 1990 to complete the excavation on this group of houses and they uncovered a unit of three houses, covering an area of 225m², along with a street to the east and a large open area to the west. They belong to one group as they have common wall between houses 50 and 51, 51 and 52, and 52 and 53. Houses 51 and 52 are seen in Fig.22a (from left to right), and house 53 is seen on the extreme right in Fig.22b, along with houses 51 and 52 on its left.

In house 51, as one enters from the street, there is a plastered double basin built over a pediment of mortared stone. This basin, after the excavations, has been covered for the sake of protection from any damage, by a wooden box, as seen on extreme left, in Fig.22 a,b. The basin with its pediment can be seen in Fig.22d (Photographed through the metallic mesh fixed over the box). In the same room on the left side corner of the wall, opposite the basin, an hearth has been located. It has been constructed over a rectangular plastered platform extending almost to the entire length of the horizontal wall, of house 51, seen in Fig.22c. Stones are protruding from the shallow plastered platform.The hearth is semi-circular in shape and is attached to the wall. Excavation at house 51, uncovered the basin and hearth. Adjacent to the hearth, on its right side, are found two lumps of plaster over the platform.House 51 had an entrance in the rear wall also.This seem to be a deviation from the normal plan of the Sar settlement houses, so far uncovered. In this house the British found a seal depicting the art of sexual intercourse. Though this seal has not been illustrated by the British in their preliminary report, but has been published separately by Crawford (1991:225-260). Another interesting find from house 51 is a lid, of steatite vessel, having dot-and-circle motif. Vessels of this designs have been found the Gulf states and are exhibited in the museums of Al Ain, Dubai, Ajman, Ras-al-Khaima, Fujaira, etc. Stone vessels with similar design from the Gulf state of Umm al-Qaiwain have been recently illustrated by Boucharlat etal (1988:16 Fig.2).

The plan of the house 52, situated next to 51 on the south east side similar to its predecessor but its rear wall seems to have been demolished. In this house also was found

Fig. 21a (Above) House I during excavation by the British team (1990) (Photo Courtesy : Bahrain National Museum). Fig. 21b. (Centre) House. I Ovens are seen adjacent to the walls. Fig. 21c. (Below) House 3 with a circular oven in the corner.

158

Fig. 22 a   (Above) Houses 51 and 52.
fig. 22b   (Middle) Front view of houses 52 and 53.

Fig. 22 e An 'L' shaped stone wall enclosure at the entrance to house 53.
(Jane Moon, one of the Directors of the London-Bahrain Archaeological
Expedition 1990-92 is seen within the enclosure).

a plastered hearth at similar location as in the previous house. The British excavators suggest that this house fell in disuse and later on house 53 was built to it south-east house. Further it seems that after it was abandoned it was used as passage, as evident from the nature of the deposits recovered from here. The plan of house 53 is different and much bigger than its predecessors.Most of it was excavated by the Bahraini-Jordanian expedition and what was left-over was completed by the British. The latter have observed that it is the largest house found so far in the Sar settlement. It has four rooms and a courtyard with a compound wall on the back-side. Different from the previous houses, its entrance has on "L" shaped stone wall forming an enclosure (see Fig.22e) for the doorway. It might have been a portico. In this house also were located a plastered basin, and a hearth.The exceptional features of this house suggest that it belonged to a high official of importance. The big courtyard suggest that it might have been meant for public gathering or meetings.The door of these houses open in a street which runs in both directions:one end continues right up to the front of the temple, and the other end continues upto the third group of houses (100-101) and may be beyond the present limit of excavations.So where the street ends cannot be stated at present.

The third group of houses (Fig.24d) where the British excavated during their first season is a unit of two houses 100-101. Of these, only one, house 100 was completely excavated, while other partially. These houses are situated on the opposite sides of the main road (see Fig.24), which is linked to the temple. Subsequent excavation of second season 1991 by the British have revealed that there is a row of houses on the two sides of the road and that the houses 100 and 101 at the head of the row, lie at the northern-end of the road. The British have suggested that these two houses (100-101) have at least two distinct phases. Similar to the other group of houses, mentioned above, the layout of these houses (100-101) is also rectangular having two areas, the 'L' shaped outer area of the entrance and inside a small rectangular room. In house 100 two plastered basins of different heights are located on the right wall, slightly away from the doorway. Next to the door of the inner rectangular room there is a small plastered feature (Fig.23a), may be to serve as a stand. The door opened inward is evident from the door socket (Fig.23c) found inside the doorway of house 101. Also seen in the illustration is the raised stone threshold of one step.No step stone was found inside the doorway. In house 100 one stamp seal depicting a person in a s sitting posture and drinking through a pipe was found. Due to stone robbing the house 101 has been damaged considerably. In the inner room of this house was found one small pink pearl of size 4.02 mm. Like house 53, this house also has a walled 'L' shaped enclosure at the entrance.(Killick, Crawford, Moon, etal, 1991:121-126). A pit, an oven and a rectangular basin found in the area behind house 101 are shown in Figs.23b-e.

The schematic plans of the houses excavated by the British during their two seasons of 1990-91 are shown in Fig.24 b, d; and those of the buildings adjoining the temples are shown in Fig.24a. The plan of the commercial complex is shown in Fig. 24e and Fig.24fg is that of houses 100-109 excavated during 1991.

160

Fig. 22d (Above) Basin with its pediment, adjacent to external (Photographed through mettalic mesh).

Fig. 22c   (Below) Hearth over a plastered platform in house 51.

Fig. 23c (Above) A door socket inside the doorway of house 101.

Fig. 23d (Below) A circular pit in a house behind house 101.

The British team during the second season 1991 of excavation at Sar settlement site, brought to light an 'industrial complex' (so-called by the them). (Killick, Moon and Crawford 1991 - unpublished field report). I would prefer to designate it as a commercial complex rather than an 'industrial'. The complex is located to the north of houss 1-3 and is not only linked to them but is found to be continuation of housing unit. The common wall of houses 2 and 3 conects the complex. See plan in Fig.25. Beyond the connecting wall and the rectangular room is the commercial complex.Further north with an opening on the right side leads to the main room of the commercial complex. It has a semi-circular storage tank (Fig.25a) with opening on the back side from the other room.The tank seems to be of some liquid with basins attached to its semi-circular wall, which served as outlet for extracting the fluid. In the back room hearth and basins are found. The central room opens into the alley (see Fig.25c) which leads to the temple on the eastern side. While the doorway on the left side of the central room leads to the kitchen of the commercial complex having hearth, bake oven, trough, basins and pits. Here several stone crushing tools were found by the British. The bake oven is seen in the corner of the room in Fig.25b and an hearth is seen attached to the left wall in the foreground.It is oval in shape, broader at one side and narrower at the other, as seen in Fig.25c in the foreground. This room has two out side door ways and facing them in the outside space basins and other installations have been found along with heaps of remains of fish and shell fish and lots of ash and rubbish. This place, immediately on its discovery the British named it as "the sea-found restaurant", as the remains indicate that it was associated with the large-scale preparation of sea-food. The north west wall of the commercial complex constitutes one of the walls of the alley which on the east north end leads to the temple. The alley is not of uniform width.It is narrower on the side of the kitchen of the complex and bends in at the central hall and from here it is broader, as seen in Fig.25f,d. Also seen in the figure is the parallel wall, on the extreme right, running opposite to the commercial complex, which form the alley. On the right side of the wall of the alley, extreme right in Fig.25d, is most probably, a toilet and to its north are several storage pits. Probably this was a public toilet meant not only for the people of the commercial complex but also for the pilgrims to the temple; as it is situated on the alley linking the temple at close proximity.With in the central hall there is a semi-circular room, but its entrance seems to be from the other side of the back room on the extreme right. In this semi-circular room there is a large storage tank of some liquid.Since there are basins on the other side in the central hall around the semi-circular wall of this room, perhaps there is some connection of these basins with the storage tank. Probably the liquid was drawn from the tank through these basins. The complex located so close to the temple, must have been catering to the needs of the pilgrims visiting the temple. And the four rooms, areas 12-4 and 20 between the houses 1-3 and the commercial complex, might have been used as residence of those working at the complex. Excavation on house 53 was continued by the British during the second season also and it turned out to be a very large house with five rooms and enclosed courtyard behind (see Fig.22c).From the house adjacement to house 53, informs Harried Crawford,a bun-shaped copper ingot was discovered. This piece, she says, is very close in size and shape to those found by Weisgerber

Fig. 23a. (Above) A plastered stand in house 101 and inner doorway.

Fig. 23b. (Left) A rectangular basin in the second house behind house 101.

Fig. 23e. (Right) An oval shaped oven in a house behind house 101.

in Oman.(Crawford, personal communication).

An unusual small room, as seen in the top left corner of Fig. 25e was uncovered during the second season by the British. Its walls are plastered from top to bottom, as seen in Fig.25f., except the floor.Instead at the floor, at the bottom, was a large quantity of burnt date kernels.This room was probably, as supposed by the British team, a form of madbas, or date-press, occasionally cleaned out by lighting a fire at its bottom. As seen in the fig. 25e, this room is located at a distance, away from the residential houses, (a standard two room house in also seen in the centre of the photograph). This implies that the room had some commercial function as evidence by the finds from its storage tank. Several layers of plaster flooring is found in one of the houses as seen in Fig.25g. While in another house plastering with marks in found on the side wall, as in Fig.25h.

RESUME

The building so far exhumed at Sar settlement area fall into five main classes, *viz.*, (1) Temple; (2) Administrative-cum-Residence; (3) Dwelling houses; (4) Commercial complex; and (5) isolated structures.

The structural features of the temple is absolutely different from all the buildings so far uncovered at Sar and its architecture and plan are discussed in the next section in this chapter.

The buildings on the three sides of the temple separated by narrow lanes on the three sides, north-west, west-south and south-east may be categorised as administrative-cum-residences for two reasons. Firstly, the buildings with several rows, especially to the north west and south east, are too big to house the administrative offices of the temple. Secondly, since hearths and ovens have been found in these buildings, it is obvious that the temple officials used it for the residence as well.

The size of the three buildings on the three sides and the dimensions of their rooms vary not only between them but when compared to the other regular dwelling houses uncovered at the Sar settlement on the other side of the street. The general plan of these two buildings on the north west and south east seems to be similar with entrances from the rear, west south sides and not from front, like that of the temple itself. They have both long and small rectangular rooms, with two external door-ways (The plan is incomplete). The structure on the west south side is comparatively small, with may be two rooms only. Possibly it was meant for the menial staff employed at the temple or for the guards at the temple. Excavation at Sar, conducted by the British team, are in rapid progress. Every season or year, the size of the settlement is growing and new finds and pattern of settlement are brought to light. The two season of 1990-91 and 1991-92 have revealed that Sar settlement was, to a certain extent, well planned town. The excavators (Killick, Crawford, Moon etal, 1991:134) state

SĀR SETTLEMENT _ HOUSES

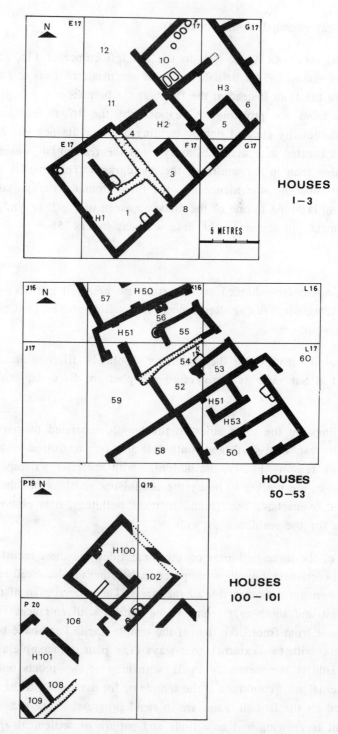

Fig. 24   Plans of houses excavated by the British team (1990-92). (Based on plans in Field Reports 1990-92 Ms) by the Directors. (H. Crawford, R. Killick, J. Moon)

that there are good evidence to the effect that the settlement was laid out with some measure of fore thought and that its organic growth was controlled. This inference is based on the street pattern and the housing blocks which are of uniform plan. Irrespective of the directions, the streets run at right angles; and all the houses or others buildings, uncovered so far, were built along one of these two axes.A glimpse of the schematic plan of the settlement in Fig.25, will elucidate the point. The most striking characteristic features of the settlement lay-out plan are: the block and unit system of building houses; all rectangular shape, uniformity in house plan as well as dimensions.Except one house (No.53), there is consistency in the size of the dwellings, which are of two-roomed tenements.One outer "L" shaped room, and an inner rectangular room. The internal area is about 35 square metres.However, the average floor area is about 40 square metres, comprising the court and the roofed area. (Crawford, personal communication.). From the schematic plan of Fig.20, it is evident that the basic layout of the Sar settlement shows regular orientation.This comprises two distinct elements: on the north, rather north west, the temple complex built on the highest part or the site, with a long axis running north-south, and to east-west; and dominated by it, a lower town, comprising the dwelling houses as well as a commercial complex linked to the houses. The streets were laid out with controlled skill; although they are not in precise alignment. The smaller streets were at right-angles to the main street. There seems to be some standardization in the measurements of the streets. The principle and the largest (north-south) being nearly double the width of the smaller ones (east-west). And the four alleys also have almost same width. Thus suggesting certain rule in the coordination of the measurements of the principle streets, side street and alleys was maintained as a distinguishing factor, may be based on the importance and volume of traffic it served. Since the site has not yet been fully excavated it cannot be said whether the town or site was rectangular or square and whether there was a surrounding wall or not for security purpose. Further, future excavation may probably reveal houses on the other sides of the temple.Nothing can be predicted about the final over-all plan of the Sar settlement. Again, consistency with regard to location, construction and size of the domestic fixtures, such as, plaster basins, hearths, benches and bins etc., has been maintained.

The layout plan of the commercial block, though linked at the south to the dwelling houses is quite different from those of the regular houses, as is evident in Fig.21. Obviously it was so designed to suite the commercial needs and its functions. In the fifth category of the structural remains in the one small room with some special functions.

The excavators, the British, have not drawn any parallel of the Sar settlement plan in their report, both published and unpublished. However, I am of the opinion that the lay-out plan of the Sar settlement had been influenced by the Mohenjo-Daro and Harappan settlement pattern of Indus Valley Civilization, where we find plan laid out on the grid. Sar settlement does not seems to have been influenced by the Mesopotamian pattern which show random growth, and not controlled growth as found as Sar.

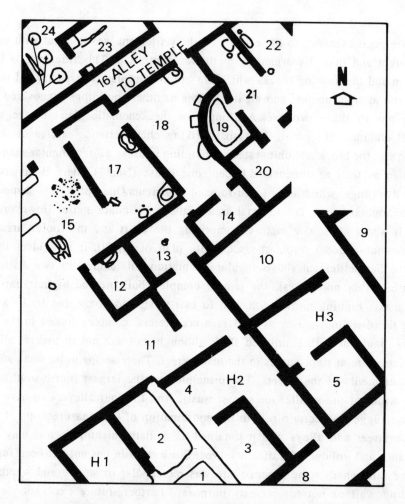

Fig. 25   Plan of the commercial complex near the Sar Temple. (Based on the plan
in the Field Report 1990-92 of the Directors of the British team).

☐ Basin   ▭▭ Pair Of Basins
○ Bin
◉ Hearth
⬭ Oven / Bake Oven
⦿ Pits
▯ Plastered Feature
☐ Stone / Stone Bench
⊖ Storage Pot
▭ Trough
🛢🛢 Water Proof Bins

Fig. 25a (Above) Commercial complex with storage tank in the centre.

Fig. 25b. (Below) Rooms adjoining the commercial complex with pits and ovens. The street leading to the Temple is in the fore-ground. (Photo : Courtesy Jane Moon).

Fig. 25c (Above left) Oblong and oval shaped ovens in the room of Fig. 25b.

Fig. 25d (Above right) Street leading to the temple between commercial complex and probable toilets.

Fig. 25e (Below). House with plaster (extreme top left). And House 50-53.

Fig. 25f (Above Right). Plaster on the wall of a house.

Fig. 25g. (Below). Plaster flooring in one of the houses.

Fig. 25h. (Above right). Plaster on the side of the entrance with marks.

However, in one aspect, use of rough lime stones in building walls, Sar settlement differs from Indus Valley, Mesopotamian and Tepe Yahya where mud bricks were used.Thus implying this technique did not reach Sar or otherwise it was not feasable and full opportunity was made in utilizing stones easily available locally.

(3)   DIRAZ HOUSES

Diraz is situated almost at the extreme north west corner of Bahrain. Eastward from the village of Diraz, stretches a large area of sandy hillock where Bibby and Glob found millions of potsherds. Close to the village is the Diraz well and from it Bibby and Glob found pottery dated to the third mellennium.B.C., thus attesting occupation of the site and existence of settlement at Diraz during this period. (Bibby, 1969:67-69). The site at Diraz, which lies about half-a-mile west of the Barbar mound north of the Budyia road, was excavated in 1972 by the Bahraini team under the direction of Abdul Kader Al-Tikriti.The original area of site is considered to have been nearly 100 acres.However, much of this is now occupied by the modern villages and gardens.Thus the total area uncovered by the excavation was about 40 square meters only, to a depth of three and half metres to the virgin soil.Diraz has yielded traces of architecture, and about five houses have been identified.It is observed that houses adjoined each other or at least two sides and open areas have been found, the walls were built of unshaped stones, or rough filled foundations and were plastered on both the faces internally and externally the houses were roughly rectilinear in plan with traces of rooms flanking a courtyard. Three individual portion walls have been found in one large house. But their height suggests that they were not up to the roof level. Al-Tikriti suggests that the roofs were most probably low gables of brushwood and mud, as found even to day in villages.The floor were generally composed of packed silt on a bed of sand. Storage bins and ovens, similar to those found at Sar settlement, have been found in Diraz houses.One of them had a tone of plaster.Two doorways with recessed jambs have been noticed in one of the houses. There was a flat stone set behind the western wall with a slit above, which might have served as a corridor. No appurtenances were found with the doorway. However, stone door sockets have been found at other places of the site. These houses were destroyed partly by the later occupation of the sites.However the traces of houses suggest that Diraz was a village. The artifacts recovered from the houses indicates, says al Tikriti, that Diraz was contemporary with Barbar assemblages and may be dated between 2500-2000 B.C. But al Tikriti finally concludes that the Diraz site was occupied in the beginning of the third millennium B.C., and hardly later than 2500 B.C.

The artifacts found were Dilmun seals, pottery, copper bronze arrow heads and spear heads and some pieces of stone vessels.Huge quantity of shell of several varieties and fish bones found at occupational levels at Diraz suggests that it was a fishing village.This is the only village, so far discovered,which is related to both, the Cities (I and II) Qal'at al Bahrain as well as Barbar temples.There seems to be no evidence of agriculture at Diraz, save a few number of querns, rubbing stones and storage pits., However, it is not certain that this material were used for agriculture purpose.It is quite possible that these were as well used for storing food. (Al-Tikriti, 1972:12; 1973:4-6).

The British expedition under Mc Nicoll (1973-75) made excavation in Diraz east and a trench square N15 of size 9x9 m. brought to light architecture.Within the trench three "column bases" were found, which were built of rubble set in mortar, diameter 1.10-1.20 m., maximum height 0.60m.The columns stand 2.3 m. apart.Two other possible "columns bases" were found with the square N15, and another definite one was outside the trench to the south-east. Beside these, in the eastern section was found a rectangular structure, built of cemented stones and plaster faced, which could be either a plinth, wall end or some other structure. The only other architectural feature of N15 was a short stretch of a gypsum plastered wall face in the west of the trench. Mc Nicoll observed that the function of these architectural features is uncertain and possibly the "column bases" did in fact support a roof; but no traces of roof beams, tiles or other materials were found. The Dilmun pottery and Umm an Nar sherds recovered from the trench suggests third millennium date for the architectural features. That the area of Diraz east seems to have been occupied or more likely used as a burial ground during early third millennium is attested by the recovery of chain-ridged ware and also by the style of the seals. (Mc Nicoll, Ms.9f. Unpublished Report)

(B) TEMPLES

Exacavations have brought to light, so far, four temples which fall under the purview of our period. These are: the Barbar temple, the Diraz temple, the well-temple of Umm es sejur and the Sar temple settlement. There seems to be another temple at Sar grave complex, but it is of a later date and hence out of the purview of our period. Recently Pierre Lombard (personal communication) has hypothesized that the large building of City IV at Qal'at was a 'Temple' of middle and late Dilmun. See above under   City IV, for details and plan.

(1)   BARBAR TEMPLE

When the submit of the large 3 meter high gravel mound near the Barbar village, mentioned earlier by Durand in 1890, was removed by the Danes in 1955-56, three superimposed temples were uncovered. The area covered by the temple precints was 3600 square meters. During the first year of excavation the Danes found three temple buildings super imposed one above the other, the earlier building having in each case been demolished to the foundation before the new temple was built above them.When the inner precints of the two uppr temples (II, III) were exposed by the Danes, the earliest temple was uncovered. In Fig.2 is illustrated partly excavated plan of temples, constructed by Kristian Jappesen of the Danish team. The composite plan of Barbar temples is illustrated in Fig. 1.

The first temple, Temple I, was constructed on top of the artificial mound of clay and sand and its surrounding wall appears to have formed a square with sides about 20 meters

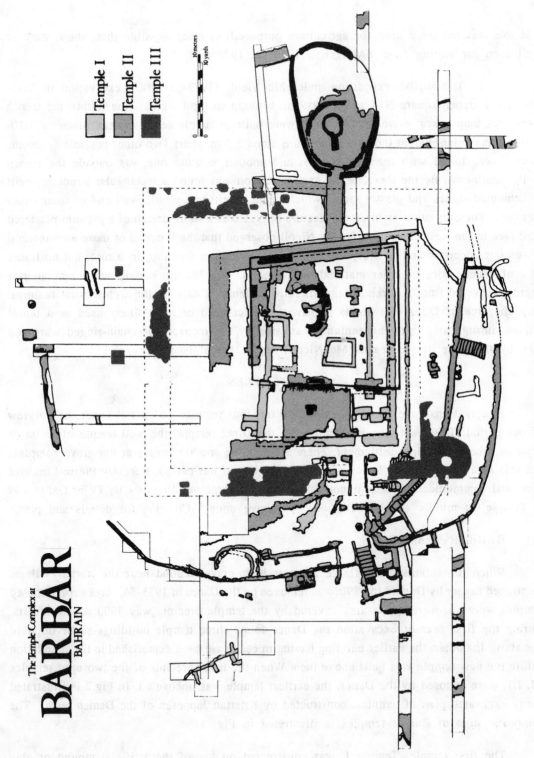

Fig. 1. Composite plan of Barbar Temple Complex. (From "The Temple Complex at Barbar-Bahrain", 1983. Ministry of Information Bahrain).,

long. Outside this wall towards both south and east were other buildings. On the western side stood the eight large plinth-blocks.Temple II had an inner core, approximately square and measuring about 25x25 metres, with a wall thickness of slightly over two metres. The wall was built of solid ashlar, finely cut rectangular blocks of stone of various sizes but carefully fitted together and joined together with gypsum mortar.Here there was an outer complex, with a stone-set ramp to the west. (see Fig. 3). It is noticed that stone from the Temple II were utilised in bulding the Temple III.The latter has a smaller inner court measuring 16x16 meters. On the western side of this courtyard are remains of a few rooms.One of them has a width of 3 meters, while its length cannot be known, as stones have been robbed away. This west chamber in Temple III is illustrated in Fig. 8. This room might have been of the earlier temple, Temple II. Around Temple III was built a massive wall of unshaped blocks set in gypsum plaster. It seems that the wall constituted a square area of 40x40 meters (externally). The dimensions of the wall are approximately four meters in width and faced with massive rectangular blocks of stone. And beyond the wall was placed two large plinth stones.Eight large cut blocks of Temple I are set up in a double row by its western side. These block run under a ramp ends up from west to Temple II. (see II in Fig. 6), and this ramp is in turn topped by the outer wall of Temple III. (See III in Fig. 6). These stone blocks of dimensions approximately 1 x 0.5 x .5 meters, have two square holes cut in the upper surface, and are of similar types as those of Temple III. However, two blocks at the northern side of the site, one of slightly varying size and one of them has, in addition to the large square holes, a smaller circular hole in the centre of one side near the edge, as seen at extreme right in Fig. 6. In these holes was found a sleeve of copper sheating filled between the space.Through the sheating rows of copper nails have been driven, with the points inwards, along with the remains of wood. Obviously, the function of the nails was to secure wooden support in the holes in the stones.These wooden supports are about 20 cms. in diameter. Glob believes that the stone blocks acted as foundations for human figures, wooden statues of gods, with one foot fitted into each of the holes. In the case of the block with the third hole, is feasible, supposes Glob, that the figure held a staff or the like. One of these blocks has rock carvings, as seen in Fig. 7. (Glob, 1954:149-153; 1955:190-192). The rock art on the fill with-stone on the Barbar temple is similar to the Bronze Age rock art found in Saudi Arabia. (See volume I in this series, Chapter IV).

As seen in the illustration, Fig 2, the square surrounds a central area, possibly a court yard, which is partly paved with sand stone. It measures 14x18 meters, internally. In the middle of this area, stands the remains of two circular structures (D-E) linked together, as seen in Figs.7, 8. It is a double circular altar and an offering table stood in the centre.To the south stood three cult-stones shaped like the anchors, as seen in Fig.11, on top extreme left (Only two are vissible in this figure.). The altar stone are almost 80 cms. in height. One of them at the time of excavation stood in situ, while the other lay over turned, but the mark left by its foot was visible in the paving. In front of these stones was a small square stone trough, apparently not far from its original position, B.(Fig. 2). Behind the

174

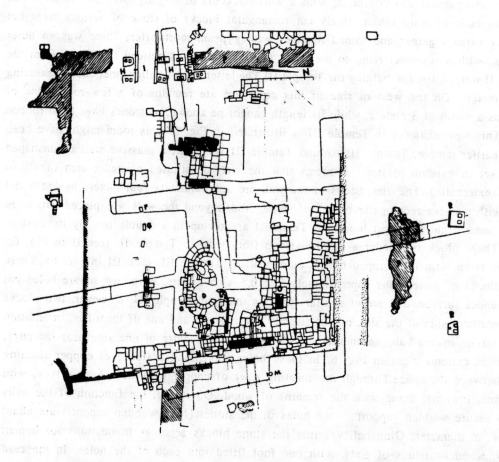

Plan of the excavated portion of the Barbar temples (plan constructed by Kristian Jeppesen). Temple I:
H plinth-stones to statues, L altar complex, M east wall. Temple II: K circular altar, I ramp, N east and
north walls. Temple III: A pit of offerings, B altar and altar-stones, C, F, G pierced stone blocks, D–E
circular structure, O east and north inner walls, P west and north outer walls, R plinths for statues.
Earliest structure: S stone setting.

Fig. 2   Plan of exvacated portion (1955).

(After K. Jeppesen and P.V. Glob, *Kumal*, 1955).

eastern half of the circular altar, there was a stone of about 80 cm, but over turned.It was rounded at the top and pierced by a round hole, C (Fig.2). Similar stone was found in situ at the south-western corner of the inner courtyard,F. In the north eastern corner of the countryard there was a pit bordered by slabs standing on edge along its south and west sites, A. Below the two circular altars (Figs. 10, 11) on the western side, were found remains of another stone circle obviously it was of an earlier temple. Its surface was about one meter under the level of the upper courtyard. Glob states that they could follow the section trench of their earlier phase of the temple building, and about one meter further down, till another building level was identified. Foundations of the walls surrounding the earliest structure were found in the southern part of the trench.These structures are identified as temples on the basis of their distinct features, such as altar-stones and other artifacts found in the inner courtyard.How these altar stones, which were slightly hollowed at the top, were originally used, cannot be definitely stated, says Glob.It is presumed that a seat originally rested on the hallow top.This is quite possible, as Mesopotamian seals, depict the god seated on a stone of similar form, with a square altar before his feet, while he receives the offerings from the people.This is attested by the objects of offerings discovered during excavations, which were found scattered around the square pit opposite the altar stone and the altar. It is probable, says Glob, that the perforated stones also had same firm action within the cult of the temple.(Glob, 1954:149-153; Bibby, 1969: 72-74).

The Temple Oval at Barbar is shownin Fig.5 . This was discovered on the eastern side of the mound during the excavation of 1955-56 by the Danes.The upper edge of an oval wall, says Mortensen (1956:195-198), connected the temple by a ramp of about 5 meters in length and 1.5 meters in breath. Above a yellow-grey gravel stratum a floor of about 10 cms thick of a course greyish plaster, was found at the base of the structure. On the eastern side of the plaster, was a soft claylike layer containing pebbles.And at the centre of the western side of the struture was a low platform (A in the figure), which was with regard to the circular stone structures. During Caspers (1973b:75-79) draws parallel with those of brick at Mohenjo-Daro and at Chanhu-Daro and in the centre of these stone structures, she believes that a date-tree was planted there with religious motive.Her observation is based on the fact that both in Sumer and Indus Civilization tree was sacred and its worship was practised and Dilmun was greatly influenced by these two civilizations. This is attested by depiction of date-tree on Dilmun seals.She concludes that religious ceremonies doubtless related to the veneration of date tree were centered round the two circular stone structures at Barbar which stood during Temple II period in the centre of the courtyard about 15 cms. height above the floor level. A rough circular wall of unshaped stones and plaster is built around the platform.This wall is about 10-15 cms. in thickness and its height is 3-5 cms.The diameter of the circular space within the wall space is 1.8-2.2 meters.On the western side of the platform a rectangular bock (B) of plaster is situated . It is about 1.6 meters in length. Possibly it was also a platform. Both the platforms, circular and rectangular, are enclosed by a wall (C) almost circular of about 6.5-7.5 meters in diameter. This wall of about 20-25 cms. in

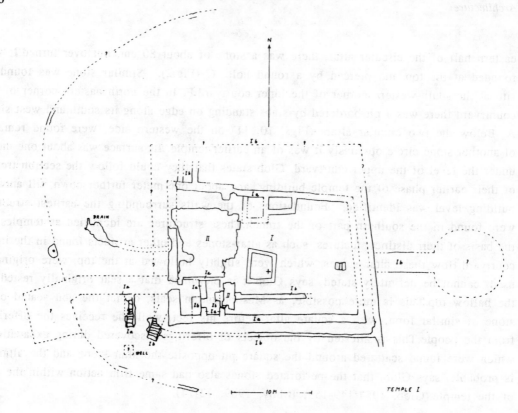

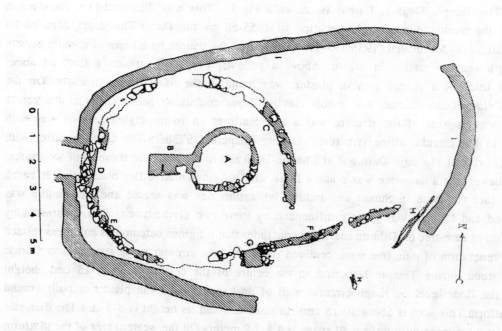

Fig. 3 (Above) Plan of Barbar Temple, I ab (After H. Anderson, 1986).

Fig.5.   (Below). Oval temple.

height is 40-45 cms. in width. There is an opening (D) at a lowest step of the ramp.On the western side of the wall on the south eastern side is the outer circular wall (E); and a straight section of the lowest circular wall. Between E and F is a square block (G) of size 60 cms. At the extreme south east end of the oval parts of a drain have survived. It is of irregular dimensions. Its depth is 10-15 cms.and width, 5-10 cms. Greyish plaster is found on the walls and bottom portion.It seems that it was originally covered. All these features are surrounded by asymmetrical oval wall (I). However a portion of the oval wall is missing at its north east and south west points. The thickness of the wall varies from about 50-70 cms; and its maximum height is 105 cms. From this oval wall the temple has been so designated by the Danes, who have distinguished three building phases. Mortensen suggets on the basis of the grey-black level and deposits of greyish gravel found in both Temple II and oval temple, that the oval is contemporary in all its phases, with Temple II. This is attested by the fact that both the earlier and later ramps lead up to this building.From this oval building a large number of red ridged pottery was found. Important finds were: bases of reddish-ware, nine pottery beakers (broken above the base). two rim-sherds, large quantity of thin buckled sheating and nails of copper or bronze, a tanged arrow head, fragment of a tanged dagger etc.

With regard to the function of the oval structure, Mortensen compares it with two Mesopotamian oval temples as possible parallel to the Barbar oval. These are the oval temples of Nin-Khursag at al 'Ubaid and at Khafajah, east of Baghdad.They both are contemporary with that of Barbar oval. However they are comparatively larger than Barbar oval and the building materials also differ. The Mesopotamian temples consists of cult-building, surrounded by one or more asymmetrical oval walls and connected with the surrounding structures by a ramp or a stairway. They show in plan a certain measure of agreement, while they have also several details in common. The possibility that the Barbar oval, like the contemporary oval temple of Mesopotamia, suggests Mortensen, had a cult-function .This inference is attested to a certain degree by the objects found at Barbar. Thus, the remarkable broken bases might have been used in cult ceremonies and the scores of animal bones found explain as the remain of sacrificial animals. (Mortensen, 1956:195-198).

Several excavations by the Danish expedition have revealed that there is clear evidence in the stratigraphy of the large tell at Barbar for a sequence of three temples.The general structure is : a "high temple" with a double stepped platform, an upper square one and a lower oval one, and two wing structures, a basin to the west, and an enclosure to the east. This, says Anderson (1986:166), is paradigmatic for Temples I and II, whereas Temple III just seems to consist of a single square platform. The idea of a double-temple is born by the existence of the NE-Temple. The fact that the temple is in five building-stages is corroborated by the five stages of the temple well in the south west corner.The structural plans of the three temples, Temple I, Temple II and Temple III are illustrated in Figs. 3, 4; while the composite plan of these three temples is shown in Fig. 1. The successive retaining walls

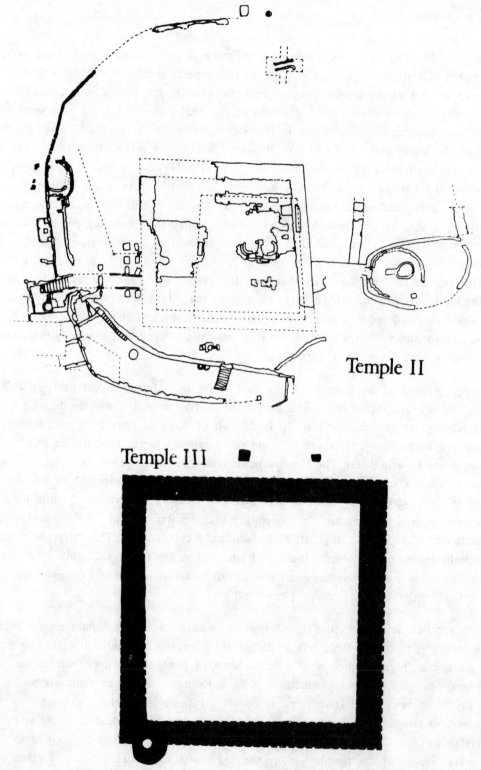

Temple II

Temple III

Fig. 4. Plan of Barbar Temple II, III (The Temple Complex at Bahrain", 1983).

of the lower curved platform of Temple II are seen in Fig 9. The flight of steps led from the ground level up to the terrace of Temple II. °Excavations have established, as detailed above, that at Barbar there were three stone built temples superimposd one above the other. Obviously implying successive rebuilding at the same site and over earlier structures. This practice is characteristic of the Sumerian temples of Mesopotamia. Temples I and II are approximately of the same size. Temple III which covers a greater area is over Temple II. While Temple I is under the floor of Temple II. Doe (1986:186) says that the Temples I and II, when surveyed during the original excavation found to have been built comparatively of small stones and had a plaster floor. Whereas, Temple II was built in large squared masonry and its floor was paved. The different types of masonry, the method of construction and the workmanship of the cut stone, the ashlar facing stone of the southern perimetre wall and the Apsu chamber sugests, says Doe, that a technological change took place during the period of building Temple I and Temple II and the use of small stones continued in building of the later temple. It seems that Barbar temple is the only temple with Sumerian religious and architectural affinities, so far, discovered to have been built in stone. The people who built Barbar temple's foundations, walls, and flooring with stone seems to have been unfamiliar with stone masonry but being familiar with clay brick construction, adopted level courses in building. The north wall of Temple I is built of roughly hewn small stones, uncut blocks of irregular size and coursed.

The masonry of Temple II exhibits fine cut stone work and edging of the foundation. This is evident from the in situ walls on the east and north, having large rectangular cut stone in the foundation. On the west of the temple are remains of well cut slabs paved on plaster screeding. At some part of the walls proper bonding was not made and the heavy weight of the stones provided stability. But at some places proper binding was made. Importance to horizontal courses was given. However, proper attention was not paid to the alternate 'breaking' or offset vertical joints for lateral strength. At some places the joints continue almost vertically through several courses. This implies the workers or the builders were inexperienced. The masonry at the western side of the southern oval wall is seen in Fig. 12 and that on the terrace of Temple II in Fig. 13., The use of small stone to replace clay blocks in Temple I, says Doe (1986 : 191), a Sumerian influence in the design of the first two temples, and that the use of cut stone in Temple II implies that the craftmen were outsiders where building in stone was in vogue.

With regard to the dating of the Barbar temples, a possible terminus antequem for the construction of Barbar Temple III, lies in two C-14 results of 2080 - 100 and 2050 - 100. The date for the Temple I seems to fall within the transition of late Protoliterate D to Early Dynastic I, *viz.*, 2900 B.C. This is suggested by the presence of solid-footed, clay goblets in the foundation deposits below the first Barbar temple, which can be compared with pottery beakers dated in Mesopotamia, *viz.*, ca., 9200 - 280 B.C. A second adjunct is that of a painted Protoliterate D (or Jamdat Nasr) sherd. *viz.* ca. 2900 B.C. from the construction

Fig.6. Western side of Barbar Temple showing plinth stones for statues (I); ramp of the temple (II); outer wall of temple III (III); stones from the earliest building level (A). (After P.V. Glob, 1955)

Fig. 7. (Below) Plinth-stone for statue with carved figures - Barbar Temple I. (After P.V. Glob, 1955, Courtesy Jutland Archaelogical Society).

Fig. 8. (Above) West chamber in Temple III (AFter P.V. Glob, 1955, Courtesy : Jutland Archaelogical Society).

Fig. 9. Steps from ground leading to the terrace of Temple III.

Fig.10, 11.   Circular altars of Barbar Temple.

F'.g. 12. (Above) Masonry of the Barbar Temple on the western side of the southern oval wall.

Fig.13. (Below) Column base at the terrace of Temple II.

Figs.14,15. The `Apsu, the stone chamber built over the holy spring.

Fig. 16. (Above) Part of the oval structure on the eastern side of the temple complex.

Figs. 17, 18. (Centre, Below) Diraz Temple. Remains of circular and rectangular columns.

of the first temple.   (Mortensen, 1970 : 395-97; Caspers, 1975:71)

In the walling of 'Apsu' (Figs. 14, 15) also fine cut stone blocks were used on the western side. Further, the practice of using larger and thinner stone slabs at the same time is evident from the Apsu's wall. (Doe,1986 : 188).

Doe observes that in the later phase of Temple II when a proper square stone was not fitting properly with the adjacent stone, a piece of stone was inserted. This feature is evident in 'Solid' stone walling and also in the ashlar facing of the southern oval 'platform' well. Chisel finishing for smooth surface is evident from the ashlar masonry on the western end of oval wall. Random sized uncut stone were used in the inner terrace wall which follows an oval perimetre of Temple II. A ramp of cut stones leads upto the floor of Temple II. Master craftmenship is evident from the rectangular cut stone platform or altar with two circular plinths on the paved floor of Temple II. (Doe, 1986 : 198f).

On the western side of the Barbar temple, through the western ramp leads down to a 'well-temple' (Figs. 14, 15) in the centre of which there is a stone vessel with three holes in the sides first above the bottom to allow the sub soil-water to run out of it. As seen in the illustration, the apsu (the Abysr of subterranean waters), the stone chamber built over the holy well or spring.   This unique structure,states Andersen (1986 : 176), represents 'apsu', and that the temple-apsu is well known from the texts. It has been atributed to the special dwelling of Enki, the god of the subterranean fresh water ocean, also called 'apsu'.

Since dedication was never found in the Barbar temple, Andersen (186:175) suggests that the interpretation of the Barbar temple has to rely upon the architecture and in a wider sense upon the identification of Bahrain with Dilmun and a geneal background in the Sumerian culture.   The idea about the architecture and Sumerian cultural back ground is acceptable and we have sufficient evidence for it. However the idea of identifying Dilmun wholly with Bahrain is not acceptable in view of the discussion already mentioned. (Chapter II, *Supra*).

Considering the architecture of Temple I and II, the oval Temple, Andersen, like Mortensen draws comparison with those of provincial Sumerian style with traditions going back to temples like the one of al'Ubaid which was dedicated to the mother goddess, Ninkurzag. The stone architecture, the axes of orientation, the interior of the sanctuary etc., consitutes the local features. The myth of 'Enki and Ninkurzag' provides the spiritual traditions and point to the three deities worshipped in Dilmun. These were the divine pair of Enki and Ninkurzag, and Enki's son Inzag.

The location of Barbar temple at fresh water spring is indicative of the numinious power which gave the impules for the cult. A basin was built over this spring and here water-cult took place. Apsu is the abode of Enki as the god of wisdom. He there administers the 'mes' and as the Lord of the apsu he is also the god of the springs which dispense fresh water and fertility. Enki became prominent god of purification and lustration magic by the power of water to cleanse. The holy ablutions which took place in the apsu of the temple yielded the life spending power of its water. Further, a Nippur hymn refers to a temple of a god of wisdom in Dilmun (Andersen, 1986 : 176f). Regarding the affinity of Barbar temples, Potts (1990 : I, 172) discusses the opinions of Alster, Mortensen and Andersen and comes out with his own suggestion to the effect that the temples at Barbar may have been sacred to the Sumerian deity Utu and his Semitic counter part Samas. This inference of Potts is based on two facts. Firstly because the word 'Barbar' where the temples are located, seems to be alien to Bahrain; as, there is no plausible Arabic etymology; and secondly, the word seems to be of Mesopotamian origin from the temple of Samas, called e'-barbar. Thus, the word 'Barbar', with two long vovles otherwise unexpected in Arabic may be an Arabicized version of the non-Arabic name for a Samas temple. Moreover, it was Utu who, in the myth 'Enki and Ninhursag', provided Dilmun with fresh water. (For an argument on Pott's theory, see *infra* chapter X,p,309). The architectural features of the Barbar temples and the artifacts recovered from the foundation deposits reveal Mesopotamian influence to a large extent. This is obvious because the religion of Dilmun itself was greatly influenced by that of Mesopotamia. (See chapter X, pp. 386 ff, *infra*). In fact, the civilization of Mesopotamia served as a prototype and an"Alma Mater", as rightly observed by During Caspers (1975 : 70). All the architectural features at Barbar temple are comparable to similar characteristics of Sumerian temple construction of Early Dynastic times, *viz.*, 2900 - 2400 B.C. Examples of temples with an oval outline are the oval temple at Khafajah, Ninhursag temple at al 'Ubaid, the Inana temple VII at Nippur and the oval temple at Al-Hibba. Further, the Sumerian practice of foundation deposits, is also found itn Barbar temple, where clay beakers and various copper weapons in the case of the second temple have been found deposited. Again, the Sumerian practice of building new temple or shrine over the older ones is also found at Barbar, were Temple III was built by dismantling Temple I, retaining the central cult complex and building new altars rasied above it (Glob, 1954 : 150-152, During Caspers, 1975 : 70; Rice, n.d.28). For the chronology of the Barbar temples see *supra* chapter II,p.43f and Table I at p.45.

(2)   DIRAZ TEMPLE

In the Diraz east, the British team led by Michael Roaf, in 1973-75 excavated the temple dated to the third millennium B.C. Though at first the remains appeared to be a building, but the discovery of an altar, partly broken, established that it was a temple.The temple has rows of large columns of limestones, which originally stood inside it as seen in the Figs. 17, 18. The area of columns has structural remains on two sides at north and south. The schematic plan of the temple complex along with the remains of the structures on its two sides is shown in Fig. 21. There are in all the nine circular columns in pair of four rows and one additional on the extreme left row or in two .horizontal rows of four columns each and again one additional column on the extreme right. In the centre of one of the horizontal

Fig. 19. (Top) Rectangular hall at Diraz Temple.

Fig. 20. (Centre)Remains of rooms at Diraz Temple.

Fig. 22. (Below) Umm es Sujur Temple.

rows, there is a square column or base. The structure had sufficient columns, uniformly spaced, to take load of the roof, as such there does not seems to have been any functional need for this square columns; and moreover for the purpose of symmetry there is no square column in the opposite row. Hence, we may presume that there was no square column to the full height upto the roof. But it was a base of much smaller height, may of the same existing height, as seen in Fig. 18, and most probably it severed for placing the altar. Nothing can be said with certainty as excavators' report is unpublished and was not available to the writer for reference, inspite of best efforts to procure it. The whole temple complex appears to be rectangular with two rectangular structures of dissimilar sizes and of different functional purposes. However, these structures does not seems to have any external doorways or openings. They have doorways from inside the main temple's central area. The only entrance to the whole complex is from the south end, adjacent to the southern structure. Inside the southern structure, there seems to be another smaller structure, with entrance on the opposite side at the south end, while this structures entrance from the central area of the temple is at the north end. Inside this inner room, there is a rectangular base in the corner. Probably it was for altar, and may be this inner room was the actual worshipping area. At the north end of the temple complex is a big rectangular hall, with entrance from the main temple hall. Incomplete walls continue behind this hall. Possibly the complex extended further at its north end.Michael Rice, based on Shaikh Haya al·Khalifa's personnal communication, states that inside was a large stone and mortar basin adjacent to the building, though this was suspected of being later in date than the building itself, perhaps of the late Babylonian period. Sherds from pottery of this time were found and in one of the rooms the burials of at least five persons dating from late Babylonian times were found. An empty snake bowl, similar to that found at Qal'at al Bahrain was also found here. Two stamp seals were also found. (Rice, 1985: 157f).

(3)   UMM ES SEJUR TEMPLE

During the reconnaisence of Diraz, the Danish team found a hallow site surrounded by stone blocks, some of them were over a metre along and all of them were carefully shaped to a rectangular form. This hallow is called by the local people as "Ain Umm es Sejur", and it was once a spring. When the stones were dug, the Danes found their resting on virgin sand, without the slightest sign of foundations or buildings in association with them. A sondage from the top of the bank immediately besides the stones descended through clean sand until it reached, at a depth of 3.27 ms. a layer of loose stones which clearly marked the original surface, after which it descended for a further 1.66 ms. through undisturbed water laid sand to the level of the water table, the water welling up pure and warm.

Danish excavation at the well revealed that it was not an ordinary well but in fact 'Water-temple', associated with religion prevailing on the island during the ancient times. In the slopes of the south east corner of the hollow two parallel walls with a plastered surface on both sides, about 80 cms wide which were one metre apart were found.They ran about

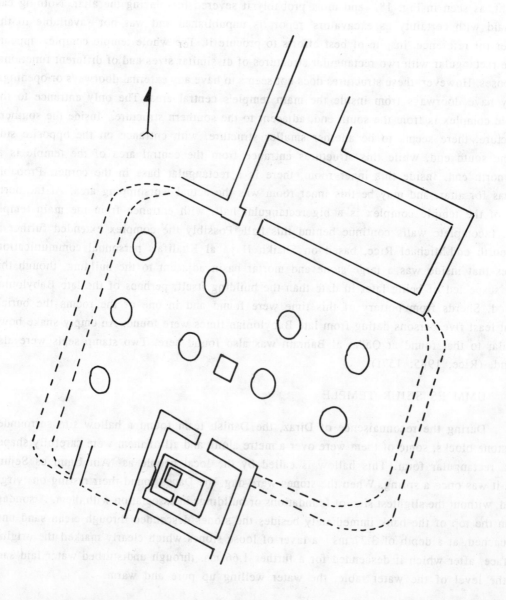

Fig. 21. Schematic plan of Diraz Temple. (Courtesy: Bahrain National Museum).

4 metre towards east and then made a turn at right angle towards the south and continued parallel at the same distance apart for about 5.10 metres, before debounching into a little room of interior dimensions of 1.48x1.4 metres.Between the walls was a sloping ramp which later developed into a staircase going down to the chamber. In the eastern wall of the chamber was a little niche, measuring 33x36 cms. and 40 cms deep.At the same level on the niche, the Danish found the first signs which indicated that the structure had a religious significance. The chamber was full of debris and among it, lay a limestone statue, a kneeling ram the head of which had been broken off (see Fig.15 in chapter VIII(D) *infra*). It is 31 cms in length and 21 cms in height.In the same debris was a little oblong stone block, hollowed at the top. It resembles the small incense burners of modern day. Obviously this stone also had the same function as an incense burner and possibly it was originally in the niche. In the floor of the chamber was a large squared stone (1.28x1..02 metres), with a circular hole of 72 cms in diametre, and round it was a stone 12 cms wide and 2 cms height. This stone was the well-head and 53 cms, deep in the central hole was the surface of gushing spring of sweet water. The well stone was 33 cms. height and below it the well-shaft was continued by another 79 cms deep which rested upon sand.

A number of potsherds of red-ridged ware and portion of an alabaster bowl were found from the gap between the edges of the well-head stone and the sides of the chamber. On the fourth step up from the chamber stood another limestone ram identical to the one found earlier. It is possible that these two flanked as kneeling rams entrance to the temple. The tiny well-chamber cannot have been built as part of the original system of water-supply, says Bibby. He further states that the bull statues, the incense burner and the niche suggest that this was a holy-well, a little water temple.On the basis of the red ridged ware found in the well-temple, Bibby has dated it to the third millennium B.C. (Bibby, 1954:160ff; 1965:68f). During Caspers (1975:753 1986:298) has suggested first centuries of the third millennium B.C. as the likely date for the ram statues.

During Caspers (1986:286-304) draws parallels between the animal figures of Mesopotamia and the Diraz rams. She says that two rams of Diraz may appear to belong to the local Gulf production but she suggests that the original artistic concept is from Mesopotamia, where such representations were made during the close of the fourth millennium B.C. During Caspers also draws parallels between the raw statues found in the lower town of Mohenjo-Daro in the Indus Valley and the Diraz rams. There is some similarity between the rams of Diraz and Indus Valley. However she comments that the modelling of the two Diraz rams in rather rudimentary and that they are possibly unfinished products of an artist from outside Dilmun's cultural sphere, belonging to a locality across the Gulf. At the same time During Caspers also suggests, alternatively, that the overall appearance and the clumsy and unnatural posture of the two reclining animals could be a product of a local artist, who where not familiar with the anatomical features and characteristic features of this breed of animals which might not have been indigenous to the Dilmun environment.

Recently (1991) this temple site and its surrounding are being excavated by the Japanese team, comprising: Masatoshi A.Konishi, Takeshi Gotoh and Yoshihiko Akashi.The temple site after its re-excavation is seen in Fig.22.

(4)   SAR TEMPLE

The excavation conducted by the joint Arab expedition of Bahrainis and Jordanians in 1985 brought to light the Sar temple at the Sar settlement site. Their report is still unpublished and author's best efforts to procure it were futile.The information here on the Sar temple is based an author's personal survey of the site and on the reports of Killick, Crawford, Moon etal (1991: 107ff) also their unpublished field reports for 1991 and 1992.

The temple, located on the northern half of the settlement and at the heighest elevation, is trapezoidal in shape, with a loop at the north western corner. (Fig.23). The bulge or loop viewed from out-side is seen in Fig.34. It is strange why such construction was made. Possibly it is the result of several careless rebuilds.It measures 16.5.m in length and 6.1m. in width at the front entrance side or the north east end.However, the width increases gradually from north east to the south west end, were it is 9.25m. These dimensions are as stated by the British team (Killick, Moon etal, 1991:114).   Crawford (Personal Communication) informs me that the temple measurements are 17.30mx7.5m. and the irregular shape of the temple she attributes to heavy modifications at the west end at a later date. The walls have foundation trenches (Killick, personal communication). Inside the temple there are three columns in a row, mid-way length wise, as one entres from the doorway at the north east end. In the centre was originally square column, which was subsequently modified to round shape. This is flanked on either side by a square column, on the left side in the illustration; and a round column on the right side. The three columns are not equidistant, the left one is near to the central column than the right one.The central column which was originally square was modified to round shape. Since originally there were two square columns, it is possible that the third column too was square; but might have been modified subsequently to round shape in a perfect way, so as to appear now in a perfect round shape. The covering of stones added subsequently to the middle column is dintinctly seen in Fig.28. Also seen in this column is the flat face (on the right) of the square above the altar. Thus indicating that the square columns are of earlier phase and the round one of later phase. Further it is clear that symmetry and uniformity was not maintained in building the temple strucuture.

Two altars are located within the temple, as seen in Fig.23. Of these, one is constructed against the south eastern wall (Fig.25) and the other against the middle column (Fig.24). The latter one is slightly larger in size than the former. The altars (Figs. 26, 27) are crescent shape built over a small platform, built of stone and plastered. About the altars, the remakrs of excavators (Jordanians and Bahrainis)is not known as the report is not available. But the British (Killick etal, 1991:114) have suggested the design of the altars as stylised rendering of bull's horns, as an attribute of deites shown on contemporary seals. This does not seem

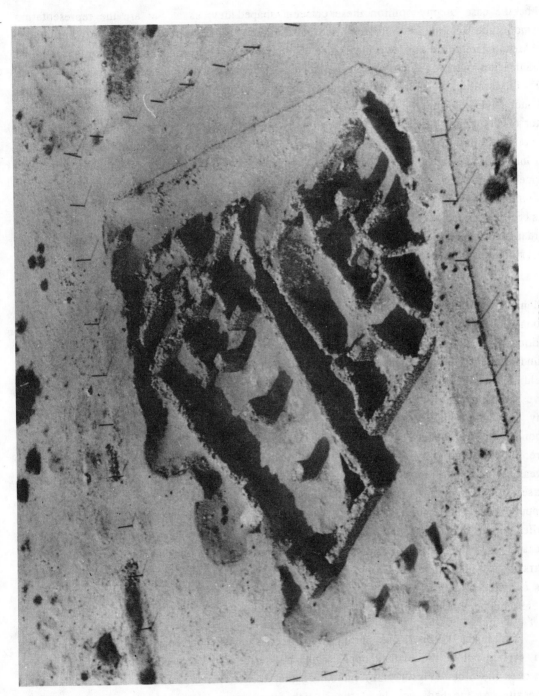

Fig. 23. Sar Temple, after excavation, in 1985.
(Courtesy : Bahrain National Museum.)

to be the case. In my opinion these crescent shaped devices at Sar are the representation of moon-god and not of bull deity. Since Dilmun civilization was profoundly influenced by Mesopotamian culture, we may trace the Sar symbols' origin in Mesopotamian religion. In Sumerian mythology moon-god has always been represented by the crescent. (Cf. Pritchard, 1954, illustration Nos.158, 518-520); also Buren (1945:190ff) for the crescent as the symbol of moon-god. During the third millennium B.C. in Mesopotamia Nanna or Suen- a name later on contracted to Sin- the first born son of Enlil, was the the moon-god. Nanna seems to refer to him specifically as the full moon, Su-en, as the crescent, and yet a third name, As-im-babbar, as the new light. (Jacobsen:1976:121). Thus, we may conclude that the crescent shaped altars at Sar temple represent moon-god.The god Nanna in Bahrain is attested from a Dilmum seal depicting the annual bull game associated with the said god. This seal Dilmun has been illustrated by Ali Akbar Bushiri. (1956/86:13). In the absence of excavator's (Bahraini-Jordanian) report, and other textual evidence, noting can be said about the form of worship and ritual performance.

The altars, the British say, had earlier phases and where the plaster of the base had fallen on the side, they found burnt deposits containing fish vertebra. (Killick, Crawford, Moon, etal, 1991:114). Obviously, the small platform in front of the altar was latter's continuation and was meant for sacrificial purpose. Further, recently (1992), the British have found existence of an earlier altar against the central column. (Killick, Moon, Crawford, Field Report, 1992, Unpublished). Regarding the presence of two altars in the temple, we have three possibilities. Firstly, since the fish vertebra was found besids one altar, we may conjucture that this particular altar was used for sacrificing animals etc. While the second altar was meant for worship. And may be they had a statutette of the deity placed here. However, no deity so far, has been found here. Further excavations of the temple may reveal the true phases. Secondly, since the British sounding has brought to light earlier phases of the temple, below the visible one, on the same plan, of an earlier period (Unpublished Field Report, 1991:8), it is possible that one of the altars belonged to the earlier temple and the second altar was built at a new place, leaving the older or earlier one as it is, and was not desmantled as a reverence or for respect. The difference in the altars is also indicative of two phases. But the two altars are on the same floor level.In this case the possibility of both belonging to the same phase cannot be ruled out. Thus in the absence of authentic evidence any thing is possible.

Latest (1991-92) 'deep-sounding' down to the under lying bed-rock, a depth of almost 4 m. carried out by the British, opposite the middle altar have revealed three temple levels, one over the other (Figs.31, 32) indicating that the temple was rebuilt three times at the same site. At the bed rock level the British found some 'chain-ridged' pottery typical of City I levels at Qal'at al Bahrain. The excavators conclude that Sar might have its origin around 2,300 B.C. At the bottom of the sounding a skeleton of a mongoose was found. (Moon, personal communication, Chand, 1991; Killick, Moon and Crawford, 1992 Field Report,

Figs. 24   (Top and Centre) Altars and Three columns of Sar Temple.
Fig. 28. (Below) Entrance of Sar Temple.

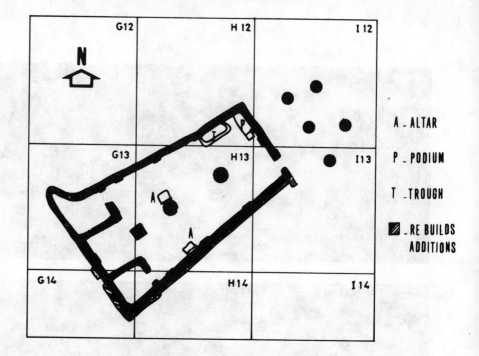

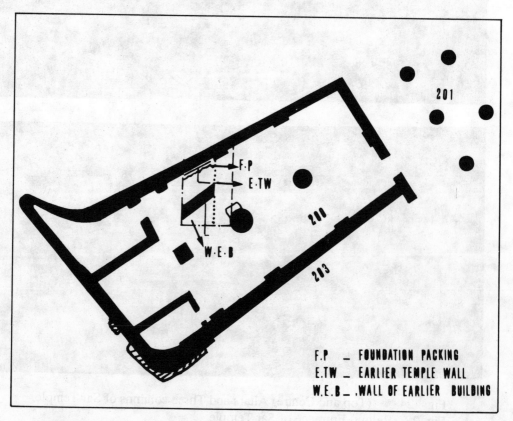

Fig.25 Plans of Sar Temple and walls of earliar Temple
(Based on Plans of R.Killick, H.Crawford, J.Moon, et al, 1991-92).

Unpublished). Thirdly, it is quite possible that both the altar belong to the same phase/temple. There was no restriction to have only one altar in a temple. No fixed rule was laid down to have one altar only. There could be number of altars depending upon the exegency and social necessity. It is also possible that some one has built the first altar and soon after wards or later on the chief preist or the chief of the locality/settlement wished to dedicate and desired to built another altar during his time.

A rectangular through in found attached to the north western wall, left of the entrance side of the temple, as seen in Figs. 28, 29.   Most probably this trough was filled with water which might have been used for washing or cleaning once hands and feet on entering the temple before proceding to the altar for worship. Such type of plastered trough in a temple in Mesopotamia was meant for incinerating the remnants of sacrificial. *E.g.*, temple at Warka of Jamdat Nasr period (LLyod, 1978:55; Moortgart, 1969, 11, Pl.7).

Immediately on the right side of the entrance along the eastern wall of the temple are a rectangular podium and a base or block (Fig. 30). The top and sides of the podium has gypsum plaster. A soundage made by the Jordanian-Bahrain team had revealed, states Killick etal (1991:114), that the base of this podium is well below the highest extent floor level of the temple.Thus implying that the podium was present during the earlier phases of the temple. A portion of the upper surface of the plaster seem to have stuck to something that was placed over the podium and was transfered when those articles were lifted away. From the rectangular impression on the podium surface, Killick etal (1991:116) speculates that these are the impression of the base of statues. This is quite possible. However, so far the excavators have not found any statues or their parts from the temple.The absence of statue(s) from the temple may be explained as follows. As per the ancient customs the stattues of gods were taken out on a certain day in a year or so in a procession for public audience; and it is possible that these were never returned to the temple, may be due to some mishap. The soundage made by the British at the podium reveals that there is another 60 cms. of floor deposit and this indicates earlier phases of the temple. This is confirmed by the second sondage.

Inside the temple on the western side, there are two small rooms (Fig. 23). These seems to be later additions; and one of them was possibly meant for the preists. But in one room opposite to the entrance, thick plastered flooring with circular basins pits have been found (Fig. 32). Possibly these were meant for washing the statues of the god. However, the excavators, the British, in their latest report (1992, Field Report, Unpublished) have suggested that the plastered depressions were probably used to support jars, containing the food and drink offerings used in the temple rituals and that the room was used as stores. Near the entrance to this room Jane Moon discovered foot-print of a child in white plaster on the floor of the temple.The print is of the upper part of the foot and the four largest toes were clearly vissible. It is about 9 cms wide and Moon believes it is of a child 10 years old. It is contemporary with the temple.(Moon, personal communication; Chand:1991).

197

Figs. 26,27. Cresent shape altars at Sar Temple.

Fig. 29. (Top) Trough at Sar Temple. Fig. 30.(Centre) Podium at Sar Temple.
Fig. 31. (Below) Room at the rear of the temple with plaster flooring and basins.

Fig. 32. Trench in the Sar Temple revealing three phases. (Author in the Picture)

Fig. 33. (Above) Column bases and foundations in front of the Sar Temple.

Fig.34. (Centre) Loop wall. (outer view).

Fig. 35. (Below Loop wall. (inner view).

The central open space between these two rooms and the back west-south wall of the temple i.e., the space in the fore ground opposite the square column was most holy and sacred place of the temple and here, as per the ancient belief, the holy spirit of the god resided.

On the entrance side in front of the temple faced there are five circular columns, as seen in Fig. 23, 33, in two rows of three and two. However the columns are not symmetrically aligned.The spacing between the two columns at the front row is greater than those in the rear, closer to the temple wall. May be they supported a porch at the entrance.It was here the public waited for worship or reverence to the god. As per the ancient practice the public was not allowed inside the temple premises.The religious rituals were performed on their behalf, by the servicing preist.As we know from an inscription of the Assyrian king that Shalmeneser III (858-824 B.C) came to Kutha in Babylon to worship the god Nergal, he humbly made the prostration at the door of the temple, offered his sacrificial lamb and gave the required gifts. (Luckenbill, 1975, I No.624; Oppenheim, 1944:546). Obviously impling that he was not allowed to enter the shrine. But there are same exceptions. Adjacent to these columns bases remains of a room (s) are found (Fig. 33). May be these were of a guard-room for those on duty at the temple for safety and protection. The plan of the Sar temple suggest Mesopotamian influence. This is evident from the following parallels: Like the Sumerian Temple city, we have a Sar temple Town; like the Sin temple at Khafaje, like those of Protoliterate levels in Eanna precinct at Warka, which are 'ground-level' temples, so do Sar temple is; like the temple in Eridu which continued to be built on the old ground plan, the Sar temple was also rebuilt over the plan of the earlier phase, provision of altars, trough, podium etc. in Sar temple is similar to those in Sumerian temples; and podium at Abu Temple at Tell Asmar is against one of the short walls, so do we find at Sar; if it is proved (by future excavations) that the two altars at Sar belong to two phases of the temple, then it implies that the position of altar was shifted in the latest phase, and this practice has a precedent in the case of Abu Temple at Tell Asmar, when it was re-planned the altar was transfered from the west to the east side; each city in Mesopotamia had its own temple, so do we find temple in each city or town, at Sar, Barbar, Diraz etc., to cater to the needs of each city or town, though there is no exact replica of Sar temple in Mesopotamia, but we find vague parallel in at Khafaje (Level V and VI) as well as in Abu Temple at Tell Asmar (earlier and Archaic Shrine I). (Moortgart, 1967; *passim*; Falkenstein:1974, *passim*). Contrary to Mesopotamian temples, we have not found, so far, at Sar any relief nor art nor even a statue. The plan of the Sar temple is also similar to the temples of Megiddo (Palestine) dated to the early Bronze Age. (cf. Pritchard, 1954). Finally, inspite of foreign influences, the Sar temple is indigenous in its character as the Dilmun civilization itself which is regional in character and culture.

CHAPTER V

TUMULI AND SUBTERRANEAN BURIALS

Bahrain contained the largest prehistoric burials in the world and they are of unique characteristic among the world cemetries. As such archaeological expeditions, before the coming of the Danes in 1953, was confined to tumuli. In 1878-79 Captain E.C. Durand (1880:189f) investigated one of the largest mounds at 'Ali, and a few smaller mounds in the same area. He was followed, a decade later, by Mrs. and Mr. Theodre Bent; and in 1903 by M. Jouanian from Belgium Colonel. Prideaux investigated 67 mounds on behalf of the Archaeological Survey of India. During early 1920's Major Daly excavated a few mounds near the north west coast which were earlier reported by Durand. In 1925-26, Ernest Mackay, on behalf of the British School of Archaeology in Egypt, excavated 34 tumuli, around 'Ali area. P.B. Cornwall from Harvard University came in 1940 and excavated a large number of tumuli in fullfilment of his research for the doctorate degree. Cornwall (1944:103) estimated the tumuli to 50,000. The presence of enormous number of burial mounds (see Fig. 1 in this chapter and map 5 in Chapter II) made Bahrain to be called as "Island of the Hundred Thousand Burial Mounds" (Glob, 1954:100). The mounds were considered earlier as one of the riddles of history. To account for this large number of mounds, various theories have been advanced by different persons. Bent (1890:1ff) theorized that the tumuli was built by the Phoenicians. But this was disproved by Hogarth (1920:46) and Mackay (1929) who theorised that the people buried in the grave chambers at Bahrain were natives of the Arabian main land. He concluded, as he did not find any settlement, that Bahrain was not inhabited at all during the period when the grave mounds were built, but was surely used as a burial-ground for people living on the main land of Arabia. Cornwall (1944:177f) tried to disprove Mackay's theory on the grounds that similar tumuli exists in Al-Hasa, eastern Arabian main-land and at other places, indicating that the deceased of the main-land were buried in the main land itself. Recently also we have found similar tumuli in Dhahran, eastern Arabia, and similar type of artifacts, as found in Bahrain tumuli have been found in Dhahran as well. (Zarins and al Badr, 1986:19ff).

The Danes did not believe in the interpretation of Bahrain as a sepulchral island and to investigate thoroughly, despatched an expedition in 1953. (Glob:1954:101). The Danes were successful in their expedition (1953-1965) and the uncovering of the flourishing cities at Qal'at al Bahrain, from third millennium B.C,. till the pre-Islamic times with evidence of advance civilization which proved that Bahrain was not the land of the dead but the land of the living (Bibby, 1969:18).

The Danish expedition excavated a large number of tumuli from 1954 to 1965. The Department of Antiquities of Bahrain undertook excavations of the tumuli and other burial complexes from 1969 and since then they continue work every year at different burials. The Arab expedition under Moawiyah Ibrahim came in 1979- 79, followed by that of Rafique

Mughal of Pakistan in 1980-82. Larsen came in during the later half of 1970s for research for his doctorate thesis and excavated a large number of mounds. The Australians, Philip J. Habgood in 1981-82 and Edwin Brown in 1982, excavated numerous tumuli. Anthony Lowe, from Britian came in 1982-83. Though the main objective of the London-Bahrain expedition 1990-91 is the Sar settlement site, however, they are excavating a few tumuli in collaboration with Khalid al Sindi of Bahrain National Museum. Regarding the total number of burial mounds that are present in Bahrain different scholars have estimated differently. Prideaux (1912:128) estimated in five figures, Cornwall (1944:103) estimated it at 50,000. Bibby (1954:100) doubled this figure to 100,000. Larsen (1983:45) based on an ariel survey estimated as 172,013 tumuli. Ibrahim (1982:1) doubled the figure of Bibby, i.e., 200,000.

Frohlich's figure was slightly less than that of Larsen, i.e., 172,093. Out of this figure about 150,000 area assigned tentatively by Frohlich to early Bronze Age (2800-1800 B.C.). Besides these mounds, there are large number of other types of burials, below the ground, which also belong to this period. (Frohlich:1986:62f). Frohlich's study is based on calculations of average life expectency, derived from the study of burials. Lamberg-Karlovsky (1982:46) amplified the views of Mackay and Cornwall and contradicted those of Bibby (1969:18). He concluded that there is insufficient indigenous settlements (at that time) to account for the enormous number of burials in Bahrain, and that the tumuli represented an elaborate funery cult reflected in Sumerian literature as Dilmun. Thus Lamberg-Karlovsky propounded that the deceased in the Bahrain belong to the greater Mesopotamian population and included the populations of northern Arabia.

During-Caspers (1984:1ff) captioned her paper as "Dilmun- International Burial Ground" and examined various theories about Bahrain's tumuli. She agrees partly, with Lamberg-Karlovsky that Bibby's belief that the burials exclusively belong to the Bahrain population is not acceptable, if we were to consider the Bahrain population as being native Dilmunits. Yet, she is hesitant to accept Karlovsky's theory that these internents belonged to deceased of Greater Meso-potamians who were transported, either dying or dead, from Mesopotamia to Bahrain or to the eastern Arabian coastal strip to be buried there, either for religious or for other purposes.

The Danish excavations have brought to light seven cities at Qal'at al Bahrain dated from third-millennium B.C. to the modern times. Recently the joint Jordanian-Bahrain excavations have brought to light (1985) existance of settlement at Sar, most of which has been uncovered most recently, 1990-92, by the British team and still excavations are in progress. In view of these settlements it is quite clear that Bahrain was continuously inhabited by the indegineous population, immigrants from the Arabian main land and foreigners from Mesopotamia and possibly from other lands as well. As such it is almost certain that the tumuli belong to those inhabiting Bahrain island as attested by Frohlich's research and that it was not an international burial ground nor that for the Arabian main land. This is also attested by the tumuli of similar nature found in the Arabian main land and that there was never dearth of land in the Arabian main-land for burying their dead. There does not seem to be any reason for the people of main land to carry their dead across the sea to an island and bury there. Since we have scores of texts of Mesopotamia about Dilmun and giving minute details of different aspects, people, kings, religion, myth, gods, items of goods traded etc., but none of them, to the best of my knowledge, mentions carrying of the dead from Mesopotamia to Dilmun or Bahrain for burial purpose. As such in the absence of any textual evidence, we cannot say that Bahrain was burial ground for Mesopotamian dead nor it is proper to call it an international burial ground.

Concentration of burial mounds and burial complexes are scattered over a wide area in northern half of Bahrain at numerous places (see map). Bibby (1954:132) rightly remarked that : there are places in Bahrain where in every direction to the horizon nothing meets the eye but thousand upon thousand of burial tumuli. Excavations or investigations at major complexes have been carried out. Major tumuli and other sites which fall within the purview of our period-Bronze and Iron Ages, are the following: 'Ali, Buri, Al-Hajjar, Hamad Town, Hamala North, Janussan, Kharzakhan, Al-Magsha, Rifa'a, Sar el-Jisr or Sar, and Umm Jidr. These are scattered mainly in six major fields. Besides these, there are several mounds and burials of later period. Hellenistic, at the sites of Barbar, Dumistan, Shakhoura, etc. Since they fall out of purview of this volume, they are not discussed here. It is proposed to describe here the tumuli and burials complexes firstly within-grave pattern, secondly within cemetry pattern, and thirdly regional pattern. In order to have a clear idea of different types of tumuli and burials, mode of construction, etc., within each site or cemetry, it is proposed to describe the graves of each site seperately. This facilitates evaluation of cultural data and characteristic feature of each site and the differences found between sites of different chronological periods and of the same period as well.

The Bronze Age burials of Bahrain may be broadly classified architecturally into two categories - (1) Mounds above the ground; and (2) burial below the ground. The first category may be further classified chronologically into two types: (1) Early Type burial mounds; and (2) Late type burial mounds.

The reasons for burying the dead above the ground, and building a tomb is attributed by Mackay (1929:137), firstly to the nature of the soil in the island which is exceedingly scanty and in some areas only two feet deep; and secondly to the religious reason, a possibility. This resulted in the preparation of rock tombs for the dead and hence we find enormous number of tumuli. Where the burials are under the ground at few places, may be there the soil is deeper and facilitated digging below the ground and possibly the practice of burying have changed from above the ground to below the ground. However, so far only at two or three sites graves below the ground have been found. The earlier type of burial mounds are those which contain chambers without cap-stones and the chamber is located inside the ring wall. In the late type burial mounds cap-stones are found and the chamber is located within the ring wall, both these categories of mounds contained either a single burial chamber or multiple burial chambers. They had, either one ringwall or a complex system of interactive ringwalls, mostly found in association with multiple burial chamber systems. They possibly also had a simple or multiple subsidiary burial chamber located outside the ringwall systems. An important characteristic feature of these mounds is that they all belong to a general construction pattern of having a central burial chambers surrounded by ring walls. (Frohlich, 1986:52). Below the ground burial complexes are clusters of chambers placed below the present ground surface that were not covered by distinct or well-developed mounds. Cornwall (1942:103ff Ms.) divided the Bahrain tumuli into two principal divisions: firstly, small crude mounds made of slabs of rock. In diameter these mounds seldom exceed 10 feet and their height averages between 4 to 5 feet. Secondly, large mounds of gravel and lime stone chip. These tumuli vary greatly in size, but the majority are from 21 to 42 feet in diameter, and from 6 to 8.5 feet in height. Mounds of first category generally are situated inland on the heights around central basin; while the mounds of second category are located close to the sea shore, and these are numerous on the flat north western corner of the island. Among them is a small group of very large tumuli, situated close to the village of 'Ali. They range from 49 to 82 feet in height and up to 100 feet in diameter at the base. Some of the second type of tumuli are encircled by a circular ring of gravel, which stand at present to a height of 2 feet, having a thickness of about 20 feet. The mounds and the rings are separated by about 65 feet. The purpose of these rings might be to protect the mounds. The rock mound are built around a very crude cist or a few stones which define a small grave, sufficient in size for a contracted body or a secondary burial. These mounds do not, as a rule, contain a distinct burial chamber. Other types of tumuli do usually have one or two burial chambers. These types are quite well built. The internal arrangements of the secondary category of tumuli may be classified into five classes: cist chamber; plain chamber; chamber with (one to four) receses; double chamber; and shaft entrance. More common type of mounds found in Bahrain during the Bronze Age and Iron Age are differentiated as "Barbar mounds". Lowe (1986:74ff) has described these high conical form mounds as follows : structurally they are mostly single burials with a centrally-built chamber covered by capstones and surrounded by a narrow ring-wall. Both, the ringwall and the chamber were built of un-worked limestone blocks. The fill between the ringwall and the burial chamber is earth. The construction of the Barbar mound is often marked by a small mound which for sometime stood around the chamber, presumably while it waited for its internment. Subsidary burials of infants and sub-adults were sometimes placed to the south of the mound against the outside face of the ringwall. The orientation of the chamber was calculated by astronomical determination has been suggested by Cornwall (1952:137-45). Other types of burial graves are discussed under different mounds, e.g., alHajjar, Rifa'a, Hamad Town, Sar, al Maqsha etc.

(1)   'ALI MOUNDS

Situated in a large grove of palm-trees the village of 'Ali stands on a high eminence

206

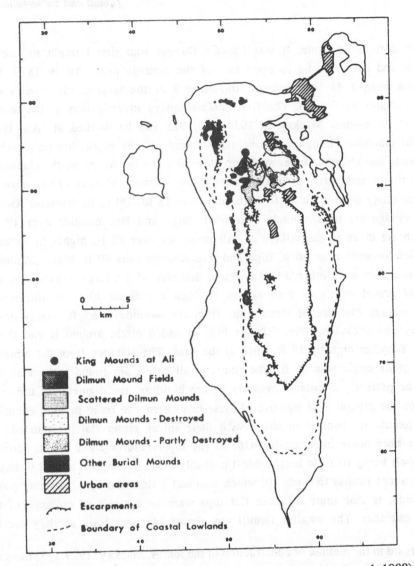

Fig.1 Distribution of Dilmun Mounds (After J.C.Doornkamp etal, 1980).

Fig.4 The 'King Mound' at 'Ali.

from which it derives its name. It was Captain Durand who first brought to attention the tumuli at 'Ali and he was first to open two of the mounds near 'Ali in 1879. Prideaux, during 1906-08 opened 44 'Ali mounds, including 9 of the largest. (See rough sketch of 'Ali Tumuli complex in Fig. 2). The first comprehensive investigation of the mound field was caried out by Earnest Mackay in 1924 and 1925 and he worked at 'Ali. He opened a series of 30 mounds. Though his conclusions were off the mark, his publication about different mounds and chamber-types still provides basis for the future work. Mackay worked partly at 'Ali tombs and partly at smaller ones in the vicinity. Mackay (1929) observes that the tumuli size range from 4 to 26 ft. high, and from 18 to 100 ft. in diameter. One mound, close to the village are nine mounds over 66 ft. high and five mounds over 49 ft. high. Mounds which are close to the village of 'Ali measures over 82 ft. high. In its immediate vicinity are nine mounds over 66 ft. high and five mounds over 49 ft. high. Mounds which are at a distance from each other, Mackay found that size of the large tumuli were encircled with a ring of gravel debris as high as two ft. high and about 20 ft. in thickness at the ground. The average distance of these rings from the mounds is 65 ft. Only one mound which Mackay had excavated (No. 30; see Fig. 2) had a circle around it and the size of this was 5 ft. 8 inches high by 19 ft. thick at the base. The distance from the tumulus itself to the inside of its circle was 66 ft. The rings, in all cases, are found to be very carefully set out and one perfectly circular, obviously before building, the diameter of the circle was first marked on the ground. The purpose of these rings seems to be to prevent encroachment. Most of the tumuli are conical in shape with their apices either flat or rounded. Flat top seems to have been made intentionally. One of the top measures about 35 ft. across, while the tumulus itself being 40 ft. in height. Most probably these flat-topped tumuli were provided with shaft entrances similar to tomb 10, which also had a flattened apex. Another possibility, Mackay suggests, is that some of these flat tops were as a result of collapse of the roof of the upper chamber. The smaller tumuli are almost twice as long as they are broad.

With regard to the method of construction of the tombs, Mackay (1929:137) has suggested that the tumuli builders of Bahrain does not seem to have been at all skilled in the preparation of stone for building. However, this conclusion of Mackay was made prior to the discovery and with out the knowledge of the stone structures at Qal'at al Bahrain and Barbar temples. Mackay's statement cannot be generalised. May be the builders did not pay attention for proper cutting and finishing of the stone used within the tomb as they were to be covered up eventually.

The lower chambers in the large tombs as well as a few of the smaller ones, were built partly below the surface of the natural rock. This, as Col. Prideaux (1912) has suggested, extraction of stone to build the tomb itself, as the cause. The quarrying left a hallow in the ground, and in this hollow was built the sole, or lower, chamber. The rock base or flooring of all the chambers was roughly levelled and the walls were executed on this rough base. Generally large stones were used for the base of the walls, and each course was placed in

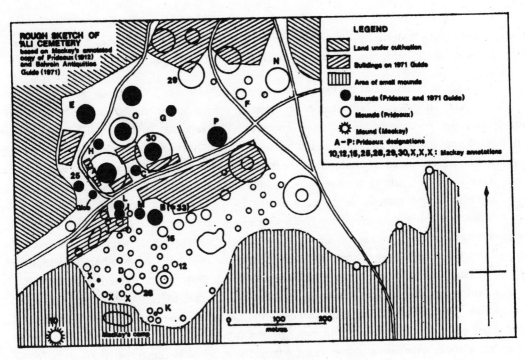

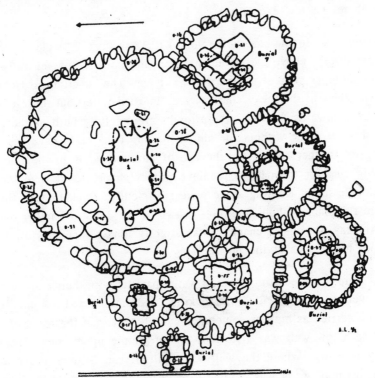

Fig.2 (Above) Sketch of 'Ali Tumuli Complex'. (After Julian Reade and Richard Burleigh, 1978).

Fig.5 (Below) Sketch plan of seven burials at Buri, Tell 20. (After Anthony Lowe, 1982)..

position, backed up externally by gravel and pieces of stone. These stones has a horizontal slaty cleavage which helped in its easy extraction from its bed, majority of which are square.

The interior chambers of the tumuli, Mackay (1929:138) has divided into seven categories, as follows: cist chambers, plain chambers, chambers with one niche, with two niches, with four niches, double chambers, and shaft entrance. The recesses in the smaller tombs were certainly of too small in size to accommodate an intact burial. The larger tombs had large recesses and were able to accommodate the burial and even in majority of cases, the burial would have to be in a sitting portion as found by Durand. In practically every case, recesses were larger in height than in depth or breadth. In the smaller tombs they appear to have been set out a definite measurement. Their width and height is nearly always the same. The common measurements average, 13.5 inches. In some measurements vary. In all the tombs, the roofs of the recesses were some distance below the roofs of the chambers to which they belonged. This varied in different tombs. In all cases they were covered with large slabs of rock which, in the smaller rescesses, generally sufficed to roof the recess throughout. Two roofing slabs were usually used to cover the larger recess. The recesses were carefully constructed on the chamber itself. In most of the tombs they were built of dry walling and had either a rocky floor or a gravel one. Where the tomb was plastered, the recess too was plastered, however there are few exceptions.

Large tumuli only had double chambers (No. 10,12,15 in Figs. 2,3) The upper chamber is always placed immediately above the lower chamber, and both are of generally the same size. The flooring of the upper one seperated the lower one. The superimposed chamber are always well built. The sides of the lower chamber are almost parallel, but those of the upper one are slightly inclined inwards. Walls of these tombs are carefully built as they are, were constructed of flat slabs of stone without the aid of mortar. This might have been with the idea to avoid collapse. Another reason for the use of battered walls in the upper section of the tomb probably was for the need to achieve proper shape. Large size blocks were used to cover the double tomb. Roofing stone were sufficiently thick to take the load. In every case they were flat slabs without dressing. In two of the double chamber tombs (Nos. 10,15) opened by Mackay, the upper chamber was slightly longer than the lower one, and the extention in both tombs was at the north.

All the tombs were provided with flanking walls, parallel with their entrances, to keep back their gravel covering. These walls form a kind of dromos to each tomb. In double tombs, these walls are carried as high as sometimes even higher than the roofs of the upper chambers. In this case a low wall was also built on top of the upper inlet. The walls are roughly built of dry masonry. Where the wall was built of small stones,it has collapsed. The object of these retaining walls was evidently to keep the entrance of each tomb open until it was required. This is a proof that the tomb was built before the individual died and occupied it. However, these walls were allowed to remain after the tomb chambers were

210

Fig.3 'Ali Mounds after Excavation. (Above left Tumulus 6, above right Tumuls 15 and below Tumulus 15). (After E.Mackay in M.Rice 1984).

Fig.6 Excavation in progress at Buri, 1990, by the Department of Antiquities, Bahrain.

blocked and were never demolished.

In every tomb the walls are of dry stone masonry. But in some larger chambers, as the Nos. 10, 15, 25 and 33, the crevices between the stones are either pointed with gypsum cement to improve their appearance or are entirely covered with a plaster of that material. The material for this cement is called juss in Bahrain, as in Mesopotamia, was available on the island. This was used only for finishing the walls and not for building stones. A gypsum plaster was also used in larger tombs as a pavement. (Nos, 10,15,25,33). Most of the tombs had either plain irregular rock floors, or a floor formed of a gravel laid on the rock. Majority of the tombs were found with entrances securely closed with a wall of stones. A definite threshold of stone blocks was laid down immediately before the entrance of the tomb. Peg or beam holes have been found in some of the tombs, ranging in size from 2 to 2.5 inches in diameter. The doorways of the tombs are all oriented in one direction, namely, approximately to the south-west. However, there are considerable divergence in the orientation of the tombs, the axes of the chambers varying from 25° to 78° from the north.

Mackay found several types of artifacts within the tombs ; such as : pottery, bronze weapons, ivory and wooden objects, etc., and these are mentioned in relevent chapters (VI-VIII) in this volume.

The 'Ali tumuli has been dated, on the basis of ceramic parallels and ivory, by Reade (1978:78) to Ur III or Isin Larsa periods (ca. 2100-2000 B.C.).

The Danish expedition under Glob, Crabb and Larche undertook during 1962-63 investigations of mould field south of 'Ali and selected two areas, about one kilometre apart comprising forty- one mounds. They defined the 'Group' as a selection of mounds within a smaller part of the dense mound field. The location of Group A was about 300-400 metres southeast of the southern most of the large 'Ali mounds. They excavated 19 mounds which were partly removed earlier. The remaining mounds were intact. These mounds with the exception of one or two, were found to be broken into during the prehistoric times and were partly plundered. The mounds were rather low in their structure, less than 2 metre high, most of them were less than 1.50 metre. However, their diameter was larger comparatively, generally about 10 metres and several of them had much larger diameter up to 20 m. They were built of large roughly cut blocks in 3 to 6 courses with smaller stones in between them to tighten the walls. They were caused by sand and gravel. The chambers were mostly over 2m. in height. The orientation was almost east-west, and where ever there was entrance, it was in the west end. With the exception one, all the chambers had alcoves, generally one or two at the east end. However, in one exceptional case there were no less than four side-chambers, two at each end. The side chambers might have been meant for keeping gifts or provisions. In two side-chambers a pot was found. The chambers were roofed by the capstones. Smaller ones had the alcoves, limestone rock served as the floor which was never dry. Both floor and walls were plastered in the chambers with four alcoves. Only one case of ringwall at

Fig.7 (Above) A large stone vessel is exposed.
Fig.8 (Centre) Built tomb at Buri
Fig.10 (Below) Al-Hajjar Subterranean Grave Complex.

the foot of the mound was found. In these mounds the remains of the dead were in bad state of preservation. In one grave alone it was possible to acertain that the body was placed in a flexed position. None of the graves were empty. Generally a few human bones were found in each. Animal bones were also found in most of them (Bibby, 1964:107; Frifelt, 1986:127-129).

From the dense mound field of Group B, south of 'Ali and one kilometre south west of Group A, twenty two tombs were not much lower, but their diameter was not more than 7m. The chamber built of medium to small, usually unfashioned block in three to four courses and covered with capstones was less than 2m in length. No alcoves were found in these tombs, some had one or two niche (s). The Group B tombs, like those of Group A, had bed rocks as the floor with sand or gravel scattered over it. The construction of Group B tombs is modest and poorer than those of Group A. But they have additional details of ring wall at the foot of the mound. The absence of ring wall in Group A is attributed to the thick deposits among the dense mounds that washed down over the centre and covered the old surface and the low surrounding wall. These deposits made the mounds appear lower than they were built. The difference between graves of Group A and B with regard to design and contents, is attributed by Frifelt (1986:133) to two/three possibilities: chronological and or social. The tombs of Group A are close to the 'Ali Royal Tombs', (Fig.4) not only in proximity but also in contents: alabaster, ivory, carnelian, metal, ostrich egg shells, strainer jars. Caspers (1980) finds affinity between her Hamala North tombs and 'Ali tombs with the common find of goblet of fine red ware with black cross-hatched butterfly motif. While Firfelt tries to match this with the find from the Suq-Sunayal graves in Oman dated by her to about 2000 B.C. Thus she dates Group A mounds of 'Ali to ca. 2000 B.C. While she dates graves of Group B to an earlier period on the basis of the squat brown jar and partly purple paint. Neither of these two are known from other graves. (Frifelt, 1986:131-133).

(2)   BURI MOUNDS

In December 1981 an Australian team, invited by Shaikha Haya al Khalifa, then Director of Antiquities and Museum, dug in Bahrain on the 'New City' site at Buri. Simultaneously, on the site a Bahraini team excavated. Anthony Lowe, a member of the Australian team, stayed on in Bahrain as part of the Bahraini team from February 1981 to April 1982 and excavated Tell No. 20 at Buri. The information of Buri mounds given here is drawn from Anthony Lowe's report (unpublished) 1982. Lowe's report is captioned as : "A Burial Mound at Buri". While in the opening sentence, with reference to the previous work of the Australian team, he states that they dug in at the 'New City' site at Buri'. Lowe seems to be confused over the 'New City' and 'Buri. May be because the tumuli field of these two sites stretched continuously, undivided. Further, the mound dug by Lowe being in close proximity to Buri, he might have designated it as 'New City' site at Buri. The mounds of the New City, which was later on named as Hamad Town are discussed seperately (see *infra*). But since Lowe

214

Fig.9a-b "Double Storey" graves at Buri. 1991

clearly captioned his report as "A Burial Mound at Buri", it is detailed here. However, since there was no dividing line at the time of excavations, this mound in as well be grouped under 'New City' or Hamad Town. Now, a highway divides the tumuli. North of the highway is the tumuli of Buri; while to the south is that of Hamad Town.

The mounds at Buri are relatively lower and are of varying diameters. They are not built much higher than the top of their grave chambers. Generally, the chambers are either rectangular or ovoid. Alcoves, are rarely found. They are built of stone blocks. No mortar was used. A circular stone-built ring wall around the graves is found in most cases. Rock and rubble fill was placed between the ringwall and chamber and also out-side the ringwall. Ringwall construction varied between courses of larger and smaller stones. Where large rocks were used to built the ring wall, the latter was closed to the chamber, than those where smaller rocks were used.

The mound, tell No. 20, is 0.8m. in height and 10m. diameter before excavation did not gave any indication, says Lowe, that it was just a normal single burial construction. Eventually it turned out to be made up of seven burials (Fig.5). Six of these were grouped around the main central burial, the largest and having complete ring wall. The six subsidiary burials, each had a chamber surrounded by its own ring wall, adjoining the main ring wall, and /or to other subsidiary ring walls. Small rocks were used in building up the ring walls of the chambers. Earth and rocks had been placed outside the ring wall to support it and to continue the downward slope of the mound. The internal dimensions of the six chambers, and their capstones etc., are as follows :

TABLE 1

Burial No.	Length m.	Width m.	Wall Height (Internal)	Ring wall Diameter m.	Level of chamber Below ring wall m.	Capstone size m
1	1.65	0.80	0.20-0.61	4.70	-	-
2	0.50	0.30	0.35	-	0.15	-
3	0.60	0.30	0.26	-	0.16	0.35
4	0.65	0.40	0.40	-	-	0.35
5	0.9	0.45	0.37	-	-	-
6	0.8	0.35	0.50	-	0.18	0.47
7	0.9	0.40	0.40	-	-	-

The size of these burials indicates that they were used for infants to young children. This probably explains the lack of skeletal evidence - the high degree of un-calcified bone would not lend itself to preservation in the soils. The orientation of the six burials (Nos. 1-6) is towards east-west; while that of the seventh one is towards north-east-south-west.

Bone was diserned in only one of the six subsidiary burials. So far twenty other burials were excavated at Buri. Of these only two produced any skeletal remains. This absence of bone leads to the speculation that the subsidiary burials were added later on in case they might be needed. But Lowe's contention is that mounds were built with 'somebody' in mind and that they were in demand when they were built. The use of capstones also implies that the chambers had been used. Nearly all the subsidiary chambers yielded grave objects: shells, in burial Nos. 2,4 and 7; pottery vessel in 5. Those from 3 and 6 might have been leached out as they were badly disturbed. All the burials had pottery, which has many parallels with that of Sar and Umm Jidr; although the Buri mounds seem to pre-date those of these places.

The date attributed to Buri mounds was at first thought to be as early as 3000-2800 B.C. Certainly they are earlier than the Dilmun (Barbar) type mounds as they do not contain the characteristic Dilmun round-based cylindrical bodied pots common in these. Habgood (1982, unpublished report) gave the mounds a pre-Barbar to Barbar I date (2300-2100 B.C.).

Lowe's report is appended with Frohlick's osteological report. According to the latter all the osteological material has been replaced by inorganic material derived from the ground and the visible traces suggest the placement of the body on its right side, with the cranium in the southern corner, the vertebrae and ribs (which were partly visible) along the southern longwall and the lower extremities in the south western part of the grave. However, no traces of the upper extremities, the innominable bones, or dental material have been identified. The placement of the assumed lower extremities suggests dis-arrangement by either rodents or thieves. The size of the skeletal material suggests an infant between three mouths and one year. However, lack of bones and dental material prevent from estimating exact age. The reports of excavations conducted by the Bahraini team at Buri are not available.

The second foreign expedition was that of Japanese, Masatoshi Konishi, Tekashi Gotoh and Yoshihiko Akashi of the Japanese Archaeological Mission to Bahrain during 1987. They excavated two burial mounds at Buri site near Buri village, north of Hamad Town. This Buri site (see map) is in fact the northern extention of the Hamad Town site, but had a few bigger mounds which could be estimated to be little different in their inner structure from the smaller ones. The one selected by the Japanese for excavation is a typically small burial mound. It is 1.9 m. above the ground level and 9.4 m in diameter. It was covered by the whitish soil with gravels all over. It was surrounded by a ring wall beneath and a stone chamber. Excavations revealed that the stone chamber is of 'T' shape with two alcoves to both sides of the end wall. The main axes of the stone chamber is about 82° east. However, the orientation is east-west, as in the general practice. The main chamber's width on two ends is 65 and 76 cms. and is rectangular in shape. Its length is two metres. The end wall with alcoves is 142 cms. in width. The two alcoves are not of uniform shape and size. The left is comparatively smaller and is of irregular shape. The average width of the alcove 20 cms. Rough hewn stones and chipped stones were used in building the wall of the chamber. The Japanese did not find any trace of mortar in building the wall. The front and end walls are almost vertical. However, the side walls are sightly carvelled due to the heavy load of the capstones over them. The inner height of the chamber is between 60-85 cms, with the top centre a shallow concave. Four big size capstones were placed over the chamber. The largest measures 110x75x35 cms. and the smallest 55x50x27 cms. Below the top most capstones are the stones which covered the top of the alcoves. Skeletal remains were found to be heaped up on the bed rock, by the side of the end wall nearer to the left side alcoves. No artifacts were found within the mound. (Konishi, Gotoh, Akashi; 1989:4-6). The second Buri tumuli which the Japanese team excavated is one of the few highest and biggest in the Buri area. It is about 4 m. high above the ground and 19m. in diameter. It was completely covered by the soft whitish soil with loose gravels. It was situated about 242 m. from the first tumuli, mentioned above. On excavating it was found that the ring wall was about 12.2 m. in diamter, thus forming almost a perfect circle. This speaks about the perfect workmanship. When the walls were un-earthed, it was found that the second or middle walls of the shaft formed a rough square with round corners in shape. The deepest and lower most wall is rectangular and smaller in shape. This formed a sort of terrace, 40-70 cms. wide from the bottom of the upper one. The burial chamber is 2.75 cm long, 1.1m wide and 1.4m high. The main axis of the chamber coincides with that of the shaft, it has east-west orientation. At the end wall are two alcoves, left and right, measure 40x35 cms and 35x30 cms. respectively. The total plan of the stone chamber seems to be symmetrical and well-ordered and made the Japanese excavators to consider this tumuli well planned before hand. The ceiling is made by placing one single big stone over the end wall as well as the two side walls of the alcove. These stones over the alcoves form the same row as the other first row of stones supporting the capstones which are four large rocks. The floor of the chamber is flat, and is about 1.5m. below the deepest floor level of the shaft outside. The chamber rests on the deep-cut pit into the natural soil. Skeletal remains were scattered at the end wall and close to the alcoves. The bones are of two males differing considerably in age. No artifacts were found inside the mound. The two mounds excavated by the Japanese does not provide any clue to dating. However, the finds from the neighbouring mounds suggest a date of third milleminum B.C. (Konishi, Gotoh, Akashi, 1989:4,7-12). Recently during 1990, the Antiquities Department of Bahrain carried out excavation at Buri mounds. Figs. 6,7 illustrates excavations in progress and reveals the outer circular wall of the graves. Here built-tombs as seen in Fig. 8, were discovered. "Double storey" graves at Buri are shown in Fig. 9 a-c. The excavation was in progress when the author visited the site. Report is not available.

Al Hajjar Graves

Fig.11 (Above)capstones on the graves.

Fig.12 (Left) Alcove.

Fig.13 (Below) Curved wall inside a grave.

(3)   AL HAJJAR SUBTERRANEAN GRAVES

The discovery in 1970 and excavation of the al-Hajjar grave complex (Fig. 10) introduced new dimensions in Bahrain's Bronze Age archaeology for it has several characteristic features not found at other sites. These characteristics are : they are the earliest graves in Bahrain dated ca. 3000 B.C., they are collective graves designed for more then one corpse, the remains of ten corpses were found in one, they had doorways to facilitate entry; they followed different design in the form of "L", "U", "T", "V", "E", as well as straight graves, the shape of the graves were modified and expanded according to the exegency and were reused.   For the first time (1970) seals were found with the corpses; and they were rich with artifacts of archaeological importance. (al Tarawaeh, 1971:6). Yet another characteristic feature of al-Hajjar graves is that they are situated within the popular area, centre of cultivated north plain, al Hajjar village.   Thus, the strict division between a land of living and land of the dead cannot be supported any longer, says Salles (1991, Ms. unpublished).   The report of excavation has not been published so far since 1970. Al Tarawaeh's short note and Michael Rice's papers (1972, 1988) are the only sources which provide us with some details of al Hajjar graves.   Subterranean graves at two sites, al Hijjar I and al-Hijjar II were found cut into the rock bed (Fig. 11). Except one, all the graves in al Hajjar I are of rectangular shape. However there does not seems to be any consistency or uniformity in the size, as they vary, as they were not planned, in fact they were built haphazardly.

One grave is "E" shape. All the sections are apparently of the same period and on the basis of artifacts recovered, it is dated to third millennium B.C. An interesting selection of seals was found from these graves. The graves range in depth from 1.10 to 1.85 m. In one case of 1.65 m, the original depth appears to be 2.20 m. Each grave had low surrounding walls over which capstones were placed. Of the two capstone (Fig. 11) the smaller one was over the entrance side, while the large one over the other end. They were cemented made up of lime, sand and ashes. Thirteen out of 14 graves were plastered inside. Steps were found in side eight graves. The excavators of al Hajjar, Fayez Tarawaeh and Abdul Aziz Fakhroo, numbered the first complex of fourteen graves in sequence as they opened them. The most interesting and unique grave is No. 2, which is E-shaped.

From this "E" shaped grave two seals, one Dilmun type and the other Neo-Babylonian type were found. Besides variety of pottery and round bowels, bronze arrowheads, engraved ivory and gold rings were found from this grave. Grave No 1 had yielded seals of Jamdat Nasr, Nuzi style etc. Other graves too have yielded other types of seals. Some of the graves of al Hajjar 2, differ from those of its neighbour al Hajjar 1. Comparatively they are smaller, shallow square pits dug into the bed-rock. Some of them have been blocked by a type of stone portcullis. This characteristic feature is absent in al Hajjar 1. One of the grave had a skeleton lying on its left side, with the hands joined before the face. Adjacent to it was a small inverted bowl and next to it is a Dilmun seal. Accordingly the burial is dated to the end of third or early second millennium B.C. Graves with captones and alcove are shown in Figs. 11,12. The inside of the grave is shown in Fig. 13. A few al Hajjar graves belong to later Hellenistic period.

(4) HAMAD TOWN TUMULI

In December 1981 an Australian team, led by Philip J. Hobgood (University of Sydney), invited by Shaikha Haya al-Khalifa, then Director of Antiquities and Museums (Bahrain) excavated burial mounds at the 'New City' site. The team worked from December 1981 to February, 1982. Habgood's report (Unpublished) is titled : "Report for the Australian Expedition to Bahrain 1981-82: the excavations of the New City Mound Field". And the second season's Australian team's report (Unpublished) by J. Edwin Brown, Judith Littleton and Robyn Stocks, is titled "Eighteen Mounds at the New City site, 1982". Both the reports does not specify or mention any where to which 'New City' the mounds belong. However, Hobgood states in the openning para of the report that the New City mound field is situated between the town of Ar Rifa'a al Gharbi, the village of Buri and lies directly south of the large tumuli field at 'Ali. The grid reference, he gives, is 50°30'E and 26°08'N., the site is bisected by the large wadi. The mounds are located between the 25 meter and 15 meter contour lines on either side of this wadi and would number over 250. From the personal discussions with Shaikh Haya al Khalifa (former Director) and 'Ali Akbar Bushiri, it is learnt that the 'New City' is the 'Hamad Town' (Madinat Hamad). However, when one reads Anthony Lowe's report the matter becomes confusing. Lowe was one of the members of the Australian team during 1981-82. After the team left Bahrain, Lowe continued to stay at Bharain and undertook further excavation as part of Bahraini team. His report entitled: "A Burial mound at Buri" (1982, Unpublished), states in the opening sentence : "In December 1981 an Australian team, invited by Shaikha Haya al-Khalifah, Director of Antiquities and Museum, dug in Bahrain on the 'New City' site at Buri". This implies that the site of Australian team was not Hamad Town but Buri. Again while dating the Buri mound (p.3) Lower states "Philip Habgood, the leader of the Australian Expedition 1981/82, gave the mounds a pre-Barbar to Barbar I date (c. 2300 - 2100 B.C.)" and refers Habgood's report (p.14) in the notes. This clearly implies that both Hobgood and Lowe worked at the same site and that according to the latter the site was Buri.

This confusion of the site arises due to two reasons. Firstly, at that time, 1981-82, when the Australians worked, the site area had no name and that a new city was planned there, it was generally called as New City site. Secondly, the mounds stretch over the entire area and there was no separation or division between the Buri mounds and New City mounds. Demarcation between the two was made by the highway constructed later on, thus dividing the mound field. Those north of the highway belonged to Buri; and those south of the highway are of the 'New City' named Hamad Town, about 1984. Under the circumstances, the New City mounds are considered as that of Hamad Town, and the mounds, lying north of the highway and Hamad Town, in close proximity to Buri, as that belonging to Buri. A general

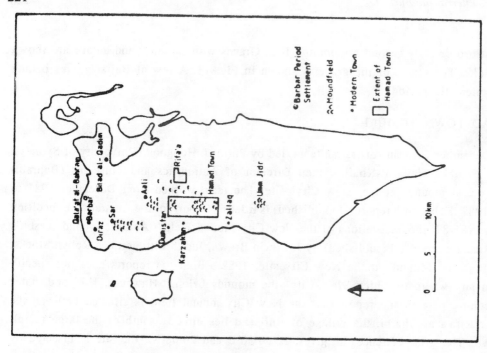

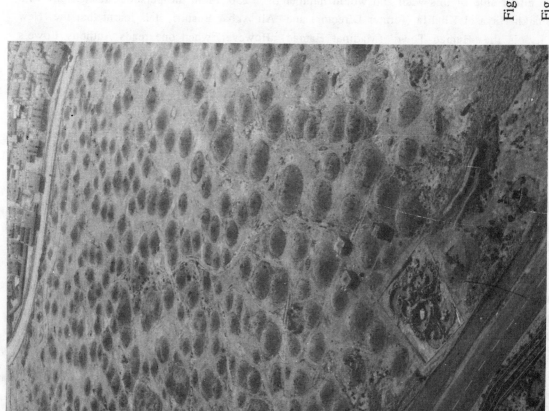

Fig.14 (Left) Hamad Town Burial mounds. A general view. (After De John Lawrence, 1985).

Fig.15 (Above) Territorial extent of Hamad Town Mound field. (After Anthony Lowe, 1986).

view of the Hamad Town mound field is shown in Fig. 14. The territorial extent of Hamad Town is shown in Fig. 15; and its mound field is shown in the sketch in Fig. 16. Excavations at Hamad Town were conducted during 1981-85, by three teams, the Australians, (1981-82), the Bahraini's (1981-85) and the Indians (1984-85). They worked separately on different mounds of Hamad Town which comprises a vast area. Reports of the Australians and the Bahrainis are not published until today; while that of the Indian team just published in 1991. The Bahrain Department of Antiquities, during 1980-81, excavated twelve mounds at the site. The results of these excavations, has not been published, nor available for reference. They continued further excavations during 1981-82. With the growing threat of the destruction of the mounds caused by the proposed building of a new city on the site, two teams, one Australian and one local were employed to rescue the archaeology. The Australian team was assigned several mounds that were considered to be typical. They were located in an area 115m x 85m. and bounded by the wadi edge on the east, a track on the west side and two intermittent water courses. They excavated six mounds. (Fig. 23). Details of Hamad Town tumuli given here are derived from Habgood's (1982) unpublished report of the Australian team. He has classified the Hamad Town mounds into two basic types, in accordance with their size and number of courses of stone used in building the ring wall and the positioning of the ring wall in relation to the burial chamber. The first type of mounds have ringwall that is positioned close to the burial chamber and which are constructed of basically one course of large stones. Fig. 17 illustrates type one mound and shows chamber plan of mound No. 5. The second type of mounds are those which had a ring wall constructed of two or more courses of relatively small stones which is located a reasonable distance away from the burial chamber, as seen in Fig. 18. A few of these two types of mounds are described here, based on Habgood (1982).

In the category of type one there are three mounds, Nos. 1,4 and 5. Mound 1 is of medium size being 0.92 m. in height and 9 m in diameter. The east-west section of the mound from the south side is shown in Fig. 23. The burial chamber is basically rectangular in shape and has an east-west orientation. Its internal dimensions at ground level are, length 1.74m., width 0.83 m., and height 0.81m. Relatively large stones were used in constructing the chamber of 2-3 courses, on top of one another, so that the eastern and western ends corbel inwards 0.22m, and 0.30 m., respectively. The wall rest upon a layer of semi-compacted clay and pebbles. No capstone was found over the chamber, the latter was surrounded by a ring wall of one course of large stones, except on the southern side, which had two courses of smaller stones. The ring wall was almost circular with diameters of 4.29m and 4.30 m. in east-west chamber. Its height is 0.33 m, and width 0.45m. The burial chamber was filled with earth within which there were two distinct layers. The first, 0.40m, deep, had sand and rocks. The second layer, 0.20m, deep, consisted of a clay and small pebbles. Within this second layer the burial was found. This consisted of a partly articulated flexed skeleton of a human and a very fragmentary and disarticulated sheep skeleton. The human skeleton remains consists of : part of cranium, two phalanges of the hand, a number of rib fragments, a number of arm bone fragments, four vertebrae, the left hip bone, two femurs, a patela, two tibiae, two fibulae, and a number of bones of the feet. The sheep remains consisted of two halves of the lower mandible, a number of teeth and numerous other fragmentary bones. The gracility and small nature of these bones and the possibility of an unfused epiphyses of a bone suggest that they belong to a young animal. This dis-articulation and fragmentary nature of the upper part of the human skeleton and of the sheep skeleton and two pottery sherds suggests that tomb was disturbed in the past. At the lowest level of the chamber were found two very small sherds of a coarse grained, sand tempered pottery. It has a red colour and would seem to have been fired at about 800°C. No other finds were recovered from the chamber.

Mound 4 is of medium size being one meter in height and 8m. in diameter. It has a central chamber and a subsidiary chamber. The former is oval in shape and has a basically east-west orientation. Its dimensions at ground level are, length 1.06m, width 0.84m, and height 0.92 m. The chamber wall is built of three courses of rough stones placed one on top of another so that the eastern and western portions corbel inwards 0.07m, and 0.09m, respectively. The wall rests on a layer of semi-compacted clay and pebbles. The chamber lacked any form of capstone. The central chamber was surrounded by a ring wall consisting of a single course of large stones which on the northern side are rectangular in shape and placed on one of their long sides. This gives a flat outer and inner face to the ring wall. On average the ringwall is 0.54m. away from the chamber. The maximum height of the chamber is 0.44m but near the subsidiary chamber, it is 0.56m. Likewise the width at the two positions is 0.45m and 0.15 m respectively.

The central burial chamber was completely filled with earth within which there were three distinct layers. The first 0.32m, deep consisted of sand and large stones and contained a number of fragmentary sherds of a well lavigated, fine grained, red coloured ceramic that was fired at about 10000°c. The second layer, 0.25m deep, consisted of semi-compacted clay and rocks while the third layer, 0.35 m. deep, consisted of compacted clay and small pebbles. This lowest level contained the burial which consisted of an almost complete and articulated flexed skeleton of a human and a partly articulated skeleton of a sheep in the north west corner. The human skeleton was laid on its right side. The arms were drawn up towards the face and the legs to wards the body. Some bones were missing or very fragmentary. The lower portion of the face was also very fragmentary. It seems to be of an adult male. Small sherds of pottery from the upper level of the chamber fill and the large stone that is missing from the ring wall suggests that the chamber was disturbed in the past. No other finds were recovered from the central burial chamber.

In the second category also three mounds were excavated. viz., Nos. 2, 3 and 6. Mound 2 is a large size mound (Figs. 22,23) 1.06m, in height and 12m. in diameter. It has a central chamber and a subsidiary chamber. The central burial chamber is ovoid in shape with a north west-south east orientation. There is a large alcove projecting from the north eastern

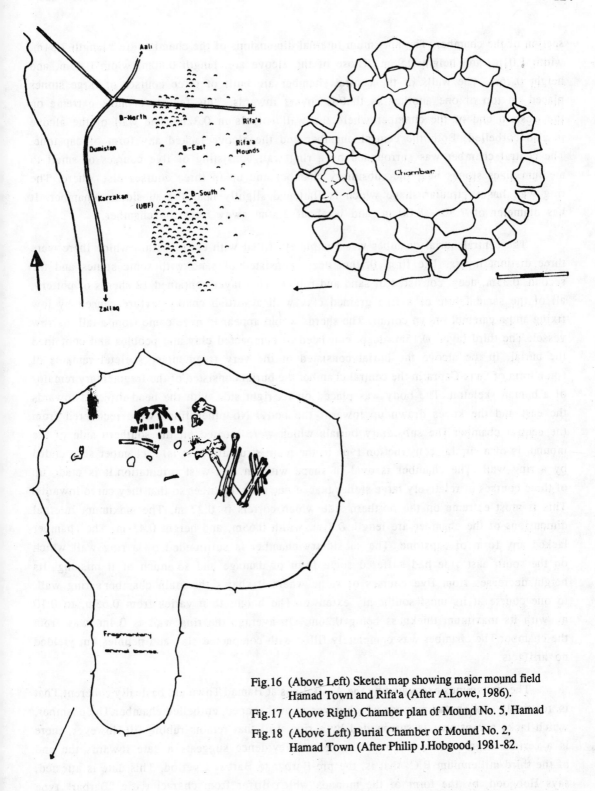

Fig.16 (Above Left) Sketch map showing major mound field
        Hamad Town and Rifa'a (After A.Lowe, 1986).

Fig.17 (Above Right) Chamber plan of Mound No. 5, Hamad

Fig.18 (Above Left) Burial Chamber of Mound No. 2,
        Hamad Town (After Philip J.Hobgood, 1981-82.

section of the chamber. The maximum internal dimensions of the chamber are : length 1.51m, width 1.01m, and height 0.96m. Those of the alcove are: length 0.80m, width 0.45m, and height 0.76m. The walls of the central chamber are built of three courses of large stones placed on top of one another so that it covers inwards. This feature is most extreme on the western end of the chamber where the wall corbels in 0.32m. The wall of the alcove is also corbelled. Both the central chamber and the alcove lacked any form of capstone. The central chamber was surrounded by a ring wall consisting of five courses of small to medium sizes stones near the subsidiary chamber and up to three courses else where. The ring wall has a circular shape which is flattened slightly near the subsidiary chamber. It has diameter of 7.30 - 8.00 m. and is about 2.30m away from the chamber.

The central burial chamber was completely filled with earth, within which there were three distinct layers. The first, 0.10m, deep, consisted of sand with some stones and the second, 0.35m, deep. consisted of sand and rubble. This layer contained 12 sherds of pottery, all of the same fabric of a fine grained clay with a softish chalky texture caused by low fixing and a caremel brown colour. The sherds would appear to have come from a tall, narrow vessel. The third layer, 0.15m. deep, consisted of compacted clay and pebbles and contained the burial. In the alcove the burial consisted of the very fragmentary skeletal remains of some form of Ovis-Capra.In the central chamber the burial consisted of the fragmentary remains of a human skeleton. The body was placed on its right side with the head directed towards the east and the knees drawn up towards the body. No other finds were recovered from the central chamber.The subsidiary burials which were located on the southern side of the mound, is of a similar construction type to the main structure.That is, a chamber surrounded by a ring wall. The chamber is oval in shape with an east-west orientation.It is made up of three courses of relatively large stones placed one over the other so that they curve inwards. This is most extreme on the northern side which correls in 0.27 m. The maximum internal dimensions of the chamber are length 0.8 m, width 0.65m, and height 0.45 m. The chamber lacked any form of capstone. The subsidiary chamber is surrounded by a ring wall which on the south east side had suffered some form of damage and so much of it missing. Its height decreases from five courses of stone where it shares the main chamber's ring wall, to one course at its most southernly extension.The height then varies from 0.65m. to 0.10 m. with its maximum thickness being 0.26m. On average the ring wall is 0.4m.away from the chamber.The chamber was completely filled with compacted clay and pebbles but yielded no artifacts.

The six mounds excavated by the Australians at Hamad Town are basically coherent.That is, relatively small broad mounds which cover an oval shaped, corbelled chamber.The chamber, which lacks a capstone, is surrounded by a ring wall that retains rubble fill.However, there is a certain degree of variability. The ceramic evidence suggests a date towards the end of the third millennium B.C. that is, the pre-Barbar to Barbar I period. This date is attested, says Hobgood, by the form of the mounds which differ from characteristic "Barbar" type

Fig.19 (Top) Hamad Town grave of five sections.

Fig.20 (Left) Inter-connected graves form 'E' shape.

Fig.21 (Right) Steps in graves

(Courtesy : Bahrain National Museum)

Fig.22 a,b,c Skeletal remains in the 'E' of Fig. 20.

228

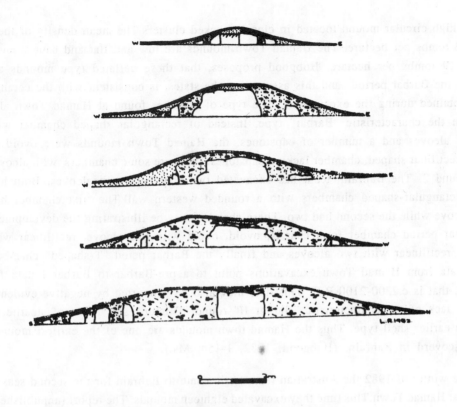

Fig.23 Mound size Comparison. Hamad Town.
(After P.J.Hobgood, 1981-82, Unpublished report).

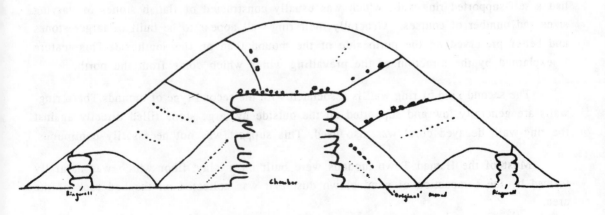

Fig.24 A typical Barbar Mound Section. (After A.Lowe, 1986).

which is a high circular mound located in closely packed clusters.The mean density of these tombs is 53 tombs per hectare. The Hamad Town mounds are low and flat and have a mean density of 19 tombs per hectare. Hobgood proposes, that these deflated type mounds are earlier than the Barbar period and this assumption, he states, is consistent with the ceramic evidence obtained during the excavations. The type of chamber found at Hamad Town also differs from the characteristic "Barbar" type. Instead of rectangular shaped chamber with one or two alcoves and a number of capstones, the Hamad Town mounds were ovoid or sometimes rectilinar shaped, chamber lacking capstones.There are some chambers with alcoves such as mound 2. The Bahraini team has excavated two chambers with alcoves. Both had basically rectangular-shaped chambers with a rounded western wall.The first chamber had only one alcove while the second had two. These chamber may be illustrating the development of the Barbar period chamber form.That is, ovoid, ovoid with one alcove, rectilinear with one alcove, rectilinear with two alcoves and finally the Barbar peiod "T-shaped" chamber. All these data from Hamad Town excavations point to a pre-Barbar to Barbar I date for the mounds, that is c.2300-2100 B.C. This date may also be supported by negative evidence such as the lack of the characteristic "Barbar II" round "Dilmun" seal made of steatite or the possibly earlier shell type. Thus the Hamad town mounds are one of the earliest mounds thus far discoverd in Bahrain. (Habgood, 1982, 1-15m Ms.).

In the winter of 1982 the Australian team again came to Bahrain for the second season to excavate at Hamad Town.This time they excavated eighteen mounds. The report (unpublished) is entitled: "Eighteen Mounds at the New City Site, 1982," for the second season is by J.Edwin Brown, Judith Littleton and Robyn Stocks.They had accompanied Habgood team earlier. The report is unpublished and the information derived here is from the said report.Brown etal have divided the mounds in to two types, characterised by the ring wall. The first type had a self-supported ring-wall, which was usually constructed of flatish stones of varying sizes and number of courses. Generally their ring-wall appear to be built of larger stones and better preserved on the north side of the mound than on the south side.This feature is explained by the direction of the prevailing winds which come from the north.

The second kind of ring-wall is associated with the second type of mounds.These ring-walls are generally low and supported on the outside by large stone filled directly against the ring-wall, decayed coral was also used. This support was not necessarily continuous.

Most of the Hamad Town mounds were built on a 'clay' floor which was naturally formed by the compaction of wind blown dust that was collected on the bed rock of the area.

It is not proposed to describe here the details about each mound.However, the main characteristic features of these mounds are tabulated in Table II, based on Brown etal (1982 83). A casual glance at the table reveals the following features of these mounds: The diameter of the ring wall varies from one meter to nearly six and half meters.The height of the ring-

Fig.25 Hamad Town. Skeleton on left lateral with fenerary gifts.
(Courtesy : Bahrain National Museum).

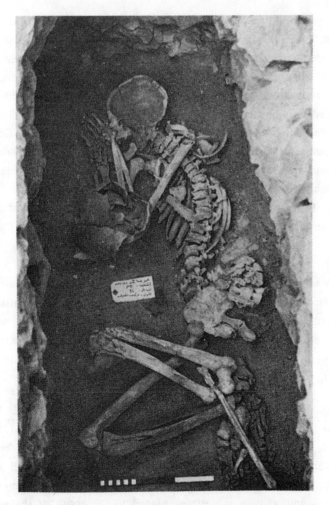

Fig.26 Hamad Town. Skeleton in a flexed position with broken pots.
(Courtesy : Bahrain National Museum)

wall varies from as low as 0.20m. to as high as 5.3 m. The number of courses of stone used in building the ring-wall was usually one to three or the dimension of the chamber varied considerably.As many as seven shape of chambers were constructed.They are rectilinear, oval, round, square,'D','T' and 'L' shaped. That consistency in orientation was not an essential factor is evident from these mounds, where orientation varied from 28° to 100°. Construction of alcove is limited to a few cases, four out of 28 mounds excavated. Burial remains and burial gifts too are few. Most probably the mounds were disturbed and robbed in the past. Only in one case a Kassite pot was recovered.It is presumed by the excavators that capstones covered the chamber which were empty except for the body and burial goods.The excavators have not suggested anydate for the mounds or have given any details of ceramic analysis. However, they have stated that sherds of pottery earlier than Kassite pot, were recovered from a lower depth of tell 35-1.So, we may tentatively date these 28 mounds to early second millennium B.C.

Anthony Lowe, one of the members of the Australian team that excavated inBahrain during 1981-82, remained in Bahrain after the teams departure and joined the Bahrani team tocontinue further excavations at Hamad Town during 1982-83.As a result of his two season's excavation of 55 burial chambers (33 Barbar and 22 Rifa'a) he wrote the report entitled: "Bronze Age Burial Mounds on Bahrain", in September 1984 (unpublished) for the Bahrain-National Museum.Revised version of it was subsequently published in 1986 (Lowe, 1986:73-84). Excavation at Hamad Town has revealed two main types : the common Dilmun (Barbar of Lowe) type and another hitherto over looked type which, Lowe (1984:2) designated as 'Rifa'a' mound.The Dilmun mound are typical with high conical form of which several hundred are in the south of Hamad Town south of the high way. This field was code name B-North in the excavation. (See Fig. 15).Dilmun mounds as found to the south of Hamad Town (B-south) are mainly of low shape. The Rifa'a type mounds are generally low, flat and uneven, structurally characterised by rock fill between the burial chamber and ring-wall and with very few exception lack capstones. Since black-on-red painted wares have been recovered from these mounds they are locally known either 'Umm an-Nar' or 'Jamdat Nasr' mounds.The Rifa'a mounds are situated to the east of Rifa'a where they can be seen dotting the slopes that run down into Hamad Town. They spread to the northwest and south west of Rifa'a. In Hamad Town they were found in scattered fields, extending to the western edge of the site. The B-south mounds in 1982-83 season were excavated on the eastern side of the mound field opposite Karzakan. (Lowe, 1984:Ms.)

Structurally the Barbar mounds are mostly single burials with a centrally built chamber covered by capstones and surrounded by a low ring-wall. Both ring-wall and chamber were built of un-worked lime stone blocks. The fill between the ring-wall and burial chamber is earth. The construction of the Barbar mound is often marked by a small mound which for some time stood around the chamber presumably while it waited for its internment. Subsidiary burials of infants and sub-adults were sometimes placed to the south of the mound against the outside face of the ring-wall. Grave pottery from the two main mound types at Hamad

232

Fig.27 An incomplete skeleton of a human body.
Hamad Town (Courtesy : Bahrain National Museum)

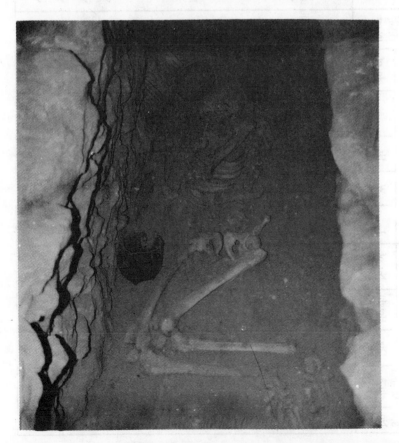

Fig.28 A skeleton in kneeling position, with five funerary goods.
(Courtesy : Bahrain National Museum).

TABLE II : MAIN FEATURES OF HAMAD TOWN MOUNDS

S. No.	Mound No. Type I	Ring-wall			Chamber						Finds				
		Dia. M	Height m.	No. of Courses	L. m.	W. m.	Ht. m.	shape	No. of courses	Orientation	Bone	Pottery	Other	Alcove	Capstone
1	15	6.05	3.4	3	1.64	6.4	0.83	Rect.	3	70°	Yes	Yes	-		
2	22	1.95	1.6	1	0.68	6.1	0.24	"	1	68°	-	-	-	-	
3	27	2.83	2.4	2-3	1.40	8.6	0.51	Oval	3	70°	Yes	-	-	-	
4	35-1	6.8	5.3	3	1.35	1	0.70	T-shape	3	28°	-	Yes (Kasite pot)	-	1) N.alcove 6.2x40x63-length 3220 210 cm 2) S.alcove 62x48x60 145°	Yes
5	35-2	1.86	1.9	2	0.50	0.42	0.42	Rect.	3	68°	-	-	-	-	-
6	35-3	3.43	0.33	3	1.05	0.58	0.42	"	2	60°	-	-	-	-	-
7	35-4	1.0	0.31	3	0.41	0.32	0.30	"	2	65°	-	-	-	-	-
8	35-5	1.27	0.36	3	0.49	0.47	0.47	Round	4	-	-	Yes	22 Beds	-	-
9	35-6	1.47	0.20	3	0.53	0.4	0.28	Square	2	40°	-	-	-	-	-
10	36-1	5.0	0.3	1-3	1.8	1.1	0.57	Rect.	2-3	62°	Yes	-	1 Bead	-	-
11	36-2	1.6	0.25	1-3	0.82	0.48	0.35	'D'	2	58°	Yes	-	-	-	-
12	42	4.5	0.36	1-3	1.41	0.95	0.54	Oval	2	100°	Yes	Yes	-	-	-
13	A-14	4.30	0.23	3	1.58	0.74	0.34	Rect.	2	80°	Yes	-	-	72x42x57 360°	-

TABLE II : MAIN FEATURES OF HAMAD TOWN MOUNDS

S. No.	Mound No. Type I	Ring-wall			Chamber						Finds			Alcove	Capstone
		Dia. M	Height m.	No. of Courses	L. m.	W. m.	Ht. m.	shape	No. of courses	Orientation	Bone	Pottery	Other		
14	A-41	4.30	0.23	3	1.58	0.74	0.34	Rect.	2	80°	Yes	-	-	-	-
15	A-64/1	3.8	0.33	2-3	1.38	0.68	0.51	Oval	2	54°	Yes	Yes	-	-	-
16	A-64/2	1.66	0.20	1-2	0.77	0.52	0.32	'D'	1-2	72°	-	-	-	-	-
17	A-64/3	-	0.23	1	0.70	0.74	0.32	'D'	1-2	80°	Yes	Yes	5 Beads	-	-
18	A-64/4	1.68	0.23	3	0.72	0.50	0.43	'D'	3	38°	-	Yes	-	-	-
19	A-64/5	1.23	0.20	2	0.68	0.43	0.40	Rect.	1-3	37°	-	-	-	-	-
20	A-65	2.65	0.18	1	0.69	0.53	0.25	Oval	1-2	68°	Yes	-	-	-	-
21	A-73	2.70	0.22	1	0.92	0.63	0.33	Rect.	1-2	58°	-	-	-	-	-
22	A-85	2.63	0.16	2	1.10	0.74	0.36	Rect.	2	60°	-	-	-	-	-
23	A-95	2.85	0.20	3-4	1.0	0.64	0.34	Oval	3	50°	-	-	-	-	-
24	A-44/1	5.9	0.36	1-3	1.25	0.70	0.35	Rect.	1-3	114°	-	Yes	-	-	-
25	A-44/2	3.59	0.30	1-3	1.55	0.80	0.80	Rect.	3	60°	-	-	-	40x36x36 1) 59x32x13 118° 2) 70x27x36	-
26	A-74	6.2	0.28	1-2	1.55	0.80	0.80	Rect.	3	64°	Yes	-	-	-	-
27	18	6.15	0.38	1-3	1.8	1.1	0.57	Rect.	2-3	62°	Yes	-	-	N. 64x45x40 340° S. 58x30x40 T Bar 1.90	-
28	31	6.47	0.27	2-3	1.7	0.84	0.70	'T'	3	60°	Yes	-	-	-	-

Town, the Dilmun and Rifa'a, differed markedly. Also there is significant difference in the pottery from the mounds in north and south. The Rifa'a black-on-red painted vessel found in the B-south Dilmun (Barbar) mounds during 1983-84 suggests that the B-south Barbar mounds are some what earlier than the Barbar mounds else where in Bahrain. On the basis of comparative ceramic analysis of those found in Hamad Town, Qal'at al Bahrain and at other places, Lowe concludes that the Rifa'a mounds represent burials of City I population and Dilmun (Barbar of Lowe) mounds that of City II population. However, the inference becomes complex owing to overlap. The Dilmun mounds seem to have been first constructed during late City I period. The relative chronology, Lowe expresses in the equation : Rifa'a Rifa'a/Barbar (B-south)-Barbar. (Lowe, 1986:73-80).

Skeletal remains in mounds are not only important for the study of anthropological aspects but are useful for the reconstruction of the ancient population. Such remains found in the mounds of Hamad Town are illustrated here in Fig. 29. They vividly illustrate the ancient burial practices and highlight not only the cultural aspects but reveal anthropological as well as medical/health aspects about the diseases the bones indicate. One grave consists of five sections and are all inter-connected forming on 'E' shape (Figs. 19-21). This grave seems to be a mass burial, may be of a family. The burials along with the pottery, found in the left wing of Fig. 22a or the lower space of "E" are shown in Fig 21 while those found in the right wing of Fig. 22 or the upper space of "E" are shown in Fig. 22b while the vertical space formed by the three arms of "E" are shown in Fig. 22c. As seen in this figure, from the left wall, extreme end, bones and pottery are protruding from under the right wing of "E". The steps are shown in Fig. 21. These three illustrations clearly indicate that this grave was a mass burial and was re-used.

In Fig. 25 a the skeleton is lying on left lateral aspect, there is flexion at hips and knees. The upper limbs are flexed and hands are placed in front of the face. The skeleton is virtually complete, there is destruction of right orbital cavity. Few teeth in both the jaws seen. The vertebral column is flexed. Scapulae are seen. The left hip bone and sacroiliae joints are visible but the right hip joint is covered by the femur. At the top left corner of the burial are burial gifts, a complete pot of black-on-red and a steatite bowl.

In Fig. 26, the skull, and vertebral column in flexed position are seen. Upper limbs are flexed at elbow. The hands are seen in front of face. Sacrum and right hip bone are intact. The left hip bone is not seen. The left femur is disarticulated from the hip bone. There is extension of right hip joint, flexion of both knees clearly visible. Plantar flexion of both ankles noted. The bones of foot are clearly seen but disarticulated. The body is kept in the north-south direction of the grave, facing towards the west. The skeleton is virtually complete in a few breakage. Fig. 27 is of an incomplete skeleton of a human body lying in the north-south direction of the grave. The back of body is towards the east. Face was probably towards the east. Humerus is seen in at the upper end. Few ribs are disturbed. 9th, 10th, 11th, 12th thoracic vertebrae, the 5 lumbar vertebraes sacrum, both the hip bones are seen in the normal anatomical position. The left femur is disarticulated from the hip bone. The lower end of the femur is missing. Fig. 28 shows a skeleton in kneeling position. Funerary gifts are seen placed near the head and on the side. The skeleton appears to be of a male of about 40 years of age. (Nayeem, F., 1992:91). Fig. 29a reveals the ancient practise of burying the small children first within a small earthern pot or a jar and then burying in the grave made in the earth. In the two small skeletons of childs aged 10 and 15 years are seen.

Three seasons of 1981-82 extensive excavations at Hamad Town by the Australians and the Bahrainis themselves could not complete work on all the mounds. Thus, in 1983, Shaikha Haya al Khalifa extended invitation to Indian archaeologists to dig at Hamad Town. The Indian team of thirteen archaeologists, led by K.M.Srivastava came to Bahrain in December 1984 and worked at the burial mounds of Hamad Town till the end of May 1985. Their report is now published (19a1); and the details about the construction of graves, given below, are drawn from the said report. The burial mounds at Hamad Town which were excavated by the Indian team has been divided in four main types by the excavators. These types are, cairn type having flattened top of the mound; a tumulus with filled up oblong burial chamber made of undressed stones and conical top; a tumuli with oblong burial chamber of semi-dressed stones and conical top; and tumulus of irregular chamber with flattened top of the mound. All these four categories have sub-types. This classification of burial mounds is based on differences in their mode of construction and this is briefly mentioned here for a proper understanding of Hamad Town's mounds.

The first type of mound was constructed by making a small depression in the natural soil (rock) by scooping out the area where the dead body was placed. Then a bed of earth was made for the body and the burial gifts. All this was then enclosed in a ring wall of stones. After the body was placed in the central position, the area was demarcated by the courses of stones, placed one above the other in small way so as to form a dome. The burial gift were placed in the adjoining alcove, which too have a similar dome. The chamber and the alcove were filled up with hard earth and chips of stone. Finally, the whole area, the chamber, alcove and the ring-wall were completely covered in a cairn of stones and earth. The second and third type of tumuli are completely different in their construction from that of the first type. But for the filled up oblong burial chamber made of undressed and semi-dressed stones the construction of the two was similar, say the excavators. In the second type the burial chamber was filled up and made of undressed stones. While in the case of the third type, it was filled and made of semi-dressed stones. In the fourth type of burial mounds very little attention was paid to the construction of the burial chamber and the alcove. Thus, they were irregular in shape. The filling outside the burial chamber was also a little different. It was more akin to the cairn type in which big stones were used. But for the burials in the cup-like depression with flat surface as the south-western fringe of the elevated land, the burials as a whole were constructed on a high ground. The fourth type of burials were constructed at a slightly higher land than the other three types. Limestone was used in the construction of the graves and the dead body was also placed on the bed rock of limestone. And this limestone was quarried from the field of the mounds itself. The shape of the burial chamber in the first type of burial mounds was an irregular circle. In the case of second and third type it was an oblong. While the case of fourth category, it was altogether irregular without any well defined shape. The construction of burial chambers was personally made without using mortar. However, in some cases of type two mortar used with the stones. Where the bed rock was cut deep the burial chamber was set in mud mortar. Completely undressed stones were used in the burials of first, second and fourth type. While in the case of third type, semi-hewn stones were used. In doing so, the irregular side of the stones were kept outside and the semi-hewn surface was kept inside. One interesting feature is that the interior size of the chambers was not the same at top and bottom. The chambers sides were tapering inward, so much that the top row of stones touched each other in an arch-like manner. The burial chambers in the first type of mounds have a much broader base compared to their top, where the stone projected over the skeletal remains in dome shape. The difference between the top and bottom dimension of the chamber was 30 cms in the case of first type and 35 cms in that of the second and third types. The maximum height of the chamber below the capstones was 0.70m in the case of the first type and 1.10 m. in the case the remaining three types. Four courses of stone were found in the case of first type; and seven in the case of the remaining types. The maximum length of the chambers in types two and three was approximately 3m. and the width 1.25 m. The subsidiary chambers were found in three moulds only; and in one grave there were seven. The ring-wall was not proportionately related to the burial chamber. Generally one to three courses of stone were adopted for the ring-wall. Partially hewn stones were used in the construction of the ring-wall. In some cases more than one ring-wall was found but at different levels.

Generally one alcove was built attached to the burial chamber on the eastern end towards the north forming an 'L' shape. In some cases deviation was found and the projection was towards the south. In a few graves the alcove was 'T' shaped, with projection both towards north and south. The alcove was always less in height than the burial chamber. The alcoves were covered with capstones.

Orientation does not seem to be given importance of graves of type one. In type two graves the orientation was generally east-west with slight inclination towards north and south. The orientation of the dead body along with its flexed position happened to be similar in type three and four.In majority of the graves the skeletal remains were found in disorder. The head was always towards the east, the body was placed in a flexed position resting on the right side with the right hand placed under the head. In one case only the dead body was in a fully articulated position. In two cases the right hand was not placed below the head. Along with the dead human body, body/bones of the sheep or ram were also placed in the grave. The animal remains were generally confined to alcove, but in some cases they were placed close to the human body near the head. Ritual practice and sacrifice at the time of burying the head body is evident from the layers of ash and charcoal found inside the chamber and within the alcove. These were also found outside the burial chamber, suggesting ritual practice performed outside the chamber. The Indian excavators believe that animal remains were roasted before placing them in the alcove, as evidence by the charred bones in two graves (Nos. 1742 and 1767). The most important discovery among the funerary goods was an Indus type seal, which was found almost in the centre of the burial chamber, very close to the north wall in grave No.,1757. Even though most of the graves did not yield any goods, however, a large variety of items have been found in the graves. Such as, pottery, steatite vessels, beads of different material, shell and shell rings, terracotta, crystal, agate, alabaster, carnelian, seals of shell as well as steatite, copper rings, rod and spear head. Capstones, from large to massive size were used to cover the burial chambers. They were not always uniform but were almost flat on either surfaces. Small stones were used to close the gap between the capstones. The filling inside the burial chamber and the alcove was of hard earth mixed with flat chips of stone in the cases of the graves of type I and IV. However, two varieties of filling was found in the case of type II and III graves. Some of them filled up with hard earth mixed with flat chips of stone; while some were not field at all. The chambers of the latter variety are partially filled up by the fine earth percolated from the top.

(5) HAMALA NORTH TUMULI

The tumuli at Hamala North lay at the southern tip of a mound field located in the north-west of Bahrain. The first excavation of this one-storeyed tumulus was made by Mrs. E.P. Jefferson in 1968. A large variety of funerary gifts objects recovered from these tumuli are preserved in the Department of Western Asiatic Antiquities of the British Museum, London; and some of them are illustrated here in Chapter VII-VIII. Later on, captian R.Higham opened 47 tumuli of four types, but these were located in various parts of the island and pertain to different cultural periods. Caspers (1972:11) suggests nearly 1000 year date between 3000-2900 and 2000 B.C. for the Hamala North graves on the basis of Barbar pottery from them. Again on the basis of the ostrich egg beakers, similar to those of Royal Cemetry of Ur, Caspers suggests a date between 2500-1800 B.C. for the Hamala North.

Of the four mounds, three of them are of prehistoric date. The first two are of sand and small stones with an average diameter of about 3.70m. and height of 0.61-1.20m. Inside they are beehieve shaped or corbelled burial chambers which were constructed of limestone slabs with smaller stones, filling up the gaps in between. The base of the burial chambers seems to be slightly below the ground level. The third type are pimple-shaped mounds, of different height from 1-6m., with diameters of up to well over 20m., constructed of large, roughly-squared limestone blocks laid in courses without mortar, the gaps being filled with small stones. In several cases, remarks Caspers (1972:9f), the mounds had originally been ringed by one or two concentric walls of the same roughly shaped stones. The burial chamber had usually one, two or occasionely more than two alcoves at the east end of south and north walls and near the west end of burial chamber. Finishing was made by cement coating. The alignment of these graves were generally east-west. The chambers were linked by walls to the west-facing entrance which was blocked by stones. Massive capstones were placed over the whole structure and these were generally two or three. Some tumuli were found to be of double storey with a smaller upper chamber without alcoves. The fourth category of tumuli are simply a series of individual stones built of mud or cement-lined graves, roofed by stone slabs. They were built into mounds of irregular shape at different levels with different alignments. In the first three categories of graves the position of the body lay on his right side, some time on the left and was facing north or south, respectively. The head was turned towards the eastern end of the burial chamber and the feet were towards the entrance. The heads were found to be before the face and the whole skeleton appears to lay either in a kneeling posture, or in a flexed position.On the contrary, in the case of the fourth type of category of tumuli, the position of the body was quite different. The body lay either on his left or right side, legs extended or flexed. The arms were placed across the body or at the abdomen. (Caspers, 1972:9-1980-2).

(6)   JANUSSAN MOUNDS

Janussan lies about 100m. south of the high tide line of the central sector of the north coast of Bahrain. It is a mound approximately 40x40m and 4.50m.high. It is high on the north side and slop down to the south. During 1920-26 these mounds were explored by major Daly. In 1969 rescue excavation was made by the Antiquities Department of Bahrain under the directionof al-Tikriti, but report is unpublished and also not available for reference. In 1973 excavations were made by the British team lead by Tony McNicoll. However, this report is also unpublished; but available in manuscript form. In order to test and date the burial mounds, the British made four sondings, which revealed three different burial mounds. These British have dated to third millennium B.C., on the basis of Barbar pottery found at the site.Mc Nicoll observes that the Janussan mounds contrast with other burials, as the former are situated on potentially cultivable land and the latter on the waste land.(Mc Nicoll, 1974 Ms.). The French excavated these mounds in two seasons during 1980-81. The first seasons of 1980 was led by Serge Cleuziou and the team comprised the folowing: Beatrice Andre Leicknam, Pierre Lombard, Jean Gire and Jean-Francois Salles. The latter was the head of the French Archaeological Mission in Abu Dhabi. During the second season of 1981 the French team was headed by Remi Boucharlat and Jean-Francois Salles. Khalid al-Sindi was one of the local participant on behalf of the Department of Antiquities. (Salles, 1984:11f). The French team excavated mound II A and mound III B at Janussan. Mound II A was found to be a cemetary and the French excavated eight tombs in it.These have been classified into five main types: (1) the tombs built with worked and dressed blocks; (2) the cist-tombs made of stones and mortar; (3) the tombs built with stones and mortar or mortar alone;

240

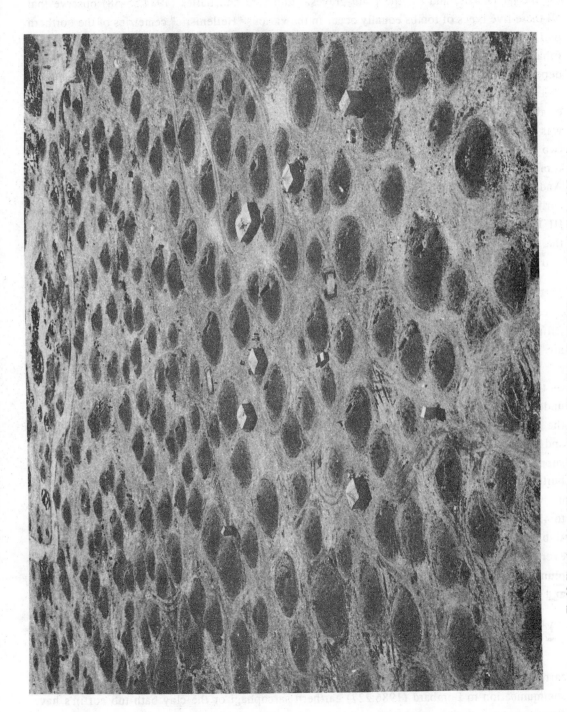

Fig.30 Karzakan Mound Field. A general view. (Photo Bruno Frohlick. Courtesy : Bahrain National Museum).

(4) the jar burials; and (5) the plain-graves. Lombard and Salles (1984:55-58) observe that all these five types of tombs equally occur in the various "Hellenistic" cemetries of the northern part of Bahrain. They have divided the mound II of height 2 m. into five phases. The earliest (phase) being Barbar level (Late Barbar, after 2000 B.,C). Phases D,E and A are of sandy deposits; while phase B is a cemetary of the Hellenistic period. French have concluded that part of these mounds have a natural origin. And if it is accepted that the construction of these hills to be completely artificial, then we must undestand the reason why the site was built up after Barbar II period, i.e., after 1800 B.C. For this, the French has made two interpretations. Firstly, Sanlaville suggests the building up of an hillock. Secondly, that it might have been the result of filling of earth rejects from the surrounding gardens cleanings. And the height of the Janussan mounds suggests that this filling might have had happened earlier than the middle of the first millennium B.C., the time when the jar cemetary mound III B was settled. No evidence of agricultural expansion, as suggested by Larsen, between the ca. 1800 and 600 B.C., have been found by the French. (Lombard- Salles, 1984:27-58; Marquius-Salles, 1984:598; Salles, 1984:137f).

The Janussan graves are of two types- the built tombs and cist-graves. The former is composed of an internal burial room built with dressed stones and an external complex filling. The latter with one rectangular cist,made with roughly dressed stones. Besides these are burial-jars for children. (The cist type and jar-burials are of Hellenistic period and fall out of the purview of this study). The burial chamber of the built tomb (T of the French) on the mound II A is 2.65 m. in length and 1.18 m. in breadth. The full height of the chamber under the covering slab was 1.65 m. Irregular slab stone were used to pave the floor of the chamber. The tomb was covered with a huge monolith slab 2.81 m. long, 0.45 m wide and 0.45 m thick, which was not lying on the top of the inside dressed walls but as a thick support 0.50 m high. The excavators suggest that the tomb was not dug into the sand, but built above the floor by first raising the burial chamber with dressed blocks and then held up with fillings of stone and juss, which they called it external walls. It seems that the tomb was made sometime before the death of the person who was buried there. The covering slab was found to be resting on a support for the protection of the burial chamber. Then every thing was covered by sand. Some important finds from the tomb was after it was plundred earlier are: a tabular bead, several iron and bronze arrowheads, an iron spear head, and remains of a scaled piece of armour.

(7)   KARZAKAN MOUNDS

A general view of the Karzakan burial mounds is shown Fig. 30. The report of excavation carried out is unpublished and not available for reference. According to Shaikh Haya's personal communication to Lombard (1986:227) earthern sarcophagi or the clay bath-tub coffin's have been recovered during excavation. This burial practise which was prevalent in the Levant and Mesopotamia also reached Bahrain. However, it was an unusual custom in Bahrain. The

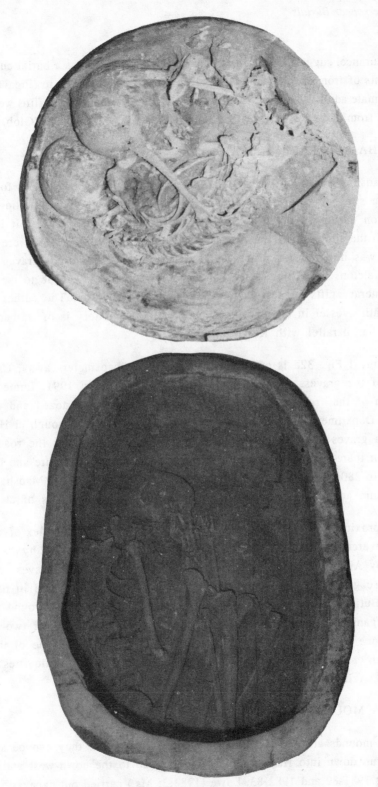

Fig.29 (Above) Two childs burried in an earthern pot.
Fig.31. Skeletons in Bath-Tub Coffins. (Courtesy : Bahrain National Museum).

very scares occurance, suggest Lombard, seems to indicate that it was a burial custom foreign to the inhabitants of Iron Age Dilmun. A bath-tub coffin illustrated here (Fig.31). Itcontains skeleton of a female adult. (Nayeem, F., 1992: 88-89). Similar bath-tub coffins were recovered by the Danish from City IV at Qal'at al Bahrain, dated to Iron Age. (Glob, 1957:166).

(8) AL MAQSHA SUBTERRANEAN GRAVES

At al-Maqsha, graves of Barbar, Kassite and later period have been found.(Larsen; 1987:77f). The site being a private property, the Department of Antiquities under took rescue excavation during 1990. It is a small site of subterranean graves. It is across the road opposite to the site of al Hajjar graves. The illustrations of Fig.32a, were taken while the excavation was in progress during October-December 1990. Eight graves are seen in Fig. 32a. No skeletons were found. Lack of human remains may be due to the acid nature of the soil. Funerary gifts suggest that human were burried here. The author found only pottery and steatite vessel in tact *in situ*. (Fig.32 b,c) The pottery is of Barbar period and one of the jar has parallel with Kassite ware.

Illustration of Fig. 32d is of adjacent graves about two meters away, Capstones are seen on each of the graves. Photographed during excavation in 1991. Immediately after the completion of the rescue excavation these graves were bull dozed and the contents removed to the Department of Antiquities.Report is not available. Though al Hajjar graves and al Maqsha graves are both subterranean and situated just across the road about 100 meters or so, but there is much difference between them, both in structure and in time. The former is dated to 2800-3000 B.C., while the latter to ca.1600 B.C. At al Maqsha only single graves were found and they are somewhat similar to the single graves of al Hajjar.

In close proximity to the al Maqsha site, another large burial complex of subterranean graves was discovered very recently and has been exacavated during 1991-92 by the Department of Antiquities by Abdul Aziz Soweilah and his Bahraini team. These graves are shown in Fig.33a-c. These graves are all rectangular in several series, arranged in parallel rows systematically. But, later on, additional graves were built haphazardly around the parallel rows of well organized graves.They are quite deep and well built.One or two appear like 'E' shaped and one in the middle of the complex is 'T' shaped. In one of the graves a cylinder seal with cuneiform inscription was found. A large variety of antiquities were found in them. (Abdul Aziz Soweilah, personal communication).

(9) AR RIFA'A MOUNDS

Ar Rifa'a mounds are situated to the east of Rifa'a where they can be seen dotting the slopes that run down into Hamad Town. They spread to the north-west and south west of Rifa'a. During 1981-82 and 1982-83, Lowe (1984:2f Ms.) carried out excavation at Hamed Town where he found Rifa'a mounds scattered and extending to the western edge of the

244

Fig.32 a   (Top) al-Maqsha Subterranean Graves - during excavation 1990.

Fig.32b,c   (Centre) al-Maqsha graves. Funerary gift pottary and stone vessel *in situ*.

Fig.32d   (Below) al-Maqsha graves with capstones, during excavation, 1991.

Fig.33a,b,c   al Maqsha (New Site) graves. During excavation 1992.

site. Lowe makes a distinction between the more common type of Barbar mounds and the Rifa'a mounds, heither to over-looked.Lowe describes the Rifa'a mounds as generally low, flat and un-even, structurally characterised by rock fill between the burial chamber and ring wall and with very few exceptions a lack of capstones. The chamber is square/rectangular, H-shaped, T-shaped, or ovoid in shape and relatively shallow. As black-on-red painted wares have been recovered from these Rifa'a mounds. They are generally called either 'Umm an Nar' or 'Jamdat Nasr' mounds. The second type of mound are the typical 'Barbar' mound of which the ideal version is the high conical form of which several hundreds have been found to the north of Hamad Town south of the high way. However, elsewhere these mounds take mainly low shape as at Sar; or south of Hamad Town they are large flattend mounds.

The Rifa'a grave mound wares were mainly restricted to the round-bodied jars, with flat bottom and out-turned rim. The vessels are thin-walled and well-fired, often orange coloured.The decorative pattern is distinctive and varies little. The zig-zag pattern of intersecting lines is found almost exclusively in the Rifa'a mounds.(see Chapter VII). The Ur type of round-bodied vessel of Royal Graves has been found in both Barbar mounds and Rifa'a mounds at Hamad Town. Lowe (1984:Ms) makes a comparative analysis of the pottery found in the Rifa'a mounds and Barbar mounds at Hamad Town and while suggesting a relative chronology, concludes that the Rifa'a mounds were the burials for the people of City I settlement of Qal'at al-Bahrain. This is evident from the decorated forms found and the absence of ridged and cylindrical jars. The barbar mounds with their ridged vessels and cylindrical jars are latest, ofcourse there is some overlap. The relative chronology Lowe expresses in the form of a equation : City I=Rifa'a mound; City II = Barbar mound - is made complex due to overlap. The Barbar mound seems to have been constructed during late City I period. Lowe dates the Rifa'a mounds to ca. 2300 B.C. - 2150 B.C., while Barbar mounds to ca. 2100 B.C. -1800 B.C. (Lowe, 1986:73-83). Since the report is unpublished more details of Rifa'a mounds are not available.

(10) SAR BURIAL FIELD

Sar burial field is one of the largest fields of burial mounds in Bahrain. A general view of graves is shown in Fig.34. It borders another burial field of Janabiyah on its west; and the two are separated by a gap of about 250m. Sar mounds estimated by aerial photographs to number more than 15,000. They are generally uniform in both shape and spacing, especially in the western part of the causeway. But this is not the case in the eastern part of the area. Here they are smaller and scattered haphazardly.The height of the mounds varies between 0.5 m. to 4m, with diameters at the base ranging between 3 to 25m. However majority of them have diameter between 6-10m. only. They are conical in shape and are regular.Some of the mounds are elongated or irregular in shape and form a group in which they are linked to each other. Some of these irregular mounds contained subsidiary burials in addition to a central one.But most of these were uncovered. The Arab expedition undertook excavations

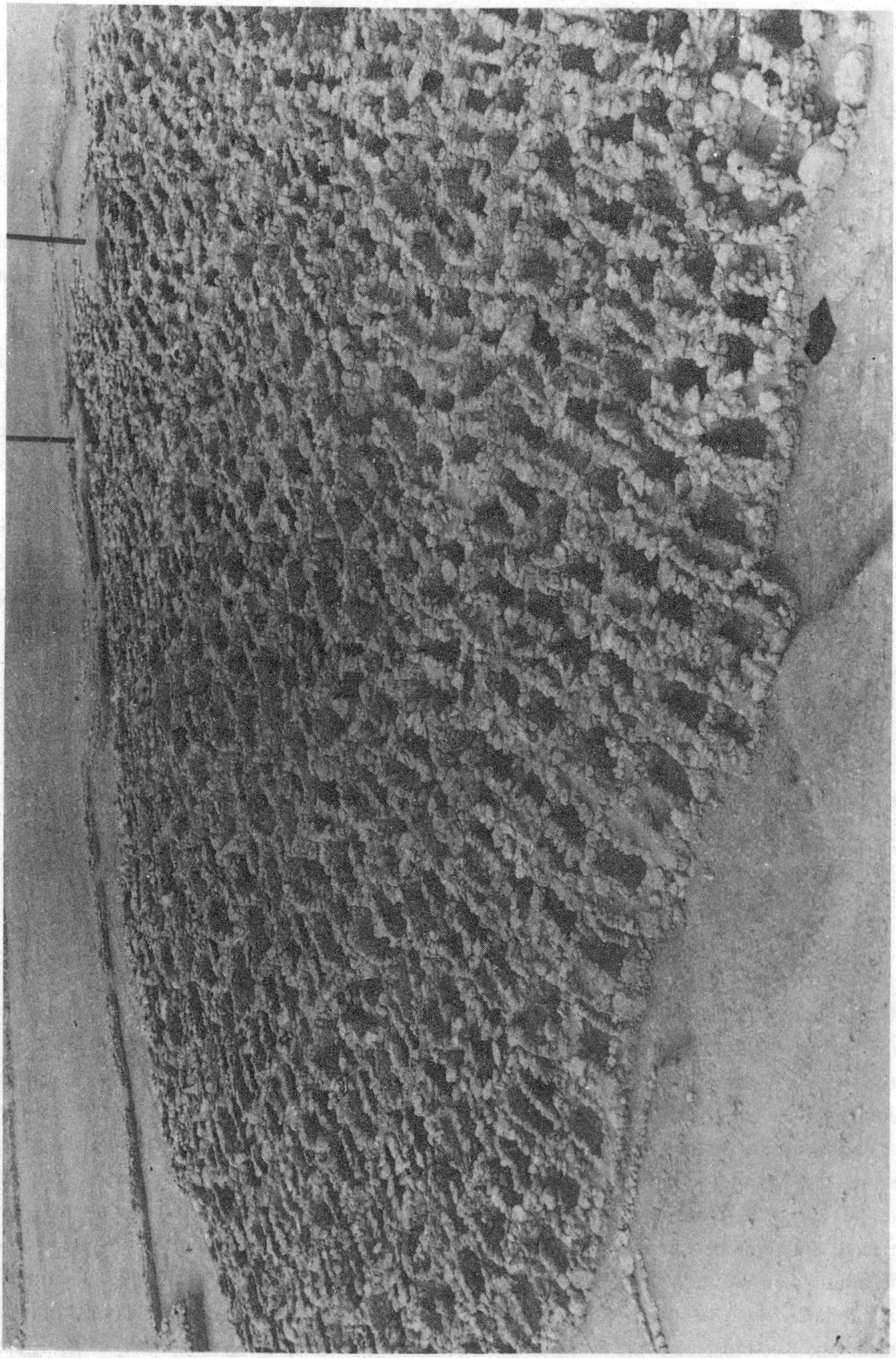

Fig.34 Sar Burial Field. A general view (Courtesy : Bahrain National Museum)

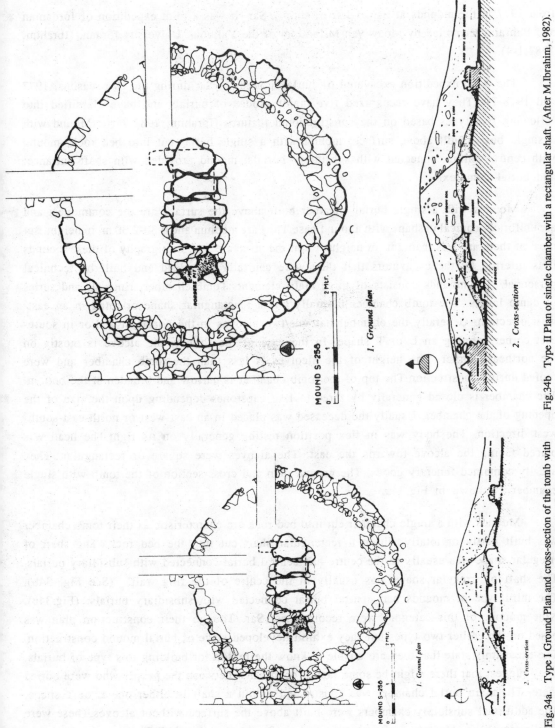

Fig.34b   Type II Plan of single chamber with a rectangular shaft. (After M.Ibrahim, 1982).

Fig.34a.   Type I Ground Plan and cross-section of the tomb with single chamber. Sar. (After M.Ibrahim, 1982).

from 1977 at the mounds at Sar el-Jisr or simply Sar. It was a joint expedition of Jordanian and Bahraini teams led by Moawiyah M.Ibrahim of the Yarmouk University,Jordan. (Ibrahim, 1982:1-4).

The Arab expedition excavated 61 burial mounds at Sar during the two seasons, 1977 and 1978-79. They have recognized five major groups of burials and have classified into following five types based on the constructional features (Ibrahim, 1982:7 ff): Mound with a single burial built above surface; mound with a single burial cut into bed rock; mound with central burial connected with subsidiary burials; mound provided with shaft entrance; and burial complex.

Mounds with a single burial chamber built above the surface are the commonest and are uniformly conical in shape with a round base.They are medium and 0.30-2.30 m. in height.But most of them are less than 2m. in height. From the structure and stratigraphy of these mounds it is inferred by the excavators that they were centrally organized and built by technical personnel. The mounds consists of three main elements:Tomb-chamber, ringwall and series of dump layers. The tomb chamber normally has a reactangular shape oriented in an east-west direction. Generally the chamber has one/two alcoves in the northeast and/or in south-east corner forming an L or T shape. In the case of the former, the alcove is mostly on the northeast corner. The height of the alcolves is less than the tomb chamber and were roofed during construction.The top of the tomb chamber is narrow and broaden at the bottom. The chamber is closed generally by three to five capstones depending upon the size of the opening of the chamber. Usually the deceased was placed in an east-west or north-east-south-west direction. The body was in flex position resting generally on its right.The head was placed facing the alcove towards the east. The alcoves were square or rectangular. They usually contained funerary goods. The ground plan and cross-section of the tomb with single chamber is shown in Fig.34a.

Mounds with a single chamber cut into bed rock are charcteristic as their tomb chamber was built partly or totally within a rectangular shaft cut into the bed rock. The shaft of irregular shape was usually in the centre had central burial connected with subsidiary burials. The shaft of irregular shape was usually in the centre of the ring wall. (See Fig. 34b). The third type of mounds had central burial connected with subsidiary burials. (Fig.34c). Nine mounds of this category were recorded ast Sar. Though their construction plan was based on the earlier two types but they exhibit developed stage of burial mound construction. The excavators state that they are unable to know the reason for building this type of burials. They suggest that there might be some family connection between the people who were buried there. The main burial chamber was constructed within a shaft in either one L or T shape. The additional subsidiary chambers were built above the surface without alcoves.These were smaller in shape. Mounds of fourth type had shaft entrance (Fig.34d).They are homogenous in their construction and are located close to each other. Around the central chamber the right wall rises upto about two metres. The chamber has built partially into the bed rock

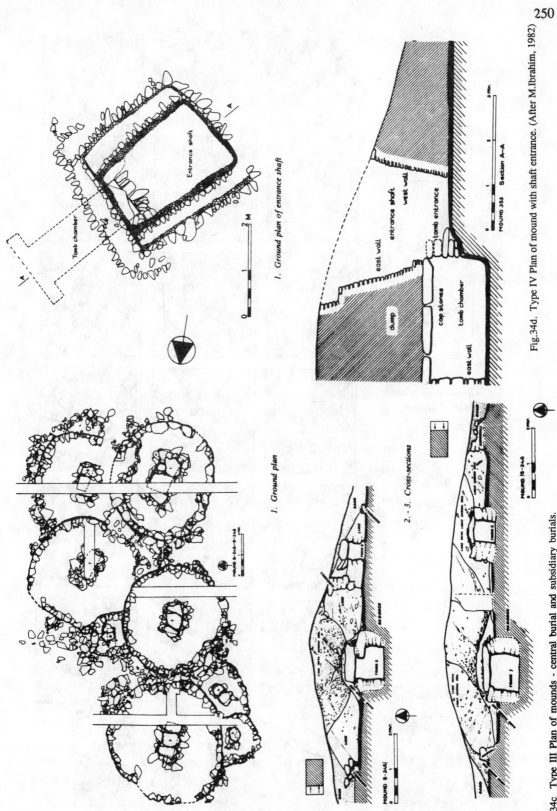

1. Ground plan of entrance shaft

Tomb chamber

Entrance shaft

2 M

1. Ground plan

MOUND 5-2+6-9-2+6-3

2. - 3. Cross-sections

MOUND 5-2+6

MOUND 15-2+6

east wall

entrance shaft

west wall

tomb entrance

dump

cap stones

tomb chamber

east wall

MOUND 359   Section A–A

Fig.34d. Type IV Plan of mound with shaft entrance. (After M.Ibrahim, 1982)

Fig.34c Type III Plan of mounds - central burial and subsidiary burials.

Fig. 34e

BURIAL COMPLEX

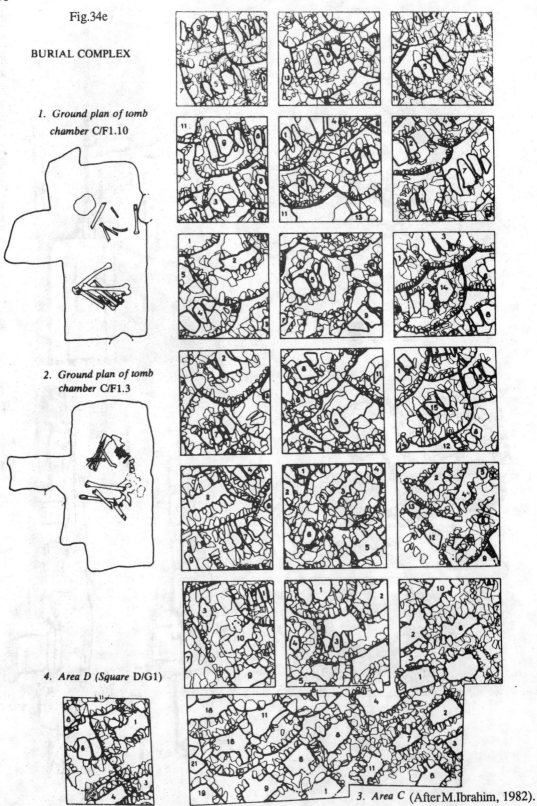

1. Ground plan of tomb chamber C/F1.10

2. Ground plan of tomb chamber C/F1.3

4. Area D (Square D/G1)

3. Area C (After M. Ibrahim, 1982).

252

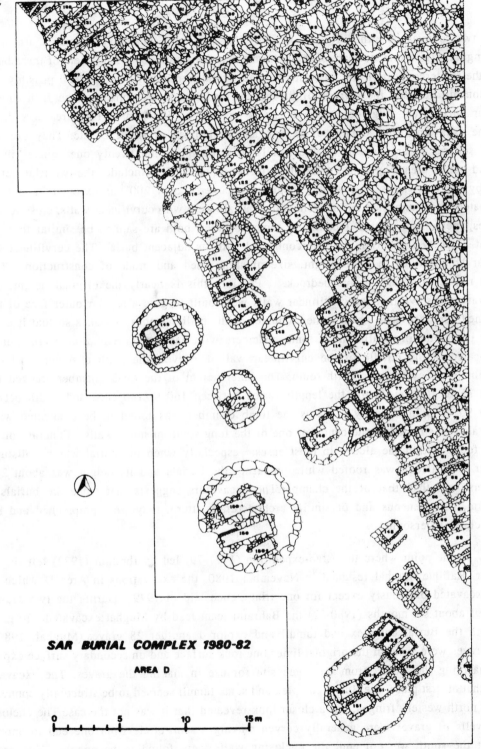

Fig.35a *Complete structural plan of the Burial Complex and the tumuli and Area D after the second season of excavation ending May 1982* (After R.Mughal, 1983).

with two alcoves of either T or L shape. However, the subsidiary chambers are always rectangular. The excavators are of the opinions that the manner of arrangement of these burials and their interconnection are suggestive of an overall structural planning and possibly some relationship between the owners of the burials.Burial complex constitute the fifth category at Sar burial field (Fig.34e) which occupies an area of 5,000 m² . This area was divided by the excavators into squares of 5x5 m. and designated as A,B,C,D, etc. They excavated eight squares in area A, six in the small burial complex and twenty one squares in area C, and one in area D, giving a total of thirty two squares. This includes the two trial trenches dug by the excavators. The Arab expedition uncovered over 200 burials out of about 1000 estimated inter-connected burials. The latter burials were with curvilinear walls, close to semi-circles, including a central rectangular tomb chamber, both are said to be similar to a great extent. Each of the burials are interconnected with its adjacent burial. The curvilinear walls appear homogenous in their height, size of stone used and mode of construction. These walls rise upto 1.3 m. above bedrock. Possibly this is nearly the original height. The excavators observe that the curvilinear walls were built to give a regular outer face of large and medium sized semi-hewn stones, chinked with smaller stones or flakes so that it curved in as in a retaining wall. The 8 tomb chambers with east-west orientation, were found to be located in the middle of the curvilinear wall. However, the tomb chambers had often a slight tendency towards north-south. The inner height of the tomb chambers ranged from about 85 to 100 cms.While the length varied between 160 to 180 cms. and width between 80 to 90 cms. In majority of cases the tomb chamber was found to be connected with a large alcove, situated in the centre of one of the long south or north walls. Funerary objects were found within the alcove in most cases; especially when the burial was not disturbed earlier. The alcove was roofed while preparing the burials and its height was about 20 to 30 cms. less than that of the chamber.The excavators suggests that since the burials are uniform, homogeneous and of similar architectural pattern, they were preplanned and built by technical personnel.

At the point where the Arab-expedition (1977-79) led by Ibrahim (1982) left the side of Sar, Rafique Mughal resumed in November 1980, the excavations in Area D which was not excavated previously except for one trial trench laid in 1979. During the two seasons, each of about six months (1980-82) the Bahraini team lead by Mughal excavated 150 graves of both the Burial complex and tumuli and explored another 28 graves.(Mughal, 1983:4). The graves were built on the original limestone rock surface and on secondary surface exposed by quarrying the stones from the same site for use in making the graves. The excavators state that at first place, the Burial complex and some tumuli seemed to be structually connected at the north western fringes; but a closer look revealed that it was not the case.The enclosing ring walls of graves were generally curved making a semi-circle from one end to another. But at the south western end, the enclosing walls were found to be angular. The graves were interconnected and were enclosed by a curved, angular or semi-circular ringwalls. Mughal (1983:11) says that the adaptation of honey comb mode of grave construction at Sar was an intentional deviation from other methods in vogue at that time, e.g., al-Hajjar, al-Maqshah

254

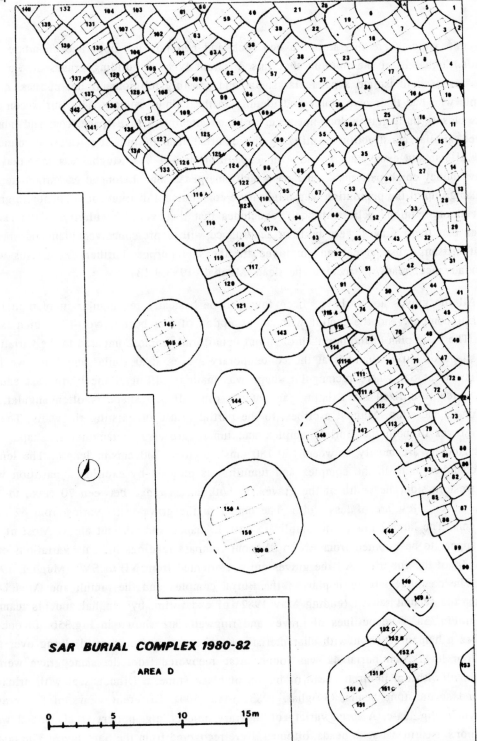

Fig.35b   *Outlines of graves and rignwalls at Sar Burial Complex with Burial numbers*

(After R.Mughal , 1983)

graves etc., which were dug into the bed rock and had no built-up grave chambers and ringwalls.Mughal is of the opinion that this different type of building graves at Sar was perhaps intended to isolate a particular social and possibly religious, if not cultural group of people who had their own status and identity in the Dilmun society. The Burial complex with its closely built graves does not seem to be an attempt to save space, cost and labour. However, similar construction re-utilizing the external face of the ring wall are found in the Sar el Jisr site excavated by the Arab expedition and at Buri.Mughal assumes that the extensive honey comb patterned cemetery which emerged at Sar, belonged essentially to one particular group of the population who might have constituted a distinct socio-economic group with common religious beliefs.Mughal concludes that the overall regularity in the layout indicates that these graves were built in accordance with a pre-conceived plan and special class of artisans must have been employed for the said purpose.Further, the graves were built in advance, ready to receive the dead.(Mughal, 1983:9-13).

All the graves at Sar have been found to be basically rectangular in plan in both the Burial complex and the tumuli with an exception of one burial (No.147) which is T-shaped. The basic plan of the burial through out is uniformly same.Compared to the variations in the shape of burial chamber at the contemporary graves at al Hajjar and Buri, we find no variations at Sar where rectangular shape was maintained.But at the north east end of graves which re-utilized the existing face of the ringwall, the shape is often angular.The cause for its variation, Mughal ascribes, to the partial re-use of existing ringwalls. The L-shaped graves of both the Burial complex and tumuli are also rectangular in shape. The burial chambers are mostly between 150-180 cms., to over 300 cms.in length. The length of the chamber, both in the complex and tumuli, was reduced by exciting a partition wall on the western side.The width of the graves, in both cases, range between 70 cms., to 100 cms., however a few are of less width. The height of the grave walls varies from 42 cms. to 107 cms. The largest graves in tumuli are both L-shaped and without alcove.Most of the graves appear to be oriented from EN to SW, but compass readings indicate variations even with in 90° of the compass. All the graves are not oriented from NE to SW. (Mughal, 1983, 2-21). The complete structural plan of the Burial complex and the tumuli and Area D at Sar, after the second season (ending May 1982) of excavation by Mughal and his team is shown in Fig.35a.. The outlines of graves and ringwalls are shown in Fig.35b. In one of the graves a human skeleton with characteristic Kassite pot (cream slipped) lying over and above floor level from burial 42 was found. Also recovered from the same grave were a steatite bowl with dot-in-circle, bead or button of black stone, a Dilmun seal with drinking scene, and seven stone beads. (Mughal, 1983; 1982, 504). Different views of Sar graves are shown in Fig.36a-c. A large variety of funerary objects, e.g. pottery, seals, metal ware and weapons, steatite vessels, beads, bitumen, were recovered from the Sar graves. The honey comb mode of construction of Sar graves is illustrated in Fig.34.

A peculiar feature observed near the Sar graves, close to the chamber and the ring

256

Fig. 36a,b,c Views of graves at Sar.

wall are a pair of vertical stones tilted inward, as seen in Fig.37a,b,c. Their purpose is not known . 'Ali Akbar Bushiri of Bahrain is of the opinion that they are 'Sun stones' with some religious/mythological motives for grave and the person buried in it. They seem to follow the shadow of the sun.

(11)   UMM - JIDR

An isolated mound field is situated at Umm Jidr in the south of Bahrain along the lower contour line of the central inner hod, on the western coast.Though isolated but these mounds are in close proximity to the prehistoric sites along the coast. A French team of archaeologist comprising: Serge Cleuziou, Pierre Lombard, Jean Francois Salles and three other undertook excavation of Umm Jidr mounds during November-December 1979.The excavators have classified these mounds into three main types, according to the shape and construction of burial chamber. These types are: Burial chamber with alcove to the north; burial chamber with alcove to the south; and mounds with simple burial chamber. The mounds of first two categories are medium sized with its base surrounded by a low stone wall. One of the mound (No.2 of French) is described here.It is 1.8m. in height and 9 m in diameter.The burial chamber is 1.70m. in length and 0.70 m. in width, with an average height beneath the capstone is 1.05 m. It has east-west orientation. Dry stone masonry was used in the construction of the walls.There are no traces of mortar.The walls slightly lean inward.The floor of the chamber has been cut 10 cm. into the bed rock and on this floor sets the foundation of the walls. This features is found in all the tombs.Rock inside the chamber is covered by a thin layer of clay.Stone slabs of large size were used for the roof.The alcove is 0.50m. in length and 0.35m. in width and 0.65m. in height.The mound was disturbed by robbers in the past.A stone ring of two/three courses high surrounds the base of the mound.The fill ranges from sand mixed with gravel to stones and earth. The burial was disturbed and the bones were scattered,only some extremities of the skeleton are preserved.From the Umm Jidr mounds the French team recovered red ware with whitish temper, typical ware of Bahrain in the third millennium B.C. Three vases with decorated horizontal ridges were found. Two globular bitumen coated baskets were also recovered along with other finds, e.g., stamp seals, soft stone beads, copper ring etc. (Cleuziou, Lombard, Salles, 1979:21ff).

RESUME

The burial mounds have been the subject of constant investigation, research and debate. They have been the cause of such speculation as to their origin. The question was whether the burial mounds of Bahrain are the exclusive cemetries of an indigenous population or as proposed by Lamberg-Karlovsky (1982:45-50; 1986:156-165) that they include the burials of peoples from surrrounding areas.This latter speculation proposed by Mackay (1929) and Cornwall (1943a) was amplified by Lamberg-Korlovskey (1986:156f) on the basis of insufficient indigenous settlement pattern (i.e. population). This theory is nullified by the excavations which brought to light Bronze Age Dilmun settlements at Qal'at al Bahrain, Diraz, 'Ali, and

Fig.37 a,b,c, Probably 'Sun Stones' at Sar graves

Sar.Since all burial mounds do not yield skeletal remains, this may because of another speculation. Regarding this Lowe (1984:10) suggest that this is due to acid nature of soil, and that over their four thousand years life span most of the mounds have been disturbed, and lack of technique and experience for excavating poorly preserved bone. These factors are multiplied in the case of subsidiary burials where the burials are of sub-adults or infants.Further, as in the case of Rifa'a type of graves where lack of capstones and shallow chambers does little to prevent the leaching and disintegration of the bones. Research and field study made by Brauno Frohlich suggests that Bronze Age burial mounds of Bahrain were a local development of the people living in Bahrain during the third and second millennium B.C. They exhibit architectural development with almost no change in its basic configuration during the period of Bronze Age.

In the absence of reliable dating method, the chronology based on the geographical location and constructional features, suggests that the early type mounds are the earliest, then comes the late type mounds, lastly the below ground burial complexes.Frohlich,tentatively suggests a period of 2500 B.C. to 1800 B.C. for these types of mounds. (Frohlich, 1986:52). Human skeletal remains were not found in all the burial mounds or their chambers.Some of them were empty.Obviously implying that human was buried or placed there.Another possibility is that biological human matrix of the bones might have decayed completely.Third possibility is that the excavator missed precise observations. It has been found that 53.7% of the burial chambers had a single alcove located at the northern or eastern corner or had two separate alcoves, one located at each of these two corners. It is noticed that in case of one alcove in the eastern corner the deceased was always placed on its left side. While bodies were found placed on the right sides in the cases where there were more than one alcove or no alcove. (Frohlich; 1986:53f).

Again the theory that Bahrain was the burial ground for the dead of the mainland is disproved by the discovery of similar type of burial mounds in eastern Arabia at Dhahran and in its surroundings. (Zarins, 1925. 25-54; 'Ali, 1988:9-28). Thus the dead of the mainland were buried in the mainland and there was no dearth of land to bring the dead across the sea to Bahrain.So, we may conclude that the burial mounds of Bahrain are those of the indigenous population. Of course with an exception of those foreigners who died while residing or visiting Bahrain were buried there.

CHAPTER VI

SEALS

Archaeological excavations in Bahrain have brought to light scores of Dilmun seals dating from third millennium B.C. The large variety of seals, rich in imagery, reveal several aspects of Bahrain's social, cultural and economic life, as well as its contacts with the neighbouring countries manifesting latter's influence in the manufacture and design of the seals. Though the Dilmun seals are related to the Indus stylistically, yet they are best interpreted, observes Lamberg-Karlovsky and Sabloff (1979:200), as indigenous products. Dilmun seals or their impressions have been found at various far off places : Ur, Larsa, Susa, Tepe Yahya, Luristan, Lothal, etc., and they bear characteristic features typical of Dilmun and not found any wherelse. Within the territorial extent of Dilmun itself these have been recorded in hundreds from Failaka and a few in eastern province of present Saudi Arabia as far as Ar-Rab' al-Khali.

Dilmun's seals played a number of different roles during the third through first millennium B.C. The purpose of seals, Halo (1981 : IX) has rightly remarked that seals were by nature legal instruments; they also fulfilled a ritual function as amulets; or as on artistic replica of an object used in daily life in the domestic, commercial, or military spheres, they served as a votive objects; and above all they were objects of art. While Porada (1980:3) has observed that in the ancient south west Asia, seals were meant to make marks on clay as signs of the ownership of property or to authenticate a document. While Nissan (1977:15), remarks that the stamp seals, which preceded cylinders had a function in the economic system. Thus, Dilmun engaged in the international trade between the east and the west needed its own stamp seals not only for foreign trade but for domestic purpose as well, for the proper functioning of its economic and administrative system.

One of the important purpose authentication of trade documents which the Dilmun seals served, and for which they were designed is manifested from an impression on a cuneiform tablet (Fig. 1) discovered at Larsa. The tablet preseved in the Babylonian collection of the Yale University (Yale), is dated to the tenth year of Gungunum, king of Larsa, i.e., 1923 B.C. (Buchanan, 1965 : 204-209; revised 1967:104-107; 1981-382). Though this seal's impression is found on a tablet in southern Babylonia, but the origin, (from which part of Dilmun) of the tablet and the seal it bears in unknown. The seal is similar to those found in Dilmun cities : Failaka (Kajaerum, 1983 : 79, No. 76), and Bahrain (Bibby, 1965 : 137, Fig. 3a). The seal is definitely of Dilmun origin. But how it reached Larsa, there are two possibilities. Firstly, the owner of the seal, Dilmunite, must have carried it, on a visit to Babylonia to finalise a business transaction and after settlement he must have impressed it by way of agreement and authentication of the deal. Secondly, the cuneiform tablet itself

Fig.1 A Dilmun seal on a Cuneiform Tablet discovered at Larsa dated to 1923 B.C. (From Babylonian collection, courtesy : Sterling Memorial Library, Yale University, Yale).

with the seal impression, might here originated in Dilmun and transmitted to Babylonia as a record of transaction and agreement reached. This is also quite possible, as several cuneiform tablets have been discovered in Bahrain during excavations.

Again, another purpose the ancient seals served was that on the package of goods transmitted an impression of seal was attached to the pakage. This, was probably, by way of identification of the sender and authentication. Caspers (1972:10) has recorded one such example of seal impression from Umma (Djokha) attached to a pakage containing some merchandise for despatch to Mesopotamia by an Indian merchant.

Archaeological excavations and surveys in Bahrain and else where in the neighbouring countries have brought to light three categories of seals (1) Stamp seals (Round steatite and other shapes) ; (2) Shell seals; and (3) Cylinder seals. The round steatite stamp seals are characteristically Dilmun seals. Some of the rectangular seals are of foreign origin may be of foreign merchants residing or visiting Bahrain. Likewise about 30 or more cylinder seals found during excavations in Bahrain are not of Dilmun but of foreign origin. Regarding the origin of cylinder seals there are two possibilities. Firstly, as they are of foreign origin, they may be of the foreign merchants residing/visiting Bahrain on business and they might have died in Bahrain, as we find them in graves along with the skeletons. Secondly, it is also quite possible that some Dilmunites might have got them made abroad and owned them. In the absence of sufficient evidence the two presumations are quite possible.

Nearly 400 Dilmun seals have been discovered, so far. It is beyond the scope and purpose of this volume to list out or describe all these seals. Here only a few important seals of different categories depicting a variety of subjects and motifs are described and illustrated in order to highlight the cultural, artistic and technical achievements of Dilmun civilization in glyptic art.

Secondly, shell seals seems to be native to Dilmun and are described here briefly. In fact Shaikha Haya and M. Rice's (1986:251ff) arguments points to the thesis that shell seals preceded steatite seals. But since these were found together with the steatite, and in the absence of proper evidence, I have dealt them after the steatite seals. In fact I feel, on the basis of archaeological evidence, Ibrahim (1982) and Mughal (1983), that the two were contemporary and were used simultaneouly by some people. Thirdly, cylinder seals have been discovered in Bahrain during excavations, first at Qal'at al Bahrain (Bibby, 1965:137) and later on at al Hajjar graves (Tarawah; Rice 970-71, 1988). Subsequently these have been found in the graves at Hamad Town, al Maqsha etc. However these are all of foreign origin (Porada, 1970); Beyer, 1989:59) and not native to Bahrain or Dilmun, as such they have been excluded from here. Most probably they were owned by the Mesopotamian officials who were residing in Bahrain to look after business or official interest. This view is further attested by the discovery of a cylinder seal recently (1992) from a grave at the new site of al Maqsha having cuneiform inscription. (Abdul Aziz Sowailah, personal communication).

Further, discovery of several cuneiform tablets in Bahrain also confirm that these cylinder seals belonged to foreigners and were brought by them for their use.

(A)   STEATITE STAMP SEALS (ROUND)

Characteristic Dilmum type seals (as will be evident from the following pages) have been found in Ur excavations by Leonard Woolley in 1928-29. In 1932, Gadd (3-22) published these seals; and in the absence of sufficient number of Dilmun seals known at that time from the Gulf and lack of other evidences, and in view of strong Mesopotamian-Indus relations, he considered them as "Seals of Ancient Indian style found at Ur". No doubt in the collection were present some seals of Indus style. But there were also present six/seven Dilmun type seals of Gulf origin. This is attested by the large number, nearly 400 or more similar steatite round Dilmun seals recovered during the excavations and surveys in Bahrain from 1945 onwards. Further, Egon Hansen's (1959:238) discovery at Qal'at al Bahrain in 1959 of a workshop for the stamp seals characteristic of Dilmun culture of third and second millennium B.C. attest that the Dilmun seals found at Ur were of Gulf origin, and obviously from Bahrain. Again the discovery at Diraz of a fragmentory blank of a black steatite seal strongly suggests that there was more than one workshop operating in Bahrain. (Caspers, 1977:54f). Following Gadd, Bibby (1958:243-246) described the seals discovered from the stratified occupation levels in the city site of Qal'at al Bahrain as "The 'Ancient Indian Style' seals from Bahrain". Bibby's description brought to light the characteristic features of these Dilmun seals. They are defined by the reverse bearing a shallow/high boss with one to three grooves and four center pointed circles. Some seals have no circles. Later on, Buchanan (1965:206, 1976:105) and Kjaerum (1980:45ff) considered these features on the reverse as the characteristics of Dilmun stamp seals.

In Fig. 2 are illustrated different types of reverse side of the Dilmun stamp seals showing boss, grooves across the boss and dotted circles. Fig. 2a has a high boss with one groove across its boss. Fig. 2b has one groove but boss lower. Fig. 2c is lower boss with two grooves. Fig. 2d has lower boss, one groove and four dotted circles, two on either side of the groove. Fig. 2e has lower boss, two grooves and four dotted circles. Lastly, Fig. 2f has three grooves and four dotted circles. I have classified the stamp seals on the basis of these reverse side features as follow : (1) Early Dilmun seals with high or low boss and with one or two grooves across the boss; (2) Intermediary Dilmun seals with low boss, one or two grooves and four dotted circles; and (3) Late Dilmun seals with low boss, three grooves and four dot-in- circles. These are the characteristic features of Dilmun seals which distinguishes them from those of contemporary neighbouring countires.

Classification of stamps seals discovered in 1954, at Qal'at al Bahrain by Bibby were considered to be similar to those found earlier at Ur. Bibby argues that the presence of identical seals at Ur and Mohenja-Daro proved that there had been contact between India and Mesopotamia during the time of Indus Valley Civilization. But he asserts that the round

264

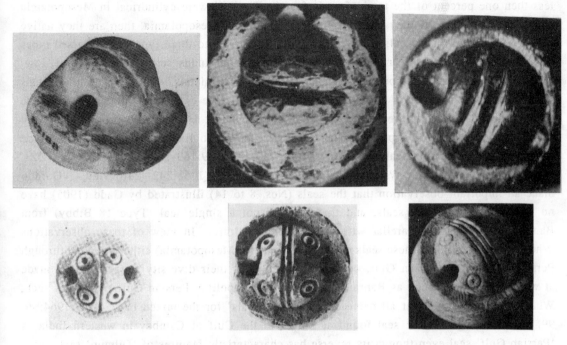

Fig.2a-f   The reverse side characteristics of Dilmun Seals.
(Above) (a) high boss, one groove; (b) lower boss, one groove; (c) lower
boss two grooves.
(Below) (d) lower boss, one groove and four dot-in-circles ornamentation;
(e) lower boss, two grooves and four dot-in-circles; and (f) lower boss, three
grooves and four dot-in-circles.

Fig.3   Indian Style Seal with a bull and Indus script from Ur.
(Courtesy : Trustees of the British Museum).

stamp seals were "foreign" both in India and in Mesopotamia. In both cases they formed less then one percent of the total of seals found. The rest were cylindrical in Mesopotamia and square in India. If they were "foreign" in India and Mesopotamia, then are they native to Bahrain ? The round seals Bibby classifies differently into three types, high bossed types with the bulls and Indus script, high bossed type without Indus script, and the third, low-bossed circle-ornamented type with designs of human and animals. However, the three seals from Mohenja-Daro were of the high-bossed type, while the two from Bahrain were of the low- bossed. All these three types of seals were found at Ur. Types one and two were found in Mohenja-Daro. Types two and three were native to Bahrain. The low-bossed type were designated "Dilmun seals" by Bibby (1958:243-47; 1969:163-166, 177, 180). Col. D.H. Gordon and Sir Mortimer Wheeler commented on Bibby's (1958:242- 246) views. Gordon made an important observation that the seals (Nos. 8 to 14) illustrated by Gadd (1905) have no resemblance to Indus seals, and that there is not a single seal (Type 18 Bibby) from Bahrain which has any parellal with the Harappan culture. In view of these observations Wheeler suggested that : these seals might have come (to Mesopotamia) either overland through Persia or from the Persian Gulf, or, more probably, as their diversity suggests, were made at various entrepots (such as Bahrain itself) of a cosmopolitan Persian Gulf trade. As such, Wheeler proposed the over all name 'Persian Gulf seals' for the mixed bag. Rao (1964:96-99, Pl. IX) designates the seal found at Lothal in the Gulf of Cambay in western India as 'Persian Gulf' seal even though its reverse has characteristic features of 'Dilmun' seals, viz., low boss, triple lines, four circles with a central dot. On the lines of Bibby, Buchanan (165:204f) also made a similar classification of these seals into three types. Type I pure Indus Style; Type II, local; imitation of the Indus style, and Type III, a homogeneous round though distinctly different but related to Type I. The backs of Type I usually have a high boss with a single groove. While Type III has a lower and broader boss with three grooves and four dotted circular decorations. Since many seals of Type I and III have been known from Bahrain and Failaka, Buchanan called them as "Gulf seals", Type II beign the earlier and Type III the later. They were named "Tilmun Group". Later, Buchanan in 1967 (104-109) revised his paper of 1965 and agreed to Wheeler's designation and called them as "Persian Gulf seals". Woolley (1982:135) designates the Ur finds as 'Gulf seals'.

The characteristic features of the Dilmun seals are described by Porada (1971:331-338), who while making comments on the seals found in the Gulf states (Bahrain and Failaka) groups them into two main groups, an 'earlier one' and a 'later one'. The earlier group, she mentions as characterised by a disc shape with a button boss pierced in one direction and divided across the other by a groove. The latter though resembles the earlier group in the basic disc shape and central boss, but the latter being comparatively much lower, wider, and has three parellel lines with four circles and dot within. In the first category humans were absent and had animals only. Humans actually gods in human form are depicted in the later category in wide variety of scenes. To this grouping we must add an intermediary group, similar to the early one but having two grooves (see Fig. 2 d, e). Mughal (1983:64-

66) following Porada (1971), classified the 22 stamp seals found from the excavations of Sar burial mounds, as 'early' and 'late' Dilmun seals. That is, seals without human figures but generally showing animals and other symbols and without well defined button backs as 'early' type; while those with human figures and incised button back are grouped as 'late' type. However, Mughal introduces new term "Early Barbar" seals and states that seals from Qal'at al Bahrain are characterised by the button boss similar to 'late' or 'Dilmun' seals with a single instead of three incised lines running across the perforation. That is by 'Early Barbar' Mughal implies late type Dilmun seals.

Mitchell (1986:278) while discussing Indus and Gulf type seals from Ur follows Buchanan's classification of Gulf seals and restricts the name "Gulf" for Buchanan's Type III seal alone. Kjaerum (1986:269) while discussing the Dilmun seals as evidence of long distance relations in the early second millennium B.C. divides the unifacial seals with doomed reverse into two types. The first type has, as an ornament, only one or two grooves diagonally across the dome. And the second type has the same design and in addition has four circles, placed symmetrically around the grooves or lines. The second type has been named as Tilmun Type by Buchanan (1965:206). While Kjaerum (1086:269) considers this nomenclature as the diagnostic for the Dilmun area during the first half of the second millennium B.C. and states that though the difference between the two type is apparently minor, but actually it has a major difference with regard to style and motifs depicted on them. Animal figures and symbols of various types are the dominant features of type I. While the characteristic featueres of type II or the Dilmun type are religious aspects - ritual scenes involving cities, cult objects and sacrificial animals. This charge in the seals seems to have occured during Ur III period towards the end of third Millennium B.C. That is, Kjaerum (1986:269) considers only the type II as Dilmun seal and not type I even thought it is also of Dilmun, irrespective of characteristic features and when the difference is minor. While Beyer (189:136f) designates both type I and type II and other types as "Dilmun seals" and groups them into four categories - first, intermediate, standardized type - late group and lastly Kassite or late Bronze Age type. He is justified in calling all Bahraini or Dilmun seals as "Dilmun seals". But Beyer's labelling of the fourth group as "Late Bronze Age type" does not seems to be proper as he has not designated the earlier types as early Bronze Age type or middle Bronze Age types. Thus assigning the fourth group alone to Bronze Age raises doubts as to whether the three other groups belong to ages or periods other than Bronze Age. As a matter of fact the entire Dilmun period falls within the Bronze Age of Bahrain covering the period from 4000 B.C. to 1200 B.C. Again Beyer's calling the third group "standardized type" without mentioning any norms of standardization leaves other three types as non-standardized. He has not given any name to the first type., while he has named the remaining three types.

Potts (1990:161-168) discusses "Persign Gulf seals and chronology" in his recent publication and distinguishes the Gulf glyptic by 'Persian Gulf' and 'Dilmun' on the basis of Wheeler's comments of 1958. The 'Dilmun' seal tradition, according to Potts is represented by the seal found in level 14 (at Qal'at al Bahain), the upper most of the two early building-levels. And the seal recovered in level 21 he states as belonging to the earlier 'Persian Gulf' group. He describes the features of the two types separately into two chapters, and lists in a table the seals of the 'Persian Gulf' published to date. The list records the seals mentioned by Gadd (1965), Bibby (1967-69), Ibrahim (1982), Mughal (1983) and others. Except Gadd, the seals recorded by the three others are those recovered during excavations in Bahrain. As late as 1990 when we have seveal hundreds of seals recovered from excavations and stratified sites from Bahrain and Failaka, I think, we should not continue to adopt the term 'Persian Gulf' seals which Wheeler had coined in 1958 on the basis of a very few seals recorded by that time, their origin being unknown, and in the absence of sufficient data for study and analysis. Moreover by the term 'Persian Gulf seals' Wheeler had implied all the seals illustrated by Bibby, a mixed bag, which included, early and late Dilmun seals and Indian style seals all emanating from the Gulf. Now Potts has divided the seals into two groups 'Persian Gulf' seals and 'Dilmun' seals. I think the former also includes the seals of latter group. Wheeler at the same time had suggested that the 'Persian Gulf' seals were made at various entrepots (such as Bahrain itself). Subsequently workshop for the manufacture of Dilmun seals has been found in Bharain (Glob 1959:238). There seems to be more than one workshop in Bahrain (Caspers : 1977:54). Now the question arises about the origin of actual place of 'Persian Gulf' Seals? Where they were manufactured? This could be no other place than Bahrain itself. Evidence suggest that they were neither manufactured in Mesopotamia nor in India even though we find Indus or Harappan script on them. These seals have no parallels at the latter place. Because they were first discovered in Ur and exact origin being unknown, but were sure to have originated from the Gulf area, they were proposed as 'Persian Gulf' seals at that time. But how can we call 'Persian Gulf' and 'Dilmun' seals when both these types of seals have been recovered at the same time from Bahrain during excavations of mounds and settlements as well as stratified sites ? When we are sure of their origin and manufacture in Bahrain it is not proper to continue to designate them with the vague or general term. A critical study of the seals discovered during excavations in Bahrain by Bibby (158:PL26, 27; 1957:143; 1966:76, 79), Ibrahim (1982:158f, Pl. 60f), Mughal (1983:531), Srivastava (1991:239); reveals that these seals are of Bahraini origin and all are Dilmun seals; but of earlier period/phase. And the seals generally accepted as 'Dilmun' seals are of later period/phase, manufactured with improved technique and design.

The diversity or differences in the features of the so called 'Persian Gulf' seals and 'Dilmun' seals may be explained as follows : (1) In the earlier phase during the initial stage of seal making in Bahrain, the maker had made the reverse of the seals by a high boss, with one/two groove(s). Later on, with the progress in seal making , modification was made by adopting a lower boss with three incised parallel lines and four dotted circles. (2) On the obverse side, during the initial period, the owners and makers of the seals have, at first thought, adopted only animals and other abstract symbols. Later on, as they improved the desiging and most probably as a result of outside influence, they started introducing human figures and better motifs, in the seal as we find them in 'Dilmun' seals. This is quite obvious as in all cases even today, things will be crude and improperly designed in the initial phases and later, as industry and faculty of the mind of the designer improved and progressed things became refined and better. Thus with advancement of glyptic art, we find Dilmun seals of better design with improved technique, elegant in appearance than the so called 'Persian Gulf' seals. (3) The depiction of humped bull (zebu) with or without Indus script in the seals, may be explained in two ways. Firstly, that the Indian traders visiting or residing in Bahrain seems to have been responsible for the origin of sealing in Bahrain or Dilmun. The seals in the possession of the Indians in Bahrain and also the round Indus seals with bull and manger design that accompanied the merchandise on its travel through the Gulf, as suggested by Caspers (1976:24f), were the model or prototype for the Dilmunites to adopt the round shape, button boss, and incorporate the similar design in the beginning. She further states that the common type of 'Persian Gulf' seals developed out of the Indus Valley impetus. The naturally rendered Indus bull with lowered head in the 'Persian Gulf seals' and later replaced by "ringed-neck" bull type, in the 'Persian Gulf' glyptic repertoire, establishes, says Caspers, Indus Valley influence and relationship. Potts (1990:165) too is of similar opinion, and attributes Bahrain-Indus Valley connection to the very origin of sealing in the Arabian Gulf region. So, we may presume, that the Indian merchants, visiting or residing in Bahrain, needed seals for their business transactions, for the authentication of documents etc., and they must have had made first their seals with bull and Indus script. Following this innovation, Bahraini merchants too must have adopted the making of seals for their personal use. And since Bahraini's could not adopt Indus script in their seals, and as they did not had any script of their own, they had to obviously resort to adoptation of animals and abstract symbols in their seals. Thus seals of earlier period with bull and Indus script may be attributed to be belonging to Indians residing or visiting Bahrain; while those with or without bull, with other animals and abstract symbols may be those belonging to Bahraini people. And both these categories of seals are also of Bahrain or Dilmun, but of an earlier period than the so called 'Dilmun' seals. The adoptation of Harappan motiffs and script to the Dilmun seal form, suggests Brunswig et al (1983:11), to be a acculturative phenomenon, similar to that occured in Mesopotamia by the adoptation of Harappan traits to the cylinder seal. Thus, Dilmun seals are a result of cultural interaction. (4) From technical point of view with regard to the technique of manufacture and characteristic features of the two categories of seals, it is observed that there are certain features common between the two categories and a critical study clearly reveals that the 'Dilmun' seals evolved from the so called 'Persian Gulf' seals. Potts (1991:168) is also of similar opinion and he too finds some degree of overlap and certain features common between the two categories. He calls such types as 'aberrant' seals indicative of transition. Earlier, Beyer (1989:137) has also noticed this feature of overlap and he called these trasitional types as 'intermediate' types, as distinct from the 'early series' and 'late series' of Dilmun seals. In view of the above argument and in view of the fact that both the categories of the seals have been found together during excavations of burial mounds and cities in Bahrain or Dilmun, the nomenclature 'Persian Gulf' seals is no more applicable.

Thus, we may conclude that all stamp seals with characteristic features of Dilmun seals on the reverse are Dilmun seals, irrespective of they having been found at Ur or Lothal or in the Gulf states. These Dilmun seals may be grouped into three types: 'early', 'intermediary' and 'late'. The seals found at Ur are also Dilmun seals of 'early; and 'intermediary' periods. They must have originated from Bahrain or anywhere from Dilmun. This is attested by the fact that recently, 1984-85 a similar seal with bull and Indus script was discovered in a burial mound during excavations, at Hamad Town in Bahrain. (Srivastava, 1991:25,239). Since they have Indus or Harappan script, they must have belonged to Indian merchants residing at Bahrain or Ur, and trading between Mesopotamia-Bahrain-Indus Valley. They do not seem to have originated form India, as such type of seals are not found in India. Further, the sequence of Indus letters or signs on the seals from Ur, have generally no perallel in Indus script, observes Brunswig et al (1983:104). As such we may classify the Dilmun stamp seals broadly into three categories - Early Dilmun seals; Transitional or Intermediary Dilmun seals, and Late Dilmun seals. Typologically these unifacial circular stamp seals may be classified into several sub-types under each. The order may perhaps illustrate evolution of Bahrain's seals from crude designing to perfect desiging.

Type I	A	-	Plain
	B	-	With perforation only.
Type II	A	-	Single Groove with perforation.
	B	-	Double Groove with perforation.
	C	-	Four Grooves with perforation.
Type III	A	-	Two Dotted Circles.
	B	-	Four Dotted circles with single groove and perforation.
	C	-	Four Dotted circles with three grooves and perforation.

In these seals the engraving has been made with a gouge, some what deep but without the use of a drill. The motifs are often inclined at an angle of 90° to each aligned on the same ground line. They have treated either in style schematically or in a naturalistic way. In the case of the second type use of tools like gouges and drills are evident from the deep engravings. (Beyer, 1989:136). The first stamp seals seem to have probably appeared during the Agade period to which there is a tendency to attribute the levels of the Qal'at al Bahrain City I. The first type seems to cover the Agade period until Ur III Dynasty when the type II seems to have appeared. (Beyer, 1989:137). The change in seals from type I to type II seems to have occured during the Ur III period towards the end of the third millennium B.C. This is evident from the seals of early type II or early Dilmun type recovered from Barbar temple II and dated by carbon-14 to 1975- 2025 B.C. and 1945-1965 B.C. This is corroborated from the Failaka evidences. Circumstances suggests, states Kjaerum, that the evolution of the Dilmun seals took place on Bahrain, but evidences indicate that their motifs to a great extent were inspired and influenced by the foreign countries such as Mesopotamia, Syria/Anatolia and India. (Kjaerum, 1986 : 269f).

(I)   EARLY DILMUN STAMP SEALS

In this category are descirbed Early Dilmun seals with distinct characteristic of a disc shape with a button boss pierced in one direction and divided across the other by a groove (Gadd, 1932 : 194ff; Porada 1971: 331ff). And the observe having a bull with or without Indus script, other animals and with abstract symbols. Such type of seals have been first discovered at Ur in Mesopotamia in 1928, then at Qal'at al Bahrain from 1957 onwards, at Lothal in India in 1962-63. All are round of white or grey steatite. The Early Dilmun seals may be grouped in two categories - (1) Indian style seals with Indus script and probably belonging to Indians having connection with Dilmun, and (2) Indian style seals without Indus script and probably belonging to people of Bahrain or Dilmun.

(1)   INDIAN STYLE SEALS (WITH INDUS SCRIPT)

Five complete seals with bull and Indus script have been found at Ur during 1928-29 excavations by Woolley. Three more seals are partly broken have Indus script in the upper portion (Gadd, 1932). May be they had a bull in the lower portion. One seal with a bull and Indus script was discovered in a burial mound during excavation (1984- 85) at Hamad Town in Bahrain (Srivastava, 1991:239). The description of the seals from Ur (Figs. 3-10) given below is based on that of Gadd (1932:3-22; 1979:115-122); and Legrain (1929:298f), they are dated to third millennium B.C. The seal of Fig. 3 is circular stamp seal, lower edge slightly broken of steatite, with highly glazed white surface. The reverse has a pronounced button boss, pierced in one direction and divided across the other by a groove. The obverse has a short-horned bull with lowered head. The upper portion has Indus-Harappan script letters, numbering five. The script is not readable and cannot be interpreted. The seal of Fig.4 is similar to that of Fig. 3 as regards the reverse side. The obverse has a bull, with a lowered head, and without a manger or anything under the head. In the upper half, along the periphery are 4/5 letters of Indus script. Fig. 5a is of glazed steatite and originally had the pierced boss at the back but not broken away, leaving only the trace of the boring. The bull is of the short-horned variety and stands over the manger. The Indus script letters are very clear on top of the bull. The Danes excavated a seal (Fig. 5b) from Qal'at al Bahrain during the 1970 season. It features a short- horn bull, in the lower half, facing right. Above the bull, in the upper half of the seal are inscribed five letters of Indus script or Harappan sings. It is round in shape of diameter 2.75 cms., thickness one cms., and boss 0.7 cms. Brunswing etal (1983:104) states that it is made of green semi-translucent steatite. The small high boss has single groove across. The excavators found it along with a cuneiform tablet. Earlier also in 1959 from Qal'at excavation of City II the Danes found a similar seal having a bull, but in bad condition, the features having been effaced. (Brunswing et al, 1983:104). The Indus inscription of this seal (Fig. 6) is crowded and not very distinct. Bull passant with lowered head. A flower shape sign or letter is more distinct on the right

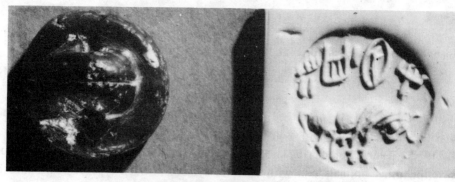

Fig. 4 (Above) Indian style Seal with a bull and Indus script from Ur.

Fig.5a (Centre) Indian style seal with a bull and Indus script from Ur.

Fig.7 (Below) Seal from Ur with a bull and Indus script
 (Courtesy : Trustees of the British Museum).

above the bull's head could be also foot-print. A few more letters are seen along with a round white spot or blob above the bull in the centre. Legrain (1929:306) suggest that the letters are pictorial signs of primitive writing. It is of grey steatite found in Ur pre-dynastic cemetery.

The seal (Fig. 7) is comparatively bigger in size. It has a diameter of 1.25 inches and height of 0.75 inches. It is of almost black steatite, but caused with usual creamy glaze which has worn off at the edges. The reverse has a boss, with single groove, and perforation. In the upper half of the seal are five Indus script characters; most prominent among them are two schematic human figures in standing posture besides each other. On the right appears fish sign (damaged). Below the inscription, in the lower half a bull is depicted in the act of mating with a cow. The head and legs of the latter are not very clear due to damage. The tuft at the end of the tail appears like an arrow- head, hanging invertedly. Three stamp seals from Ur are broken. But since their reverse has button boss similar to those described above and same as that found in Early Dilmun seals, they are mentioned here. Two seals (Fig. 8, 9) have Indus script; and in one seal (Fig. 10) a bull is visible. From the illustrations it is clear that they resemble the above mentioned seals (Fig. 3-7) in every respect. The material of seal (Fig. 8) is greenish-grey steatite; while that of Fig. 10 in brownish grey.

Two seals (Fig. 11 a, b) in the possession of the Department of Antiquities of Bahrain have bull and Indus script or Harappan signs. Caspers (1976:25. Pl. 5, 6) has published these seals and are reproduced here. The Harappan signs are schematic representation of humans in un-proportionate sizes in the two seals. However, Caspers' statement based on some one else, that the seals have "the normal 'Persian Gulf' boss with grooves, pierced holes and four dot-in-circle pattern", does not seems to be factual. As, no seal, so far, has been reocrded having Harappan signs and these features on the reverse side. Probably she has been mis-informed. Thus, taking for granted that they do not have four dot-in-circles, they are grouped here under early type, tentatively. (Caspers 1976:25, pl. 5, 6). Supposing, if the statement comes out to be true, then the seals fall under the category of late Dilmun seals. But such possibility is very remote; during late Dilmun period such features seems to have been discontinued. The seal (Fig. 12) has a unicorn bull in the charging posture, in the lower portion; and above it, a peacock, looking backwards. On top, along the circumference are four letters of Indus script. Srivastava (1991:26) has deciphered these four letters, reading from right to left as 59, 233, 25 and 1, in accordance with Mahadevan's Concordance. The reverse has a button boss with two perforations directed at either end of the bottom and groove across on the top with a diameter of 2.9 cms, the maximum height of the boss is 0.5 cms and its thickness is 1.7 cms. It is of fine grey steatite. Srivastava observes that the sequence of letters in this seal is almost similar to that from Mohenjo-Daro cited against No. 1190 on page 44 of Mahadevan's Concordance.

Fig.5b (Above left) Seal with a bull and Indus script (After A.Parpola, 1983).

Fig.6 (Above right) Seal from Ur with a bull and Indus script. (After C.J.Gadd

Fig.8 (2nd row) Portion of a seal from Ur with schematic figures of Indus script.

Fig.9 (3rd row) Part of a seal from Ur with Indus script and high boss reverse.
(Courtesy : Trustees of the British Museum).

Fig.10 (4th row) Portion of a seal with a bull and Indus script. (after C.J.Gadd, 1979)

(2)   INDIAN STYLE SEALS WITHOUT INDUS SCRIPT

The Danish, during their excavation (No. 520 LB) in 1957, within the city-wall at Qal'at al Bahrain discovered a seal (Fig. 14) having on the obverse side, figure of a bull surmounted by those of scorpion and a human foot-print. On its reverse is a dome boss with perforation and a single groove across the boss, perpendicular to the perforation. It measures 2.8 cms in diameter and 1.6 cms in height. It is of green steatite, baked, white glaze on the surface. (Bibby, 1957 : 143, Fig. 136; 1958 : Pl. XXVII; Beyer : 1989 : 140). This seal is similar to that of Fig. 6 found at Ur, but without the Indus script. The two have a bull and two naturistic symbols, a foot-print and scorpion. Same motif, but with the addition of one more animal or bovid above the bull in a vertical posture replacement of the foot print, horizontally with three figures only is found in another seal (Fig. 13). Two symbols not clear, provenance unknown. Facsimile of the seal exhibited in the Bahrain National Museum. These motifs are of Harappan influence. From the thick occupation levels of the Barbar period at the central area of the tell at Qal'at al Bahrain the Danish recovered a steatite stamp seal (Fig. 15) of diameter 1.6 cms, which is considered by Bibby (1966:76, 91) to be of well known Bahrain/Failaka type. Features not clear. There appears to be a bull at the bottom, and besides it, on the right a scorpion. If the seal is rotated by 90° and viewed, there appears probably an schematic outline of a man in dynamic posture. The Danish during their eleventh campaign, 1965, discovered, in the levelling layer above the occupation levels, nine stamp seals. One of them had the remains of the cord in its suspension-hole. The collection comprised early as well as late types of Dilmun seals. Of these five seals (Fig. 14-18) fall under this category under review. Two are of later period and two are broken. These seals (Figs. 14 - 18) are of diameters : 2.2 cms, 2.1 cms, 2.0 cms, 2.5 cms, and 2.6 cms. All are having animal motif, (Bibby : 1966 : 79, 91). Similar motif is found in another seal (Fig. 17) discovered by the Danish in 1957 at Qal'at al Bahrain, in a layer of beach sand (level 21), which soon after the erection of the forification wall had been laid immediately behind it. It is 2 cms in diameter and of black steatite, without 'glaze'. The reverse bears a high boss with two grooves and no circles. The obverse has a figure of a quadrupad, more resembling a goat than a bull, with above its back, a star like figure and, view by rotating, appears a gazelle, (Bibby, 1957 : 143, 157; 1958:244).

(II)   INTERMEDIARY TYPE DILMUN SEALS

Seals retaining the characteristic features of early Dilmun type but with the addition on the reverse by four dotted circles, two on either side of the groove are considered as transitional between the early and late types of seals, while the obverse having similar motifs as the early type with or without some modification. A few such examples are illustrated here. (Figs. 19-20). Of these, the two were discovered at Ur and two were found in Bahrain and preserved in Bahrain National Museum. The Ur finds were recorded by Gadd (1932:104f; 1979:11f). According to him the diameter of the steatite seal (Fig. 19a) is 11/16" with the

Fig.11a,b (Above) Seals from Bahrain having a bull and Indus script.
(After During - Caspers, 1976).
Fig.12. A seal with a bull and Indus script from Hamad Town graves. (Left & Centre)
Fig.13. A seal with Harappan sign and other symbols (on right)
(Courtesy : Bahrain National Museum)

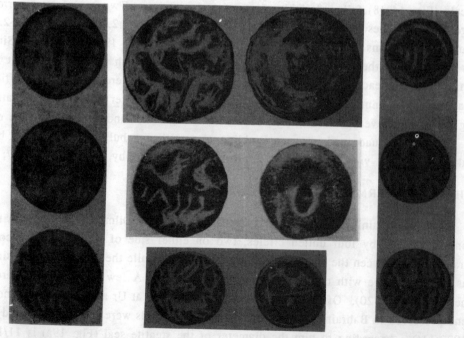

Fig.14-18 Indian style seals without Indus script. (After P.V.Glob and G. Bibby,
Kumal)

usual features. He comments that the device is puzzling. The bull with long horn is roughly depicted. There appears to be another bull, when viewed by rotating the seal by 90° The reverse has two grooves with two dot-in-circles on either sides. Regarding the other seal (Fig. 19b) Gadd remarks that is has unsually high boss and a single groove across it and in material and style it is similar to those Gulf seals found in Ur. The observe has a scorpian and, some symbols, possibly an eye or probably some characters of Indus script. Similar elleptical symbol is found on two seals of later period with three grooves and four circles with dot (see Figs. 37 a, b). It may be probably Harappan sign, but when placed vertically, of phonetic value 'P'. Below this (Fig. 19b) at the bottom there appears a symbol like 'Y', of phonetic value 'W'. On the top left margin three/four lines, joined together. But when the seal is rotated by 180° and viewed, there seems to be a schematic figure of a man. This again is an Harappan sign for 'r' (Rao, 1984 : 197).

Another seal (Fig. 20) in this cateogry has single groove of early type and four dotted-circles of the later type. Two bullmen are in fighting style with a child between them with upraised hands, as if trying to prevent the two men on his sides from attacking each other. Below the three men in the lower half of the seal is a bull with long horn facing towards left. The man on the right seems to be holding in his right hand something to protect, in a form of an arch. It is from 'Ali cemetary'. This seal is a departure from the motifs found in early Dilmun seals with the introduction of humans in the design. This seal is an intermediary or transitional between the early and later types of Dilmun seals with regard to features both on the reverse and the obverse. A grey steatite seal (Fig. 20 b) from Sar mounds has a white glaze. The boss on the reverse has two grooves and four dot-in-circles devices. On the obverse is a bull facing towards left, surmounted by two gazelles tail to head. The space between these three animals has been filled up by a scorpian. A large crescent, symmetrical to the curve of the neck of the bull is incised. While there is another one but small and thin on top of bull's head. Its diameter is 2.4 cms., height including the boss is 1.3 cms., and without boss 0.8 cms. (Ibrahim, 1982 : 82, pl. 61, 5). The collection of seals discovered by Ibrahim (1982) and Mughal (1983) from Sar burials consists of early, intermediary and late types of Dilmun seals with regard to reverse and obverse features. And thus suggesting that for a considerable period of transition from early to late type, the early types continued to be used.

(III)   LATE DILMUN SEALS

The characteristic features of the late improved Dilmun seals are : the reverse has a low-domed boss with three thin parallel grooves in the centre separting the two, on each side, dot-in- circle devices, (Fig. 2f). While on the obverse a large number of subjects and motifs have been introduced. E.g., Humans, gods, animals, abstract symbols, drinking scenes, geometric pattern, podium, altars, gate, standards, scenes in rafts in ships, erotic scences etc. The introduction of new motifs in the Dilmun seals have been attributed to the foreign influences of Mesopotamia, Syria, Anatolia etc. The motif of bucranium seems to be Syro-

Cappadocian or early Syrian cylinders' influence. The association of birds and bucranium is from the common Cappadocian motif. Drinking scenes, common in Early Dynastic times and continued into Akkadian period were also introduced in Dilmun seals of late types. (Buchanan, 1965 ; 207). Circular pattern of heads of animals is considered to be from Achaemenian imitation, (Porada : 1971: 335). The dress and the horned crowns of the gods, bullmen, monkeys, etc. menifest Mesopotamian influence as well as spiritual affinity. The representation of single figures as well as composite figures and themes on Dilmun seals is influenced by the glyptic art of the Levant. (Kaejrum : 1986 : 271f). Thus Dilmun received different cultures from abroad and by amalgamating them produced its own style. And he reciprocated and transmitted its culture to others as well. For instance, the design of Susa stamp seals were inspired by Dilmun's stamp seals, observes Amiet (1986:267). However, in some cases we find Harappan symbols of early types have been continued to be incorporated with the new motifs. Most probably such seals were owned by the Indian merchants or agents operating in Bahrain for handling trade between the east and west. Since Kjaerum (1983) has published a catalogue of Failaka/Dilmun seals by classifying them thematically by grouping into four categories, hence inorder to have a standard and uniform pattern or system of all Dilmun seals and to facilitate comparative study; I have adopted here the same classification of Kjaermn's "Group I, the Dilmun type" for describing Bahrain's late Dilmun seals. But, except for Indian style seals; because this category falls under early type and has been described above. Kjaerum has recorded only one seal having Indus inscription. I have made some changes in Kjaerum's classficiation with regard to animals and animals and men and has made some sub-classifications. Kjaerum's classification is as folows : Group I - the Dilmun type - Unifacial stamp seals (28 categories); Group II - other unifacial stamp seals (5 categories); Group III - Bifacial stamp seals (3 categories); and Group IV cylinder seals (6 categories). As far as Bahrain is concerned, groups II and III and absent, to the best of my knowledge. Also a few types or categories found in Failaka are absent in Bahrain. So, Bahrain, has Kjaerum's Group I and IV, with the addition of shell seals. The shell seals from Bahrain are described seperately in this chapter. Beyer (1989 : 135 ff) too followed a similar classification, while cataloguing Bahrain's seals, but his listing is restricted to nine categories thematically, as against 28 of Kjaerum.

RADIAL AND WHORL COMPOSITIONS

From the basin of the third Barbar Temple the Danish (excavations No. 517 AOY) discovered a grey steatite seal with three groove lines and four dotted circles on the reverse (Fig. 21a), from Bahrain National Museum. On the obverse is the radial motif consisting of necks of six horned animals which are joined in the centre of the seal by a circle with a dot in the centre. The orientation of the heads gives an impression of a moving wheel. On top between the two heads is a tree. It measures 1.1 cms in height and 2.3 cms in diameter. It has been dated to early second millenium B.C. Porada (1971:335) has drawn attention to the similarity between the radial motifs consisting of animal protomes which

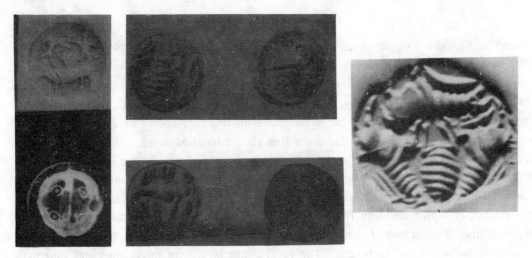

Fig.19-20 Intermediary type Dilmun Seals.
Fig.19. (Left) and Fig.20(Right) (Courtesy : Bahrain National Museum).
        (Centre) Fig.19a,b (after C.J.Gadd)

Fig.21a,b,c Dilmun seals with Radial and Whorl Compositions.
            (Courtesy : Bahrain National Museum)

are found in Bahrain, Failaka, Anatolia and Indus. (Mortensen, 1970 : 392; Kjaerum 1986 : 270f; Beyer, 1989:152). A variant of the same pattern, but difference in the central joint of the four necks of the animal was also found at Barbar Temple III. In Fig. 21b, the necks of the animals are joined by a four pointed star of unequal points. The branch of the tree is absent and the wings of the animals are modified. Another vareeant of the same pattern as in 21a is shown in Fig. 21c from Bahrain National Museum. Here the six necks of the horned animal are directly joined together without a circle or star connecting them. A seal (Fig. 22a) found at Ur during 1930-1 has an engraved face divided into four quadrants by lines, each of which terminates at the edge of the seal in some object, possibly a vase or vessel, out of which dividing lines emanate. In each of the quadrants a naked sitting figure are found. Two of these figures, clasp their hands upon their breasts. The seal measures 7/8" in diameter and 7/16" in height. The reverse has boss with three lines and four dot-in-circles. It is preserved in the British Museum. (Gadd, 1932 : 3-32, No. 9; Mitchell, 1986:286, Fig. 115).

Four stylised bulls heads (bucrania) in the quadrants of a seal (Fig. 22b) from Ur are stylistically engraved on the observe. The quadrants are formed by four forked branches springing from the angles of a small square, with some internal decoration. It was found during 1929-30 season and is preserved in the British Museum. It measures 15/16" in diameter and 3/8" in height.

COMPOSITIONS IN VERTICAL PANELS

In 1970 from a grave (No. 11 of site 1) of Al Hajjar a black steatite unbaked seal (Fig. 23a) with three incised grooves/lines across the boss with perforation was recovered. The obverse has in the central field, a vertical, chevron-patterned panel, with parallel lines. On both of its sides is a vertical motif, perhaps a palm tree, in a crude form, and a zigzag line. The pattern of the seal has been carved in a geometric style, and deeply engraved. The border is hatched pattern. It measures one cm. in height and 2.15 cms. in diameter. On the basis of similar seals from Failaka. Beyer (1989 : 156) assign this seal to the Kassite or late Bronze Age period and dates to second half of the second millennium B.C. Though the stylistic features of this seal are similar to those from Failaka (Kjaerum, 1983 : 29, Fig. 49) and dated to the Kassite period, the reverse design of only groove lines and perforation are similar to type II B-C of Bahrain and dated to late third millennium B.C. Since it is the only seal of its type so far discovered it is difficult to assign proper dating. A similar type, but with three incised lines across the reverse without dotted circles and on the obverse in the centre is the standing human figure holding something in the hands, probably candles, with parallel lines on two sides separating from a snake/serpent on the left panel and a palm leave on the right panel. (Fig. 23b). The central figure seems to be schematic. Photo from the Bahrain National Museum.

SCENES BY A GATE OR SHRINE

From the Barbar temple (N. 517 AUU) the Danish excavation recovered a grey steatite seal (Fig. 24a) having four dotted circles and three groove lines. On the obverse is a nude man standing in the middle of a vertical rectangle which could be a frame of a door or niche of a temple. The man is holding a vessel in both the hands. On the right of the frame is a scorpion; while on the left side is an antelope. It measures 0.95 cms., in height and 2.2 cms., in diameter. It is dated to early second millennium B.C. (Bibby, 1969 : Fig. 7b; Beyer, 1989 : 149). Anderson (1986 : 177) considers the naked man depicted in the above seal, to be Enki god in his apsu. At the north west part of the city wall at Qal'at al Bahrain, the Danish (Bibby, 1965, 137) during excavation (No. 520 ABA), found a grey steatite seal (Fig. 24 b) with white surface. It has triple lines between four circlets having a dot on the reverse side. The obverse side has a design of horizontally placed ladder dividing the seal into two halves, each having a bucranium, facing inwards from the opposite quadrant. Symmetrically opposite is palm, but with the addition of a human foot-print in the upper left quarter. In the middle, at right angles to the ladder is upper half of a nude man, with upraised hands. With his right hand he supports the crescent symbol. While in his left there appears to be branch of palm leaves. The replica of the man is repeated in the lower half of the seal, but inverted. This is evident when the seal is viewed by rotating 180°. Thus, in this seal there is double impression of each of the following, man, bucranium, palm, crescent, and palm leave, but only one foot-print.

SCENES BY AN ALTAR

Seal (Fig. 25a) with a nude man in half-standing and half-sitting posture on the right side of a rectangular net podium in the centre lower-half of the seal. One hand is on his waist and with right hand touching a bovid over the podium. On the other side of the podium is a horizontally hatched lentoid symbol. Provenance unknown. Photo from the Bahrain National Museum. In another seal (Fig. 25b) a nude man holds a central square net podium. Below it is a bull facing left. The reverse has three grooved lines with four dotted circles. This seal was discovered at Barbar temple during Danish excavations (No. 517 ARE). It is grey steatite seal with white surface (baked). Its height is 0.8 cms., and diameter 1.7 cms. It is dated to early second millennium B.C. (Beyer, 1989 : 149). A third example has an unsually elongated rectangular net podium flanked by the dragons on the two side with no human. From Bahrain National Museum, provenance unknown. The podium and other features in the Bahrain seals are similar to those recorded from Failaka (Kjaerum, 1983 : 36-51).

SCENES BY A STANDARD OR PODIUM

A standard naked man, schematic, holds with his left hand a podium. Over the square net podium is a crecent standard (Fig. 26a). The staff the standard does not rest directly

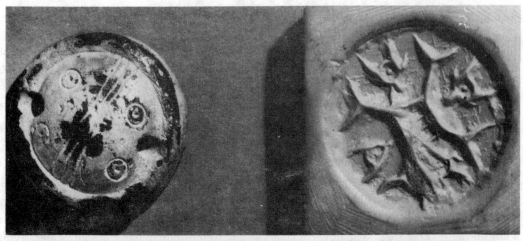

Fig.22a,b   Seals with Radial and Whorl Compositions.
(Courtesy : Trustees of the British Museum).

Fig.23a,b   Seals with Compositions in Vertical Panel.
(Courtesy : Bahrain National Museum)

over the podium. Below the latter is a bull facing east-wards. In front of the bull is a an arrow-head, half-shaded, half-black. Along the right periphery facing the bull, there seems to be a serpent, not clear. Over the head of the standing man, in an inverted posture is some animal, incomplete. This seal was found in the Barbar temple site. A seal has a central rectangular net podium flanked by two hounds and on top is the standard of crescent and sun. Besides it is some vague symbol, may be a vessel. On the two extreme sides, behind the hounds are two rectangular nets of vertical lines, supported by a vertical shaft in each case. Provenance unknown. From National Musuem of Bahrain.

SCENES WITH CRESCENT STAFF

A crescent with staff extending to the full length of the seal with a disc on top (Fig. 26b). On the sides there seems to be antelopes, not clear. From Bahrain National Museum. The disc may be representing sun.

SCENES BY A TREE, MAINLY PALM

The Danish, during their eleventh campaign in Bahrain in 1965 found nine steatite stamp-seals and one clay bull from the area within the north wall at Qal'at al Bahrain. (No. 520 AMH). One of these seals, has a central palm (Fig. 27a) held by a nude man with his right hand facing towards the palm, while with the other hand he holds a "Sheild or a Gate" symbol. On the other side of the palm is an ibex. Down at the border are small fishes. In between the tree and man is foot-print placed vertically, (Bibby, 1966 : 79), Beyer, 1989 : 150). In another example (Fig. 27b), one man, is sitting on a horizontal hatched trapezoid stool; while the other standing, both holding a central palm tree. The sitting man has a fowl in his lap. Adjacent to the standing man there is a gazelle. It is dated to early second millennium B.C. It was recovered from Barbar temple IIB by the Danish (Excavation No. 517 AQB). (Mortensen, 1970:392; Beyer, 1989 : 151). Several examples of this type of seal with palm and different scenes, flanked by animals, human sitting on either side etc. are recorded. Palm seem to have had special reference by the people.

DRINKING SCENES

Several Dilmun seals with drinking scenes have been found in Bahrain. Briggs Buchanan (1965:206) while discussing the Gulf seals has pointed out that the motif of drinking was common in Mesopotamia during Early Dynastic times and continued into the Akkadian period. Similar motif with birds and bucranium appeared on provencial Syrian cylinder seals. The occurence of various types of drinking scenes on Dilmun seals suggests Bahrain's connection not only with Mesopotamia but Syria as well. In a seal from Bahrain National Museum (Fig. 28a) two garbed men, facing each other with hatched skirts are sitting on hatched rectangular stools and holding drinking tubes leading to a common jar. Between them in

Fig.24a,b   (Left) Seals with Scenes by a gate or shrine.
Fig.25a,b   (Right) Seals with scenes by an altar
             (Courtesy : Bahrain National Museum)

Fig.26a   (Left Above) Seals with Scenes by a standard or podium
Fig.26b.   (Left Below) Seal with Scene of crescent staff.
           (Courtesy : Bahrain National Museum)
Fig.27a-b (Centre and Right) Seals with Scenes by a tree / palm

the centre is the standard, crescent with rising sun. The cresent is having a staff with two lines. It appears as a tree branch constituting the staff of the crescent. In the Bahrain Museum Guide (n.d.) this seal is dated to 2300 B.C. In another seal (Fig. 28b) of the same date, from al Hajjar graves has two garbed men are drinking with tubes from a common jar. One of them with horned head dress is sitting on a small stool, while the other man is standing. Beyer (1989:146) considers the former as a god while other as an ordinary man. It is strange that god and a commoner drinking from the same vessel. A stylized foot-print is on top centre above the jar. The foot is similar to that in Failaka seal (Kjaerum, 1983 : No. 177, 178), but in the case of Bahrain seal the foot fingers appear reversed. A bird is depicted behind the seated person. Below them at the bottom centre is a gazelle facing left. According to Beyer, it is grey steatite, baked, with traces of white surface, height is 1.1 cms and diametre 2.4 cms. It has three lines and four dotted circles on the reverse. In another seal (Fig. 28c) in the Bahrain National Museum two garbed seated men, seated on a hatched rectangular stools and wearing vertically hatched skirts, and holding drinking tubes leading to a common vessel at the bottom. Between them and the tubes, in the top centre is a gazelle facing eastward. Provenance unknown. In another seal (Fig. 28d) two seated men with hatched skirts seated on stools hold short drinking tubes leading to a common jar placed between them at about the knee height. On top centre, above the tubes is a symbol of radiating sun. At the bottom, in the centre, below their feet is gazelle in running posture and facing eastward.

Contrary to the above mentioned four seals, in one seal (Fig. 28e) only a single person is depicted with a long drinking tubes from a jar. He is having a hatched skirt and is seated on a hatched stool with a back-rest. In front of the drinking man is a gazelle looking backwards with a bent neck. Behind the seated drinking person is one nude standing man holding or supporting the arm of the man in front of him. The reverse has three lines with four dotted circles. Provenance unknown. From the Bahrain National Museum.

From Sar al Jisr excavations of graves the Arab Expedition (Ibrahim, 1982) recovered seals of which one has a drinking scene. In it (Ibrahim, 1982 : 159, Fig. 2) two schematic men sitting on stools, one opposite the other, with a jar between them, drinking through tubes leading to their representative blob heads. Between their heads on top centre is the representation hand/foot. The common jar seems to be enclosed in a 'V' shaped stand. From the Sar Burial complex, one seal with drinking scene was recovered out of the twenty two stamp seals. It shows two human figures drinking from one vessel with long tubes. On top in the centre star is depicted. It is dated to ca. 1923 B.C. (Mughal, 1983 : 66, PL. XLVIII, 3). In another seal from Sar a standing man is shown holding a long tube from a jar; but not in the actual act of drinking. An impression of a circular stamp seal on a Bitumen was discovered by the Danish at Qal'at al Bahrain during their excavations (No. 520 ABV) of 1964. The impression has a representation of a drinking scene of two persons seated on stools with back rests. The drinking tubes are represented two curved lines emanating

Fig.28a-e   Seals with drinking scenes.
(Courtesy : Bahrain National Museum)

Fig.29a-c   Seals having Naked men with symbols and animals.
(Fig.29a, after J.C.Gadd; others courtesy : Bahrain National Museum)

from a vessel of square shape. In the space between the tubes is a bull bucranium and over it two curved lines. The seal impression measures 2.7 cms in diameter, height 1.35 cms., length 3.2 cms., width 2.6 cms. It has holes for passing string (Bibby, 1965 : 137, 147; Beyer, 1989 : 147).

NAKED MEN WITH SYMBOLS AND ANIMALS

During the fifth excavations campaign (1957-58) the Danes discovered in Barbar, in the rubbish level south of the south wall of the upper temple a steatite stamp seal (Fig. 29a). On the obverse are two naked men standing, facing each other, and holding a sheild or gate symbol between them and holding lances or spears. On top is an elleptical symbol, like an eye. May be Harappan symbol for 'P' but engraved horizontally. At the bottom beneath the gate symbol is a swimming bird. The reverse is domed, pierced, and decorated with three parallel lines and four dot-in-circles. At the time of its discovery in 1957-58 it was considered by the excavators to be the first seal found in the third millennium B.C. culture levels in Bahrain. (Glob, 1958 : 141, 144, Fig. 5). A seal from the Sar burial mounds depicts a naked man in the centre (Fig. 29b) in dynamic posture, holding a sheild or 'gate' symbol in his right hand, while with the left dragging an animal by the neck. The head of the animal seem to have been chopped off. At the bottom, between the space of the man's legs is an impression of foot, placed horizontally. The point of the heal is conneced to a circular blob. All these features are enclosed in an ornamental circular frame.

The British during the excavation of Sar settlement in 1990-91, discovered a seal (Fig. 29d) from house 1, area 2. It measures 2.2 cms. On its obverse are two naked men. On their left is a large fish with open mouth. The other man has a vessel in his right hand and the left hand on an a antelope, looking backwards. Between the necks of the two men, is a small crescent. Above the latter, with some space or gap, on top, is sun symbol, partially radiating.

From the Barbar Temple III B basin, a Barbar pottery sherd of red clay was recovered bearing a seal impression. The seal has the motif of a beardless standing man flanked by two ibexes, which he holds them by their neck. The sherd measures 7.5 cm. in length. the diameter of the seal is 2.2 cms. It is dated to early second millennium B.C. The practice of applying seals on pottery for ownership purpose is extremely rare. (Mortensen, 1970 : 385; Beyer, 1989 : 144). In the above mentioned four seals (Fig. 29, a, b, c, d) naked men are depicted as main or prinicipal characteres along with the animals. In some seals animals took the main feature with naked men as secondary character. In one such type of seal from Karana, a bull in the lower centre half is depicted with three crounching gazelles above and besides, extending to the full width of the seal. On top is a small crescent. In the right margin a naked standing man is shown in low profile. Besides the head of the man is some animal or bird in smaller size. It appear as if the man is releasing the bird with his left hand. Another seal (Fig. 29c) has a serpent flanked by two dragons on

287

Fig.29d-e Seals with Naked men and animals (Courtesy : Bahrain National Museum)

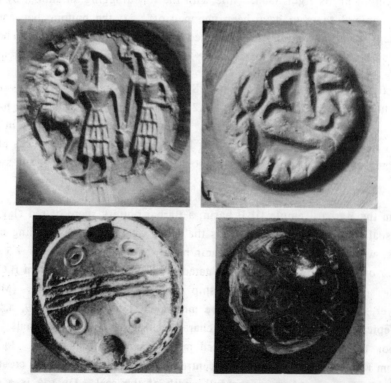

Fig.30,31 Seal from Ur with garbed men or bullmen with animals.
(Courtesy : Trustees of the British Museum)

either sides. On two sides in the margin are two naked men in standing posture, holding some device. On top, in the centre is the crescent, which the serpents support. Form a house (No. 1), Sar settlement the British team discovered several seals, one of them is illustrated here (Fig. 29e). It shows a naked man standing with a spear in his hand trying to attack the two rampant gazelles. the bodies of the latter are crossed at the waist giving an X shape appearance. Symmetrically opposite to the man on the right side is the third animal, looking at the gazelles. At the crossing point of the two gazelles in the centre, there is a vertical staff supporting the standards of crescent on top. The diameter of the seal is 2.16 - 2.67 cms. (After Crawford, 1991 : 260).

GARBED MEN OR BULLMEN WITH ANIMALS

During Ur excavation of 1925-6 a seal (Fig. 30) was discovered from the loose soil close to the surface. It is of light grey steatite with the usual creamy surface. It measures 2.2 cm., in diameter and 1.15 cms., in height. The scene depicted seem to be sacrificial. Two garbed men facing left and holding a vessel between them and the one on the left holds by neck the goat-like animal. The skirts, which the men are wearing, has three rows of vertical lines, resembles the characteristic early Sumerian garment of fleece. Further, as Gadd (1932 : 9f) remarks the style of delineating the heads and the attitude of goat would be entirely normal as Sumerian. Gadd further comments that the interest of this seal resides in its combination of a Sumerian device with form and material which are no less clearly those of the Indus Civilization. The reverse is characteristically Dilmun type. It is preserved in the British Museum.

Another seal (Fig. 31) from Ur (1926-7) bears a long-horned Ox below an uncertain object, probably a quadruped and a rider at right angles to the Ox (counter clock-wise). Gadd (1932 : 10) presumes that it is an attempt to show the Ox(s) in a couching position, when seen by rotating by 90°, anticlockwise. If that was the motive then the head of the second bull is turned back, and the remaining space, was perhaps meant for another animal or a bird, as the practise in the Sumerian art. (Gadd, 1932 : 10; Mitchell, 1986 : 282f).

GOD OR HERO BETWEEN TWO ANIMALS OR PROTOMES

An enthroned garbed god, Legrain (1929 : 299), states moon-god, wearing a horned crown facing right a seal (Fig. 32a). Behind him are bullmen standing in attendence and each wearing a triangular horned mitre and long hair tied in a roll. The god, wearing a hatched skirt is seated on a hatched stool. Below him is a passant bull looking left. Legrain suggest that it is the emblem of god. This seal (Fig. 32a) was discoverd during Ur excavation and measures one inch in diameter and 7/16" in height. Its characteristic features are of Dilmun seals. Gadd (1932 : 3- 32; 1979 : 118) remarks about this seal that the Sumerian character of the device is strongly marked by the depiction of ithyphallic bullmen, the so-called 'Enkidu' figure which is common in Babylonian cylinders of the early period. The bull-men also have horned head-dress and the moon-symbols upon poles seem to represent the door-poles that the pair of 'twin' genii are commonly seen supporting on either side of a god. Gadd observes that this seal is completely of the "Indus" type so far as material and shape are concerned; whereas the device is much rather Babylonion than India.

A seated god, facing left wearing a horned crown is flanked by two antelopes on the two sides and a bull below him is featured on a seal (Fig. 32b) from Hamad Town mounds. The skirt of the god is vertically hatched, in the margin facing the bull head is vertically hatched, in the margin facing the bull head is a tree branch; while symmetrically opposite to it, at the back side an uncertain horizontal symbol or animal is seen with two parellel curved lines emanating upwards from its back. Between this symbol and the tail of the bull is one small vertical stroke. In this seal there is neither any bull-men nor any other symbol of standard. It is preserved in Bahrain National Museum. A seal (Fig. 32c) from Buri mounds and exhibited in Bahrain National Museum has a god wearing a horned crown and seated facing right, on a stool of three outlines, each smaller than the other. In his left hand the god appears to be holding a standard of crescent, within which is a triangular symbol. Possibly a representation for a star. The god is flanked by a bull-man behind him and an antelope in front. Beneath him a bull facing right. In the margin below the face of the bull is a tree branch. The bull man appears to be holding a lance in his right hand. Both the bullmen and god are garbed. The latter has at skirt hatched horizontally with two rows of vertical lines for the upper portion, while the flounced lower 'portion, has the hatching in single row. Excavation of Sar burial complex by Mughal during 1980-82 brought to light several seals. Of these one of them (Fig. 33a) is of a seated god facing right and wearing a horned crown and below him a bull with a tree branch. On the top right margin are only heads of the animals. The god has his right hand on his waist; while the other on the head of the animal in front. (Mughal, 1983 : 66, 475) several such types are illustrated by Mughal.

From the same Sar burial complex, three seals (Fig. 33b, c, d) are recorded with heroes or men either seated or standing, flanked by animals. In two seals (Fig. 33b, c) the men are garbed with skirts of vertical hatching. While in one (Fig. 33d) the man is naked and holding the gazelles with two hands, while beneath him is the third one. In seal (Fig. 33c) the man is standing on a hatched stool holding a pipe from a vessel. The two gazelles, in front and behind him are in regardent posture. From Ibrahim's site (B/A4.2, Fig. 49 No. 4) one seal of single groove was recovered. Whereas non from Mughal's site. Both have plain boss. These two categories of seals are of early Dilmun period.

Sometimes the hero is depicted as directly standing or riding on the animals. In the seal (Fig. 34a) from Karana, garbed man, in plain skirt, facing left, is shown standing over the gazelle and holding with his left hand; with his other hand he holds a sheild or 'gate' symbol. From the National Museum of Bahrain. From one of the al Hajjar II graves, dated

Fig.32 a. (Top-L.-R.)Seals with god or hero between animals or protomes.
(After J.C.Gadd, 1979)

Fig.33a,b. Seals of god or hero with animals (After R.Mughal, 1983).

Fig.32b,c. (Below) Seals of god or hero with animals.
(Courtesy : Bahrain National Museum).

to late third millennium B.C. or early second millennium B.C., a baked steatite stamp seal (Fig. 34b) was recovered during the excavation conducted by Fayez Tarawaeh and Abdul Aziz Fakhroo. It is baked steatite seal with characteristic features of the late Dilmun seals on the reverse. The observe has a scene of a short bearded man with head-dress standing on the back of a gazelle, with lowered head facing right. The man is wearing a "Kaunakes" skirt. The man is flanked by a naked man behind him and a regardant gazelle in front. It measures 2.55 cms. in diameter and 1.15 cms. in height. (Rice. 1972, 60f; 1988 : 84, 93; Beyer, 1989 : 145). The British expedition during their second season of 1991-92 discovered several interesting steatite stamp seals. One of the seal (Fig. 34c) has a grabed standing figure of a man flanked by two bouncing gazelles on two sides. The man is facing towards right. While the two animals face in the opposite direction. On the left, below the animal, there is a foot-print along the margin. The man is wearing a skirt, hatched by vertical lines in four sections.

ANIMALS WITH FOOT-PRINT AND OTHER SYMBOLS

From an area with in the north wall of at Qal'at al Bahrain nine stamp seals were discovered during 1965-66 season (AML520) by the Danish team. Of these one of them (fig. 35a) has two animals and a foot print. The main figure is the bull facing left. Above him, placed vertically (may be viewed by rotating the seal 90° anti-clockwise) a goat. In the margin, behind the tail of the bull and below the feet of the goat is the foot print pointed downwards. Its diameter is 2.3 cms., and height 1.15 cms., from Bahrain National Museum. It is dated to end of third millennium or early second millennium B.C. (Bibby, 1966:79,92; Beyer, 1989- 142). Another seal (Fig. 35b) having a bull, surmounted by another quadruped with a head resembling that of a cock, and above a footprint, a scorpion and an uncertain symbol was discovered at Diraz by an engineer in 1953 in Bahrain on the surface of the desert near the burial mounds. It is 2.6 cms in diameter of grey white steatite. The reserve bears a shallow boss with three grooves and centre-pointed circles. (Bibby, 1958:244).

Seals of steatite similar to Dilmun seals have been recovered from the excavation at Tepe Yahya in Iran. Lamberg-Karlovsky (1970:67) describes it as a "Persian Gulf" seal of steatite with button-back perforation on the reverse and a bull, ibex, and crescent moon on the obverse and states that it has close parellel to the one reported from Bahrain of the same composition as recorded by Bibby (1966:79f). Later on, this seal (only the obverse) has been illustrated by Lamberg-Karlovsky (1983:pl. XXVK); 1974:289) which was found in a house of period IV B building, the lower most dated to 3000-2500 B.C., (Lamberg-Karlovsky, 1973:26). Since the reverse side details on the boss of the seal from Tepe Yahya is not known, it is difficult to classify it. But according to the dating of this Proto-Elamite settlement, it fits into our classification of ealry Dilmun seal. However, in the absence of reverse side detail, this seal, on the basis of Lamberg-Karlovsky's remarks, is described here. The origin or the place of manufacture of this seal is not known. but considering the recovery of three other items, unfinished stamp seal of steatite; blank stamp seal, with rear attachment (Lamberg-Karlovsky, 1970, P1.25, E, I; P1.26, N). It becomes obvious that seals were made at Tepe Yahya or at least some activity was going on. May be an attempt was being made. And in that process, influence of early Dilmun seal is evident. This may be the result of Dilmun trade in steatite or chlorite with Tepe Yahya, the latter being the source of supply of steatite. In a seal (Fig. 35b) from Bahrain National Museum a foot-print extending almost the size of the seal is engraved on top. Below it there appears to be an antelope in dynamic posture facing left with a branch of tree in front of his face. Behind the two main features is a crescent facing right.

PASTORAL SCENES

A seal (Fig. 36) from Sar displayed in the Bahrain National Museum has a bull in the lower half, with a tree above him. The tree is flanked by two animals, with their faces upwards, touching the top of the tree. Facing the bull, in the lower left margin is an elongated foot-print. Further, between the heel of the foot-print and the fore-legs of the bull is an inverted symbol of crescent engraved with a thick outline. Comparatively the pastrol scene of this seal is quite different from that of Failaka. (cf. Kjaerum, 1983 : 100ff).

ANIMALS WITH HARAPPAN SIGN AND OTHER SYMBOLS

The Harappan signs found in the early and intermediary type (see Fig. 19, *supra*) seems to have continued to be adopted in a few seals of late Dilmun period. Most probably they belong to the Indian traders resident or visiting Bahrain or Dilmun. The characteristic features of the reverse side are same as the late Dilmun seals. However, their design on the obverse appears to differ considerably from the common seals of late Dilmun period described here. The seal (Fig. 37a) from Hamad Town has a bull as a main feature. On its top is a radiating sun with a dot within the circle. In between these two features, on the left, in the margin is the elleptical sign, may be Harappan sign, engraved almost vertically. The sign is repeated at the bottom margin facing the bull. There is difference in shape of these two signs. The one above is broader; while the other is narrower and elongated. The body of the bull is partially hatched by vertical lines. In another seal (Fig. 37b) from the Bahrain National Museum, the elleptical sign, may be Harappan sign, has been given more prominent and is engraved in the centre of the seal. Above and below the sign are two antelopes/gazelle crounching head to tail. In front of them is a tree branch. The upper one is more clear and bigger in length.

Amiet (1986 : 266, Fig. 87) has reported earlier a seal discovered in Susa (Fig. 37c), of exactly the same design as we find in Bahrain's seal of Fig. 37b from Hamad Town. The elleptical sign is in the same position in the centre. However, the animals, though the very same style, but seem to be goats. Since we find exactly the same type of seals both from Bahrain and Susa, it is quite possible that the seal found at Susa had originated

Fig.33c,d (Above) Seals with god or hero with animals (After R.Mughal , 1983)

Fig.34a-b   (Below) Seals of god or hero with animals.
(Courtesy : Bahrain National Museum).

Fig.34c. (Left) A seal with garbed man and gazelles.
(Courtesy : H.Crawford, R.Killick, J.Moon, 1992).

Fig.36   (Right) Seal with pastoral scenes. (Courtesy : Bahrain National Museum)

from Bahrain. Further, the possibility of origin from Failaka is excluded as so far, we have not found such a type of seal from Failaka. Likewise, it is quite possible that this seals from Susa (Amiet; 1986:266, Fig. 88,89 etc.) also might have originated from Bahrain.

ALL ANIMALS

A late Dilmun style seal (Fig. 38) was discovered by Rao (1963:96-99) at Lothal, an important harbour-town of the Indus Civilization at the head of the Gulf of Cambay on the west coast of India. It is of steatite of light grey colour with a creamy surface. The reverse has characteristic features of late Dilmun seals. The obverse has two jumping goats or gazelle-like animals regardent and flanking a double-headed dragon. It has no script nor symbols. Though discovered in India, but in motiff and characteristic features of reverse, are entirely different from those of the normal square seals of the Indus Civilization and from the Sumerian cylinder seals. Rao observes that it is neither wholly Indian nor Sumerian in workmanship. It measures 2.25 cms. in diameter and 1.2 cms. thick at the centre. The reverse has a perforated boss covering almost the entire surface and divided by triple lines between four circles with a central dot. The carbon 14 date for a charcoal specimen from the late levels of the structural phase III of Lothal 'A' is 3985 B.P. ± 115; i.e., 2023 B.C. ± 115. As such Rao dates this seal, a surface find, to Lothal's phase III (2000 - 2200 B.C.) and concludes that it is unlikely to have reached Lothal's earlier phase than phase IIA. (Rao, 1963:96-99; 1986:376f).

From the north west part of the city wall at Qal'at al Bahrain during Danish excavation 1965-66 a seal (Fig. 39a) of grey steatite, was discovered. It measures 2.32 cms., in diameter and 1.25 cms in height. A very large domed boss with three lines and four dot-in-circles are on the reverse on the obverse probably a lion seems to be attacking a gazelle at the bottom. The latter's mouth appears to be open. On top, is a monkey trying to attack the lion. Seal in the Bahrain National Museum. (Beyer, 1989 : 144).

Eight birds/ducks form a whorl combination along the circumference of the steatite stamp seal (Fig. 39b) with their heads in the centre and within the centre of the space formed by their heads is a circular device with five sections. Between each pair of the birds (for one on the lower left not visilbe) along the periphery are crescent symbols, pointed outwardly of varying sizes depending upon the space. The neck and head of all the birds is turned towards right. The circular symbol or device in the centre is exactly same as the Harappan sign found on Indus seals. One such seal is illustrated by Mackay (1976:Pl.XVII (15)). In a seal (Fig. 39c) from at Hajjar, there is a serpent in the centre of the stamp seal, extending to the full size of the seal is flanked on either side by two pairs of antelopes, one above the other facing the one opposite the other. No symbols. Bahrain National Museum. During the second season 1991-92, of Sar settlement excavation, the British team led by Robert Killick discovered an exequisitely - carved rectangular seal (Fig. 40a) having four prancing horned bulls. In the centre, two bulls one above the other crouching head to tail are depicted.

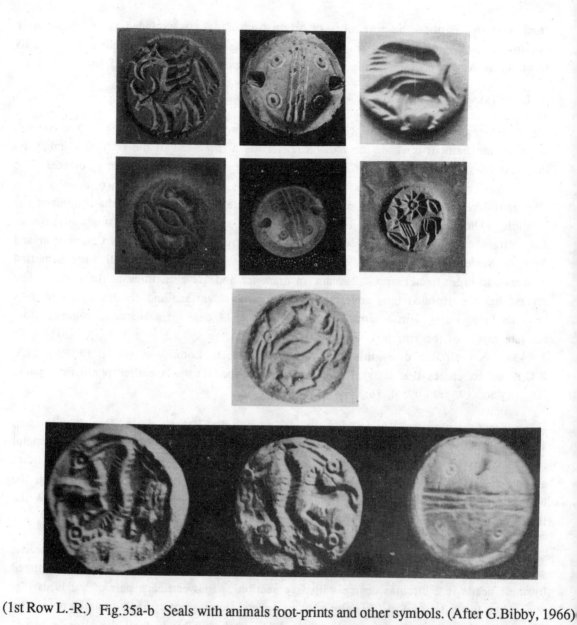

(1st Row L.-R.) Fig.35a-b Seals with animals foot-prints and other symbols. (After G.Bibby, 1966)

(2nd Row) Fig.37a,b Seals with animals and Harappan sign.
(Courtesy : Bahrain National Museum).

Fig.37c. Seal with Harappan sign and animals. (After P.amiet, 1986)

(Below) Fig.38 Seal with animals only. A Dilmun seal from Lothal (India).
(After S.R.Rao, 1963).

They are flanked on the two sides, left and right by two similar animals, with the head of the left one is upwards, while that of the right one is downwards. (Killick, Crawford, Moon, 1991, Unpublished field report).

Four bulls in different position and of different sizes are shown on a seal in Bahrain National Museum. One in the lower half of the seal is the major one facing right. Between his head and fore-legs, a small baby-bull is depicted creeping along the periphery of the seal, facing left. In the upper half, on rotating by 90°, clock-wise, two bulls, are shown at a distance from each other. The Department of Antiquities of Bahrain possesses a seal having three Harappan style bulls. Caspers (1976:25; 1979:65) published this seal. She states that the reverse has grooves, pierced holes and four dot-in-circle pattern. The seal is damaged and not clear. The same seal has been also published by Parpola. (Burnswig et al, 1983 : 164, Pl. III No. 10).

SCENES WITH RAFTS OR SHIPS

Two schematic figures of men with round blob heads, standing in a ship, on either side of the mast is depicted on a seal (Fig. 41a) from Hamad Town and displayed at Bahrain National Museum. On top of the mast is the crescent symbol. The men are flanked by a tree branch. At the bottom, below the ship, is one serpent in zigzag style, moving towards left. In another similar seal (Fig. 41b) two schematic standing men are holding the mast of vertical 'Y' shape from the opposite direction. One of them on the right, seem to carry some tool, like an hammer. There is nothing on top of the mast. Beneath the ship, there appears to be a monster with a tail and with six snakes, three or either side, emanating from his body. There is some difference between the shape of the two seals. The earlier one is of a simple design. The second one has the ends pointed upwards, and two shape metallic rods are projecting out from the right side of the ship.

DIFFERENT MOTIFS

From the Ur excavations of 1930-1, a peculiar seal (Fig. 42) was discovered from the upper rubbish Kassite (?) level, over one of the houses in the residential area. A nude man as a water- carrier, hung on either side of the yoke across his shoulders and the third is below the crook of his left arm. Two stars, one on either side of his head are shown. The entire design is enclosed by thin curved lines, like brackets, on either side on the periphery of the seal. Gadd (1979:118) states that this is unmistakable example of an hieroglyphic seal, a legend in the form of a fully developed pictures, and is unique steatite stamp seal with characteristic late Dilmun style on the reverse. Paroda (1971:336) comments on this seal and says that the relation of the water carrier with his two skins or jars to a sign of the Harappan script is very obvious and further states that Egyptian representations of water carriers are quite similar.

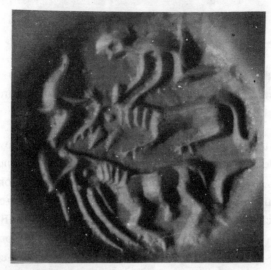

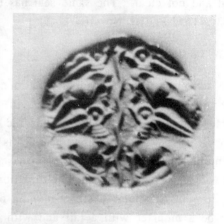

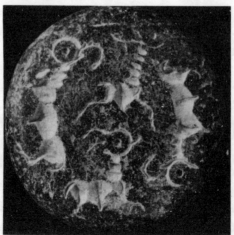

Fig.39a-c   Seals with animals only. (Courtesy : Bahrain National Museum)

Fig.40   (Below) A seal with animals from Sar settlement.
                (Courtesy : Directors : London - Bahrain Archaeological Expedition,
                                    1992).

From the Barbar temple II B, the Danish recovered during excavations (No. 517 AOX) a seal (Fig. 43) having the design of five imbricated squares on the obverse side. Around the square on the sides are galeods or worm like animals. It is dated to second millennium B.C. From Bahrain National Museum. (Beyer, 1989 : 150). The British during their first season (1990) of excavation at Sar settlement discovered five seals from house 1 alone. One of these is unique in design or motif. It has a seated human holding a pan balance over a long-necked round bottomed jar placed on a stand. Another man on opposite side watches the balance. The seal is slightly convex shaped, like a bun. Its diameter is 2.61 - 2.67 cms. (Crawford, 1991 : 259).

EROTIC SCENES

A few scenes depict erotic scenes. One such example (Fig. 45) was discovered in a stratified occupation level 14, City II at Qal'at al Bahrain by the Danes during their excavation of 1957. It is 2.1 cms. in diameter, 1.2 cms in height. (These measurements are according to Beyer (1989:148 No. 267); while Bibby (1958:244) has stated as 2.6 cms and 1.1 cms. diametre and height, respectively). It is of grey steatite with a white glaze. The obverse has a phallic naked man standing over a podium and behind a nude women with legs apart and hands on feet (viewed by rotating seal by 90°). Behind them is a gazelle, head to tail along the margin of the seal. Behind the woman on top is a hatched lentoid. The reverse has a low boss with three parallel lines and four dot-in-circles. (Bibby, 1957 : 143, Fig. 13a, 1958 ; 244; Beyer, 1989:148). A seal depicting sexual intercourse and illustrated by Erlenmeyar (1966:26) has several Harappan signs. Its reverse is characteristically late Dilmun seal features. Another seal showing sexual intercourse was found at Barbar Temple III B by the Danes during their excavation of 1969. For the illustration of this seal see : Mortensen (1970:392, Fig. 8); Porada (1971 : Fig. 7); (1986:176, Fig. 43); Beyer (1989:148, No. 288). Recently, from the Sar settlement also the British discovered from a house (No. 51) a seal depicting scene of sexual intercourse. Harriet Crawford has illustrated and described this seal (Crawford, 1991 : 261).

(B)   OTHER SHAPES - RECTANGULAR, OVAL, CONICAL ETC.

During the second season (1991) of excavation at Sar settlement by the London-Bahrain expedition, a unique rectangular seal (Fig. 46) of black steatite was discovered by the British team from one of the houses. The obverse has a podium in the right centre and a horned animal extending along the left and beneath the podium. The reverse has a triangular shaped pointed boss with three grooves and four dot-in-circles. It measures approximately 2.5 cms. (Jane Moon, personal communication).

Stamps seals of various shapes, other than round have been recovered from Bahrain. These shapes are oval, pyramidal, conical, hemispherical, oblong, hemispheriod etc. These have been listed and illustrated by Beyer (1989 : 162-164). Though these seals have been

Fig.41a,b (Above left) Seals with scenes of rafts or ship.

(Courtesy : Bahrain National Museum).

Fig.42-45 Seals with different Motifs. (42 After J.C.Gadd 1979;

43 (Below) Courtesy : Bahrain National Museum; 44 Top right)

Courtesy : Jane Moon, 1992)

recovered in Bahrain during excavations of Qal'at al Bahrain or burial mounds, or other graves, they do not bear the characterisitc features of the Dilmun seals on the reverse nor obverse. As such they have not been included here. I believe they are of foreign origin. They are usually of Neo- Babylonion period. (Seventh-sixth centureis B.C.).

(C)   SHELL SEALS

In 1964, the first shell seals were discovered by the Danish from the tumuli south of 'Ali. Fossil sea shells were carved into the shape of the Dilmun steatite stamp seals; and the natural spiral sides of the shell formed the obverse of the seal. (Bibby, 1964 : 107). Subsequently shell seals were discovered in burial graves of Sar, al Muqsha, Hamad Town, Umm Jidar, Karazakan, etc. (Khalifa and Ibrahim, 1982 : 37f; Mughal : 1983). Shaikha Haya (1986:251ff) made a detail study of the shell seals discovered in Bahrain and the details here are based on her study. Shell seals are made from the conidae species distinguished for their variety. Colours, surface, and most important, the size and thickness of their bases. Shaikha states that since it was difficult to classify them in chronological order, she had classified them in accordance with development of inscriptions carved on them. Thus she has classified them into two groups, with two and three sub-groups for the two categories, respectively. The characteristic features of the first category is that after polishing on all sides, the obverse appears spiral in shape. This feature is important for using the shell as a seal which is made round by scraping and rubbing. The reverse sides depended on the type of seal used. Rubbing it on smooth stone would result in required shape and five characteristic types on the reverse, as mentioned here : (1) having half-circles covering the whole of the surface and has a natural recessed pattern of a spiral, which ends at the apex in a circular shape on each side of which it is pierced by two longitudinal holes. (2) In this category the reverse has a pyramid-like cupole covering the entire reverse side and ending in an apex with a sharp tip. (3) A small hump in the middle is formed on the reverse of this type. However, sometimes it is flat or rounded. (4) In this type a small pyramid in the middle is found. (5) This type has completely flat reverse and appears like a disc pierced by two longitudinal holes. Seals of second category of the first group are comparatively smaller in the size than the first category and they were made by the same technique. The obverse of the seal shows a raised natural spiral shape, while the reverse is flat but apex slightly raised. The second group, in accordance with the technique of engraving, is classified into three categories. They are almost similar to the types mentioned above except for the incorporation of some animals motifs. Some of the shell seals are illustrated. (Fig. 47)

Shaikha Haya (1986 : 260) observes that if we assume that the shell seals of Bahrain are the origin of all flat circular chlorite stamp seals, then the inscriptions of the shell seals represent the distinctive character of their owners before this area was exposed to external influences (round steatite stamp seals). She is trying to suggest that shell seals preceded steatite seals of Dilmun. However, as she has stated herself (186 : 257) that shell seals, so far have not been found in domestic occupational sites (Cities I-IV of Qal'at al Bahrain) or temples, but only in burials. This implies that they are later than the cities and temples. If they were earlier than the steatite seals, then they should have been found in the stratified levels of Qal'at. I think they did not precede steatite seals by but were used simultaneously some or rather little percentage of the population, as they are not found in abundence, in hundreds as steatite seals but only handful have been recovered.

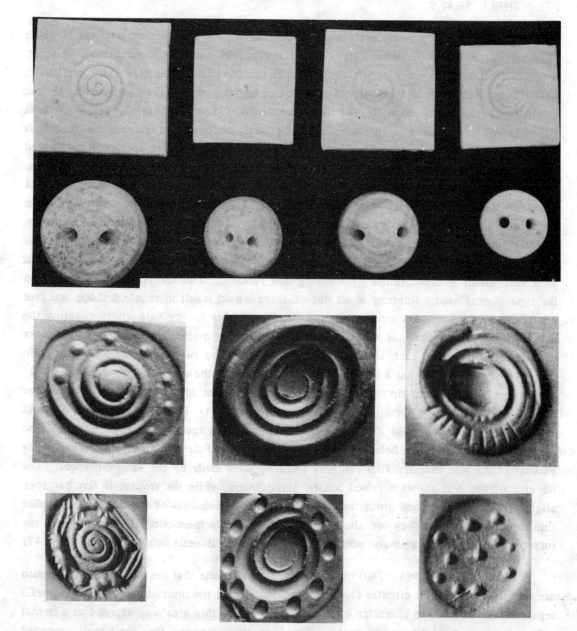

Fig.46   Shell Seals (Courtesy : Bahrain National Museum)

CHAPTER VII

POTTERY AND SOFT-STONE VESSELS

(A) POTTERY

Pottery had a very important role in the daily life of the people of prehistoric and protohistoric Bahrain. In archeological research it is an important factor in the dating of Cities and Qal' at al Bahrain, Sar settlement, Barbar and other temples, and the burials. The study of Bahrain's pottery has been made here in three chronological phases of periods: Early Dilmun (3000 - 1700 B.C); Middle Dilmun (1700-1200 B.C); and Late Dilmun (1200-400 B.C). However, strict demarcation cannot be made as some of the pottery, e.g., 'grave jar' (Fig.12d) was continued to be used almost throughout all the periods of Dilmun. A large variety of pottery spreading over a period of three millenniums has been discovered in Bahrain. It may be broadly classified into two major categories: (1) Foreign/Imported Pottery; and (2) Indigenous Dilmun pottery. In chronological order one of the types of foreign/imported pottery found in Bahrain is the earliest, as such, it is given precedence over the indigenous type in consideration here. Foreign/Imported pottery found in Bahrain may be sub-divided into four categories: 1) 'Ubaid and other pottery of Mesopotamian origin; 2) Umm an Nar pottery of Emirates; (3) Harappan or Indus type; and (4) Wadi Suq Omani type. Besides these there are decorated pottery of unknown origin; and plain and painted pedestalled beakers of unknown origin.

THE EARLY DILMUN PERIOD

I   FOREIGN POTTERY

(A)   'UBAID AND OTHER POTTERY OF MESOPOTAMIA

Chronologically, the earliest pottery discovered in Bahrain at al Markh and Diraz, belongs to prehistoric 'Ubaid culture. 'Ubaid pottery and 'Ubaid sites in Arabian Gulf were first discovered by Burkholder and Golding in 1968 and they number 17 in 1970. Masry (1974) added numerous sites to the list through his investigation and excavation. The Mesopotamian painted pottery culture called the 'Ubaid by Sir Leonard Woolley after the site of al-'Ubaid, four miles to the west of Ur, where he discovered huts characterised by chunks of reed impressed plaster and by hand made pottery painted with bold design in black or dark brown on light clay, buff or reddish when it was over fired. This type of pottery belongs to the second part of the 'Ubaid period (ca. 4300-3500 B.C). (Porada, 1971:294; Lloyd, 1978:37f). The 'Ubaid period has been conventionally classified into four distinct phases based on the major changes in architectural temple sequence at Eridu. These phases are gradual transformation of the early 'Eridu' designs. The four phases are: 'Ubaid 1 (Eridu, from virgin soil, level

XVIII level XV); 'Ubaid 2(Hajji Muhammed, levels XIV to XII); 'Ubaid 3 and 'Ubaid 4 phases corresponded to earlier and later stages in the development of the conventional culture, which reached its peak at the time of temples VII and VI. (Lloyd, 1978:4f; Oates 1986:80). These four phases are dated by Lloyd (1978:36) as follows: 'Ubaid 1 (ca. 5000 B.C); 'Ubaid 2 (ca.4,5000 B.C.); 'Ubaid 3 (4000 B.C) ; and 'Ubaid 4 (ca. 3,800- 3,500 B.C).

The first 'Ubaid sherd, a surface find, was discovered at Al- Markh on the west coast of Bahrain, in 1971, by a visitor from Saudi Arabia. The British expedition led by A.W.Mc Nicoll and Michael Roaf during 1973-75, (Report unpublished) found 'Ubaid sherds. These have been listed and illustrated by Roaf (1976:152f, Fig.7). These are described here (Fig. 1), based on Roaf, as follows:-

Grey-green with fine sand and straw temper, black paint, but partially eroded; buff close straw tempered body sherds with plain pierced lug handle and two broken mending holes, cream/grey-green slip; grey-green ware body sherd with 7 mending holes; grey-green ware with 2 broken mending holes; grey-green ware with cream/grey slip with a filled down edge; yellowish grey- green ware, rim, thin grey-green ware, rim, slightly eroded; grey-green ware with black paint; grey-green buff ware, grey - green outside, orange buff slip inside which is filled down, diameter between 22-16 cms., thin buff ware rim with fine sand temper, cream slip inside and out, diameter ca.10 cms., grey- green ware, rim, hand made wet smoothed, diameter ca.12 cms., grey-green ware ring base fragment; grey-green ware, edge filled down; thin grey-green ware ring base, diameter 4 cms., thin grey-green ware rim, black painted band inside and outside of rim, diameter 6 cms., buff ware with orange buff outer surface with 4 mending holes; grey-green ware rim, diameter between 22-17 cms., thin grey-green ware ring base; grey-green ware rim with plain pierced lug handle; grey-green ware body sherd with black paint; grey-green ware fragments of ring base with possible band of black paint on base; grey-green ware rim; grey-green ware carinated body sherd; thin grey-green ware body sherd with black paint; grey-green ware, body sherd from neck of vessel; grey-green body sherd; and pale buff ware rim with painted band inside and outside.

Specimen of 'Ubaid pottery from al Markh resembles, according to Joan Oates (1978:4ff; 1986:85), the pottery of Hut soundings of southern Mesopotamia at the end of 'Ubaid and at the beginning of the Uruk period and thus the earlier phase may be dated to ca.3,800 B.C. (Roaf, 1974:501; 1986:85). However J.Oates (1986:85) concludes that the contact between 'Ubaid Mesopotamia and Bahrain perhaps dates as early as the end of 'Ubaid 2, most evident during 'Ubaid 3, and probably continued during 'Ubaid 4, and came to an end at the very end or 'terminal' phase of the Mesopotamian 'Ubaid.

Neutron activation, petrographic and electron microprobe analyses carried out on 'Ubaid sherds (discovered by the British Expedition) from Bahrain by J.Oates etal (1977:227- 234) have shown that the sherds tested both plain and painted examples were made in Mesopotamia, often quite specifically from southern Mesopotamia. Oates etal infer that more than 50 per

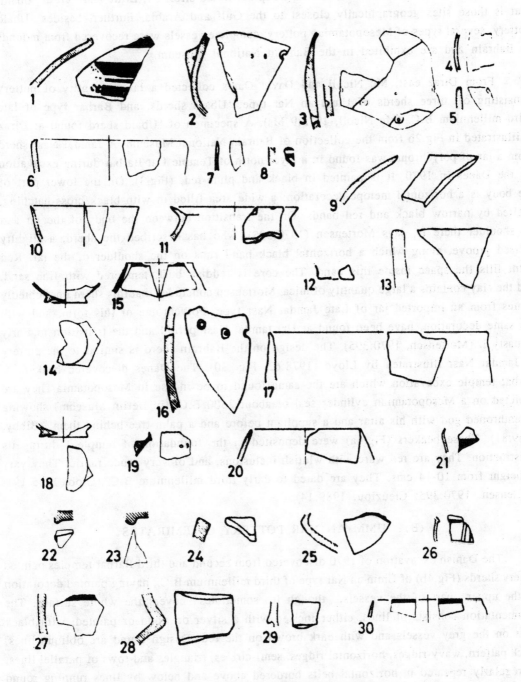

Fig. 1. 'Ubaid potsherds from al Markh. (After M.Roaf, 1976).

cent of the 'Ubaid pottery sherds from Bahrain, Saudi Arabia and Qatar can be shown to have come from the southern most known group of 'Ubaid sites, Ur, Eridu and Tell al 'Ubaid, that is those sites geographically closest to the Gulf and Arabia. Further, besides 'Ubaid pottery, several types of Mesopotamian pottery, complete vessels were recovered from mounds in Bahrain and are exhibited in the Bahrain National Museum.

From Diraz east, Mc Nicoll and David Oates collected a large quantity of pottery consisting of: three sherds of Umm an Nar type, 'Ubaid sherds, and Barbar type of late third millennium B.C. (Mc Nicoll, 1975:9 Ms). A specimen of 'Ubaid sherd found at Diraz is illustrated in Fig.2b from the collection of Bahrain National Museum. A Jamdat Nasr sherd from a jar of polychrome was found in a layer north of Temple I at Barbar during excavation by the Danes in 1970. It is painted in black and plum-red, (Fig.3). On the lower part of the body is a horizontal metope-decoration: a wide area filled in with black cross-hatching, limited by narrow black and red bands. On the transition between the body of the jar and its shoulder there is, says Mortensen (1970:395), who has described the sherd, a slighlty incised groove, along which a horizontal black band runs on the shoulder of the jar. Red paint fills the space inside this band. The core is reddish buff, tempered with fine sand, and the clay contains a large quantity of mica. Mortensen concludes that this sherd undoubtedly comes from an imported jar of Late Jamdat Nasr type. Polychrome of this form, and with the same decoration, have been found at Ur, Jamdat Nasr period and the transition to Early Dynasty I. (Mortensen, 1970:395). The design on the Bahrain sherd is similar to the pottery of Jamdat Nasr illustrated by Lloyd (1978:62, Fig .30). The Danes discovered beakers at Barbar temple excavation which are the same found to be in use in Mesopotamia.They are depicted on a Mesopotamian cylinder seal of about 2300 B.C. (in Berlin Museum) showing an enthroned god with his altar and a suppliant before and a palm tree behind them. (Bibby, 1969:81). These beakers (Fig.4a) were deposited in the foundation of temple I during its construction. They are red ware with whitish inclusions, and of very crude fabric. They vary in height from 10-14 cms. They are dated to early third millennium B.C. (Glob, 1955:191; Mortensen, 1970:395; Cleuziou, 1989:14).

(B) 'UMM AN NAR POTTERY OF EMIRATES

The Danish excavation of 1970 discovered from second and third Barbar temples painted pottery sherds (Fig.4b) of Umm an Nar type of third millennium B.C., having painted decoration on the upper part of the vessels, though it sometimes covers the whole surface. The ornamentation consists of lines, either incised with a silver or wood or painted, with black paint on the grey vessels and with dark brown on the red. Design found are oblique lines, check pattern, wavy-ridges, horizontal ridges, semi-circles, triangles and rows of parallel lines, all regularly repeated in horizontal belts bordered above and below by lines running round the vessels. (Thorvildsen, 1962:219). From the bed rock (*farush*) levels of City I at Qal'at al Bahrain, Bibby (1969:81f) found a rim sherd (Fig. 5, left) which is exactly same as the one found at the Umm an Nar settlement off Abu Dhabi (Fig. 5, right). They are virtually

Fig. 2a. 'Ubaid sherds from al Markh. (Courtesy : Bahrain National Museum).

Fig. 2b. 'Ubaid sherds from Diraz. (Courtesy : Bahrain National Museum).

identical, thus suggesting influence of Umm an Nar culture at City I. However, it does not imply complete identity of civilization. Dilmun culture is quite different from the Umm an Nar. On the contrary, not a single sherd of Dilmun's characteristic chain-ridge ware has been found in Umm an Nar. Painted Umm an Nar pottery was found by Bibby to occur through out City I levels at Qal'at al Bahrain and they terminate sharply with the building of the city wall. Typical of Umm an Nar ware are large globular vessels decorated with raised ridges, called the meander pattern and all are painted with its black-on-red chevrons and drooping triangles. (Bibby, 1986:111ff). Cf., Thorvildsen (1962:213ff) for specimens of typical Umm an Nar pottery recovered from the Umm an Nar settlement and Frifelt (1970: 357ff;1971:296ff; 1975:Figs.10,11). The very same pottery, as found in Bahrain, has been recently recovered from the tombs in 'Ajman of Umm an Nar culture, dated to third millennium B.C. They are on display at the museums of al 'Ain and Ajman. (Cf. al Tikriti, 1989:89ff, pls.50-53). From City I Bibby (1986:113, Fig.29) could recover only painted Umm an Nar sherds. Subsequently, excavations of burial mounds and graves in Bahrain produced complete vessels (Fig.6) of Umm an Nar pottery with meandering pattern, some of these are illustrated here from the Bahrain National Meseum. The pot of Fig.6a is from al Hajjar subterranean graves dated to early third millennium B.C. The vessel of Fig.6b is from a burial mound of Hamad Town dated to late third millennium B.C. The pots of Fig.6c,d, are from the burial mounds of Hamad Town. The flat bottomed pot of Fig.6e is from the burial mounds of Sar. Another variety of pots is from Sar (Fig.6f); amid a slightly different pattern (Fig.6g) with horizontal bands across the middle of the vessel comes from Hamad Town mounds. (Information on provenance: Khalid al Sindi, personal communication). From the Rifa'a mounds, Lowe (1986:77) recovered painted Umm an Nar type pottery similar to the one Bibby found at City I levels at the Qal'at al Bahrain, levels 29 to 22. The Rifa'a mound ware is mainly restricted to round- bodied jars, with flat bottom and out-turned rim. The pots are thin-walled and well-fired, often orange coloured. Lowe observes that the decorative pattern is distinctive and varies little (Fig. 6h). A series of horizontal lines border a wavy line and further down on the shoulder of the vessel a zig-zag design of interesting lines. The decoration restricted to the shoulder and upper body of the vessel is found nearly in all Rifa'a mounds. The association and the proximity of Umm an Nar painted wares and Rifa'a mound type wares in City I supports the dating of this mound to Umm an Nar period of 2500-2000 B.C. (Friefelt, 1975:392; Cleuziou, 1980:26ff). In Bahrain we find Umm an Nar painted pottery, which in turn was greatly influenced by the Harappan pottery. (Cf. Cleuziou, 1984:371-371, de Cardi, 1983:50ff).

(C) HARAPPAN OR INDUS TYPE

One painted sherd from a large jar of fine well-fired orange ware with black festoons and a chequer (Fig.7) was found in a burial mound at 'Ali. It has no parallels in Bahrain. But resembles those from Harappan culture, and similar sherds were found in the Harappan levels at Balakot. (Freifelt, 1986:129ff).

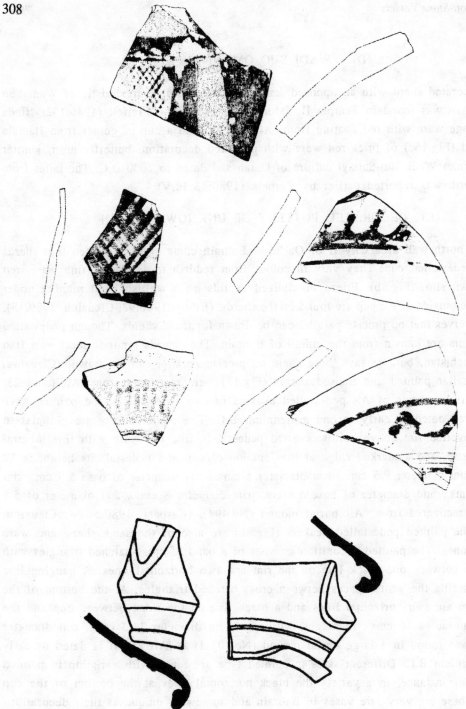

Fig.3. Polychrome Jamdat Nasr sherd from Barbar Temple I. (After P.Mortensen, 1970,
Fig. 4b. Painted sherds from Barbar Temple II and III. (After G.Bibby, 1969).
Fig. 5. Two Rim sherds from pre-city I Qal'at al Bahrain (left) and from Umm an Nar
settlement (right) off Abu Dhabi. (After G.Bibby, 1969).

(D)   WADI SUQ OMANI TYPE

A decorated sherd with an opposed semi-circular pattern, characteristic of Wadi Suq phase in Oman was found in Temple II. (Mortensen, 1986:181). Freifelt (1986:132f) finds a jar of orange ware with red coating from 'Ali (Fig.8a) and a cup or goblet from Hamala North mound (Fig.16c) of brick-red ware with plum-red decoration, butterfly motif similar or to those from Wadi Suq-Sunayl culture of Oman and dated to 2000 B.C. The latter from Hamdala North was reported earlier by Caspers (1980:43 Pl.V)

(E)   DECORATED POTTERY OF UNKNOWN ORIGIN

From north wall area City II of Qal'at al Bahrain come eight decorated thin sherds of several pedestalled cups.They vary in colour from reddish to yellowish fine ware, red to light brown slip. (Fig.8b). Frieze of stylized caprids on a whitish band running under the rim on the outside of the cup are found on the sherds. (Bibby, 1966:92; Cleuziou, 1989:15). Cleuziou observes that no precise parallel can be drawn for these sherds. Though pedestalled cups or beakers are known from the tumuli of Bahrain. The caprids reminds south east Iran or even Baluchistan, but, he says, here again no precise parallel can be drawn, (Cleuziou, 1989:15). Similar painted and incised sherds (Fig.18) were recovered from 'Ali tomb 28. From the burial mounds of Ali pedestalled beakers of two types, plain and painted have been recovered dated to early second millennium B.C. The plain beakers are globular in shape with everted rim above hollow everted pedestal in fine red ware with fine mineral temper, red slip, and a marked ridge at the junction of cup and pedestal. Its height is 12 cms., maximum diameter 9.5 cms., rim diameter 8 cms., and diameter of base 5.8 cm., rim diameter 8 cms., and diameter of base 5.8 cm., rim diameter 8 cms., and diameter of 5.8 cms. It was recovered from 'Ali burial mound (No.494). (Caspers, 1980:5, 34; Cleuziou, 1989:22f). The painted pedestalled beakers (Fig.8e) are also of the same shape and ware as the plain ones. The painted decoration consists of a band of cross-hatched triangles with concave base between one black line on the rim and two horizontal lines. A hanging line of small dots fills the white spaces between cross hatched triangles. At the bottom of the cup also there are two horizontal lines and a black line on the ridge between cup and the pedestal. It measures 16 cms., in height, with maximum diameter 11.3 cms., rim diameter 9.8 cms. It was found in a large burial mound (No.203 I) at 'Ali and it is dated to early second millennium B.C. Different sizes in painted type are found with variation in painted decoration. For instance, in a variety the black horizontal lines at the bottom of the cup are absent. These are very rare vases in Bahrain and somewhat unique as their decorations have not been found on other types of pottery. Three decorated and grey slipped pedestalled goblets were also found in a grave at Sar el Jisr. (Ibrahim, 1982, 147, 211). They are similar to those found in north eastern Iran, Afghanistan and south western central Asia during the third millennium B.C. and also similar to those found in south eastern Iran and Baluchistan around the turn of the third-second millennium B.C. (Cleuziou, 1989:23). A variety pedestalled goblets and spouted bowls from different places have been illustrated and compared recently

Fig. 6a-d. Umm an Nar pottery with meandering pattern from burial mounds of Bahrain (Courtesy : Bahrain National Museum)

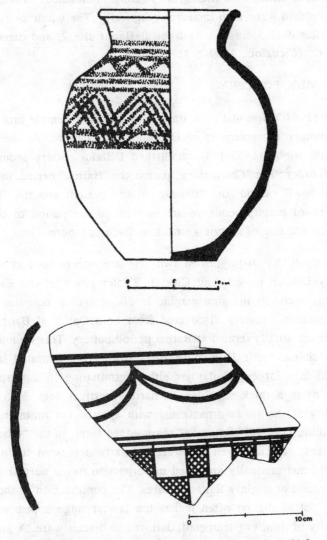

Fig. 4a. (Above) Pottery Beakers from Barbar Temple I. (After P.V.Glob, Courtesy
: Jutland Archaeological Society)

Fig. 6h. (Centre) A decorated pot from Rifa'a mounds. (After A.Lowe, 1986).

Fig. 7. (Below) A Indus type sherd of large vessel from 'Ali mound.
(After K.Frifelt, 1986).

by During Caspers (1989:13-31); and Bahrain material resembles these foreign specimens.

From al Hajjar grave (No.89) comes a cylindrical vessel (Fig.8c) with four small vertically pierced lugs, to which correspond four small holes in the base for passing strings for suspension. It is a fine red ware with red slip. It is decorated with black painted two bands of alternate groups of oblique lines separated by horizontal lines. Horizontal incised lines decorate the neck and the box. Its height is 12.8 cm, base diameter 9.5 cms., rim diameter 7.2 cms. It is dated to early second millennium B.C. and resembles those from southern Mesopotamia and those found in early second millennium B.C. grave in Oman. (Cleuziou, 1989:24). Another jar of unknown origin is reddish ware with inclusion (Fig. 8d). The whole body is covered with impressed cupula. Height 18.5 cms. It is from al Hajjar site 2, and dated to middle of second millennium B.C. (Cleuziou, 1989 : 41)

II.   INDIGENOUS DILMUN POTTERY

Danish excavations (1954-70) at Qal'at al Bahrain and Barbar Temple brought to light a variety of indigenous pottery characteristic of Dilmun/Barbar culture. At the end of the 1957 season of excavation, Bibby (1957:158) established Dilmun pottery sequence in the following six chronological order : The "Chain-ridge" period, the "Barbar" period; the "Caramel-ware" period; the "glazed-bowl" period; the "Islamic-palace" period; and the "Portuguese" period. The first three type of pottery sequence are relevent to the period of this volume. While the other categories are out of purview and not discussed here.

On the ceramic basis Bibby distinguished two separate occupations at Qal'at; City I, an early phase of early Dilmun period, and City II, a later phase of the Early Dilmun period. The ceramics forms found in the stratigraphic levels of Barbar temples were found to be identical. The characteristic pottery discovered from both Qal'at al Bahrain (City I, and II) and Barbar Temples are usually termed as Barbar period pottery. This we may designate as 'Dilmun pottery'. The characteristic Dilmun (Barbar) pottery is illustrated in Fig. 9 a-f. The dominant type (9a) is a large globular jar either terminating in a simple, slightly thickened, incurving rim, or in a thick shoulder, or narrow vertical neck 3- 5 cms., high and a rolled rim. The body of the jar is ornamented with applied horizontal ridges either of the "chain" pattern, or more rarely of continuous sharp-edged form. In the "chain - ridged" the parallel horizontal ridges were not even but were regularly depressed to form a chain like pattern, which appeared and gradually increased in porportion to the normal ridged ware (9g). The jars have either round or slightly flattened bases. The continuation of the horizontal ridges right down to the foot of the jar often makes the lowest ridge appear a ring base. The pottery is predominantly of thin, grit-tempered, dark-red to biscuit ware. A greyish white slip is some time found. All pots are wheel made. They are dated ca. 2500 B.C. (Bibby, 1957:156- 158; 1969:141).

The ware which is completely dominant in all the three Barbar temple levels is

312

Fig. 6e-f Umm an Nar pottery from burials of Bahrain.
(Courtesy : Bahrain National Museum)

Fig. 8b. Painted sherds of unknown origin. (After G.Bibby, 1966).

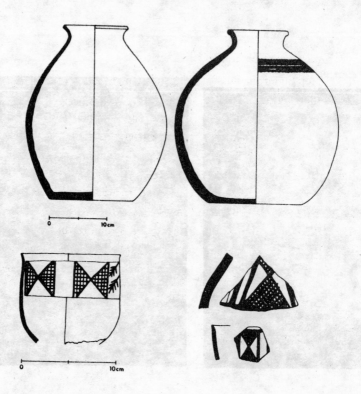

Fig. 8a. Wadi Suq Omani type pottery jar from 'Ali mound. (After K.Frifelt, 1986).

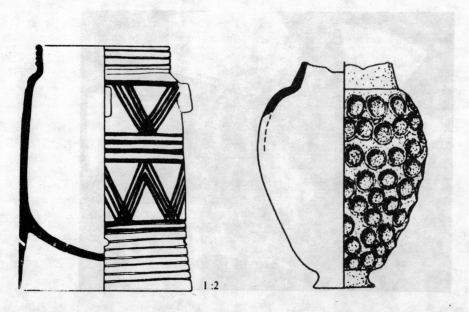

1 :2

Fig.8d-e. Painted jars of unknown origin (After S.Cleuziou, 1989)

Fig.8c. Painted pedestalled beakers from 'Ali mound.
(Courtesy : Bahrain National Museum)

Fig.11. Dilmun (Barbar) pots from Barbar Temples
(From "the Temple Complex at Barbar, Bahrain", 1983).

characterised by a hard reddish or red-brown surface covered with horizontal ridges (9b). It is characteristic of the Barbar/Dilmun culture. Bibby (1957:156) observes that the "chain-ridged" phase developed gradually into true "Barbar" phase. In this type the ridges are not sharp edged or of a "chain" pattern; but were round topped (9h). These were not applied to the pot, as in the previous case, but were built up from the paste by the finger-pressure. Some times a cream slip was added. The large globular shape of the previous type was still overwhelmingly dominant. However, greater variation was found in the rims and were carefully designed. The neck terminated in an out- turned rim of triangular section. The rim was made more thicker and was either rounded or narrowed to slightly upturned edge. They are dated to late third millennium B.C., the date of the Barbar temples (Glob, 1955:188, 192, Bibby, 1957:159; 1969:113). Three pots, recovered from the Barbar temple and identified as 'Barbar ware', same as Fig. 9b are illustrated here in Fig. 11 from the Bahrain National Museum. Similar pots are recovered from burial mounds in Bahrain. Sar (Ibrahim, 1982), Mughal (1983), al Hajjar (Rice, 1988) Hamad Town (Srivastava, 1991) etc. The third type characteristic pottery from City I is the small shallow bowl with a flat base and a straight outward-sloping wall terminating in a very short vertical wall and a slightly out turned rim. (9c). They are yellow-buff and straw-coloured, straw- tempered. They are less than 9 cms., in height and less than 15 cms., in diameter (Bibby, 1957:159; 1969:141d).

The fourth type is a hole-mouth jar, (9d) red-ware with sand temper, light yellow halves occur around individual sand grains and was found in City II. Bibby describes it as a large vessel, as big as a pumpkin and shaped like an egg, of red clay and decorated with horizontal ridges perhaps half an inch apart. The top of the pot was simply a round opening in the broad end of the egg, the rim being thickened around the opening. (Bibby, 1969:113). The fifth type of Barbar ware was common in both City I and II. It is a hole mouth jar with a short spout (9e). It is neckless vessel with a simpler, thinner rim, it is un-ridged, apart from a ring or two around the opening. They are always plain, generally with a short spout, about half an inch in height, just below the rim. (Bibby, 1969:242f).

The sixth category of characteristic Dilmun ware is a large baseless vessels with angular ridges below the rim (9f). It was of the usual red clay and bottom implies that it was meant for sinking below the floor of the house, to serve as a storage jar for some dry goods, e.g., grains. The open bottom would allow free drainage and would help to keep the contents dry. (Bibby, 1969:142). The typical Barbar pottery is a sand and lime-tempered ware, hard fired, but in the early phases seems to be rather brittle. The filling seems to have been often irregular. This had resulted in colour variations ranging from bright red to greyish and even dark red and brown wares have been found in Temple II b and III in the later phase. (Mortensen, 1986:179).

The Barbar pottery has been found not only at the cities of Qal'at but also in various burial mounds, subterranean graves, and settlements in Bahrain, but has been discovered abroad, in six Early Dynastic III A graves of the Royal cemetary at Ur, in the 'a' cemetary

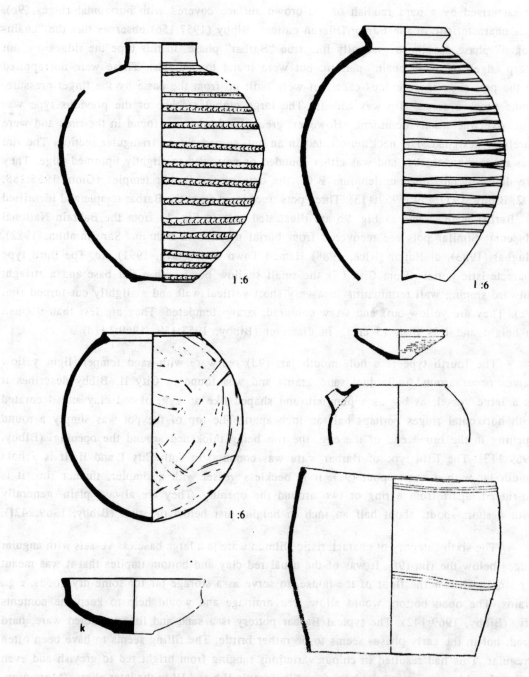

Fig. 9a-f. Characteristic Dilmun pottery. (After G.Bibby, 1969).

at Kish and Khafajah in the Dayala region, all of Early Dynasty times, early third millennium B.C. (Casper, 1971/72, 11). The main characteristic of pottery recovered from City I and City II is that very much of the City II pottery is red ware decorated with parallel ridges, while City I has ware of much the same type decorated with regularly squeezed and depressed ridges, the pattern that Bibby called 'chain-ridge'. This ware was found to be present from the very earliest level under the *farush* up through the whole City I, and in the first two levels of city II. There it overlapped with the plain-ridge ware, which commenced sharply with City II. Mixed with the chain- ridged ware and plain red sherds of City I, Bibby found some 50% of other wares. The vertical distribution of different types of pottery, chain-ridge, meander-ridge, Umm an Nar painted, plain- ridge, polychrome striped, and stemmed gazelled beakers, recovered from levels 31-8 from the city wall at Qal'at is indicated, as given by Bibby (1986:110), in Fig. 4, in Chapter II, *supra*. Chain-ridge ware was discovered from City I having chain pattern alternatively flattened and pinched together. The rim of the necked vessels was not triangular in section, but was simpler, just slightly rolled. The neckless vessels has a simpler, thinner rim, they had a tendency, in the "Barbar culture", to be unridged, apart from a ring or two around the opening, and the ware alway plain, often with a short spout, about half an inch in height, just below the rim. They have been dated to circa 2500 B.C. Bibby observes that generally "chain-ridging" was less common than the plain ridges. (Bibby, 1969:141f). The chain ridged ware and plastic decorations of small knobs or vertical or wavy bands across the horizontal ridges were found exclusively in Temple I (Mortensen, 1986:179).

"Barbar ware" has its own characteristic features; however it has its parallels in India. A type of pottery technically closely resembling "Barbar' ware and like it bearing horizontal ridges by finger pressure, observes Bibby (1957:160), is of frequent occurance in the graves of cemetary H at Harappa in the Indus Valley. However, the Harappan pottery is much taller and has a more curved neck than the pure " Barbar" type.

During the excavations at the Barbar temple, Bibby (1969:74) found remarkable uniform sherds of thin red ware, almost all decorated with low horizontal ridges about three quarters of inch apart, all seemed to belong to almost globular, round-bottomed pots of height between one foot to one and half. Many fragments of the rim were also found indicating that the pots had either been neckless, ending in a broadened rim at the top of the egg- shaped body, or else had a short neck with an out turned rim triangular in section. This pottery was named "Barbar pottery" by Bibby as it was very distinctive and easily recognizable. Thus, two major types of pottery of City II and the Barbar temples has been recognized by Bibby which is also found in the Failaka township. One of them also occurs frequently in the grave mounds of Bahrain. They are dated to circa 2000 B.C. To this pottery Bibby assigns a "Culture" which was eminently recognizable and very uniform-large vessels, as big as a pumpkin and shaped like an egg, of red clay and decorated with horizontal ridges perhaps half an inch apart. In one variety the top of the pot was simply a round opening in the broad end of the egg, the rim being thickened around the opening. In the other variety there was a short

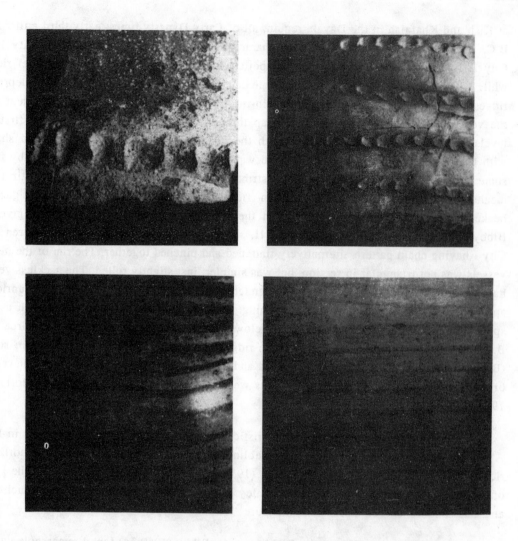

Fig. 9g-h. Types of ridges. (Courtesy : Bahrain National Museum).

neck at the broad end, ending in an out-turned triangular rim. These have been designated as "Barbar culture" (Bibby, 1969:114). The three types of pottery, red ridge ware, chain ridge ware and black on red painted ware, Larsen (1983:215) divided them into three periods in accordance with the levels at Qal'at as follows: Pre-Barbar (levels 30-26); Barbar I (levels 25-22), and Barbar II (levels 22-17). To the pottery of Bibby's City I and City II, Larsen (1983:214) refers to the assemblages as 'Barbar I' and 'Barbar II'; while to the pottery earlier than Barbar I in the north wall sequence, he has grouped as 'pre- Barbar'. The distinctive "Barbar ware", he describes as a sand- tempered, red ware with yellowish halos occuring around individual sand grains. The yellowish halos seem to be the results of a secondary mineralization around sand grains, suggests Larsen. Hojlund (1986), re-examined the ceramic sequences from City I and II at Ras al Qal'at al Bahrain and correlated them more exactly with the Barbar temples. Both, chain-ridged and ridged wares, the characteristic of Temple I ware, were also found in City II A. There are some similarities between pottery from Barbar I and II A on one side and Akkadian and Ur III pottery especially from Nippur and from the Diyala and Hamrin regions in Mesopotamia on the other side. Mortensen (1986:183f) draws parallel between several types from Temple IIb and the Isin-Larsa phase at Ahmed al-Mughir and other sites in the Hamrin plains, and between the pottery from the NE-Temple at Barbar and sites in Susaiane, especially the Simashki phase at Farukhabad, dated roughly between 2100-1900 B.C.

Hojlund (1986:217f) makes a comparative study of pottery from Qal'at al Bahrain and Barbar temples with that from Failaka and proposes sub-division of Bibby's City II into six periods and City III into two periods and demonstrates occupational continuity on the Qal'at from City II to City III, i.e., from the third millennium till at least about 1500 B.C. and might be entire second millennium B.C. He makes a distinction between different periods of City II on the basis of types of pottery used/recovered from the divisions. The first period, City IIA is characterised by plain jar rims. In City IIB triangular rims with a concave upper surface are found. City IIC pottery is typical with still thicker hole-mouth rims with a concave bevelled front. City IID is characterised by some low-necked jars with thick triangular rims. Between City IID and F seems to be a gap. Hojlund is of the view that there is pottery in the Qal'at material which typologically can fill in the gap. City IIF is characterised by elongated and smoothed triangular rims, slender, pointed, 'up-turned' hole mouth. In City IIA-D the potters worked with the hand techniques and used the fast wheel only for small painted cups and beakers. In City IIF there is a change and we find several larger shapes made on the fast wheel and nearly always painted or decorated with very fine ridges on the shoulder. Hojlund finds close resemblance between City IIF pottery of Bahrain and Failaka 3A pottery which follows Barbar tradition and states that City IIF lacks the Babylonian shapes, which is found on Failaka in period 3A. (Hojlund, 1986:217-219). City IIIA (of Middle Dilmun period) is characterised by the elongated, smoothed triangular rim and the plain jar rim, plus a few hole- mouths, all in hand made technique. But inventory has wheel made quadrangular rims of different sizes. These shapes are attributed to Mesopotamian origin. City III B also

Fig.9i,j. Dilmun pottery.

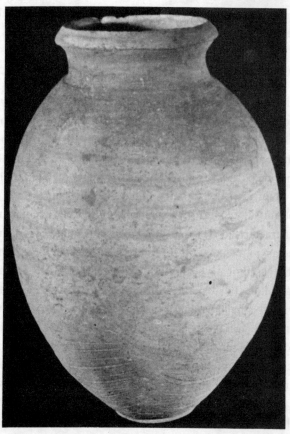

320

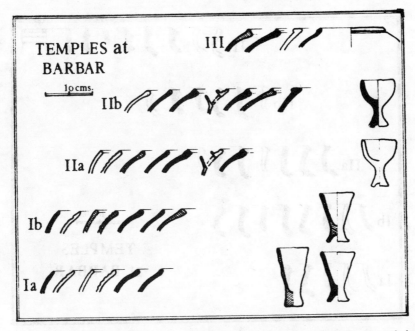

Fig. 10a   Red Dilmun (Barbar) ware, showing development of hole-mouth jars and goblets from Barbar Temple Ia to III. (After P.Mortensen, 1986).

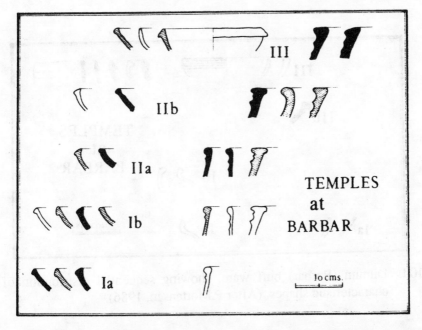

Fig.10b.   Red Dilmun (Barbar) ware, showing sequential development of bowls, cooking pots and pithoi. (After P.Mortensen, 1986).

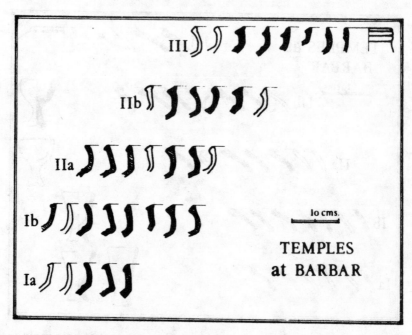

Fig.10c. Red Dilmun (Barbar) ware, showing sequential development of collard jars. (After P.Mortensen, 1986).

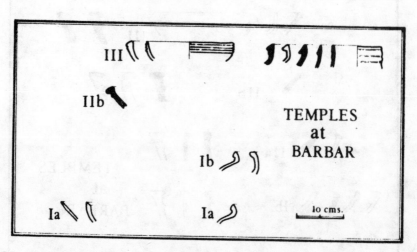

Fig.10d. Dilmun (Barbar) buff ware, showing sequential distribution of some characteristic shapes. (After P.Mortensen, 1986).

Fig.12a-d.   Globular Jars from Sar Burial Mounds.
(Courtesy : Bahrain National Museum).

Fig.13a-c Pottery from burial mounds. (Courtesy : Bahrain National Museum)

has several Mesopotamian shapes, tall goblets etc. which resembles Failaka 3C. (Hojlund, 1986:221f).

The characteristics of the hole-mouth jars of the red Barbar ware is the development from plain or slightly rounded rims in Temple Ia and b to rather elaborate thickened or flat rims in Temple IIB and III. Fig. 10a shows (after Mortensen, 1986:180) a series of goblets and profiles of the hole-mouth jars arranged in horizontal rows by temple phases, starting at the bottom with conical beakers of Temple Ia. The most common type are illustrated in black, less common types are shown by hatched lines; and rare specimens are illustrated in outline (Mortensen, 1986:180). The sequential development of bowls, cooking pots and pithoi of the red Barbar ware are shown in Fig. 10b (after Mortensen, 1986:181) along with a series of bowls on the left. These are most common in Temple II a and b. The sequential development of the rim-profiles of the classical Barbar jar with a vertical neck is illustrated in Fig. 10c (after Mortensen, 1986:182). Typical for the early phases are the high-necked collars with a plain or triangular rim. Shorter collars are the characteristic features of Temple IIB and especially Temple III. Their collars are with thick triangular lips often heavily drawn down along the outside of the rim. Barbar buff ware appear in Temple III in a variety of shapes in buff ware as well as in the local red or reddish brown ware. This variety is rare in Temple Ia, Ib and II. The sequential development of some characteristic shapes of the Barbar buff ware is shown in Fig. 10d. (after Mortensen, 1986:182).

From Qal'at al Bahrain comes other type of pottery as well. The sondages made by the French team at Qal'at al Bahrain revealed not only occupation levels but brought to light cultural levels. The ceramic ware recovered from these soundages constitute an important archaeological material. Kervran et al (1987/88 : 13- 38) discovered two groups of pottery. The first group was of light red beige ware with predominantly mineral temper comprising. Large jars with everted rims; medium size jars with short necks and triangular rims; basins in a variety of forms; bases of jars or basins, which are flat, plain, and string cut; goblets of crude make with string cut bases. The ware ranges from light-red to light-brown. They are heavy, compact, with silicuous temper. The excavators suggests that this corpus resembles those of Kassite period of Qal'at. The second group is of buff, yellowish or green ware with predominantly chaff temper. The corpus consists of wide-mouthed, neckless jars with pedestal or deep ring bases. Along with these jars were found varients of a unique type or rim: oblique, widened to the outside, with a light ledge below the rim. The size of the jar mouths ranged from 27 to 44 cms., the thickness of their walls range from 2.5 to 3.0 cms., and the mean height of these pedestal bases is 6 cms. Besides these there were also smaller jars and basins. The latter are found in different sizes and shapes. Some of them have vertical handles like those of baskets and this type of handle appears to be more in Bahrain's pottery. The excavators find parallels of their ceramic corpus with those from Susa, Failaka and Hajar bin Humeid (Saudi Arabia) dated between 11th/10th century to 4th/3rd century B.C.

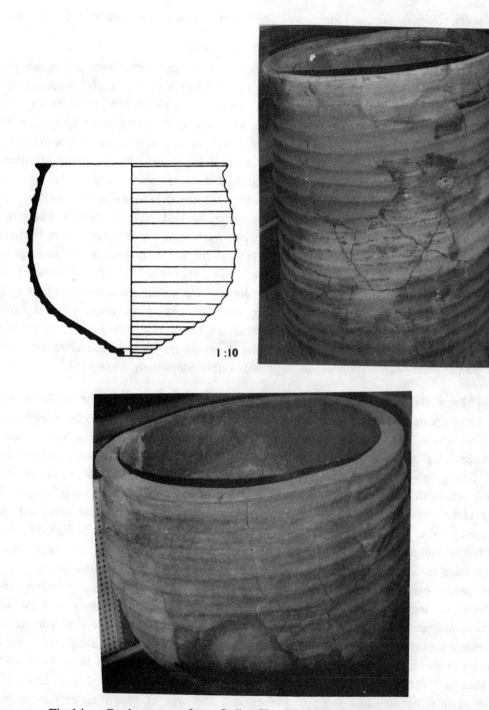

1:10

Fig.14a, Basin pottery from Qal'at City I (a,b) and canalization pottery (c).
(Courtesy : Bahrain National Museum and after S. Cleuziou 1989)

Archaeological excavations throughout Bahrain have produced scores of Barbar/Dilmun ware, as well as other types of pottery which were in use during the Early Dilmun period. Some selected specimens are described here in order to highlight the cultural development in Bahrain during the period under reference. Most of these specimens are from Bahrain National Museum, and some (Figs. 15-21) are from the British Museum.

From the burials mounds of Sar was recovered a large painted Jar (Fig. 12a). It is oval with small flat base and a short neck. The rim is thick and overturned with wide mouth. Two horizontal ridges are on the neck. It is a brown ware with red painted bands on greenish wash surface from neck to nearly the base. It measures 28.6 cms., in height and the rim diameter is 12.8 cms., (Ibrahim, 1982:72, Fig. 38/7). Another globular jar (Fig. 12b) of smaller size appears to be painted ware but the paint seem to have faded. It is also from Sar graves. A globular ridged jar (Fig. 12c) from Sar has a small flat base and short neck, out turned thick rim, wide mouth. It has horizontal ridges from neck to bottom.

The most common type of Dilmun's funerary ware found in the burial mounds or subterranean graves is a fine red ware (Fig. 13a) with cylindrical body and round base. It is of very fine fabric, made of well lavigated clay. It is an almost vertical neck but thickened externally with a raised line or cordon and upper half of the neck is generally incised with horizontally drawn lines. External surface is smooth. The neck at the shoulder is usually thick on the inner side as if the vessel was made in two parts and joined at the neck. These vessels are generally very well fired to various shades of red colour, but usually bright red, and slipped on the external surface with deep red, or light red or a dark colour. The jars are found in various shapes and sizes from elongated or almost conical body, to globular shape. Since the ware is not found in settlements, it is believed that it was made specially for burials and it is found in almost all the burials in Bahrain. It is dated to late third and early second millennium B.C. (Mughal, 1983:62). A similar jar, and a fragment of rim recovered from the 'Ali mounds is illustrated in Figs. 17c, 18a (Reade and Burleigh, 1978:82). Their parallels are found in Mesopotamia during late third and early second millennium B.C. (Cleuziou, 1989 : 19). From the 'Ali mounds (Group A) was recovered a thin-walled oval-shaped jar (Fig. 13b) with a roundish, pointed sagging base, a sharply carinated, almost horizontally inturned shoulder, a short vertical neck and a flat-topped, everted rim. It is made of pale reddish-buff clay, well lavigated, with whitish-cream slip and wheel made. A similar jar (Fig. 16b) was found from the Jefferson's graves in Hamala North. (Reade and Burliegh, 1978:82; Caspers, 1980:4,43; Freifelt, 1986:129f).

From the excavation of al Hajjar subterranean graves was found a pear shaped jar (Fig. 13c) with straight cylindrical neck rim rounded and base pointed. Dark red slip on outer surface. Neck seems to have been made seperately and attached. From the same graves a globular jar (Fig. 13d) was recovered. It has a short cylindrical neck with a triangular rim, light brown ware. Dark brown slip on the outer surface. Small flat bottom.

Fig.15a,b Painted Jars from 'Ali mounds. (Courtesy : Trustees of the British Museum).

Fig. 16a-e. Painted and plain pottery from 'Ali mounds (a,d,e) and Hamala North (b,c). (Courtesy : Trustees of the British Museum).

From Qal'at comes two types of basin pottery in red ware with whitish inclusions. The first type (Fig. 14a) from City I is a large ovoid basin with rounded bottom, horizontal rim, four thick horizontal ridges on the body, and inner portion seems to have been coated with bitumen. Its height is 60 cms., and maximum diameter at the top is 80 cms. It is dated to third millennium B.C. The second type is from City II but with thick horizontal ridges from top to bottom (Fig. 14b). It has reddish wash outside, ovoid basin with horizontal everted rim, round bottom, slightly pointed having a small hole. Its height is 51 cms., while diameter at rim is 56 cms. It is dated to second millennium B.C. The Dilmunites had a special category of pottery for the purpose of canalization or draining well. It is a red ware (Fig. 14c) with whitish inclusions, rather course fabric. It is cylindrical in shape with nearly parallel walls. Thick ridges are on the outside. Thick rim. It was recovered from Qal'at, City II and is dated to second millennium B.C. (Cleuziou, 1989:14f).

A distinctive type of Qal'at City II pottery is the globular cooking pot of light red ware with whitish inclusion, reddish wash outside, hole mouth opening, with triangular thickened rim inside and bottom slightly pointed. It measures 31 cms., in height, maximum diameter 30 cms., and mouth diameter 15 cms (Cleuziou, 1989:16). This type of cooking pot with slightly base (Fig. 19) was recovered from Jefferson grave mound at Hamala North. It has no neck and has a tiny rim which is slightly convex on the outside and concave on the inside. It is made of a brownish-red, grit tempered, brittle clay. There are traces of burning on the lower part as well as on the inside. Its height is 0.17, 1m., and the diameter of the rim measures 0.12,3 m. The thickness of the rim is ca. 3cms., (Caspers, 1980:3,43). A distinctive type of Qal'at City II Pottery is a plain jar. It is red ware with whitish inclusions, elongated ovoid jar with cylindrical neck, triangular rim, narrow flat bottom. It is 42 cms., in height, maximum diameter at mid height is 25 cms., diameter of the bottom is 6 cms., and diameter of the top opening is 12.5 cms. It was recovered from Qal'at City II and is dated to early second millennium B.C. (Cleuziou, 1989:18). Similar type of plain jar was recovered from the 'Ali mounds. (Fig. 17d) from tomb 16. It is red-brown ware with many white grits; cream slip on the exterior and inside rim. Extent height 37.3 cms., rim diameter 12.5 cms. (Reade and Burleigh, 1978:81). And a similar type of plain thin-walled jar (Fig. 21) but with shallow ridges in relief around the top of the shoulder was recovered from the Jefferson grave of Hamala North. It has a small ragging base, a short straight neck and a simple out turned rim. It is made of a dirty-cream coloured clay with a greyish tinge and is well- fired. Its height is 0.40,5 m., diameter of the rim 0.13 m. (Caspers, 1980:4,44).

A few examples of scarce painted jars have been found in Bahrain which are dated to early second millennium B.C. An ovoid jar was found in City II of buff ware with grey core, fine mineral temper, red slip outside except on a reserved band between the two heighest groups of horizontal lines, rounded bottom. It is decorated in black paint of three groups of horizontal lines, crossed by groups of eight vertical undulated lines. An effect of polychromy is provided by the horizontal band reserved in buff on the shoulder. In height it measures 38 cms. while its maximum diameter is 38 cms, diameter of the neck is 9 cms., (Cleuziou,

328

Fig.17a-d A variety of pottery from 'Ali mounds. One of them has a filter built into the neck. (Courtesy : Trustees of the British Museum).

329

Fig.18   Painted and plain pottery sherds from 'Ali mounds with a strainer.
(Courtesy : Trustees of British Museum)

1989:21). Mackay (1929, Pl.VIII No. 24) discovered an almost similar jar (Fig. 15a) in a tumulus 28 at 'Ali. It is a sandy brown ware with occasional flacks of mica; exterior covered with a red paint or slip on which the design is painted in black. Extent height 44 cms., rim diameter 12.7 cms. (Reade and Burleigh, 1978:82).

In the al Hajjar graves dated to early second millennium B.C. painted jars were found during the excavations of 1970. It is a smaller globular jar with slightly painted bottom, cylindrical neck, everted rim, red ware with whitish inclusions and red slip. The decoration in black paint has three horizontal lines on the neck, one horizontal line at the junction of shoulder and neck and interrupted undulating line above four horizontal lines on the shoulder. (Cleuziou, 1989:22). From the 'Ali mounds excavated by Mackay (1929) comes a large red-brown jar with occasional white paint and having a band of wavy lines (Fig. 15b) in purplish paint around the collar of the jar. The same paint, now flaking, originally covered all the exterior and inside of the rim. Its extent height is 36 cms., rim diameter 14 cms. It was found in tomb 14 along with the upper portion of the jar of of Fig. 17b. It is also red-brown ware with many white grits, cream slip on the outside and inside rim, and having band of combed inclusion around collar. Its extent height is 15.5 cms., and rim diameter 13.4 cms., (Reade and Burleigh, 1978:81). Another jar (Fig. 17a) has a filter built into neck and comes from the 'Ali tomb 21. It is red-brown ware with many white grits, cream slip roughly smeared on exterior and across the filter. It has two slightly slanting strokes incised on the neck. It measures 34.5 cms., in height and 10.8 cms., rim diameter. (Reade and Burleigh, 1978:81). A very rare item in Bahrain is the small hemispherical bowl (Fig. 22a) found in the large burial mound (No. 203K) at Ali along with the pedestalled beakers. It is a fine red ware with red slip, flat bottom and slightly everted rim. It is polished outside. Its height is 4.3 cms., diameter at the bottom 3.6 cms., diameter of rim 7.6 cms. It is dated to early second millennium B.C. (Cleuziou, 1989:22). A jar stand was used for placing the jar over it. (Fig. 22b) It is a red ware with whitish inclusions, red slip, slightly tronoconical in shape with out bottom. The neck is concave. It measures 12cms., height, 13 cms., base diameter and 13 cms. top diameter. It is dated to early second millennium B.C. It is rarely found in the mound but found in the settlements (Cleuziou, 1989:20).

A globular jar with strainer neck was discovered during the Isa town rescue excavations of burial mound. It is a red ware with white inclusions, wet smoothed surface, flat bottom, cylindrical neck, with everted bevelled rim. The pot seems to have been made in two parts and joined is indicated by the ridge at the junction of the neck and body. The mouth is closed by a concave strainer pierced with several holes. It measures 32 cms. in height, 12 cms. rim diameter, 28 cms., maximum diameter at the middle of the pot. It is dated to early second millennium B.C. (Cleuziou, 1989:17). A similar strainer (Fig. 18b), or fragment of the jar, was found from the 'Ali mounds. It is also a red brown ware with many white grits, cream slip on exterior and across the filter. Rim diameter 11 cms. (Reade and Burleigh, 1978:81). And an entire jar with strainer was recovered from al Hajjar grave (No. 11). It is a pale yellow pottery. (Rice, 1988:83,91). Mackay (1929) discovered a globular jar of

Fig. 19,20,21 Cooking pot and jars from Hamala North. (Courtesy : Trustees of the British Museum).

light brown ware (Fig. 16a) with paler surface of height 14 cms. rim diameter 10.5 cms., from tomb 6. It has a pointed bottom, cylindrical neck with a ridge around below the rim. Another jar from the site but tomb 5 is a brown ware with many white grits, dark grey surface (Fig. 16d). During Caspers (1974:131ff) considers this jar as imitation of a well-known grey or black Mesopotamian type which regularly bears incised decoration. It measures 15.2 cms., in height and 11 cms., rim diameter. It has a high ring base (not apparent in the photo). Which is a distinctive feature of Mesopotamian examples. A broken jar (Fig. 16e) rim and part of the body only, is of unknown provenance (was lying in 1980 in the stores of the Bahrain National Museum when Reade visited). It is a brown ware with occasional flecks of mica, red-brown slip on the outside and inside rim, with some traces inside the body, exterior well burnished. Extent height 19 cms. rim diameter 9.6 cms. (Reade and Burleigh, 1978:82).

The British excavation (1990-91) at the Sar settlement site, which is contemporary with City II C,D of Qal'at al Bahrain, has produced a large variety of pottery, mainly Barbar ware. The commonest ware type, states Jane Moon (Killick etal 1991:127), is red clay tempered with sand and crushed shell which produced a yellow spotted effect on the surface. Almost all types of Barbar ware, except the earliest chain-ridged, have been recovered from the houses of the settlement, and are same as those illustrated above at Figs. 9b-e and 14b. Along with Barbar ware painted pottery sherds were also recovered from houses, especially houses 50-53. The painted sherds from Sar settlement are illustrated in Fig. 24a. They are described here based on Jane Moon (Killick etal, 1991:128f) as follows: (1) Fragment of a rim and upper body of a painted hole-mouthed vessel of fine red clay, sparce temper of fine girt. It resembles examples from Wadi Suq culture of Oman (See Fig. 8a above). (2). Painted sherd of buff clay, fine grit temper, orange surface out. Design in black paint with red wash below horizontal strip. The pattern of animal feet resembles Umm an Nar pottery which was greatly influenced by the Harappan style of Indus Valley Civilization. (cf. Frifelt, 1975:359ff; deCardi, 1983:60,66,78,94; Allchin, 1982). (3) Small black painted jar of friable orange clay. Wheel thrown. (4) Portion of rim and upper body of a painted hole-mouth pot of orange clay with a design of black-paint on it. (5) Rim of a painted cup with a band of purple paint on the exterior. (6) A high-fired brown clay cup with black painted bands. (7) Fragment of rim and upper body of a painted jar having gouged grooves on the neck. (8) Neck and shoulder of a painted jar of pink clay, polished and red painted with black painted design of alternate hatched horizontal band of horizontal and curved lines and leaves. Almost the same alternate hatching design and horizontal bands are found on a jar recovered from Sar burial graves by Ibrahim (1982:72, Fig. 38/4). Ibrahim calls it a butterfly design. But instead of leaves there is a snake pattern. The jar from Sar burial mounds is shown in Fig. 24b. This alternate hatching design resembles pottery found at Hili 8, period 1 and dated to third millennium B.C. (cf. Cleuziou, 1989:Pl. 22). and those from Baluchistan, outpost of Harappan culture. (cf. de Cardi, 1983:50-56).

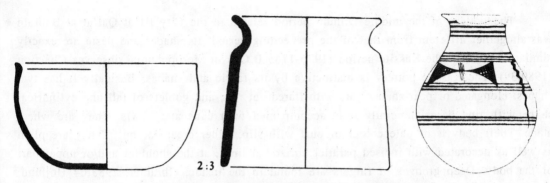

Fig. 22a,b   (Left and Centre) Bowl pottery and Jar stand pottery.
              (After P.Lombard and M.Kervran, 1989).

Fig. 24.   (Right) A painted Jar from Sar burial graves. (After M.Ibrahim, 1983).

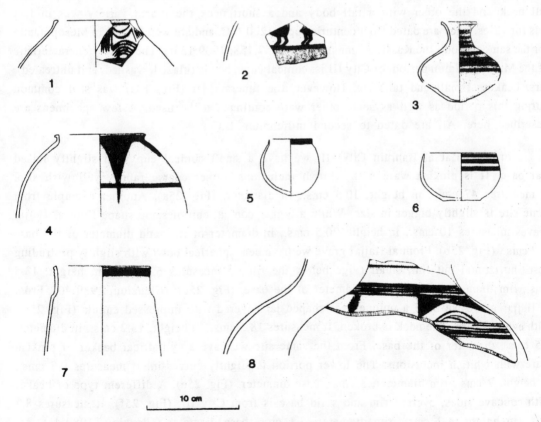

Fig.23   Painted and plain pottery from Sar Settlement.
          (After R.Killick, H.Crawford, K.Flarin etal, 1991).

THE MIDDLE DILMUN PERIOD

The pottery of the middle Dilmun period related to the City III at Qal'at al Bahrain was altogether different from that of the preceeding period. Its shapes and paste are exactly similar to those of the Kassite period (1976-1165 B.C.) in Mesopotamia, observes Cleuziou (1989:39). The Kassite pottery is distinctive by its fabric and shapes. Basically it has two shapes; elongated or pear-shaped jars with flared-out rim; and goblets of tall and cylindrical shape with ring base. Generally it is accompanied with cups and bowls. They are wheel made. Their body is of pale colour or buff with slip, either cream or buff. They are plain as well as decorated with incised parallel horizontal lines, at the shoulder and/or upper part of the body. Deep grooves of fingers are found in the inside. (Ibrahim, 1983:64 Hojlund, 1986:220). From the south western quarter of the sondage in the Qal'at al Bahrain City III Bibby discovered four types of pottery characteristic of a "Culture". The pots were all fairly thick- walled, and the clay, tempered with sand, had been fired to a warm honey or caramel colour. It was dubbed as "Caramel Ware". They comprised; bowls which were few, thick and clumsy; tall drinking vases, funnel shaped necks and narrow solid bases that often developed into regular pedestals. There were two varieties- one with a short body and a tall neck and the other with a tall body and a short neck the fourth variety was in fact lids for vases. They are dated from centuries upto 1200 B.C. and are well known in Mesopotamia for the same period - the Kassites time. (Bibby, 1957:158; 1969:136f). The pottery characteristic of the Middle Dilmun period, or City III is: conical cups, bowls (glazed, washed, and untreated), jars, beakers (small and tall) etc. However, the funerary jar (Fig. 13a) was still common during this period as well as some other ware continued to be used. A few specimens are described here. All are dated to second millennium B.C.

From Qal'at al Bahrain City III, we have a small conical cup with slightly raised flat base. It is pinkish ware with whitish inclusions, rather coarse fabric, yellowish slip. It measures 47 cms., in height, 10.5 cms., in diameter. (Fig. 25a). Another example from same site is slightly bigger in size. While a bigger conical cup of same shape from al Hajjar graves measures 10 cms., in height, 20.5 cms., in diameter of rim, and diameter of the base is 7 cms., (Fig. 25b). From al Hajjar grave we have hemispherical bowl with slightly protruding base, horizontal cut rim, small ridge below the rim. It measures 6.2 cms., in height, 13.5 cms., rim diameter, and 6 cms., diameter of the base. (Fig. 25c). (Cleuziou, 1989:40). From al Hajjar grave we have a unique pear shaped jar covered with impressed cupula (Fig. 25d), with everted base. The neck is broken. It measures 18.5 cms., in height, 13.2 cms., in diameter, 5.5 cms., diameter of the base. From the same site we have a cylindrical beaker of pinkish ware with whitish inclusions. The lower portion is slightly curves-in. It measures 9.3 cms., in height, 7 cms., rim diameter, 3 cms., base diameter. (Fig. 25e). A different type of beaker with concave sides, everted rim and solid base is from City III, (Fig. 25f). It measures 8.7 cms., in height, 4.2 cms., rim diameter, 3.1 cms, base diameter (Cleuziou, 1989:41).

From al Hajjar grave (No.1) we have pale yellowish pottery vessels decorated with

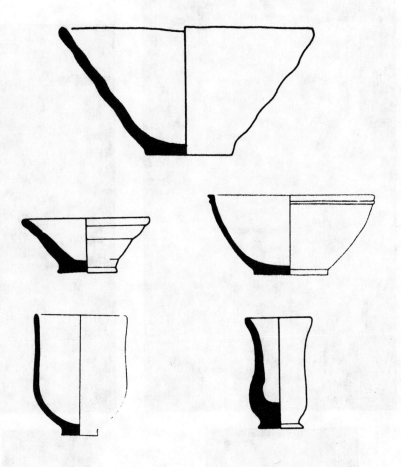

Fig.25a-e Variety of pottery - Conical cups, jars, etc. from
Qal'at City III and various graves (After S.Cleuziou, 1989).

Fig. 26a,b   (Left) Pottery jars with incised decorated lines from al Hajjar graves.

Fig.27ab (Right) Tall beakers of Kassite City III.

(Courtesy : Bahrain National Museum)

Fig.28a,b,c. Tea pots of City IV period from al Hajjar graves.
(Courtesy : Bahrain National Museum).

two sets of horizontal lines at the shoulder (5 lines) and slightly below (3 lines) (Fig. 26). It has ovoid body, cylindrical neck and rim is beaded. It has same ring base. It measures 26 cms., in height, 15 cms., maximum diameter, 6.5 base diameter. This is very common and standard type of pottery during the Kassite period in Bahrain. It is found both in the occupational sites as well as burials. (Rice, 1988:81,87; Cleuziou, 1989:46). Similar jars have been found from Sar burial complex. (cf. Mughal, 1983:473, 530). A similar jar from al Hajjar with parallel incised broader pattern from the middle of the body to the bottom. (Fig. 26b). It is from Bahrain National Museum. From al Hajjar excavations (1971-72) by Fayez Tarawaeh and Abdul Aziz Fakhroo were recovered for a gravel, a number of small, spindle-shaped, long-necked vessels with button-like bases, similar those found at City III at Qal'at. While from another grave (No. 5) of the same site was recovered a number of bell-shaped pottery jars with protrusions at the base. (Tarawaeh, 1972, Rice, 1988:81f).

From City III at Qal'at we have tall beakers or distinct Kassite goblets of Mesopotamian shapes. They are light buff ware, rather coarse fabric. It has sinuous sides and high shoulder, cylindrical neck everted rim, and small solid everted base (Fig. 27). It measures 27.2 cms., height 6.5 cms., diameter, 8.5 cms., shoulder diameter, 5.5 cms., base diameter. (Hojlund, 1986:222f; Cleuziou, 1989:43f). These beakers are found in various shapes and sizes from City III and al Hajjar graves. The tallest one recorded so far, measures 33.4 cms., in height, 7 cms., rim diameter, 0.8 cms., diameter at shoulder, and 6.8 cms., diameter at the base.

THE LATE DILMUN PERIOD

The pottery ascribed to the late Dilmun or City IV period, does not, observes Lombard (1989:52), always appear to be indigenous product. A large variety of pottery : Cylindrical vases, biconical vessels, tea-pots, spouted jugs, footed-bowls etc., that were recovered from the al Hajjar graves has strong affinity with those from Oman of the period tenth to eighth century B.C. Very little of local products have been recorded. Another characteristic pottery from City IV is the "snake-bowls". These are shallow bowls of two types and a deeper type vessel with a narrow rim (Bibby, 1969:163). A few specimen of pottery of the Iron Age Bahrain is described here. All from the Bahrain National Museum.

From al Hajjar grave (No. 29) we have an excellent piece of 'tea- pot' (Fig. 28a) or reddish buff ware. It has a carinated body and a flat bottom. The rim is everted and vertical. The spout is wide bridged with a thick lip. Its measurements are: 12.5 cms., height, 7.2 cms. rim diameter, 15.7 cms body diameter, 5.4 cms., diameter at the base and 8.5 cms., length of the spout. It is dated to tenth-eight century B.C. Lombard (1989:56) observes that this pottery and those mentioned below. (Figs. 28b,c) reflects a strong Iranian influence or connection. He further comments that nothing cannot be said about its make, whether in Bahrain or outside. Another similar specimen (Fig. 28b) from al Hajjar graves (No. 10) is a globular spouted-jug but with a side handle. From Isa town grave excavation was recovered a spouted vessel with carinated profile and light brown ware with mineral grits. It has a

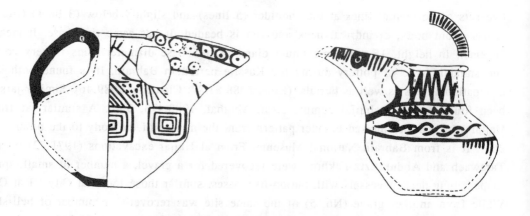

Fig.29a,b Painted and decorated spouted jugs from al Hajjar.
(After P.Lombard, 1989).

Fig.30. Pottery "Snake" bowls from City IV. (Courtesy : Bahrain National Museum).

short vertical neck, rounded flaring rim. Bottom is flat. Has light brown slip traces. Its measurements are 6.4 cms., height 6.8 cms., rim diameter 4.6 cms., base diameter, ca. 6 cms., length of broken spout, might have been a little longer. (Lombard, 1989:56f). Painted and decorated spouted jugs have been recovered from Isa town (Fig. 29a) and al Hajjar (Fig. 29b) graves. They have cylindrical necks, round flaring rims, with and without side handles. Their sizes are respectively, height 10/12 cms., diameter of the rim, 5.1/5.3 cms., body diameter, 10.3/ 12.3 cms., length of spout 74./8.1 cms., (Lombard, 1989:58). They are similar to those found in Wadi Suq grave-field (cf. Freifelt, 1975:409f); also those from Rumeilah (United Arab Emirate or Oman Peninsula) and are exhibited in the museum at al 'Ain.

The Danish excavators found one of the snake-offerings below the floor of a building representing City IV at Qal'at which were contained in pottery bowls of Assyrian types. They are dated seventh-fifth century B.C. There are some six variants of these bowls. Some of them are shown in Fig. 30. In the centre top is a globular bowl with short flaring neck and rounded rim, flat disc- base. It is 10 cms., in height and 11 cms., rim diameter. It is from City VI, Qal'at. In the foreground on the right is a bowl with strong carinated sides and flaring neck. It is 6 cms., in height, with the rim diameter of 17.5 cms. This is covered by a lid bowl which also has carinated sides and wide flaring neck. It is buff ware with sandy grits but due to over heating has become greenish. Comparatively it is smaller in size, being a lid. It is 6 cms., in height, 16 cms., rim diameter. It is also found from Qal'at City IV. On the left, in the foreground, is another bowl with carinated profile and fine sides. It has a narrow flat base. Buff ware with fine sandy grits. It is 6 cms., in height, 14.2 cms., rim diameter. It was recovered from al Hajjar graves. It is covered with a lid-bowl with flaring sides and a rounded base. It measures 6.7 cms., in height, 4.1 cms, in diameter. (Glob, 1957:160; Bibby, 1969:Pl. XVII; Lombard, 1986:228f; 1989:60f).

(B)   SOFT-STONE VESSELS

Two types of stone vessels, of steatite/chlorite and alabaster, have been discovered in Bahrain during archaeological excavations of various sites.

(1)   STEATITE VESSELS

Steatite vessels in a variety of forms with incised decorations have been recovered from excavations of Qal'at al Bahrain and from various burial mounds stretched in most parts of Bahrain. Since Bahrain does not possess any soft stone like chloride or steatite, it is obvious that finished pieces were imported from outside from Oman and it is also possible, as suggested by Tarawaeh (in his notes on al Hajjar excavations), that they were produced or carved in Bahrain, from the raw material imported from Oman mountains. (Lombard, 1986:232 fn. 24). Besides Oman there are two other possible sources. Bahrain might have possibly also received raw material and or finished goods from the Arabian mainland (outside Oman itself), where sources of raw materials for steatite have been located at a few sites. (Zarins,

Figs. 31 & 32. A selection of steatite vessels from various graves.
(Courtesy : Bahrain National Museum).

1978:67). The other source could be from the other side of the Gulf, Tepe Yahya, and/or Elam, for the both raw material as well as finished products. The workshop of these vessels at Yahya maintained a far-reaching net-work of exchange of variety of goods with the neighbouring countries. Further, it seems that the steatite bowls are of Elamite manufacture. And it appears that these steatite vessels were exchanged as gifts between leaders or communities, cities, etc., to establish and strengthen the ties of socio- cultural and political relationship. This also enabled to further trade. The steatite vessels seems to have acted as a symbol of membership in a large and far reaching network of gift-exchange; standardized offerings by one ruler to another. (Lamberg- Karlovsky, 1970:616; Kohl, 1975:18ff). An unworked solid piece of green steatite found on the surface of the Sar burial complex (Ibrahim 1982:34, Pl. 53/7) attest that steatite vessels were manufactured in Bahrain.

A selection of different forms of steatite vessels, *serie recente* (Miroschedji, 1973), recovered from archaeological excavation at the burial mounds of Sar and Hamad Town, from Bahrain National Museum is illustrated in Fig. 31. In the back row left, (a) and in the centre (c) are two carinated spouted vessels. The former with curved walls, while the latter, vertical walls. In the front row, in the fore ground are (from left to right), a greyish suspension vessel (d) with ornamentation of incised lines, single row of dotted circles, and vertical zig-zag lines, with four suspension lugs pierced vertically; a container (e) with dotted concentric circles design over the whole body; a small jar (f) with two pairs of dotted circles; and a deep bowl (g) with convex base and narrowing sides giving the upper section a bee-hive shape. On the right in the back row is a deep vessel with vertical sides and flat base. Another selection from Bahrain National Museum of steatite vessels from al Hajjar burial graves is illustrated in Fig. 32. Except the bowl, the remaining four forms have a steatite decorated lid. In the back row, on the left is a barrel shaped suspension vase (a) with a convex sides and rounded rim. It has four vertically pierced lugs, on the lower half of the body. It is decorated with horizontal lines and zig- zag lines. It measures 14.5 cms., in height 6.5 cms., rim diameter, 55 cms., base diameter. It is dated to tenth to eight century B.C. On the right, in the back row is a biconical closed vase (b) with an elegant lid, it has fine incised decoration. Has rounded rim, flat base. Its height is 7.2 cms., rim diameter 4.8 cms., the maximum width of the vessel is 10.9 cms., while the diameter at the base is its half, 5.2 cms., It is finely polished and worked piece (Lombard, 1989:67f). In the front row, on the right a bowl (d) with flaring and convex sides, tapering rounded rim, having a convex disc base. Incised decoration. On the left, in the fore-ground is a cylindrical beaker (c), with a lid, rounded rim and flat base. Has fine incised decoration of vertical slanting lines pointing upwards. In the centre is a biconical vase (e) with a lid and a small base.

A fine steatite vessel in the shape of a quadrangular pyride having two compartments and slightly converging sides (Fig. 33), is from Sar burial complex. It has a fine incised decoration of dot-in concentric circles in three horizontal and vertical rows. Its height is about 10 cms. The illustration of Fig. 34 has a similar shaped vessel but with a single

Fig. 33-35 Different types of steatite vessels (Courtesy : Bahrain National Museum)

Fig.36-38   Steatite cylindrical vessels with decorations.
(Courtesy : Bahrain National Museum)

Fig. 39 (Above) A steatite cylindrical vessel with decorations
(Courtesy : Bahrain National Museum)

Fig. 40. (Below) A conical steatite vessel with a lid.
(After Abdul Aziz Sowailah)

Fig.17-20   A selection of Necklaces from various graves in Bahrain.
(Courtesy : Bahrain National Museum).

compartment and convergent sides. It is from al Hajjar graves. The incised pattern is not fine. Horizontal lines are on the upper part and seems to be design of a flower. A bowl with a wide opening and tapering sides and smaller base is from an unknown site. (Fig. 35). It has deep incised decoration of three horizontal lines around the rim and vertical lines from rim to the base. A spouted bowel with a different pattern of incised decoration is seen in Fig. 36. Within the two horizontal lines just below the rim, horizontal angular lines pointing towards the left are incised. The lower horizontal line is supported by vertical pointing lines from the base. It is from al Hajjar graves.

A cylindrical steatite jar (Fig. 37) with deep groove below the rounded rim is from Sar burial graves. It has incised decoration of dot-in-concentric circles on each side with three vertical rows and five horizontal rows. A simple incised decoration of just horizontal lines around a beehive shaped deep vessel and found on a jar of Fig. 38. It has a convex base with sides converging towards the mouth. A unique steatite vessel from Sar burial complex has a peculiar and intriquing decoration (Fig. 39). It is a cylindrical vessel with round rim and round base, slightly convex. The sides are slightly curved in side. The motif seems to be architectural representation. The whole design is divided into four horizontal sections or panels. In the upper band the mat design has been divided by zig-zag lines, forming triangles of mat with their apex alternately up and down. In the centre of the vessel is the main motif which might be representing some structure in the mind of the designer and is chiefly wicker work. Four thick vertical lines, on either sides, to the lower line of the upper most section, form a rectangular panel with four down curving thick line facing the two set of vertical lines. Above the top curve in the inverted semi-circle space is the mat pattern. Inside the inner-most vertical panel is a cross hatched design. Above it a horizontal line which supports three double-lines connecting the lower most down curving line. At the bottom is a smaller horizontal section running around the base and filled with mat pattern. Between the top and bottom sections/panel are two horizontal panels of equal height. They have alternating pattern of vertical lines and zig-zag lines. It is quite possible that the motif might be representation of some architectural features. Similar to Bahrain's vessel, Delougaz (1959:90-95f, Pl. VI and IX), records three types of steatite vessels, one from a room of Sin-Temple IX at Khafajah; the other from 'Adab; and the third a double vase, from Susa. All three vases have the motif of vertical central panel with down curving lines and the cross hatching within the enclosure, as found in the Bahrain vase. The Susa vase was published earlier by Earnest Mackay 91932:356f), as evidence of link between Ancient India and Elam, it is dated to second period of Susa, ca. 2800 to 2700 B.C. by de Mecquenem, the excavator of Susa. In the double vase of Susa, one has motif similar to that of Bahrain, while the other has the Mohenjo-Daro's weave pattern illustrated by Burkholder [1971:Pl. III(1)] and also in volume I (138(a) in this series.

A conical vessel with elongated lid (Fig. 40) gives an elegant appearance. It has deeply incised dots within the circle. The upper portion has an alternate horizontal lines and crossed lines pattern. Major central portion has dot-in-circles in three horizontal and three vertical rows. Below the circles are four horizontal lines around the vessel; and at the base the upper

Fig. 41. Alabastar Vessels (Courtesy : Bahrain National Museum)

panel design is repeated. The bottom is round and convex. The lid has similar dot-in-circle design. The elongated cylindrical neck of the lid had four deep grooves and the top nicely shaped. Its site provenance is not known. It is illustrated on the title cover of Abdul Aziz Sowaileh's "Tourist Guide". Almost all the steatite stone vessels from Bahrain have parallels with those found in all the emirates of U.A.E. and Oman and exhibited in their respective museums. In fact most of them are identical in shape, size and decoration. If mixed up, it would be rather difficult to distinguish which is from where. (cf. Friefelt, 1975:412; Lombard, 1982, 47f; de Cardi; 1985; 225; Boucharlat and Lombard, 1985; Pls, 60, 61, 72; al Tikriti 1989; pls.55,65-68).

(2) ALABASTER VESSELS

The Danish archaeological expedition during their five campaigns (1954-58) at the Barbar temples discovered three complete cylindrical alabaster vases, and fragments of a number of others. Two of them were found in the first year in the square pit in front of the altar and altar stone in the upper temple. (Fig. 41, a-d). While the third one (c) was discovered from the building debris level in the inner courtyard of middle temple in 1958. The fourth one(d) was found in the foundation layer of Barbar Temple III. Their sizes are:

	Height	Rim Diameter	Base Diameter
a)	17.5 Cms	13.2 Cms	13 Cms
b)	28.0 Cms	12.2 Cms	14 Cms
c)	9.5 Cms	7.0 Cms	8 Cms
d)	12.5 Cms	14.0 Cms	14 Cms

The above measurements are as given by Cleuziou (1989:26). There are some minor differences between those given earlier by Glob (1958:144); but are negligible. Glob (1958:144) originally at the time of excavations had remarked that : In shape, size and material two of these vessels have closest parallels in Mesopotamia and Egypt and that similar vessels have been found at several sites, including Ur, and must have same origin as those of Bahrain. However, this statement is disputed and rejected by A.R. Lucas and G.A. Reisner (Potts, 1983:129) who considered them as non-Egyptian. Potts (130) suggest an Iranian or Mesopotamian cultural origin for these alabaster vessels. Potts opinion is corroborated by R.Ciarla's study which suggests that majority of such vases are from eastern Iran (i.e. Shahr-I-Sokhta and Baluchistan). (Howard-Cartar, 1987:86).

From al Hajjar graves we have a fine grained white alabaster suspension bowl (Fig. 42) with thick convex sides. Its rim is horizontally cut, the base is thicker, there are two lugs pierced vertically on the two sides for the suspension through a string. One incised horizontal line is around the middle of the bowl. It measures 7.5 cms., in height 11.2 cms., rim diameter, 4.8 cms., base diameter. It is dated to tenth to eight century B.C. A similar bowl was found from al Qusais (in Dubai Emirates) excavation and is exhibited in the Museum at Dubai (Cleuziou, 1989:63).

CHAPTER VIII

OTHER ANTIQUITIES

(A) METAL OBJECTS

Bahrain/Dilmun has been referred in Mesopotamian cuneiform texts as supplier of copper. Though the raw material was not available in Bahrain due to its geological composition, yet it acquired this reputation. Obviously it was procured from Oman (Wadi Samad) where several copper mining centres and settlements have been found along with huge amount of slag dumps. (Weisgerber, 1978; 15f; Costa, 1978:9ff). Subsequently, Bahrain, after acquiring raw material, started processing of copper during the third millennium B.C., as evidenced by the hoard of copper ingots found at Nasiriyah numbering nine and weighing from 0.4 to 2.45 Kg. These are exhibited in the Bahrain National Museum and one speciman is illustrated here as Fig. 1. The Danish found a copper ingot from the Barbar temple excavation. The British excavation at Sar settlement have discovered a stack of copper ingot from a house (51). (Killick, Crawford, Moon, 1991-92; Field Report, Ms.) Archaeological excavations through-out Bahrain has produced several types of artifacts of copper/bronze which were used for different purposes in the daily life during third to first millennium B.C. Some of these selected artifacts are described here and some are illustrated here to highlight Bahrain's development in the ancient times.

From the foundation deposit of the second Barbar temple the Danish found a copper adze (Fig. 2). It has a collar and a curved blade. It measures about 15.7 cms., in length, while the length of the blade in 12.6 cms. It is dated to the late third or early second millennium B.C. (Mortesen, 1970, 394: Cleuziou, 1989:28). The excavation at the north wall of City I, Qal'at al Bahrain produced a socketed spearhead of copper (Fig. 3a) measuring 37 cms., in length (Bibby, 1966:81,92). A few specimen of folded socketed spear heads and tanged spearheads of copper from burial mounds of Sar and Hamad town are exhibited in the Bahrain National Museum and are illustrated here (Fig. 3 b). Similar types of socketed spearheads have been found by the British at the Sar settlement. In a coffin recovered from what the Danes call, a Neo-Babylonian burial, at Qal'at al Bahrain, three copper arrowheads, seven copper rings and an iron dagger were found besides the dead body. (Fig. 3c). In the figure, on top right side is seen a sealstone. (Glob, 1956:168, 173). These copper artifacts from Bahrain have parallels in those found in United Arab Emirates and Oman. (cf. Cleuziou, 1975:15,22, Cleuziou etal; 1978; (Cleuziou, 1979:28). From 'Ali cemetery several items of copper and bronze were recovered. Such as, a socketed spearhead (Fig. 4a) from tomb 17, it measures 20.5 cms., socketed arrowhead (4b,c) from tomb 16, slightly damaged; their extent length is 4.75 cms., omega-shaped pins etc. (Reade and Burleigh, 1978:82). From Jafferson tumulus in Hamala North, a copper/bronze goblet was recovered (Fig. 4d). It is rimless goblet on a short, hollow, cylindrical stem and a splayed hollow foot having a concave base. The upper portion of the goblet is like beaker shape. The overall height of the vessel is 0.18 m., the reconstructed diameter of the rim is

348

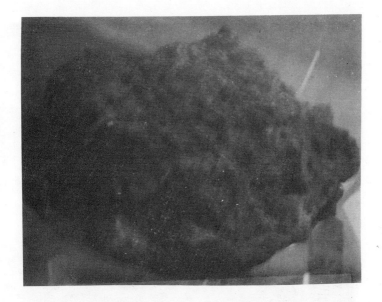

Fig.1 A Copper ingot from Nasiriyah. (Courtesy : Bahrain National Museum)

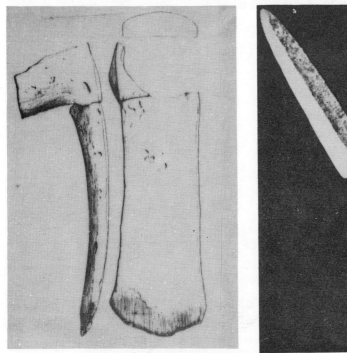

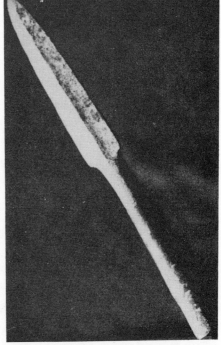

Fig.2. (Left) A Copper Adze from Barbar Temple II. (After Mortensen 1970)

Fig.3a (Right) A socketed spearhead of copper from City I. (After G.Bibby, 1966)

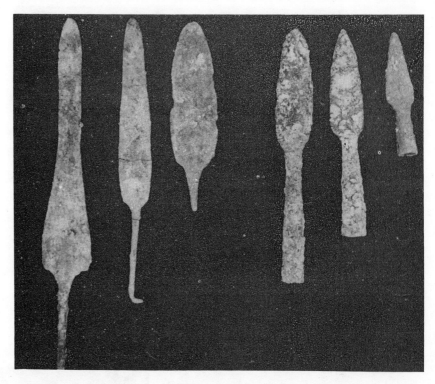

Fig.3b Tanged spearheads and folded socketed spearheads from
Sar and Hamad Town burial mounds. (Courtesy : Bahrain National Museu

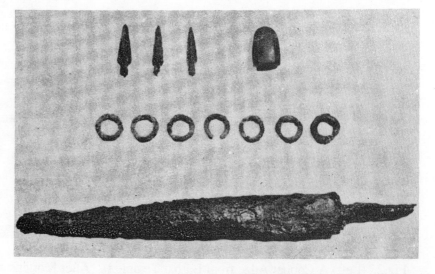

Fig.3c An Iron dagger, copper rings and copper arrowheads from Qal'at

(After Glob, 1966)

about 0.215m, 0.077 m, (Capser, 1980:5). The illustrations of Fig. 4a-e are from the British Museum.

A magnificient piece of bull-head (Fig.5) copper/bronze was discovered by Danish during the course of their second campagin in 1955 at Barbar temple. It measures 20 cms., height and 7.5 cms., wide. It was found in the corner of two foundation walls of Temple II. Along with this war a large collection of copper sheeting strips 15-20 cms., broad, all pierced with many rows of copper nails. They were lying in two layers within an area of half a square meter. Together with these were also found a copper ring and a copper band of thicker metal 4.5 cms., wide. All were buckelled and folded. The excavators believe that these strips were originally attached to an object of wood to which the bull- head was attached or mounted. (Glob, 1955:178;191f). The use or purpose of this bull-head is uncertain. It may possibly have served to decorate the sounding box of a lyre, suggest Rice (n.d.40). It is dated to late third or early second millennium B.C. (Mortensen, 1970:393ff). The bull-head was casted by lost wax process. Its interior, including the eyes are hallow, the latter might have been originally in-laid. Submit of the head, on top, has some incised decoration (Cleuziou, 1989:30). During Caspers (1971:217-223; 1975:70f) makes a comparative study of Bahrain's bull-head with five bull-heads, three from Ur Royal cemetry, one from Khafajah and one from an unknown provenance. She suggests that the bull's head from Ur and Khafajah has closest parallels in technique to the one from Bahrain, on the basis of their resemblence and similarity in size. However, she comments that Bahrain's head is largely cut generies and lacks all the elegance and naturalness found in other heads. Finally, Caspers suggests that in spite of the rudimentary modelling and the many dissimilarities which point clearly to a local manufacture, it is nevertheless obvious that a Sumerian proto-type was used to make Bahrain's specimen. The discovery of bull's head at the Barbar temple is an evidence of Bahrain's affinity with Mesopotamia; while the discovery of a bronze handle of mirror as a naked male figurine is yet another evidence of Bahrain's affinity in the opposite direction, with India. Thus, During Caspers (1973:128- 132) rightly captions her paper. "Summer and Kulli meet at Dilmun in the Arabian Gulf". Among the various copper or bronze objects found in a square pit under the north-east corner of the courtyard of Barbar Temple III, was this piece of copper/bronze naked male figurine, standing on a base which is curved at foot and cast in one single piece. The solid cast figure holds his hands clasped at the chest and measures 11 cms., in height. (Fig. 6). (Glob, 1954:148:152). This posture, suggests Nagaraja Rao (1969:218-220), is similar to those of Mesopotamian gods and has parallels with that from Chouchinak temple in Susa, which is dated to the third millennium B.C. This figurine, Rao finds to have close resemblance with the handle of a copper mirror from Mehi, a Kulli culture site in Baluchistan (now in Pakistan), which represents a stylised female figure, with breast and conventionalised arms akimo, but with the head provided only by the reflection of the user of the mirror. The only difference in these two specimen is that Bahrain's figure is male and complete while that from Kulli is female. Nagaraja Rao is corroborated by During Caspers (1973:128ff) who too finds blending of Sumerian and Harappan cultures in the statuette of Bahrain and she dates it to the beginning of the Akkadian period at the latest. This is further

351

Fig.4a,b,c Socketed spearheads from Ali Cemetery.
(Courtesy : Trustees of the British Museum).

352

Fig.4d.   A Copper/bronze Goblet. (Courtesy Trustees of the British Museum).

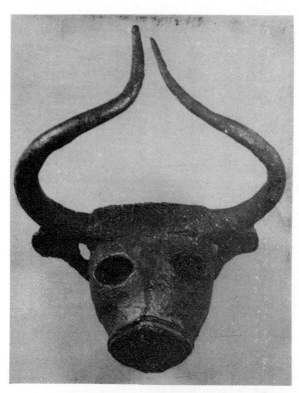

Fig.5a,b
A Bull-head of
copper/bronze
from Barbar Temple.
(Courtesy : Bahrain
National Museum).

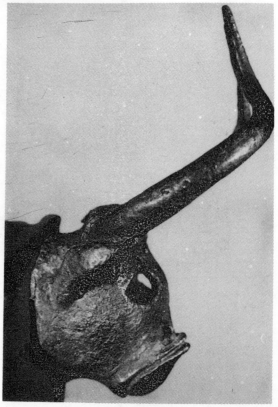

evidence by the fact that Bahrain's stattuete has several features inherent in the Early Dynastic III sculpture, in presentation, posture, ritual nakedness and contemporary tradition.

From Barbar temple comes yet another interesting piece, figure of a bird, perhaps a dove (Fig. 7). It was discovered by the Danish during their first season of excavation in 1954 at Barbar on the flags just north of the pit from where the naked male statuette was discovered. The stattuete of mirror handle (Fig. 6) and the bird (Fig. 7a) were found in the same pit. Thus, Glob (1954:152) who finds close resemblance of the stattuete with that of Chouchinak temple in Susa which has in its hands a bird/dove, believes that Bahrain stattuete of mirror handle and the bird may be of the same feature. It is possible that the Bahrain's figurine was also holding the bird/dove in the hand and might have been broken. The bird measures 12.6 cms., from breast to the tip of the tail and is 12.8 cms., high. It is of solid cast. A copper/bronze goat was recovered from the Jafferson tumulus, Hamala north, by Jafferson in 1968. It is just 2 cms., in height. It was found lying in the northern section of main burial chamber. It stands on a low base and has a loop attachment soldered to one side, suggesting its use as ornament. It is very similar to those from Harappa. (Caspers, 1987:38ff).

In a building adjoining the Sar Temple on the south east side, the British have discovered a large copper hoe (Fig. 8) weighing over two kilos. (Killick, Crawford, Moon, 1991, Unpublished Field Report) In the Sar settlement the British also found a thin rectangular copper plate (Fig. 9) with three lines across the centre but not touching the end; and has dot-in-circles, two each on the either side of the lines. Most probably it was meant for joining/revetting objects, metallic/wooden, by piercing nails through the dots in the circle. These dots-in-circles are similar those found on the Dilmun seals.

From al Hajjar graves several bronze utensils have been recovered. They vary in size and shape. They are generally bowls and dishes. They are dated to middle and late Dilmun periods. One of them (Fig. 10a) is a flattened globular vessel with wide vertical neck having ridges on the outside, bottom is round. Over the ridges a lug is attached and through it a ring hangs. Its height is 8.5 cms. rim diameter 12 cms. It is dated to tenth to eight century B.C. (Rice, 1988:81; Cleuziou, 1989:47,71). The bronze utensils of Bahrain have parallels with those from United Arab Emirates and Oman and these are exhibited in the respective mesuems. A bronze dagger from al Hajjar graves (No.1) has a blade with pointed end and parallel side. The hilt in with crescentic pommel. Its measurements are : length 32 cms. blade length 20 cms. width 3.1 cms., and thicknes 0.5 cms., the width of the hilt is 3.4 cms. It is dated to the late second millennium B.C. It has parallels with those found in Mesopotamia and western Iran towards the end of Kassite period. (Rice, 1988:81; Cleuziou, 1989:47). Similar daggers were found in the burial cairns on Umm an Nar, off Abu Dhabi. (Thorvildsen, 1962:209).

A small oval shaped rattle (Fig. 10d) of copper was recovered by the Danish during excavation of the foundation deposits of the Barbar Temple II. Its sides are pierced by triangular holes and has flat pierced lugs at both the ends. Its length is 5.7 cms., and diameter 3.2 cms.

Fig.6 (Left) A solid cast naked male figurine of copper/bronze.
Fig.7. A bird of copper/bronze. (From "The Temple Complex at Barbar, Bahrain").

Fig.8 A copper hoe from Sar settlement.
Fig.9 A rectangular copper plate.
(Courtesy : R.Killick, H.Crawford, J.Moon, 1992).

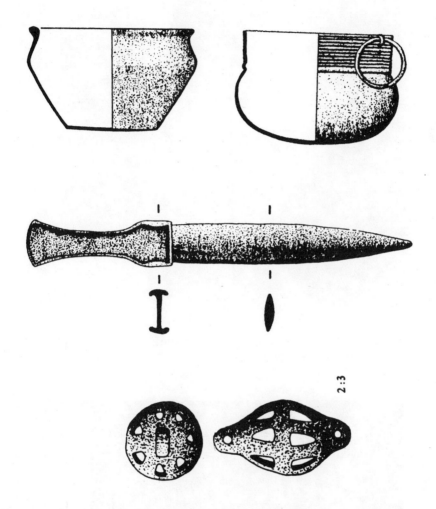

2:3

Fig.10a,b (Above) Bronze utensils from al Hajjar graves.

Fig.10c,d (Centre and Below) A bronze dagger from al Hajjar and a rattle of copper.
(After S.Gleuziou, 1989).

Fig.11,a,b,c A strainer, a ladle and a flask or situle from a coffin in City IV
(After P.V.Glob, 1956).

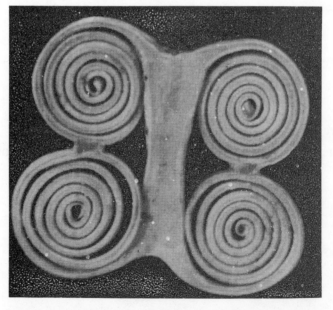

Fig.12. A golden ornament from Royal Tombs at 'Ali
(from "The Temple Complex at Barbar, Bahrain")

It is dated to late third or early second millennium B.C. (Mortensen, 1970:387,394). Cleuziou (1989:32) finds its parallel in rattles from Ur of Royal Cemetry. Rice (nd.42) suggests that the rattle indicates Sumerian's love for music in their temple ceremonies was also extended to the cults of Dilmun. In a burial-coffin recovered from the City IV at Qal'at al Bahrain, the Danish found a strainer (Fig. 11a) of hemispherical shape of 10.5 cms. diameter with an 11.5 cms. long handle, bent round at the end and ending in a duck's head. Along with it was a pouring vessel or ladle (Fig. 11b) 7 cms. high with a 25 cms. long handle, bent back at the free end and broadening out into a tongue where it meets the lip. (Glob, 1956:1771, 173). It is dated to seventh to fifth century B.C. Lombard (1986:227) finds convincing parallels in the similar specimens from Syro-Palestine and an area in North Syria. A complete set was discovered at Neirab, near Aleppo which is similar in style and composition to that of Bahrain. In the same coffin, in front of the dead body lay four objects of copper/bronze. One of them is a copper flask or situle (Fig. 11c), 19.5 cms. in height with a swivelling handle (Glob, 1956:170,173). Moorey (1980:124f) finds its parallels in specimens from Syria. Cleuziou (1989:74) suggests that it is a nice example of the type known as "Egyptian situla."

A silver hoard in a pottery vessel discovered at City IV at Qal'at below the cement floor of the palace building by the Danes during their eighth campaign (1961/62) consisted of pieces of smelted silver, portions of bracelets chipped into several pieces a number of complete rings and ear-rings, signet ring, pendent etc. The excavators believe that the hoard was apparently the stock of a silver smith buried in the ruins of the Kassite building. Conspicuous among the ornaments was a signet ring bearing Egyptian hieroglyphs. It is dated to 650-550 B.C. (Bibby, 1964:86,88, 102f)

Personal ornaments or jewellery made of copper/bronze have been found from the burial mounds. Cf. Ibrahim (1982:35, Fig. 46f), Mughal (1983:68, Fig. 27), Srivastava (1991:243). They consists of finger rings, ear-rings, etc. A tiny quatre foil meander of gold, probably a dress ornament, was found in one of the 'Royal Tombs' at 'Ali (Fig. 12). It consists of a golden tube splitted at both ends, each part is then folded in shape of spiral. The central tube is flattened and the joinning spirals are soldered. Its size is one cm. it is dated to early second millennium B.C. Cleuziou (1989:32) suggests, on the basis of Huot etal (1980), that this specimen of Bahrain belongs to a type common in Mesopotamia during the second half of the third and early second millennium B.C. It is found at Tell Brak, Assur, Mari and in Anatolia including Troy.

(B)   STANDARD

From the last two levels of City I and the first three levels of City 2, the Danish excavation, immediately within the city gate in the North Wall of a small square and a small building, each of two rooms ("Custom House" of City II) brought to light six stone weights along with 12 steatite stamp seals. Earlier (1965) also at the same site, about 20 meters away, the Danes found a cubical steatite weight of the type known from the Indus Civilization. (Bibby, 1966:92; 1970:349-353;1986:111). Bibby classified and described these seven weights (Fig. 13, here in the illustration only 6 weights are shown) into two groups by shape, three being rectangular and four spherical with two flattened sides. The particulars given by Bibby are tabulated below. Bibby concluded that these weights fall into a clear sequence of 800:400:100:16:8 : 8:1, times a basic unit (as shown in column 6 of the table), and from this scale not exceeding about 2 percent. Bibby asserted that these weights are exactly similar to those found in cities of Harappan Civilization, however, there are certain exceptions. He concludes that the "Early Dilmun" culture of Bahrain employed the same system of weights as the Harappan culture of the Indus Valley, and that the weighing activity was particularly common in the area just within the north gate

TABLE 1

S. No.	Shape	Material	Colour	Size D=Diameter H=Height cms	Weight Grms	BasicUnit 1.7 x
	1	2	3	4	5	6
1	Spherical	Marble-Like stone	Yellow-striated	D-9 H- 8.5	1,370	= 1.7x800
2	Spherical	Stone like Marble closed grained	Red	D-7.5 H- 6.3	670	= 1.7x400
3	Spherical	Lime stone fine grained	White	D-4.8 H-4.3	171	= 1.7x100
4	Rectangular	Chert-Polished	-	2.3x2.3x1.7	27	= 1.7x16
5	Spherical	Steatite	Black	-	13.9	= 1.7x8
6	Half-Cube	Steatite	-	1.8 x 1.8 x 13	13.5	= 1.7x8
7	Cube-tiny	Steatite	-	-	1.8	= 1.7x1

of the City II at Qal'at al Bahrain, especially in the building to the west of the square adjacent to the gate. Citing a cuneiform tablet from Ur (ca. 1800 B.C.), which deals with the weighing of copper çargo brought to Ur from Dilmun and mentions "according to the standard of Dilmun", and "according to the standard of the Ur", Bibby tries to establish a relation between these two standards. He works at three equations between the two systems of weights.

360

Fig.13   Dilmun Weights from City I.
(After G.Bibby 1970, Courtesy : Jutlund Archaeological society)

Fig.14 A bath-tub coffin from City IV/Karzakan.
(Courtesy : Bahrain National Museum).

(i)   13100 (+x) minas (Dilmun) (line 1) = 611 talents 62/3 minas (Ur) (line 9). As X cannot
        be less than 1/3 mina nor more than 99 2/3 minas, and reducing the Ur weights to minas,
        we get 13,100 1/3- 13, 199 2/3 minas (Dilmun) = 36,666 2/3 minas (Ur). Therefore
        one mina (Dilmun) = 2.778-2.799 minas (Ur=14,00.0-1410.7 grams).

(ii)   5502 (+x) 2/3 minas (Dilmun) (line 5) = 245 talents 54 1/3 minas (Ur) (line 10). As
        X must here be one of the multiples of 10 from 10 to 90, and again reducing the Ur
        weights, we get : 5512 2/3 - 5592 2/3 minas (Dilmun) = 14,754 1/3 minas (Ur) therefore
        1 mina (Dilmun) = 2.638 - 2.676 minas (Ur) = 1329.1348.9 grams.

(iii)   245 talents 54 1/3 minas (Ur) (line 10) + 4271 1/2 minas (Dilmun) (line 13) + 325
        minas (Dilmun) (line 15) = 450 talents 2 1/3 minas (Ur) (line 18); therefore 4271 1/
        2 + 325 minas (Dilmun) = 450 talents 2 1/3 minas - 245 talents 54 1/3 minas (ur),
        therefore 4966 1/2 minas (Dilmun) = 204 talents 8 minas (Ur) = 2,248 minas (Ur); therefore
        1 mina (Dilmun) = 2.665 minas (Ur = 1343.0 grams).

Taking average of the equations (i) and (iii) gives the result as 1 mina (Dilmun) = 2.721
— 2.732 minas (Ur) = 1371.5 — 1376.8 grams

Finally, Bibby concludes that the value in grams of the Dilmun mina is the weight of
the largest weight found at Qal'at al Bahrain (to within at most 0.5%) and to be almost exactly
on the Indus scale of weight. Lastly, Bibby observes that if the mean of equations (i) and (iii)
are justified, than it is proved with out any doubt that the "standard of Dilmun" was the "standard
of Harappa". The transliteration and translation of the Ur tablet, cited above by Bibby is reproduced
here (Fig. 13a) from Leemans (1960).

Though Bibby (1970) has reproducted the transliteration and translation of the Ur text
from Leemans (1960:38), but seems to have over-looked, while working-out the equation, the
Dilmun-Ur mina relation which Leemans has given at another place (p. 49). Michael Roaf (1982:137-
141) has tried to review Bibby's calculations and equations about Dilmun and Ur weights and
the disparity between the two which led Bibby to assume that the merchants took a commission
on the conversion of weights from one system to the other. Roaf re-examines on the basis of
the internal evidence/analysis of the text of the tablet and states that tablet under reference
records the receipt the Dilmun of a large quantity of copper weighing over 18,000 kilograms.
The consignment was recorded by one Alasum, who distributed partly to the author of the tablet,
partly on payment to Ea-nasir and Nawirum-ili. The remainder was probably to be left with
the distributor himself. The weights of copper for distribution were recorded in Ur weights
or Dilmun weights. Those in Ur were measured in talents and minas, those in Dilmun weight
were measured in minas only. The text translated by Roaf is reproduced here. (Fig. 13b) (Passage
in the translation, marked in square brackets are damaged portions of the tablet and passages
in round brackets have been inserted by Roaf to clarify the meanings). Roaf concludes and
states: that the difference between the Ur and Dilmun weight system was not confined to the

5 gín kù-babbar	5 shekels of silver
nam-KA-sa₆-sa₆-gi-dè	as a *tadmiqtu* loan
ki x-x-LAM(?)-AN	D.
mDA(?)-x ¹) AG.IM	has borrowed
5 šu-ba-an-ti	from X.
ki-AN.KAL-bi-šè	He will return the silver
šu-ba-an-ti	at a moment (yet) to be
kù gur-ru-dum	determined (?); ²)
mu lugal-bi in-pà	(This) he has sworn by the king.
10 1 ma-na kù-babbar	1 mina of silver
šà ½ UD. x ³)	from which a (the?) ½ ....,
½ ma-na kù-babbar	½ mina of silver
x-ta	.....,
na₄ig i-k u₆	for buying "fish-eyes"
15 ù(sic) níg-nam-ma	and other merchandise
sa₁₀-sa₁₀-dè	
kaskal Tilmun-na	on an expedition to Tilmun
ki *Id-din*-GIŠ.LAM	N.
mGÁL (or r í).AN.X.X ⁴)	has borrowed
20 šu-ba-an-ti	from Iddin-.....
kaskal-ta silim-ma-bi	After safe completion of the journey
šám kù im-ma-tùm	he will bring merchandise for the silver
šà um-mi-a al-dug	(and thus) satisfy the *ummeanum*.
um-mi-a TAR.ŠID(?).NE	The *ummeanum* will not recognize
25 nu-un-ta-zu-ma (read z u?)	commercial losses (?);
mu lugal-bi in-pà	This he has sworn by the king.

---

1) Probably ŠL 271 or a similar sign. It is remarkable that none of the names in this text can be interpreted.

2) Cf. F. R. KRAUS, *Symbolae Koschaker*, pp. 50 ff., B. Landsberger, JNES VIII (1949), p. 288, note 126, and JCS VIII (1954), p. 113 f., note 228, A. L. Oppenheim, JAOS 74 (1954) p. 10.

3) The sign has some resemblance to ḪA(?) in line 14.

4) There are probably two signs after AN, the former one probably considered as erased by Dr Figulla. They look most like

Fig.13a Ur Tablet about Dilmun Standard. Transiliteration and Translation. (After F.W. Leemans, 1960).

absolute weights of the units but extended to the way the units were combined and subdivided. The Ur system was sexagesimal:60 minas equalled 1 talents, and 1 mina was sub-divided into 60 shekels. The Dilmun minas, as per the Ur tablet, were combined into hundreds and thousands not into multiple of sixty; and the Bahrain (and Indus) weights suggest that Dilmun minas were normally divided into eights and hundredths; on the Ur tablet Dilmun minas were divided into halves and thirds but it seems probably that the two-thirds is an approximation of seven-eights; this difference in the weight system is also evident in the convenient equilence to Dilmun mina = 1/3 Ur mina, because Ur minas were generally divided into thirds (20 shekels) and Dilmun (Bahrain-Indus) minas were divided into eights. Roaf confirms Bibby's findings that the Bahrain/ Dilmun weights fits into the Indus system; both, according to their absolute weights and according to their shapes, for the commonest shape Indus weight is cube and the second common shape is spherical, we find in Bahrain. Roaf (1982:137ff) suggested that Dilmun mina was a weight of ca. 1,350 grams, divided into eight and one hundred. Powell (1983:141) have suggested that the best evidence is actually the implicit pattern of halving the weights, rather than precise coincidence of mass and he finds only one weight from Mohenjo-Daro actually weighed 1375 grams. As such, he suggests that Ur texts does not provide sufficient evidence for the relationship between Ur and Dilmun standards. But since the Dilmun "mina" is reckoned in the Ur text as roughly 2 2/3 (or 2 7/8 as per Roaf's assumtion) Ur minas indicates that the basic unit of the Dilmun system was incorporated in the Bahrain stone weight of ca, 1370 grams. This may also have been the basic unit of the Indus system. Rao (1986:379) also finds that the Dilmun standard of 1370 grams is five times the Lothal weight 274.4096 grams.

In 1986 Carlo Zaiccagnini (1986:19-23) tried to evaluate the absolute weights of Dilmun in relation with Indus and other weight systems. He suggests that the Dilmun mina was not sexagesimal, the division factors are 8 and 10 and their decimal multiples or sub-multiples. And that the weight of median value of 1,350 grams. (i.e. Dilmun mina) is to be considered the 100- multiple of a unit of 13.5 grams, as well as the 80 multiple of limit of 17 grams. The metrological significance of this fractioning of the Dilmun mina into 80 units of 17 grams or into 100 units of 13.5 grams will be appreciated if we consider that a weight of 17 grams will be exactly the double the Mesopotamian shekel (i.e. 8.5 grams); and whereas the weight of 13.5 grams - is exactly the double of the shekel of 6.5 - 6.8 grams. In the corpus of Indus weight there is evidence for an 80-fractioning of the mina of 1,350 gram, i.e., the unit of 17 grams. The shekel of 6.5 grams is also known from Ebla, Nuzi, Bughazkay etc., and is represented also among the Indus weights. Ebla weights provide some clues for the metrologic inter-relationship between the Dilmun standard and other "western" mina (i.e. of countries: Syria, Hittie, Ebla etc., lying west of Dilmun). Zaccagnini analyses the standards of these countries and correlates them and establishes the relation that Dilmun mina was considered equivalent of 3 "western" minas. (Zaccagnini, 1986:19-23). Weight similar to Dilmun/Indus has been found in another Gulf State, Ras al-Khaimah and it is exhibited in their museum. Dilmun weight were valid in international market, and Dilmun weight system was in use in Ebla, as attested by the texts. (Pettinato, 1981:185ff; Steiglitz, 1987:43ff).

Copy of line 1 based on Figulla's copy (*UET* V, pl. CXXIX) with Postgate's collation.

§A : ll. 1-4. ᵐA[-la-ṣum] has received at Dilmun 13,[??? minas of copper] according to the standard of D[ilmun].

§B : ll. 5-7. Out of which they had given to us 5, 5[?2]⅔ ³ minas of copper according to the standard of Dilmun.

§A* : ll. 8-9. Its weight is in total 611 talents 6⅔ minas according to the standard of Ur.

§B* : ll. 10-12. Out of which 245 talents 51¼ minas of copper which ᵐA-la-ṣum(?) has given to us.

§C : ll. 13-14. 4,271½ (Dilmun) minas of copper (are) the debt ⁴ of ᵐEa-naṣir ;

§D : ll. 15-16. 325 (Dilmun) minas of copper (are) the debt of ᵐNawirum-ili.
l. 17. Later it has been taken.⁵

§E* : ll. 18-19. In total (there are) 450 talents 2¼ minas of copper according to the standard [of Ur] which he has given.

§F* : l. 20. The remainder (is) 161 talents 4[¼] (Ur) minas of copper].

From this text Geoffrey Bibby set up the following equations :

1. §A* : = §E* + §F*
   611 talents 6⅔ minas = 450 talents 2¼ minas + 161 talents 4[¼] minas.

2. §A = §A*
   13,??? Dilmun minas = 611 Ur talents 6⅔ Ur minas.

3. §B = §B*
   5,5?2⅔ Dilmun minas = 245 Ur talents 51¼ Ur minas.

4. §B + §C + §D = §E*
   5,5?2⅔ + 4,271½ + 325 Dilmun minas = 450 Ur talents 2¼ Ur minas.

There are damaged numbers in equations 2, 3, and 4 which relate the Ur and Dilmun minas, but by combining equations 3 and 4 we get :

$$§C + §D = §E* - §B*$$

$$4,596½ \text{ Dilmun minas} = 12,248 \text{ Ur minas.}$$

Fig.13b Cuneiform Text about Dilmun Standard. (After M.Raof, 1982)

Another set/system of weights which were current in Bahrain during early second millennium was that of Mesopotamia. Four typical Mesopotamian weights, one barrel shaped and three spindle shaped of polished haematite have been found during excavation of al Hajjar graves. Their specifications are :

Length (cms)	3.9	3.2	2.1	4
Maximum Diameter	0.9	1.3	0.6	0.7
Weight (grams)	8.5	16.4	2.1	5.6

(Cleuziou, 1989:35).

(C)   COFFINS AND BURIAL JARS

During the first two seasons of their excavations (1954-54) the Danes discovered sarcophagus, burried inside a large building at Qal'at al Bahrain, which was later designated as City IV. The coffins (Fig.14) were 0.6m, broad and 0.9m and 1 meter long and 0.65 m and 0.63 m. deep. They were formed of poorly baked clay, coated inside and outside with bitumen. (Glob, 1954:168, 1956, 172). Since we find several thousands of burials in Bahrain, the burying of the dead inside the large, building seems to be rather strange with no sound reason. The use of coffins seems to be alien practice. It was prevalent in lower Babylonia and other places, (Budge, 1975, 182f). Since coffins were used and buried inside a building suggest that it may be of some important person from abroad, as evidenced by the rich furnishings. It is quite possible that he was burried in a coffin for transhipment to his native place, probably in Mesopotamia; but when it was not possible he was burried in the building. Similar coffins have been recovered from other sites in Bahrain, e.g., Karzakan (Lombard, 1986:227). These coffins are similar to those found in Mesopotamia. (cf. Mecoun and Haines, 1967. Pl. 157; Oates, 1958:m.VI). Glob (1956:173) dates then coffins to eight century B.C. on the basis of an agate seal discovered from the coffin, which came into use in Mesopotamia during late Neo-Assyrian and Neo-Babylonian times. This seal shows a male worshipper with a full beard and raised hand, turned towards the tree of life. Between them there is a figure of a fish, and above them the winged solar disk. Lombard (1986:227) suggest that the dating of Glob seems to be rather early. He proposes a slightly later date.

(D)   STONE SCULPTURE AND TERRACOTTA FIGURINE

At Umm es Sujor or the well-temple, the Danish during their first year of compaign (1954) discovered two lime stone statues of kneeling rams (Fig. 15) of 20 and 21 cms. in height respectively. One of them was found on the staircase and the other in the well-chamber below. They were decapitated; obviously when the well was destroyed during later times. The excavators could not find traces of their head. They are well marked and have well shaped ridge in front. They have a flattish tail cut in low relief and thick-set roundish body. The excavators also found at the head of the staircase on either side, an empty pedestal. They are sufficiently large

366

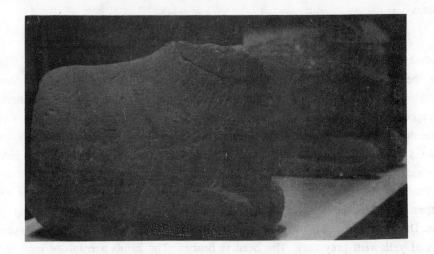

Fig.15   Rams from Umm es Sejur Temple.

(Courtesy : Bahrain National Museum).

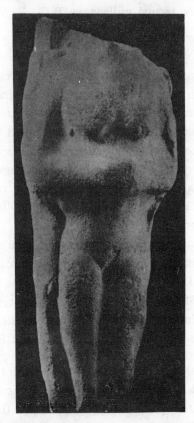

Fig.16   A female figurine from Qal'at (North wall).

(After S.Cleuziou, 1989).

to accommodate one of ram statue. (Bibby, 1954:162; 1969:Pl.3b). During Caspers 91975:68) remarks that the modelling of the rams is rather rudimentary. This may imply unfamiliarity with the working in the medium of limestone. And on the other hand, the prominent chisel marks may suggest that the statues were incomplete or were unfinished products of a workshop. Poor workmanship is evident from the crude rendering of anatomical parts. The rams are dated to first centuries of third millennium B.C. on the basis of the discovery of the red-ridged Barbar sherds in the sand which filled the gap between the edge of the well-head stone and the walls of the well chamber. Caspers suggests that Mesopotamian art served as a prototype for these rams of Bahrain. (Caspers, 1975:58-75;1976:8-38). A female figurine of terracotta (Fig. 16) was found by the Danes within the North Wall of Qal'at al Bahrain. It is 9 cms. in (preserved) height and is of yellowish grey clay. The head is broken. The hands are folded over the belly. Bibby (1966:82,92). It is dated to early second millennium B.C. (Cleuziou, 1989:33). A typical Sumerian style, naked statue of male was found at Tarut island (Saudi Arabia) in close proximity to Bahrain. (Rashid, 1970:159ff; also illustrated in Vol.I p.163 in this series). Several terracotta figurines of male and female have been recovered from Thaj. (Gazder et al, 1984:p.109ff, Pls.81f). Cleuziou (1989:33), on the evidence of Barrelet, finds parallels of Bahrain's figurine in those from Tells in Mesopotamia of early second millennium B.C.

(E)   JEWELLERY

Beads of different shapes and materials of stone, including agate, carnelian, mottled, amethyst, glass, paste etc., have been found in scores of burial mounds and graves. Barbar Temple, City IV in Bahrain (Mughal, 1983:481f; Ibrahim, 1983:481f; Rice, 1988, *Passim*, Srivastava, 1991,202f). These beads of different varieties and in different colours were used by the women for making different types of jewellery. Most common being necklaces and bracelets. Other material used was lapis lazuli, crystal, shell and bronze. Etched carnelian beads, agate lapis lazuli were semi-precious stone of origin from India and Afghanistan. These were traded from India to Gulf and to Mesopotamia and are found in Bahrain. (Caspers, 1972a:83-98). Pendant and necklaces have been recovered from several graves in Bahrain. Cf., Ibrahim (1982:218); During Caspers (1980:Pl. XXIII, XXIX) etc. Some of these specimens using different types of beads in different shades and colour, and different shapes, biconical, tabular, flat, round, barrel-shaped, pallet-like etc., are illustrated here (Fig. 17-20) in order to heighlight the cultural taste and society of the Dilmun people during third-first millennium B.C. Similar type of jewellery has been discovered from various sites in United Arab Emirates and are exhibited in their respective museums at Al'Ain, Dubai, Ajman, Sharjah, Ras al Khaimah and Fujairah.

An interesting pendant of mother-of-pearl in the shape of a bird was found in the Higham tumuli, which lies east of Buri, and north of the Hamla road. The schematically rendered bird has a suspension hole perforating the upturned wing. It measures 0.01, 1x0.12,7 m. and has an overall thickness of 0.001-0.002 m. (Caspers, 1980:13, Pl. XXIII).

368

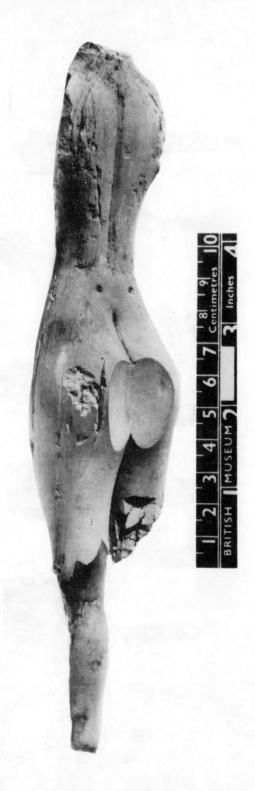

Fig.21 Ivory figurine of naked women from 'Ali cemetery.
(Courtesy : Trustees of the British Museum).

369

Fig.22 A selection of ivory objects from 'Ali Cemetery.
(Courtesy : Trustees of the British Museum).

370

Fig.23 Ivory fragments having incised pattern from 'Ali Cemetery.
(Courtesy : Trustees of the British Museum).

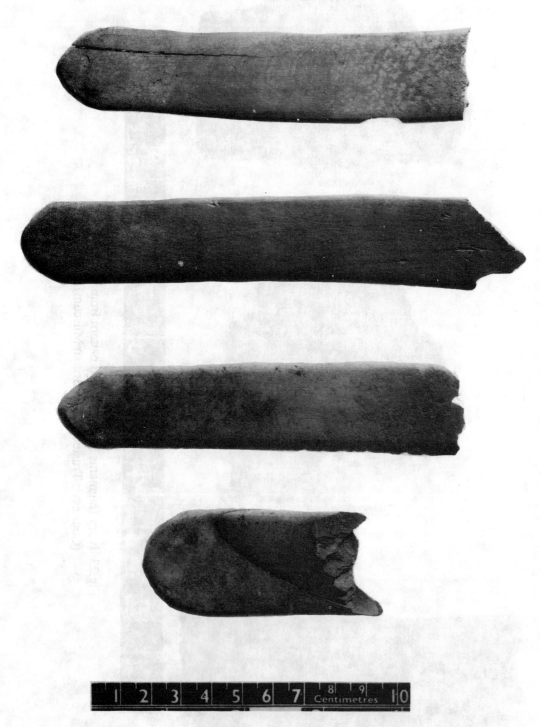

Fig.24 End pieces of spatulas of ivory from 'Ali Cemetery.
(Courtesy : Trustees of the British Museum).

(F)   IVORY OBJECTS

The 'Ali cemetery excavated by Mackay (1929) produced a large number of ivory objects. And some pieces of ivory and objects were also found from the Higham tumuli (grave 36). The objects from the latter are: a ivory comb, square ivory plaque, ivory needle-shaped pin, etc. (Caspers, 1980:15, Pl. XXIV). From tomb 12 of 'Ali cemetry Mackay recovered the back of an ivory figurine, apparently of a naked woman (Fig.21). Extent height 22 cms. She is elegantly stylized, but her most distinctive feature, is the pair of small depressions on the back at the waist. The figurine seems to be wearing garment. As there appears to be the line of garment hanging from her left shoulder and arm across the chest. This type of dress is common in south west Asia during different periods. A few more ivory objects from 'Ali are illustrated in Fig.22. They are: top row (L to R): a modelled fragment representing upper torso of a drapped man (ht 3.4 cms); bull's hoaf on a pedestal (ht 3.5 cms); a solid oval fragment, with two dowel holes in right side (ht. 4.7 cms); fragment with incised circles. (ht. 2.4 cms). Middle row (L to R) : a fragment with trade of incised pattern (ht. 3.3 cms); a modelled fragment, probably an arm or leg, (ht. 1.9 cms); a modelled fragment, possibly an arm or leg (ht. 2.9 cms); a modelled fragment, arm or leg (ht. 3 cms); rounded fragment with tenson at one end, possibly the arm or leg of a composite figure (ht. 4.8 cms) fragment with trace of raised pattern. Bottom row (L. to R): a fragment of pedestal, with part of the left foot of open work human figure on top (ht. 2.2 cms); a fragment of pedestal, with possible part of foot an top (ht. 2.8 cms); also a open work fragment, with perforation (ht. 3.1 cms); another open work fragment with broken perforation (ht. 2.7 cms). Three fragments with incised pattern (Fig. 23) seems be of a circular box. They have hallow incised decorations which do give an idea of the subject or figure. Regarding the larger piece (on left), Reade and Burliegh (1978:77) consider it to be a seated or dancing figure, wearing a dress which has a chain pattern and a hatched border. The other two fragments seems to be related to the first one, and together with more, may make up a box. In this context it may be mentioned that during 1940-41 Cornwall (1946:10) found an ivory box in the tombs. Mackay (1929) discovered from tomb 26 at 'Ali eight end-pieces of broken spatulas. Four of these are illustrated here in Fig. 24. Their lengths are : 13.5; 13.3'16.5 and 7.8 cms. Marks of wear on some of the edges suggest the action of rodent's teeth. (Reade and Burleigh, 1978:78-80). It is obvious that the source of ivory was India. But it is not known whether Bahrain imported raw material and worked or obtained finished products. But since fragment of an elephant tusks was found by Mackay (1929:15) in tomb 12 at 'Ali and again by Bibby (1970:179) at Qal'at al Bahrain City II, it is evident that Bahrain also imported raw material and probably worked on it.

CHAPTER IX

THE DILMUN STATE

It has been already discussed (Chapter II, *supra*) that the evolution of Dilmun took place in three phases during the course of late fourth and third millennium B.C., and its geographical entity as well as its centre was changing. Firstly, during the late fourth and early third millennium B.C., Dilmun comprised the east Arabian mainland and its littoral with its centre at Tarut island, secondly, during the late third millennium B.C., the centre shifted to Bahrain island; and thirdly, around 2000 B.C., Failaka was colonised and incorporated into Dilmun while Bahrain continued to be the centre or capital. This privilege Bahrain never relinquished in the millenniums that followed. Further, Failaka being in close proximity to Mesopotamia and other trading centres of the Levant it developed into a second major centre of Dilmun, next to Bahrain. This is evidenced by the large number of seals and cuneifrom tablets discovered at Failaka (Kjaerum, 1983). In fact it was a front line point of Dilmun in the north with proximity to the Mediterranean littoral. (Calvet, 1991:9 Ms). Economic and diplomatic texts suggests, says Howard-Carter (1987-115), that there may have been Dilmun merchants or perhaps a trading post, in southern Mesopotamia. Again when Tarut was Dilmun's centre, Bahrain must have been definitely functioning as an entre-pot or a trading station and must have been involved, (as attested by the discovery of Jamdat Nasr sherds at City I at Qal'at al Bahrain), in the trading activity between the east and the west. Otherwise, suddenly it would not have become Dilmun's capital. The activity and facilities at Bahrain must have justified for it being choosen as Dilmun's centre. The causes for the decline of Tarut entreport are not known. But one of the reasons, which Piesinger (1983:832Ms.) attributes for Tarut's decline as possibility, is the lack of ethnic ties betwen the Dilmunites and the Akkadian may have disrupted the special relationship which the Dilmunites enjoyed earlier, and cutting off of the middleman by Mesopotamia and the Indus during this period by their direct contact. At any rate, during this period the main entrepot of Dilmun was in the process of shifting from Tarut to more convenient and deeper port on the off shore islands of Bahrain. Thus, strategic location of Bahrain contributed much for shifting Dilmun's centre to it. Further by late third millennium, Ur III period, City II at Qal'at al Bahrain was flourishing with stronger Mesopotamian as well as Indus contacts (as evidenced by the archaeological finds of these places at City II) and Dilmun regained its monopoly on the maritime Gulf trade between the east and the west. Consequently, a society of Dilmun civilization was gradually evolving and this is manifested clearly in archaeological discoveries of the period, already mentioned in above (Chapters IV-VIII).

We find the origin of early Dilmun state (as mentioned earlier in Vol.I. p, 173, in this series), constituted by several islands on the Gulf coast: Failaka, Tarut, Bahrain itself, possibly other islands, parts of east Arabian littoral, and some areas of the Arabian mainland (see map 1 in Chapter II *supra*, and map 8.2 in Vol.I (p. 163) for the territorial extent of Dilmun. Thus, Dilmun state originated in third millennium B.C. as a kind of political and cultural federal union in the Arabian Gulf, as suggested by During Caspers (1973b:5; 1973c:4). And such a vast state whose territory stretched not only along the sea coast but extended far into the mainland of Arabia could not have existed, functioned, and flourished without any government or central administration. But we have no evidence. Discovery of Dilmun archives, hopefully in future alone can enlighten this most important aspect of Dilmun state. However, the other aspects of being a state are manifested from the following functions; issuance of its own seals and weight, operation of a custom house, town planning, religious cult, building and maintenance of temples, trade and culture relations with foreign rulers/countries, appointment of tax collector, as attested in Archaic text from Uruk dated to 3200-3000 B.C. (Nissen, 1986:338); sending of messenger or rather envoys to foreign courts, etc.

After shifting the centre to Bahrain and settling down, the Dilmun state took gradual shape during its formative period from late third millennium to early second millennium B.C. And by 1780 B.C. or may be earlier, it assumed full status of state-hood with a king at its helm. This is attested by the mention of "King of Dilmun" in a text from Mari (Syria) about the distribution of Oil to the palace where the king of Dilmun was residing on a visit to the Mari court during the reign of Iasmah-Adad; and this text is dated to ca. 1780 B.C. by Charpin (1984:92,No.61). The text is silent about the actual name of the Dilmunite king. Nor there is any other reference, so far, regarding his particulars as the Dilmun king with his capital at Bahrain. He must have, I presumed, administered or managed the affairs of the government of the Greater Dilmun through his agents or officials. Probably, he must have divided the Greater Dilmun into administrative zones/regions for the proper functioning of business and to have control; political, administrative and commercial, considering the territorial extent of Greater Dilmun, as mapped by Zarins (1986:237). (See Map Chapter II *supra*). We may venture to divide broadly Greater Dilmun into following six zones or regions, as they might have been probably at that time. Even more also possibly existed. Bahrain (capital); Failaka (second centre, northern headquarter); group of coastal islands including former centre Tarut; littoral between Failaka and Tarut/Abqaiq area; al Hasa and other adjoining regions into Jabrin Oasis, in Arabian mainland, and Qatar.

Hojlund (1989:45-49) discusses various aspects which contributed to the formation of the Dilmun state during the transition between the periods of Qal'at I and II at Qal'at al Bahrain. These periods he has fixed on the basis of relative percentage of pottery belonging to the Barbar tradition and to the Mesopotamian tradition found at Qal'at. One of the reasons for the formation of the Dilmun state, Hojlund states: should perhaps rather be sought in a condition general to the settled communities along the Gulf coast, namely the threat from the nomads of the mainland. This he suggests from the point of view of international trade, in which Dilmun was involved, and its protection. As such, Hojlund states that centre of Dilmun was shifted from the east coast of Arabia to Bahrain, which was easier to defend. But I think that the earlier centre of Dilmun, Tarut island, was also equally safe as an island like Bahrain. Both are similarly situated. As such, threat from nomads may not be the cause for the shift of centre from Tarut to Bahrain. Further, the Arabian littoral and parts of the eastern Arabian mainland, several hundreds of kilometers were within the Dilmun territory. These nomads, under the jurisdiction and control of Dilmun may not have been a threat. One possibility is from the nomads residing far interior in the mainland. But this possibility is ruled out as, they were not in direct contact and both Tarut and Bahrain were well protected from the Dilmun territory extending deep into the eastern Arabian mainland, where Dilmunites lived. Dilmunites' settlements in east Arabian littoral and mainland is well attested by the existence of tumuli in and around Dhahran, similar to those found in Bahrain and with similar practices and funerary gifts found in these tombs. (Cornwall, 1952:140; Zarins et al, 1984; 'Ali, 1988). Several Dilmun seals have been found in this region at Naqdan in Rub'al Khali, about 110 km. east of Jabrin, which was within Dilmun's territory. (Golding, 1974:28f).

On the basis of Qal'at al Bahrain's chronology of period I and II, Hojlund (1989:45ff) states that Dilmun state existed from about 2200 to 1600 B.C., when Dilmun was exposed to strong Mesopotamian influence. This period he has divided into three phases: Phase I ca. 2200 - ca. 2000 B.C.; phase II ca. 2000 ca. 1800 B.C., and phase III : ca. 1800 - ca. 1600 B.C. He has suggested that, during the first phase, Dilmun was under the influence of Indus Valley; during the second phase, under the influence of Mesopotamia and political power in Dilmun was taken over by the Amorites who were present at Bahrain; and during the third phase, decline in trade, with a few characteristic features which he attributes to dessertion of the southern Mesopotamian cities and political condition in the Indus Valley and in Oman. However, Hojlund (p. 54) does not take into consideration nor mentions the consequences or after affects of the abandonment of City II at Qal'at, some time in the first half of the second millennium B.C., about 1750 B.c., according to Bibby (1969). That is the missing link City IIE of his chronology. (Hojlund, 1986:224). There was a hiatus in the occupation at the Qal'at - City II. At least 400 years of settlement are unaccounted for in the archaeological sequence. The break in the ceramic sequence, states Larsen (1983) is abrupt. Barbar II levels are often overlain by Hellenistic and later occupations. The immediate successor to the Barbar period was the Kassite dynasty of Mesopotamia. At Qal'at Bahrain the Kassite buildings, dated to the late second millennium B.C., overlie the Barbar sequence, which dates to little later then the Isin-Larsa period. (Larsen, 1983:80).

Hojlund (1989) stops at 1600 B.C. To his three phases (from 2200- 1600 B.C.) of Dilmun state, we may add a few more phases, from 1600 to 400 B.C., as follows, in order to complete our period of prehistory and protohistory : (1) ca. 1600-1480 B.C. - period of decline in trade. No mention of Dilmun in Mesopotamian texts;   (2) ca 1480 - 1240 B.C. - Kassite domina-tion of Dilmun (City III period), under Mesopotamian viceroys; (3) ca 1240 - 705 B.C. - No record about Dilmun in Mesopotamian text. Dilmun state continued to exist and functioned of its own, probably; and (4) ca 709 - 400 B.C., Dilmunite kings regain power. (Bibby 1969; Mortensen, 1987/88:15; Reade, 1986:325-334; Lombard 1986:225-232; D.Oates, 1986:429).

During the phase from 1600-1480 B.C., there seems to be a decline in Dilmun's trade

Fig.1   A Cylinder seal with impression, naming Kassite Viceroy/Governor of Dilmun.
(Courtesy : Trustees of the British Museum).

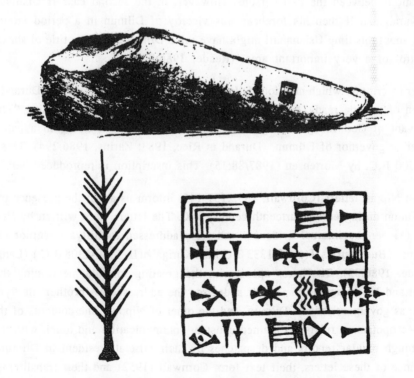

Fig.2   An inscription on black stone mentioning Rimun and his palace.
(After Capt. Durand 1880, in M.Rice, 1984).

with Mesopotamia due to the collapse of Old Babylonian Empire and there is no mention of Dilmun in Mesopotamian text. During the phase from 1480 - 1240 B.C., the coming of Kassite rule in Mesopotamia brought about a change in the Dilmun state and its relations with the former took a new turn. With commercial interest, the Kassites initiated measures to establish stronger relations with Dilmun state. Thus Kassite increased their involvement in the affairs of the Dilmun state and to exercise full control and check over the trading activities they tried to exert political pressure. This they achieved by appointing their own officials as residents or viceroys in the Dilmun state. This is evident from the cuneiform texts, one on a seal and two on tablets mentioning names of Mesopotamian officials as governor/viceroy of Dilmun. The cylinder seal (Fig.1) is from the British Museum and was published by Juliean Reade (1986:332). She states that the seal has a detailed text mentioning the name and ancestry of a man called Ubalisu-Marduk, son of Arad-Ea, grandson of Ushurana, (—) and great grand son of possibly a more remote descendent of Usiananuri - (—) who bore the title Shakkanakku, viceroy of Dilmun. Ubalisu-Marduk, owner of the seal, held an office under a king called Kurigalzu. Reade argues that the latter could be Kurigalzu I or II. In the case of the former, the date would be 1400 B.C., and in the case of the latter, it would be 1332-1308 B.C. Since in the seal it is stated that Ubalisu-Marduk is a descendent of the original viceroy Usainanuri, Reade works out, in the first case, the date of 1480 B.C., and for the latter, by considering a gap of four or five generations between the two persons. However, in the second case if Ubalisu-Marduk lived under Kuraigalzu II then his forebear was viceroy of Dilmun in a period around 1420-1410 B.C. So, about this time Usiananuri might have ruled Dilmun, with the title of shakkanakku, implying control of a very important area. (Reade, 1986:332f).

Another inscription which mentions Dilmun's governor was discovered by Durand in 1879. The inscription of a stone reads: e-gal ri-mu-um-ir in-z-ak lu a-garum. Meaning "The palace of rimun, servant of God Inzag of Aagarum". Implying that Rimun living in a palace could be only a ruler or governor of Dilmun. (Durand in Rice, 1983; Zarins, 1986:294). This is dated to ca. 1600-1500 B.C. by Mortensen (1987/88:15). This inscription is reproduced here in Fig.2.

The two Nippur letters (Cornwall, 1952:137-145) inform us about the presence of Kassite officials at Dilmun during early fourteenth century B.C. The letters were written by Ili-ippashra from Dilmun (as per the internal evidence) and were addressed to Ililiya governor of Nippur during the reigns of Burnaburias II (1359-1333 B.C.) and Kurigalzu II (1330-1308 B.C.). (Langsberger, 1965:76; Reade, 1986:33). The letter opens with the greeting formula mentioning the names of gods Enzag and Meskilag and the writer addressed the addressee as 'brother' implying equal status of both, as governors, one of Dilmun, and the other of Nippur. The contents of the letters suggest that Mesopotamian rulers maintained constant communication and touch with the affairs of Dilmun through regular reports and despatches by their officials resident in Dilmun. Owing to the importance of these letters, their text form Cornwall (1952) and their transliteration, and translation by Goetze (1952:142-145) are given (Fig. 3) for their detailed study. The first letter mentions a few names of the persons who were present in Dilmun, (the place of origin of letters) at that time. They are Iltanu, Sinu-nuri, Nawir-Uras, and Iddin-Nerigal. The first name

Ni. 615

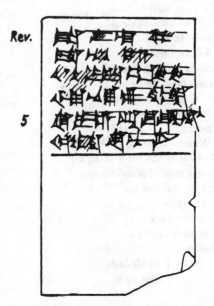

Ni. 641

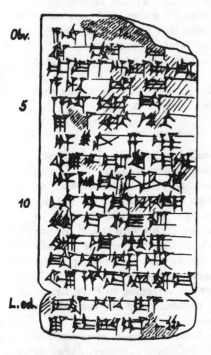

Fig.3 Nipper Letters-Text, Transliteration and Translation.
(After P.B.Cornwall, and Goetze 1952, Courtesy :
"Journal of Cuneiform Studies").

Ni. 615

Transliteration

obv.
1 [a-na I-l]i-li-ia [qí-b]í-ma
2 [um-ma] 'Ilī-ip-pa-aš-ra aḫu-k[a-ma]
3 [a-na] ka-ša lu šu-ul-mu
4 ᵈIn-zag$_x$ ù ᵈMes-ki-la-a[k]
5 ilū^{meš} ša Tilmun^{ki}
6 na-ap-ša-ti-ka li-iṣ-ṣ[u-ru]
7 ['Il]-ta-nu ša il-la-k[a a-ta-]mar
8 ù [Su]-te-tu it-[t]a-ba-[al-kat-m]a
9 il-la-ka a-la-ka ša [. . . . .].
10 [a]n-ni-ti ul qí-pa-ku i-na-an-na
11 [a-na B]ābili ul-te-te-ši-ra-[š]i⁷
12 [la-m]a waraḫ Elūli e-te-bi[-i]r
13 [i-]ka-ša-ad-ma la-mu-ú-a-a
14 [K]A.LUM Aḫ-la-mu-ú it-tab-lu
15 ù it-tu-ú-a-a mi-im-ma
16 [ša] e-pe-ši-ia ia-nu
17 ù ālu^{ki} 1-en e SU.SU-x[.]
18 i-na li-it āli^{ki} ša ú[- . . . . . .]
19 i-na ᵈSin-nu-ri ki-i[. . . . .]
20 ù bīt ili ša eš-[. . . . .]
21 bīt [x] ᵈNi[n- . . . .]
22 ù [bīt]u la-bi[-ir-ma i-na-aḫ]
23 i-na-an-na mi-i[m-ma ul]

rev.
1 ki-in-tum i-teʔ-pu[-uš aḫ-šu]
2 na-di ù ul-tu uₐʔ[-mi an-ni]
3 šu-na-ti i-ta-nam-m[a-ru]
4 ù qa-tu-tu ša eka[lli]
5 a-na 5-ši-šu i-te-la[-am]
6 i-na-an-na šum-ma i-na x[. . . . . .]
7 mi-im-ma a-na pa-ni-ia
8 ip-ta-ri-ik mi-na-a ep-pu[-uš]
9 a-na šarri iš-ša-pa-ar
10 at-ta a-na [. . . . . . .] qí-bi-ma
11 a-na 'Nawir-ᵈUraš [l]i-li-ik-[ma]
12 bīta ša-šu li-iṣ-bat-ma li-ik-ši[-ir]
13 ù šum-ma a-na 'Iddin-ᵈNerīgal
14 li-iš-pu-ru-nim-ma ālu^{ki-meš}
15 ša a-lik ur-ki-ti i-na pa-ni
16 ša-šu-ḫi i-ba-šu-ú
17 [bīt]a ša-šu li-iṣ-ba-tu
18 [li-]ik-ši-ru
19 [. . . . .]. ki pa-la-ḫi
20 [. . . . .] ul aq-bi

Translation

[1] [To Il]iliya speak! [2] This is what Ilī-ippašra, thy brother, said: [3] [Unto] thee be well-being! [4] May Inzag and Meskilak, [5] the gods of Tilmun, [6] guard thy life!

[7] Iltānu who will arrive [I have m]et. [8] Also [the Sutean woman(?)] has crossed (the sea) and [9] [she] will arrive. Of the coming of this [Sutean woman(?)] I am not (so) sure. Now [11] I have directed her to Bābil. [12] [Before] the month of Elūlu draws to a close [she] will reach (there). [14] Around me the Aḫlamû have carried away the dates, [15] thus with me there is nothing that I can do. [17] But a single town must not be allowed to remain pillaged(??).

[18] In the town which I [. . . . .], when from Sîn-nurî [I heard] — [20] and the temple I h[eard about] [21] (is) the house of Ni[n . . . .] — [22] the house was ol[d and had collapsed]. [23] Now he has done [no]thi[ng] at all(??), he [let it] go. And from that day on [3] they keep seeing dreams [4] and the destruction of the palace [5] has been indicated for a fifth time. [6] If now in . . [. . . .] something he has prevented me from achieving, what could I do? [9] Should he be sent to the king? [10] Speak you to [. . . . . .], [11] so that he may go to Nawir-Uraš. [12] May he get to work and repair that house. Or may they write to Iddin-Nerīgal — towns [14] of (his) retainers exist near . . . . — [17] and may they get to work and repair that house.

[19] [I have spoken] respectfully; [in a way that might offend you], I did not speak.

Commentary

obv. 1:   Reading according to F. R. Kraus.

obv. 4:   Misread *Sad-di-la-ak* by Unger, Reall. d. Vorg. 13 (1929) 313. It seems that, because of Ni. 641, for the sign 'sag' a value *zag* is to be posited. This variant and the one to be found in Šurpu VIII 20 make it certain that the spelling of the name is phonetic.

obv. 7:   Reading according to F. R. Kraus. — Restoration of the last word is uncertain.

obv. 8:   *Su-te-tu*(?). This is more likely a gentilic than a proper name, at least if at the end of line 9 the same

[Su-te-t]i⁷ is to be restored. *Sutētu* may stand for *Sutītu* and denote "Sutean woman".

obv. 10: Meaning uncertain.

obv. 13: *la-mu-ú-a-a* is not known to me from other passages, but the construction is good Cassite and like *it-tu-ú-a-a* in line 15.

obv. 14: [K]A.LUM, i.e. *suluppī*.

obv. 17: *e* should be negation; it is normal in negative wishes. The verbal form that should follow is apparently written ideographically and may be meant to be read as a stative. SU.SU is *šallu* "despoiled" according to Meissner,

SAI 94; cf. Delitzsch, Sumerisches Glossar 249 s.v. sud.

obv. 18: Restore either "I am living in" or "I am responsible for"??

obv. 20–21: For these lines a collation of S. N. Kramer was also available; it confirmed Kraus' readings throughout.

obv. 20: The restoration *ša eš*[-*mu-ú*] is, to judge from the preserved traces, likely.

rev. 1: The meaning given for *kintum* is merely a guess and may be wrong.

rev. 5: Literally: "has come up, emerged".

rev. 8: Literally: "has blocked".

rev. 16: *ša-šu-ḫi* (or *ša šu-ḫi*) remains obscure to me.

Ni. 641

Transliteration		Translation
obv. 1	*a-na* ¹*Il-l*[*i-ia*]	To Ill[iya]
	qí-bí-ma	speak!
	um-ma ¹*Ili-ip-pa-aš-ra*	This is what Ili-ippašra,
	a-ḫu-ka-ma	thy brother, said:
5	*a-na ka-ša*	Unto thee
	lu [*š*]*u-ul-mu*	be well-being!
	ᵈ*In-za-ag*	May Inzag
	ù ᵈ*Mes-ki-la-ak*	and Meskilak,
	*ilū*ⁿᵉˢ *ša Tilmun*ᵏⁱ	the deities of Tilmun,
10	*na-ap-ša-ti-ka*	guard
	li-iṣ-ṣu-ru	thy life!
	Aḫ-la-mu-ú	The Aḫlamū
	ša na-ka-ri	certainly talk
	ù ḫa-ba-ti-im-ma	to me
lo.e.	*it-ti-ia*	only of violence
	lu i-da-ab-[*b*]*u-bu*	and plunder;
rev. 1	*ša sa-la-mi*	of conciliation
	it-ti-ia	they do not talk
	ul i-da-ab-bu-bu	with me.
	ù be-lu ú-ḫi-bil	The lord put it upon me
	ki-i e-ri-šu-šu-nu-ti	to ask them,
	ul id-di-nu-ni	but they did not comply.

Commentary

obv. 8: This seems to be the reading that is paleographically most probably. Cf. Šurpu VIII 20 (H. Zimmern, Beiträge zur Kenntnis der babylonischen Religion, p. 42f.) "ᵈ*En-zag* ᵈ*Mis-ki-mis*" in a list of deities that have to do with water.

rev. 4: A collation by S. N. Kramer confirms Kraus' copy.

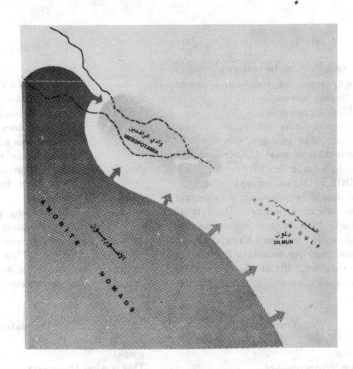

Fig.4 Migration of Amorites.
(Courtesy : Bahrain National Museum).

Fig.5　Cuneiform Tablets from the Kassite City III at Qal'at al Bahrain.

seems to be that of a merchant or a messenger; but the other three names are of men holding positions of authority in Dilmun and may be either officials or nobles who have been granted territory there. These persons may be Amorites or Mar-Tu who migrated to Dilmun around 2000 B.C. (Fig. 4) They are mentioned in cuneiform tablets recovered from Qal'at al Bahrain (For Amorites or MAR-TU connections with Dilmun, see Vol.I in this series pp. 141-145). These pure Akkadian names in the Nippar letters, implies clearly, infers Cornwall (1952:139), that in Dilmun's administration the key positions were held not by indigenes but by Babylonians. That is Kassite rulers of Mesopotamia did not simply appoint a viceroy to govern, but had taken over full political as well as administrative control of Dilmun by appointing their officials to various administrative positions or offices of the Dilmun administration. Further, we may conclude that for proper functioning and to run the administration of Greater Dilmun there might have been sufficiently large number of Mesopotamian officials working and residing in Dilmun. Obviously they maintained their own system for communication in their own language, as evidenced by several cuneiform tablets (Fig. 5) discovered in City III at Qal'at al Bahrain. They deal with administrative aspects and trade and mention names of several Amorites or MAR-TU. Further, for the purpose of authentication of offical records or attestation of business transactions they used thier own personal cylinder seals which they brought or carried with them from their country. This accounts for the large number of (more than 30) cylinder seals of foreign (Mitanni) make found in City III at Qal'at al Bahrain and in various graves, e.g., Al-Hajjar, al Maqsha etc. A few specimen of these seals are illustrated here (Fig. 6) to elucidate the point which suggests that to a great extent the Dilmun administration and the state were run by foreigners under foreign influence. These seals are from Bahrain National Museum. A seal recently discovered (1992) f rom the new site of al Maqsha bears cuneiform inscription. (Abdul Aziz Soweilah, personal communication).

The cuneiform tablets and cylinder seals both of them being foreign to Dilmun civilization, attest the presence of Mesopotamian nationals in Dilmun for a cansiderable time. And their discovery from the graves suggests that they lived and died in Bahrain, living behind their legacy. From the foregoing details about Mesopotamian governors exercising control over Dilmun implies that the latter was in a sense a province of the former. And probably Qal'at al Bahrain was Kassites provincial capital; as revealed by the abundant archaeological evidence and Kassite architecture at Qal'at al Bahrain. It seems that Kassite- Babylonia was the region first national state; and Dilmun for a time formed its part. The later second millennium pattern adumbrates that of the first millennium B.C., when Mesopotamian empires incorporated surrounding lands, including Dilmun. This incorporation of Dilmun into Kassite administrative structure suggests, Eden (1986:214f), implies a analagous incorporation of Dilmun into Kassite's relation of production. He further states that these relations mainly centered on land, collection of agricultural taxes and on labour obligations, where lands were held by the crown or granted to others. This implies forcible extraction of agriculture surplus by Mesopotamian's bureaucratic coersion. This is confirmed by the concern voiced by Dilmun's governor in a letter to his counter part at Nipper (Edens, 1986:214f).

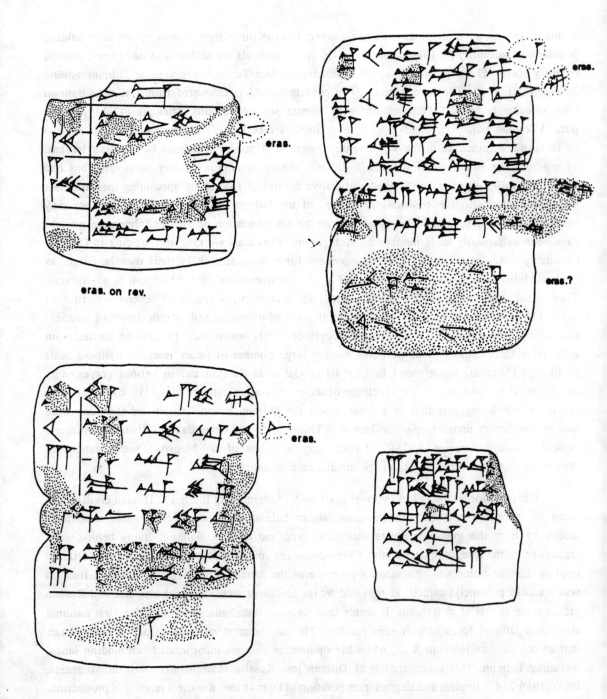

eras.

eras.

eras.?

eras. on rev.

eras.

Fig.5   Text of Cuneiform Tablets. (After Jesper Eidem 1986, unpublished).

During the phase from 1240-709 B.C. Kassite domination ceased to exist in Bahrain. As such, the Mesopotamian records are silent about Dilmun which is not at all mentioned. However, Dilmun state did continue to exist and Bahrain was occupied during this period, as evidenced by the ceramic analysis of Qal'at al Bahrain carried out by Mortensen (1987/88;13ff). The phase from 800-400 B.C. seems to have witnessed revival of power under Dilmun kings, named Uperi, Qane, and Hundaru. (Kessler, 1983:154; Howard- Carter, 1978:96) and a Dilmun kingdom emerged. The Dilmun kings are mentioned in the Assyrian records. Letters written by Assurbanipal's general Bel-ibni mention Hundaru, as king of Dilmun. Another letter Assurbanipal wrote to Hundaru offering him kingship of Dilmun. In order to assure his allegiance in the conflict between Assyria and Babylonia. Obviously, at that time Hundaru was Mesopotamian governor and Dilmun must have been made his province earlier by Nabopolassar or by Nebuchadnezzor II, because a "governor of Telmun" (Luen.Nam Sa Tel-Munik) is mentioned in administrative documents dating to the 11th year of (567 B.C.), Nabonidus (Openheim, 1954.16f). However these Dilmun kings seem to have owed alligence to Mesopotamian rulers. Thus, when 709 B.C. Sargon II crushed the revolt of Sealand dynasty and asserted his sovereignty over Elam, Kaduniash, Cheldea, and Bitiakin, down to the borders of Dilmun, being afraid of the impending danger, Uperi, in order to reconciliate Sargon II, sent an ambassador offering submission and sent tribute and gifts to the latter. The ambassador of Dilmun who took tribute to the Neo- Assyrian king was I'idru, a court-official with the title Lumu- ri-ib-ba-nu. (Oppenheim, 1954:16f). Thus implying that Dilmun's king had a regular court, court officials, special titles of officials, etc., and maintained regular administrative and diplomatic offices. And since the designation L mu-ri-ib-ba-nu reccurs in the Neo-Assyrian legal documents, it is obvious that Dilmun's court and its offices were moddled on the lines of Mesopotamia. (For more reference of suzerainty and nominal allegiance in Khorasabad texts of Assyrian rulers, see Chapter II *supra*.) Qana was the second Dilmun King who sent tribute to Assyrian ruler Esarhaddon between 680 and 670 B.C. Kessler quotes an excessive formulaic list of titles which includes "King of the kings of the lands of Dilmun, Magan and Meluhha". Esarhaddon's laying of tribute from Dilmun King Qana is mentioned in another inscription. In Nineveh archives relating to the period of Ashurbanipal, we have a list of tribute and letters to Dilmun king stating that Hundaru dutifully paid tribute to him in kind in the form of large amount of copper, kohl, parts of mountain sheep and pieces of wood. (Kessler, 1983; Howard-Carter, 1978:95f). The Assyrian rulers hyperbolic claim over the suzerainty of Dilmun may be just theoritical notion only. For all practical purposes the kings of Dilmun might have been independent. As per the practise of those days, the Dilmun king paid tribute and its payment may not imply complete suzerainty and surrender of political as well as economic authority or rights.

Now the question arises about the territorial limits of the Dilmun state. What it was during third and second millennium B.C. might not have been the same during the first millennium B.C. Either it encampassed larger territory or shrinked in size. The 'border' of Dilmun state has been discussed by several authors. It was earlier considered to be in the southern most Mesopotamia. Howard-Carter (1987:94) has suggested that Dilmun in the Neo-Assyrian period

384

Fig.6 A selection of Cylinder Seals of Mesopotamian officials or other persons,
discovered in Bahrain/Dilmun. (Courtesy : Bahrain National Museum).

consisted of the basic kingdom located in Bahrain, where there are substantial archaeological remains of an administrative buildings at Qal'at, as well as a number of Assyrian graves. She suggests to exclude Failaka from Dilmun on the ground that there are no traces of Neo-Assyrian material on the island or the mainland. But she finds traces of a Dilmun "town" north of Kuwait, south of Euphratus.

Finally we may conclude by classifying the evolution of Dilmun state into following periods/phases. Here it may be mentioned that the Dilmun as an historical entity probably originated around 6000 B.C., with the onset of southern 'Ubaid culture's involvement in the east Arabian littoral, as suggested by Zarins (1986:247). And this 'Ubaid culture spread to Bahrain also in early fourth millennium B.C. (Roaf, 1976:144). The Dilmun state had two main periods of its existence - the Tarut centre period (ca. 6000-2200 B.C.) and the Bahrain centre period (ca 2200-400 B.C.). The details of Tarut centered period fall under Saudi Arabia's pre-history (cf. Piesenger, 1983, Ms.) The Bahrain centered Dilmun state may be grouped under following nine phases, as already discussed above.

BAHRAIN CENTERED DILMUN STATE

Phase I : ca. 4000-3000 B.C.	Pre-City	'Ubaid Influence
Phase II : ca. 3000-2200 B.C.	City I	Trading Station, Umm an Nar Influence.
Phase III : ca. 2200-2000 B.C.	City II, A.B.	Indus Valley Harappan influence. Amorites take over political power.
Phase IV : ca. 2000-1800 B.C.	City C,D, Missing E. ca 1750 B.C.	Dilmun Kingdom. City II abandoned, Mesopotamian, Syrian contacts and influence in seals etc.
Phase V : ca. 1800-1600 B.C.	City II F City III A.	Migration of Amorites. Decline in trade. Mixed influences.
Phase VI : ca. 1600-1480 B.C.	City IIIA.	No mention in Mesopotamian text. Dilmun continue to flourish. Rimun Dilmun King(?)
Phase VII : ca. 1480-1240 B.C.	City IIIA.B	Kassite Domination. Kassite governors of Dilmun : Usiananuri and Ili- ippa-shra.
Phase VIII : ca. 1240-709 B.C.	City IV	Uperi King of Dilmun. Neo-Assyrian vassalage and influence
Phase IX : ca. 709-400 B.C.	City IV.	Dilmun Kingdom. Dilmun Kings: Qana, Hundaru. Governor : Neo-Babylonian

CHAPTER X

RELIGION

Archaeological excavations in Bahrain have revealed much about Dilmunite's religion during third through first millennium B.C. in all its aspects in advanced stage of development. Dilmunite's religion and its practice is manifested in the temples, Dilmun seals, snake bowls, burials and several other objects of religious scope that have been unearthed in Bahrain. Above all this, paramount evidence for Dilmun's religion comes from the texts of Sumerian and Akkadian myths/legends which reveal the names of gods that were worshiped by the Dilmunites. It was Sumerian mythology that greatly influenced Dilmun's religion and its cultural values. Dilmun's religion and its pantheon may be said to originate from Sumerian myths which characterized it as holy. The initial lines of the Dilmun myth reads as follows (after Kramer, 1964:49). "The holy cities - give(?) them to (?) him (Enki?) as his share, The land Dilmun is holy, Holy Sumer - give (?) it to (?) him as a share, The land Dilmun is holy. The land Dilmun is holy, the land Dilmun is pure, The land Dilmun is clean, the land Dilmun is holy."

There are no texts revealing Dilmun's religion. Thus our knowledge is limited to little more than a few pointers. Dilmun's religion has to be gleaned and understood from the following aspects as evidenced from the archaeological discoveries: Dilmun's pantheon; temples; gods in human form; animal representation; symbols/motifs; priests and rituals; sacrifice; and burial customs.

DILMUN'S PANTHEON

Names of Dilmun's gods have been preserved in the cuneiform texts of Sumerian myths and in few fragments with cuneiform inscription found in Bahrain, Failaka and abroad. From different text we learn about the following deities of Dilmun; Enki, Ninsikulla, Ninhursag, Enshag (Inzak) and his spouse Meskilak, Utta, Lukhamun. Out of these only three deities seems to have been important to the cult-centre in Dilmun, the divine pair, Enki and Ninhursag, and his son Inzak, (Andersen 1986:175). Hither to on the basis of Cornwall and Kramer Meskilak was considered spouse of Inzak. However, recently Reiner (1974:234), on the basis of new texts dealing with the Sumero-Akkadian Hymn of Nana, has suggested that Meskilak is not the spouse of Inzak as the former being a male deity and that Suluhhitu was the wife of both Inzak as well as Meskilak. However so far this name has not been found in any texts or myth relating to Dilmun.

Besides the above mentioned divine figures, we find worship of astral deities, Sin and Shams in Bahrain. Further the cult of the snake goddess Mush on Bahrain is evident from a cuneiform tablet recovered from Qal'at al Bahrain City III. (Eidem, 1986:1ff; Andre,1989:172). For the tablet and its text see Fig.5 (bottom left) in chapter IX, *supra*. Mush or Nirah was a minor god in Mesopotamia and worshipped mainly in De and Nippur Mc Ewan, 1983

386

cited by Eidem, 1986 Ms). These deities are in fact of Sumerian origin, as will be evident from the myths cited below, and were associated with Dilmun, the paradise land of Sumerians. Thus, the Dilmunites were polytheists.

Enki, the great Sumerian water-god incharge of the seas and rivers, is most intimately connected with Dilmun. One of the myths - "Enki and Ninhursag" is a eulogy of Dilmun, described as both a land and city, where the action of the story takes place. What was wanting in this land of innocence and bliss was sweet water. The myth has the prayer of Ninsikilla, the tutelary goddess of Dilmun, to Enki, former's husband and father, to supply Dilmun with water Kramer (1955:37; 1964:48). The translation of the myth has been given at pp.22-27 in chapter II, *supra*. From this myth it is clear that Dilmun was famous for cleanliness, purity, and it was the water god Enki who played a leading role in the religion of the two lands - Sumer and Dilmun, observes Kramer (1964:48). Another myth. "Enki and the world order", mentions Dilmun. The relevant passage reads: "He (the god Enki) cleansed and purified the land of Dilmun, and placed Ninsikilla (goddess) in charge of it" (Alester, 1983:61; Kramer, 1964:48). Kramer states that the very name of the goddess whom Enki placed in charge of Dilmun is a Sumerian compound word whose literal meaning is "the pure queen". Enki and his wife (Damkina) reposed in Dilmun is evident from the myth cited earlier (in chapter II supra). (Langdon, 1964:194). In Dilmun, the paradise of gods, eight plants were made to sprout by Ninhursag, the great mother goddess of the Sumerians. She succeeded in bringing these plants into being by an intricate process involving three generations of goddesses all begotten by Enki. As the latter wished to taste these plants, his messenger, the two two faced god Isimud, plucked them and brought to his master to eat. This angered Nishursag who pronounced the curse of death against Enki and then disappeared from the realm of gods. Enki fell ill and when on the verge of death the gods held an assembly to rescue Enki. Through the mediation of a fox the mother goddess Ninharsag was brought back to the realm of gods to heal the water god. She made him seat by her vulva and after inquiring which eight organs of his body ache, she brought into existence eight corresponding deities. They are: Abu, Nindulla, Ninsuutud, Ninkasi, Nazi, Dazima, Nintil and Enshag (Inzak). Thus Enki was brought back to life and health. Inzak was made the lord of Dilmun., (Langdon, 1964:202; Kramer, 1961: 54-59; 1964:45f). (see pp.34f *supra*). Again in the myth, "Enki and the world order" in which Enki organizes the affairs of the world and in doing so, the first lands to draw the attention was Dilmun along with Magan. The myth (after Kramer, 1964:50) reads "The Lands of Magan and Dilmun looked upto me Enki/Moored (?) the Dilmun - boat to the ground (?)/Loaded the Magan-boat sky high". After Dilmun, Enki blessed Sumer. Thus suggesting importance of the former. In fact, the last line of the Enki-Ninhursag myth suggest, as observed by Rice (1983:109), Dilmun as the place of assembly of the god, their meeting place, and so far as the Sumerians were concerned the place of their origin.

Inzak seems to be the chief deity of Dilmunites. An inscription directly linking Inzak with Dilmun was found on a stone fragment, only one inch long at Cythera island. It is

in five lines and is dedicated to the god Inzak by king Naram Sin of Dilmun ("Tilwun").
It was first recorded by Joannes Calucci in a letter dated October 3, 1849, addressed to
Hamilton and published by M. Leake in 1850. Gerold Walser (in Herzfeld, 1968:62). Walser
believes that this inscription is the trace of a sailor from Phoenician coast who had gone
to Dilmun as well as Greece. The transliteration and translation of this inscription is now
published and commented upon by Butz (1983:119f). It reads: "For the god Inzak/of Dilmun/
Naramis in/son of I piq-Adad/for his life". A cuneiform inscription (see Fig.2 in chapter
IX,supra found by Durand (1880:189f) in Bahrain in 1879, mentions "Palace (of) Rimun,
servent of (the god) Inzak, man (of the tribe of) Aqarum". The god Inzak is the same Enshag,
born to Enki in the myth cited above, and became lord of Dilmun. Inzak is also known
from another source to be the name under which the Babylonian god Nabu was worshiped
in Dilmun. (Legrain, 1925:290; Cornwall, 1946:6:1952:141). To the birth of Inzak, Alester
(1983:59) assigns the date of the third Dynasty of Ur. Glassner (1984:40,48f) interprets Agarum
found along with Inzak in an inscription, as the name of Failaka island and makes differentiation
between Inzak of Agarum and the Inzak of Dilmun. Inzak is mentioned in the greeting
formula in both the Nippur letters (Cornwall, 1952:141; Dalley, 1973:83). (For the text
see Fig.3, in chapter IX, *supra*). It reads "May Inzak and Meskilak, the gods of Dilmun,
guard thy life". The letters are dated to the time of Burnaburias (ca.1370 B.C.).

A fragment of chlorite bowl with cuneiform inscriptions seems to have probably the
name of Inzak. (Andre,1989:170). A few fragments with cuneiform inscriptions found at the
northern centre of Dilmun, Failaka, mention Inzak. Of these fragment, a steatite bowl, has
the inscription: "Temple of Enzak" and a pottery sherd mentions "god Inzak." Two seals
having cuneiform inscription mention Inzak (Kjaerun, 1980:51; Alester, 1983:42). However,
these seals are not characteristically Dilmun seals. As such they have not been taken into
consideration here. Though several cylinder seals have been found during excavations in
Bahrain within the jurisdiction of Dilmun, but they are of foreign origin. (Porada, 1970;
Beyer, 1989:157, 159, Glassner 1984:36:48). As such I have excluded the testimony of cylinder
seals with cuneiform inscription mentioning god Inzak and found in Bahrain and Failaka.
In view of this, some arguments by some scholars based on the inscriptions on the cylinder
seals found in Bahrain or Failaka, that the deities are exclusively of Dilmun is untenable.
Moreover, Landsberger (1944:434;1974:9) clearly stats that Dilmun "Possessed deities with
authentic Sumerian names, such as the chief god En-zak and his spouse Me-skil-ak". Again
that Inzak was not exclusively Dilmun deity is also proved by the fact that inscriptions with
the name of Inzak have been found outside Dilmun in Susa (Vallat,1983:93ff). The inscription
reads as follows: *I-din In-za-ku., Ku-un-In-za-ki.* To the above inscriptions from Susa, Potts
(1990:I,227) adds three more *Inzaki, Wa-tar-In-za-ak,* and *Ku-un-In-za-ki* from the personel
names of the Elamite Onomasticon dated to the Old Babylonian period. Besides the inscription
of Inzak at Susa, a temple dedicated to him has been recorded dated to the first half of
the second millennium B.C. (Vallat, 1983:93). However, Potts suggest that so far, at Susa
no temple of Inzak has been positively identified on the grounds that no native Elamite deities

were similarly honoured at Susa at that time. (Potts, 1990:I,227). Since the Sumerian god Inzak was posted at Dilmun, obviously he became popular as god of Dilmun. Inzak is also mentioned in letters from the Kassite period. (Unger, 1929, cited by Cornwall, 1944:157). Inzak had a consort and her name was Lakhamun. A text according to Cornwall (1944:158), gives this as the name of the Sarpanit of Dilmun. Also, according to the Cythera text Lakhamun is linked with Inzak as "the gods of Dilmun". Burrows (1928, in Rice, 1984:176) suggests that identification of Lakhamun of Dilmun with Sarpanit "implies the silvery scales of a mermaid or fish goddess". Thus the myths reveal that the religion and gods of Dilmun are the same as that of Mesopotamia.

During the early Sumerian times various lists of gods existed, and about the middle of the third millennium B.C., a standard list was drawn up. First in this established order is the high god, Anu (meaning heaven). As per the Babylonian Epic of creation, the genealogy of Anu is traced from Apsu, the underworld ocean. He was styled 'Father' and 'King of Gods'. Anu had a consort named Antu, but during the historical period her place as the cansort of Anu was filled by Innina or Ishtar. It was believed that from the union of Anu and Antu, whose Sumerian name means 'the earth' were born the under world gods called the Anunnaki, and the seven evil *utukki* or demons. Anu's sacred animal was the heavenly bull. The second member of the great Babylonian triad of deities was Enlil, meaning 'wind-storm-god'. The chief centre of Enlil's cult was the temple at Nippur, called Ekur, 'the House of the Mountain'. The third of the leading Sumerian deities was Enki, or Ea of the later texts, the god incharge of the abyss. Enki was the god of the waters, and was thought of as having his abode in the apsu. The chief of Ea's cult was Eridu at the head of the Arabian Gulf, the oldest of the Sumerian cities. Ea's attendant was Mummu the craftsman-god; and his consort was the goddess Damkina, and his son was Marduk. Fourth among the creating deities was the mother - goddess, Ninhursag, also known as Ninmah. She plays an important role in the creation of man and in another myth she starts a chains of divine births in Dilmun, the paradise of gods. (Hooke, 1962:12ff; Kramer, 1963:117ff).

The second group of Dilmunite gods consisted of the astral deities, the Moon and the Sun, though there is no textual evidence for these group of deities in Dilmun; however; they are inferred from the altars found in the temple at Bahrain and motifs or symbols found in the Dilmun seals. The worship of moon-god, Sin is evident from the two altars found at the Sar settlement site. One of the Dilmun myth mentions Utu, the sungod. The worship of moon-god sin in Dilmun is evident from a liturgical hymn from Nippur. (see *infra* on temple for more details). On the basis of god Inzak and her spouse Meskilak's myth taking place in Dilmun, Landsberger (1944:434) had suggested overseas origin of the Sumerians. Rice (1985:104) suggests that the veneration Enki, the lord of Abyss, and patron of the fishes, might have originated in Dilmun, and from there they might have travelled to the Sumerian lands. This accounts partially for the reverence and affection with which the Mesopotamians held Dilmun as the paradise land.

TEMPLES

In ancient Bahrain, as in all other contemporary cities, temple were originally constructed as dwellings for the deities. Like all human beings who lived in homes/houses, so did the gods. Temples, therefore, were an essential part of the community life because it was here that the divine touched the human, where the transcendent became immanent, and where the ultimate source of power became available to alleviate human weakness and requirement. It was believed that it was obligatory on the part of men to provide the physical needs of deities. That is, shelter, food, water and other necessities. In return for the human services, the god provided the former with peace, tranquility, prosperity, spritual satisfaction and guided him in his daily religious as well as social life. (Wright, 1944:42). Thus the role of the temple in relation to the people, was two - fold, cultic service and social responsibilities as well as economic grievances. (Oppenheim, 1974:107). That the temple in ancient Bahrain was the centre of religious life of the community and probably also of the state has been revealed by the archaeological excavations. All the temples, so far discovered, Barbar temple, Diraz temple, Sar temple and Umm es - Sejour, are associated with the town/city. To this list we may add the recently hypothesised by Pierre Lombard, (1993, forth-coming) temple of Qal'atal Bahrain (City IV). The religious architecture and plans with illustrations have been described above (chapter IV-B). As such it is redundant to repeat those details here. From the architectural features of these temples, we may form some idea about the cult practiced and rites performed by the Dilmunites. Each temple has its own characteristic features, both with regard to the external and internal organization. They differ in constructional features also suggesting different time periods. The altars are quite different in each one. Thus suggesting that different deities were worshipped. The Barbar temple has been attributed to Enki, the god of the subterranean fresh water ocean, also called *apsu*.

The presence of *apsu* at Barbar and other features as naratted in the myth, such as, the clay above the *apsu* makes Barbar the abode of Enki. (Andersen, 1986:176) Daniel Potts (1983:128;1990:172) has hypothesised that the Barbar temple could be the temple of the sun-god Utu/Shamas. He has tried to advance three reasons: Orthography of the name of Barbar; sun-god Utu's/Shama's association with e-babbar, and depiction of shams on Bahrain's glyptic design. Potts himself states that there is no supporting evidence to his hypothesis. Thus, in the absence of sufficient evidence, I am reluctant to accecpt Potts suggestion. Supposing if one accepts Potts proposal, then it implies dismantling of the established identification of Enki and his *apsu* with Barbar temples, and this will be contrary to the details mentioned in the Sumerian myths. That is, acceptance of Potts suggestion tantamounts to disbelieving of confirmed texts about Dilmun's myth of Enki and Ninhursag and the apsu. We can accept Potts suggestion regarding orthography of the name Barbar, but without linking it to Utu's temples in Sipper and Larsa. Further so far, no text has been found which associates the temple with the Barbar. The temples on their discovery got reputation by the name of the nearby village. Barbar village is of modern period and has nothing to do with the temple as pointed out by Rice (1983). Howard-Carter (1987:85) is also of similar opinion and states that there is no support for Potts proposal from either iconography or epigraphic sources. Potts third argument depiction of sun god's symbols in the glyptic design repertoire of Bahrain is quite true. But this could be also possible by virtue of worship of sun-god at another temple in Bahrain and may not be at Barbar temple. Like the worship of moon-god Sin at Sar temple, it is possible that sun-god was worshipped at Diraz temple. It is only an assumption, as excavator's report is neither published nor available for reference.

Inzag was placed incharge of Dilmun and the temple. One of the Sumerian poem concering the origin of civilization mentions about the temple in Dilmun, the relevent passage (after Langdon 1964:193) reads: "The two of them, whom in their land, Dilmun, they had placed, Their glory in the temple they *augmented*". The Barbar temple is the only temple so far discovered with Sumerian religious and architectural affinities and constructed in stone. (Doe, 1985:35f). The two of them in the myth refers to Enki and his consort goddess, Ninhursag; and Andersen (1986:177) believes that the two altars at Barbar might reflect the cult of this divine pair's worship. The Danish during the excavation of Barbar Temples found altar stones and "offerings", in and around the square pit in front of the altar-stone and the altar. The perforated stones found seems to have had a function within the cult of the temple, and for their significance Glob (1954c:152) refers to the ringstones of the Indus Valley civilization. Remains of ceremonial seat was also found along with the circular altar. The presence of well indicates that the element of water was essential for the cult at Barbar. The Danish recovered from the foundations of the Barbar temple deposits, which they called 'foundation deposits'. These comprised metal objects and pottery. The excavators beleive that these were votive offering to the gods made before starting the construction of the temple. Score of conical breakers (see Fig.41 in chapter VII *supra*) along with copper beakers and a gold band were recovered by the Danes from the fill of the temple platform (Glob, 1955:182,191). The solid footed beakers are similar to those found at Nipper, Warka, and Diyala, and dated to Early DynasticI (2800-2700 BC). (Howard-Carter, 1972:26). To the east of the Barbar temple complex is situated on oval structure (see Fig.16 in chapter IV-B *supra*), which is distinctly similar to an early Sumerian temple buildings. It seems that this place was meant for keeping animals, prepared for sacrifice. Carbonized remains found in the floor suggests that they were burnt as offerings to the gods. This practise is corroborated by the events related by the Ziusudra in the epic of Gilgamesh. (Rice, 1983:31). The importance of the element of water in the cult is also evident from the 'water temple' at Umm es Sejur, near Diraz. During-Caspers (1976:18) draws parallels for the presence of sweet spring water in the religious rites of the Dilmunite with that of the great bath or tank, built within the citadel of Mohenjo-Daro.

A tablet from Nippur (No.8097), cited by Cornwall (1944:52f), mentions the liturgical Hymn of Sun. In it mention is made of "the Temple of Sagnamsar which is in mount of Dilmun". It narrates how Enlil has caused his son, Sin, the moon-god, to be a shepherd. The relevent passage (from Cornwall, 1944:53Ms) reads:

14. "In the temple Sagnamsar which is in the Mount of Dilmun.
15. In the temple of the holy stylus a shephered I caused him to be (?).
16. First son of Enlil, in the land he is ruler glorious (?) hero, far-famed shepherd.
17. In the meadow a sanctuary I built; in the abode of my city Ur.
18. In the temple Sagnamsar which is in the Mount of Dilmun,
19. In the temple of the holy stylus a shepherd I have caused him to be (?)
20. It is a sagar melody.
21. Song on the flute to Sin".

In the above passage, the name Sagnamsar when translitered (according to Langdon quoted by Cornwall, 1944:53 f4.1) means *mudammik musarre* - "Temple of the benefactor of writing". (i.e. Temple of Enki) and is symbolic of the god of wisdom, Enki. This reference to "the temple of Sagnamsar in the Mount of Dilmun" is of paramount importance.

According to an inscription found at Ur by Sir Leonard Woolley, there existed a temple in Ur called E-dilmunna ("The House of Dilmun"). The translation of this inscription (after Cornwall, 1944:55) is as follows: "For Innana the lady clad in great splendour wielding all the powers, eldest daughter of Sin his lady; Warad-Sin, the prince who takes thought for Girsu with Lagash, who reverences E-barra, King of Larsa, King of Sumer and Akkad, the strong one who seeks out the (divine) oracles and executes their purpose, who builds anew the house of the gods am I; on whom Enki bestowed a wide understanding to perform the duties of the city. Because of this, for Inanna my lady, with my prayer, (I restored) E-dilmunna her dwelling of rest and of heart's delight. That the eye might see and that its interior might be light I enlarged its area more than before. Unto days to come for my life I built it; its head I raised and made it like a mountain. Over my works may Inanna my lady rejoice. Length of days, years of abundance, a throne securely based, a sceptre, to subdue the people as a gift may she grant me! ". At present there is no evidence, states Cornwall (1944:55), as to the exact location of this temple at Ur, because the inscription was found thrown down in a well. He says that E-dilmunna is mentioned elsewhere as a sanctuary of Inanna. The hymn published by Zimmern (Sumerischi Kultieder No.199) and quoted by Cornwall, reads:

31. In Nippur Duranki is mine.
32. In Ur the temple of Dilmun is mine.
33. In Girsu Zidninazag in mine.
34. In Adab Esharra is mine.

Like wise, in similar composition E-dilmunna is reckonned as the first es-dam of the goddessess in which she is brought to dwell, so that "the long days shall lengthen the short days". However, Cornwall states that Gadd and Legrain confess themselves unable to explain why this temple in Ur should be called `house of Dilmun', unless some reference be intended to the story of Enki and Nintud found in a Sumerian legend. Again the temple of Dilmun (e-tilmunna) was restored by Warad-Sin at Ur was greatly reverenced by the Sumerians and had some special significance in their religious heritage. (Cornwall, 1944, 56.Ms.; Hallo, 1969:54). Howard-Carter (1987:100f) suggests that the fact that Warad-Sin mentioned the restoration of the E-dilmunna leads one to presume that its origins were at least Neo-Sumerian in date. The foregoing details clearly attest the Sumerian myths and establish the oneness of Sumerian and Dilmunite religion and its pantheon. As such the deities of Dilmun are not exclusively deities of Dilmun alone, but they are primarily Sumerian deities and then of Dilmun. Further, in Dilmun we have not found, so far, any temple by the name of Dilmun. Whereas we have textual evidence of Dilmun temple in Mesopotamia. Most probably one of the temples in Dilmun, presumably one at Barbar was known at that time as Dilmun temple and may be its duplicate was built at Ur and called E-dilmunna. Vice-versa is also probable. This presumsation is possible because both the E-dilmunna at Ur and the temple at Barbar are attributed to Enki. All these and several other hypothesis can be confirmed only by the discovery of Dilmun archives in Bahrain.

The architecture of the Sar temple is altogether different from that of Barbar temples and appears to be indigenous in character. Two crescent shaped altars at Sar suggest worship of astral deity moon-god Sin. Burnt deposits containing fish vertebra, found besides the altar (Killick, Crawford, Moon etal, 1991:114) suggests that the small platform in front of the altar was meant for ritual or sacrificial purpose. Inside the temple on the right side of the entrace is a podium, for placing the statues/statuettes. And for washing purpose, before one proceeds to the altars is a water trough. Inside the temple are two rooms. One of them has plastered basin pits. These were probably meant for bathing the gods. While the other room was probably for priests or was meant for stores. The cuneiform inscription on two tablets (519 BIH and BJE) recovered by the Danes (Bibby, 1964:103;1966:91) from Qal'at al Bahrain City III suggests existence of three temples. Of these two seems to be dedicated probably to Nin-a....(519BIH). And the other was dedicated to the snake goddess Mush/Nirah (B.J.E.). Eidem suggests that these temples were in - or near Qal'at al Bahrain. This leads us to imagine that one of the temple found within Qal'at al Bahrain City IV could be possibly this Nirah temple. This is further attested by the discovery of snake bowls with snakes' skeletons and beads etc, from the same area. (see Fig.30 in chapter VII supra). Again the text (519 BIH) mentions a stone bowl for mixing perfumes for the "temple of Nin-a...". The names of deities are unfortunately broken, states Eidem. I suppose, most probably this Nina is the same Sumerian goddess Nina, "Queen of the Waters". (Waddell, 1976:123-125) If this could be true, then we can perhaps suppose that these two temples were located in Qal'at al Bahrain City IV.

GODS IN HUMAN FORM

The Sumerian gods, according to the myths, were entirely anthropomorphic. They were conceived as human in form, thought, and deed. In other words, they lived like humans, eat and drink, marry and raise families, had human passions and weakness. They were believed to live on the mountain of heaven and earth, the place where the sun rises, that is, Dilmun (Kramer, 1963:117). The last line of the Deluge legend mentions that the gods were transfered to the safe place, the mountain of Dilmun. (Langdon, 1964:208). (See P.36 *supra* in chapter II for the text of the passage). Dilmun's gods in anthropomorphic forms have been depicted on Dilmun seals in different form, posture and style. These seals are illustrated at Fig Nos.32a-34a,b, in Chapter VI, *supra*. The enthroned garbed god wearing a horned crown is said to be moon-god. In most of the seals the humans depicted are probably gods E.g. Fig. No.24-31. Enki himself is dipicted in his apsu in a Dilmun seal (Fig.24b, Chapter VI *supra*). Another seal in which Enki celebrates his sacred marriage has been illustrated by Andersen (1986;176). Humans in seals are represented in different scenes usually with some animals-antelope, bull, ibex, etc, favourite of the god. No sculpture nor any rock carving representing the Dilmun gods has been found in Bahrain. So far only one stone with human figures carved on it has been recorded from Bahrain. It is a plinth-stone from Barbar temple I with hallow rectangular holes for placing statues in them. On one of the sides of the plinth-stone (see Fig.7m Chapter IV-B) schematic human figures in standing/walking posture have been carved. The figures are quite unusual and do not appear to be of humans. One of them has long drooping arms from the straight shoulders, facing right in walking posture. The second one with stretched legs, and facing straight has his right arm uplifted with broad open palm. While his left arm appears partially up-turned and partially down-turned (rather confusing). The other two figures represented in a square and circular form are not clear. The Danish excavators (Glob 1955:184,191) are of the opinion that these figures possibly show the two of the statues which originally stood upon the plinth stones and we presume that they are the sketches of the two statues. If this is true then they represent gods. The remaining two figures cannot be accounted.

ANIMAL REPRESENTATION

Animals seems to have occupied an important role in the religion of Dilmun. This is manifested by their regular representation is almost all their seals. These animals are: bull, ibex, gazelle, fishes, scorpion/crab, birds and water-bird, monkey, snake/serpent etc. A very common motif in the Dilmun seals is the ibex, which is often recognised or identified with the god Enki. (See Fig.24b, 27ab and *passim* in chapter VII, *supra*,). Ram is also connected with Enki. (Langdon 1964:106). Bull is also depicted in some seals. A bull's head of copper was found in the Barbar temple. It is almost contemporary with the similar Sumerian examples. It resembles the four copper bull heads found in the Ninhurag temple at al 'Ubaid (Early Dynasty III A), the copper bull's head from Sin temple VIII at Khafjah (Early Dynastic II) and a bull from Tello (Early Dynastic III A). (During-Caspers, 1975:70f). Thus suggesting the adoptation of the Sumerian practise at Barbar. At another temple, at Umm es Sejur two lime stone statues of kneeling rams, a symbol of Enki, also suggest the importance of animals in the religious beliefs. During Caspers (1976:18) considers that these rams must have borne a direct connection with the ritual acts, or ceremonial cleanings or washings performed at a lower level in or near the spring of the temple. She draws parallel with those at Mohenjo-Daro. A stone block with hole and projection in the form of an animal head was found at the Barbar temple. The Danish excavators (Glob, 1955:185,192) consider that this was perhaps intended for tethering sacrificial beasts, as they found considerable marks of wear from the hole out to the edges. Glob considers them to be ring stones of Indus culture. This comparison is further supported, states Glob, by a some what damaged stone of the same type in which ring is emphasized by carving was found lying in the stone-querry layer. (Glob, 1955,192, Fig.8,9).

SYMBOLS/MOTIF

A variety of symbols/motifs corresponding to the deities or other religious affinities seems to have been adopted by the Dilmunites representing different ideologies of various religious groups. This is evident only from the Dilmun seals bearing these symbols. The most common symbols are: plam tree or its branch, astral symbols of crescent, sun disc, radiating sun, oval or elliptical sign, standard with crescent and sun disc, podium, gate symbol, shield, etc. (see illustrations of these symbols in the seals in chapter VI,*supra*). Different types of seals have different symbols/motifs suggesting that different religious groups or communities had their own symbol of group identification. The theme of sacred tree, as in Mesopotamia and India, had a role in the religion of Dilmun. Several Dilmun seals dipict either a palm tree or its branch as a veneration. During Caspers (1973c:78) is also of similar opinion and states that on the seals date is depicted clearly as an object of worship. According to Sumerian myths the palm tree was a gift of god Enki to Bahrain. (A. Falkusterian cited by During Caspers). She ventures to suppose that the two circular stone structures at Barbar Temple II and III in the centre of the courtyard had sacred tree-most probably date palms. Phallic symbols also seems to have had a role in Dilmun's religion. Two round-topped columns at Zallaq, near the Barbar temple suggests strongly that they are phallic symbols and they are similar in shape to the linga-shaped gaming piece made of lapis lazulli and found in the foundation deposits of votive offerings in the square foundation pit of Barbar Temple III (Glob, 1954:152;1957:126 During-Caspers, 1971:220). The linga cult at Bahrain, seems to be the result of Harappan influence where it was common practise. Phallic worship is not known from Sumerian religion. (During-Caspers, 1976:18f). Obviously this cult was introduced by the Indians residing or visiting Bahrain. And probably only Indians in Bahrain pratise this phallic cult. It may not have been a general practise by the Dilmunites. However, a stone slab found near the altar stones of Barbar Temple III with a deep cup mark to possibly hold linga raises doubt about this restricted practise of the cult. It is a slab of 64X26X20 cms, with a cup mark in the centre of 12cms. width and 6.5 cms. depth, along with a runnel of about 2 cms. width and 8 cms. depth, running out to one edge. Glob considers that possibly a linga figure originally stood in the hole. Rice (1983:138) links this phallic and snake cult in Bahrain with that of the Gilgamesh legend and puts it in an equation: Gilgamesh-Serpent Fertility-Phalloi-Snake Burial.

The worship of sun-god in Dilmun has been hypothesised by Ali Akbar Bushiri (of

Bahrain) (1979:27-35) on the basis of study of symbols on the seals mainly from Failaka and a few from Bahrain. Out of the 81 seals studied by Bushiri, he has found 38 seals to have the symbols of sun-god which he has illustrated. He has drawn parallels between the sun-god symbols of Dilmun with those from Mesopotamia, Egypt, Indus Valley Civilization, Phonecia, etc. Bushiri, after sound reasoning, observes that the people of Dilmun worshipped a sun-god, with the strong possibility that the sun-god was their main deity, the strongest of their gods. If this is true then the sun-stones found in Sar graves (see Fig.37a, chapter VII, *supra*) had a meaning and purpose. They were probably meant for sun-worship or for some ritual purpose.

SACRIFICE

Sacrificial practices and slaughter of animals in a ritual context is evident from the excavations carried out at Barbar temple complex, at Qal'at al Bahrain (City IV) and at Sar settlement temple. Carbonized remains of burnt animals in oval structure at Barbar temple attest the sacrifice of animals. (Rice, 1983:31). Burnt deposits containing fish vertebra found next to the altar suggests sacrifice of the fish. (Killick, etal, 1991:114). Practice of snake sacrifice at Qal'at al Bahrain (City IV) is attested by the discovery of special sacrificial vessels with lid and snake skeletons with beads. (see Fig.30 in chapter VII, *supra*). These vessels were deposited in pits around an altar in one of the rooms of City IV. The excavators, the Danes, haved dated this snake sacrifice at Qal'at to the middle of the second millennium B.C. The snake goddess worshipped at Qal'at may be mush or Nirah, (Andre, 1989:172). Glob (1957:126) links the snake sacrifice at Qal'at with that of Indus civilization. But snake goddess was worshiped in Mesopotamia also as evidenced by her depiction on the seals. (Buchanan, 1981:1ff).

PRIESTS AND RITUALS

We have no texts or any evidence about the presence and functioning of priests and other ministrants and officials in the temples. It is obviously that for the proper functioning and for religions practices priests and several other officials were needed. As Dilmun had several temples there must have been a regular organization of priests and other officials attached to each temple. The additional structures or buildings on the three sides of the Sar town suggest that these were definitely meant for the priests and other officials attached to it. From the plan and details of these buildings (See chapter IV-A *supra*) it is clear that these were used for residential purpose and obviousely by the temple officials. Votive deposits offerings and sacrificial remains in the temples at Barbar and Sar attest regular practice or rituals in a systematic way by the Dilmunites and conducted by the priests. The offerings comprised several types of votive objects. From Barbar temple deposit bronze objects, fragments of lapis-lazuli, long cylindrical beeds, a linga shaped game etc., were recovered. (Glob, 1954c, 152). Sacrifice of animals and fish were usually made both at Barbar and Sar temples. A little naked male figure with hands clasped at the breast from the Barbar temple reveals the typical attitude of worship of Mesopotamia being practised at Bahrain. This statuette represent a priest or worshipper ritually naked and in the typical posture of worship with his hands clasped in front of his breast, with head clean shaved and erect and looking straight. These characteristics reveals Sumerian affinities. During Caspers (1973:128ff) suggests that this figurine represents foreign influences, characteristic of Sumerian sculpture and from that of Kulli-Mehi (Baluchistan). Like wise, a female figurine from a Qal'at North wall (See Fig.16, chapter VIII, *supra*) was discovered with arms joined on the belly. It is broken. Possibly she was in ritual. The daily ritual of the temples at Bahrain, as in the case of Mesopotamia, it is presumed, must have consisted of the washing, dressing and feeding of the replicas or statuetes of deities. Then food must have been offered to the gods. Animals might have been offered and these might have been killed ritually by the priest or some official attached to the temple for the specific purpose. A cuneiform tablet discovered from Qal'at al Bahrain City III suggests functioning of officials at the Nirah temple of the snake goddess which also mentions supplies to the lady, probably for offering rituals. (Eidem, 1986:1ff;Andre,1989:172). Another tablet (519 BIH) mentions supplies to the temple of Nina. These articles were: dates, oil, honey, perfumes, etc. (Eidem, 1986:1ff). The supplies were meant for one official Abdu and other workman. Thus suggesting existence and functioning of temple organisation of workers attached to the temple.

At the temples where astral deities were worshipped, seasonal ritual or feasts might have been conducted according to the course of the sun or moon. That is, new moon, full moon and total eclipse.

BURIAL CUSTOMS

Dilmunite's main burial rite was inhumation. They believed in an after-life which is apparent from the placing of vessels (funerary gifts) with the dead, usually near the head or sometimes besides him. This practice is evident from the illustrations in chapter V (Fig.Nos.22,25,26,28,32 B.C.). (See also chapter IV-A, Fig.16). Belief in an after-life is again evident from the construction of permanent tombs or subterranean graves of solid stones which are still existing in Bahrain in several thousands. These have been built so perfectly for the after-life that they have stood the harsh test of nature for mellenniums. This is a unique legacy of Dilmunites not found any where in the world to this large extent. We have no testimony of food deposited in the vessels for the dead. However, the purpose of different types of pottery and steatite vessels placed in the graves must have been obviously for food and liquid. Archaeological excavations in Bahrain have revealed that the Dilmunites gave top priority for a good, rather permanent, tomb, or subterranean grave, a cist and an alcove and were not satisfied by having a simple hollow chamber in the ground. (see chapter V for the illustration of tombs and subterranean graves). In many cases it is observed that tombs were pre-planned and built before the death of the person to be interned in it. The planing, construction, overall regularity and uniformity of the Sar burial complex have led the excavators (Ibrahim, 1982; 28; Mughal,1983:11) to belief that the construction was pre-conceived and was through a central organization special class of artisans of religious nature. The orientation of graves and laying of the body in the graves have special religious aspects. Generally the graves were oriented from east-north to south-west. It is observed (see chapter V *supra*) that generally the body was laid on the right side, with face turned to the east. This practice reveals that the Dilmunites believed in the power of the rising sun to give rebirth or regenerate life. That is, a firm belief of after-life of the Dilmunites. Several of the tumuli excavated in Bahrain contained animal bones and some times skull of ram or of both. This suggests that as a religious rite, animals were sacrificed at the time of burial and burried together with the human. The mass burials consisting of several skeletons or their bones, of males, females and children (see Figs.Nos.19-22, in chapter V, *supra*) suggests that these were family graves and shows the importance of cult of the dead. Obviously members of the same family were burried in the same grave to retain the lifetime relationship in the after-life as well. Similar objective must have prevailed in constructing secondary graves around and attached to the primary grave. (For instance, see Fig.2, 34c, 35a in chapter V *supra*), and in burying two or more children in an earthen pot or bath-bub coffins. (see Fig.29 in chapter V, *supra*).   A few other aspects of Dilmun's religion, not mentioned above are: temple and the King or the state; temple's role in the life of the people; temple's estates; temple's source of income; etc. Information is lacking on these aspects and it is hoped that future excavations will produce new evidence and will throw light about the unknown.

CHAPTER XI
FOREIGN TRADE

ORIGIN

Foreign trade of Dilmun played most important role not only in the commerce between the east and west but also and in the development of indigenous Dilmun civilization of its own by the assimilation and diffusion of cultures that came and passed with the trade. Foreign trade of Dilmun with Mesopotamia, Indus Valley, Iran, etc, made it possible for the people of these countries to visit Dilmun and transfer their civilization. And vice versa was also true when Dilmunites visited these lands with their own evolving Dilmun culture. Lamberg-Karlovsky's (1972:229) conclusion that trade was one of the most important factor motivating the parallel but essentially distinctive rise towards urban complexes in Mesopotamia, Iranian highland and Indus Valley, is equally true in the case of Bahrain of third-first millennium B.C.

On principle three types of foreign trade of Dilmun have to be distinguished. First is the export of Dilmun's own products. Second is the export of foreign products after their procurement from neighbouring Arabian main land. Third is the transit trade of transhipped foreign goods passing between the east and west through its enterport. By way of these processes Dilmun also imported certain commodities for its local consumption. The importance of Dilmun in the international trade between Mesopotamia and Indus Valley etc., was mainly due to its strategic location, almost midway in the Arabian Gulf, natural harbour, partially protected by the small islands (now called Sitra and Nabi Salih), plentiful fresh water etc. (Cornwall, 1944 : 24). The strategic geographic location of Dilmun in the Arabian Gulf in the centre of the most ancient civilization of the world Mesopotamia, Indus Valley, Egypt and Iran enabled Dilmun to play an important role in the international trade. Cuneiform texts from the third through first millennium B.C. list (see below) as exports from Dilmun commodities such as copper, precious stones, ivory, lapiz lazuli etc., none of which Bahrain itself produced. Dilmun, had thus, acquired the reputation of an emporium for articles originating in more remote countries of the east. (Saggs, 1962 : 235). Oppenheim (1954:7) has rightly observed about Dilmun, that it served as "market Place", a neutral territory in which several parties from different regions of Arabian Gulf and neighbouring regions assembled to exchange and sell their commodities. Thus for southern Mesopotamia, Dilmun and its hinterland on the east Arabian mainland, constituted a "door way" to the eastern market to Magan (Makkan) and Meluhha for the supply of raw materials.

Lamberg-Karlovsky (1972:222-229) has examined the trade mechanism in Indus-Mesopatomian inter-relations and has proposed three different processes to distinguish this long-distance trade to be profitable. These processes are direct contact trade, exchange and central place trade. Regarding the first Lamberg-Karlovsky concludes that direct contact between traders or colonies within the Indus and Mesopotamia cannot be supported or negated due to lack of concrete archaeological evidence. The second mode, exchange, he observes, is undeterminable owing to lack of proper evidence in the differentiation of goods. Trade between the Indus Valley and Mesopotamia is best seen through the third mode, central place trade-evidenced at Bahrain and Tepe Yahya. This is attested by the archaeological discoveries made at Bahrain and discussed in chapters VI-IX, supra.

The diversity in the geographical distribution of natural resources in Mesopotamia and Indus Valley rendered them necessary for mutual supply or exchange of their commodities which were not available locally. Southern Mesopotamia lacked three commodities needed by most human societies - stone, hard wood timber, and metal ores. (Saggs, 1988:233). Besides these items, Mesopotamia imported several other commodities from different places. The imports from the Indus Valley and Magan passed through Dilmun. A geographical tablet of Sargon of Agade (2752-2697 B.C.) found at Ashur records : "The ships from Meluhha, the ships from Magan the ships from Dilmun he made tie up along side the quay of Agade". (Kramer, 1964:49). In the time of Gudea about 2500 B.C., timber was brought from Magan, Meluhha, Gubin and Dilmun, and diorite from Magan. (Cornwall, 1944; Peake, 1928:425). A text of the time (ca. 2400 B.C.) of Ur-Nanshe of Lagsh (ED IIIA) mention that timber-carrying Dilmun boats arrived at his city, Lagash. In the reign of Lugalanda (ED III B), merchants brought to Lagash copper and other merchandise in large quantities from Dilmun. Sargon, who ruled about a century and a half after Ur-Nanshe, boast that the boats of Dilmun lay anchored at the docks of his capital city Agade. (Lambert, 1953:105ff; Kramer, 1964:49f). Dilmun's exports : copper, tin, harp bear-bread etc, are attested from the Ebla texts from Tell Mardikh brought to light by Pettinato (1983:75- 82). These additional reference in Ebla texts, besides those from Sumerian texts suggests that Dilmun was a recognized cannotation in Mesopotamia, Syria etc., during the third millennium B.C. Dilmun's direct trade with Mesopotamia and its role between the Mesopotamian and Indus Valley trade is evident from the cuneiform records. The myth of Enki and Ninhursag depicts Dilmun as a land to which eight countries transport their wares : Tukris, Meluhha, Margsi, Magan, the "Sealand", Zalamgar, Elam, and Ur (Sumer). Thus revealing Dilmun's vast international commercial net work around 2000 B.C. which is the probable data of composition of the myth (Kramer, 1977:59). Archaeological evidence from Mesopotamian cities also shows existence of trade between lower Mesopotamia and and Indus Valley by way of Arabian Gulf and Dilmun during the third through first millennium B.C.

DILMUN'S ARTICLES OF EXPORT

Exports of Dilmun, especially metal, is attested in the eleven economic documents of archaic Uruk corpus. (Englund 1983:35). Dilmun's export to Ur, as evidenced by several cuneiform texts and myths were as follows : copper, bronze, silver, red gold, ivory and ivory objects, lapis lazuli, variety of precious coloured stones, several types of woods, white corals, carnelian, 'Fish-eyes" (pearls/oysters), dates (Sum Dilmun) aromatics, "Dilmun onions", plants and animals. (Oppenheim, 1954:6ff; Leemans, 1960:18ff, 121). Except dates, pearls and corals, Dilmun does not seems to have had possessed the above articles exported by it. But these articles have been attested by the archaeological excavations at Bahrain, suggesting that they were available, through imports, in Bahrain during the third-first millennium B.C. See chapter VIII for illustrations of these items recovered from Bahrain during excavations at Qal'at al Bahrain, Barbar temple site, Sar settlement site and from various burial mounds and subterranean graves. From the excavations of Qal'at al Bahrain City I and II, Bibby (1969 : 183 f) recovered several artifacts of copper, steatite, ivory, carnelian beads, etc., which were not native to Bahrain. He found copper fish hooks and innumerable scraps of unworked copper. All these items are attributed to Dilmun's imports for exporting to Mesopotamia and these objects are evidence of Dilmun's wide spread trade network during the third millennium B.C. Different commodities exported by Dilmun to Mesopotamia, along with their source of origin is given in the following table (after Piesinger, 1983:650-652, unpublished).

Commodity	Textual Source	Probable Geographic Source	Reference
1. Copper and Copper objects	Magan	Oman	(Mallowan, 1971)
2. Ivory and Ivory Objects	Meluhha	India	(Leemans, 1960)
3. Carnelian (including Kidney shaped beads)	Meluhha	N.W. India	(Gadd : 1971a, During-Caspers, 1970-71
4. Other semi-precious stones, including coral.	Meluhha	Oman, India	(Leemans, 1960)
5. Lapis Lazuli	Meluhha	Badakhshan	(Kohl, 1974)
6. Antimony (for eye paint)	Dilmun	Arabia, Iran	
7. Pearls (Fish-eyes)*	-	Arabian Gulf	(Nielson, 1958)
8. Tortoise shell (?)	-	Arabian Gulf, Red Sea, Indian Ocean.	(Bibby, 1969, (Classical Source)
9. Silver and Silver objects		Zagros (N.W. Iran)	(Mallowon 1971)

10.	Gold	Meluhha	India	(Gadd, 1971a)
11.	Magan reed (Like bamboo)	Magan	Iranian Makran (?)	(Hansman, 1973)
12.	Mesuwood (Modern siss tree)	Magan and Meluhha	Iranian and Pakistani Makran (?)	(Gershevitch, 1957)
13.	Red Ochre	-	Hormuz island	(Wilson, 1928)
14.	Aromatics, drugs, spices etc.	- India.	S. Arabia,	(Periplus)

*According to Howard-Carter (1983 : 1986; 305-310) there is no connection between fish-eye's and pearls, as such they are not one and the same).

DILMUN'S ARTICLES OF IMPORTS

Ur, in order to import the commodities listed above especially copper, exported to Dilmun the following items in exchange ; silver, garments, wool, sesame-oil, skins or leather, shelled barley, b arley mean, flour, cheese, cream etc. (Cornwall, 1944:17; Leemans, 1960:19ff;116). Ceder-wood which was imported into Mesopotamia was re-exported to Dilmun. (Crawford, 1973:233).

To the above list, Butz (1986:143-145) adds shipment of sheep leather, white and yellow goat hair and a reed basket as exports to Dilmun. (Leather Texts-BIN 939:22). Besides the above items from Mesopotamia, Dilmun imported from other places the following items, partly for local consumption and mainly for the re-export to Mesopotamia: copper, bronze, silver, red gold, ivory and ivory objects, lapis lazuli, variety of precious coloured stones, wood of different kind, carnelian, aromates, onions, plants and animals. Further Dilmun also imported a variety of soft stone vessels for local consumption. This is evident from the illustrations of foreign items in chapter VIII. Most of these items Dilmun imported from Oman, Iran and India. (Ratnagar, 1981:87ff; Chakrabarti, 1990:*passim*). Steatite for making seals and other items must have come to Bahrain from Tepe Yahya either directly or through Oman. Tepe Yahya was one of the major production centre of this material (Lamberg Karlavosky, 1970).

Pearls are one of the items of exports which Dilmun had produced through the ages. Pearling and dates were the main local exports of Dilmun. The former is attested by archaeological excavations as heaps of shells have been found in Bahrain at several places. The complete dominance of pearl oysters among the molluscs in the settlement levels indicates that the Dilmunites were chiefly interested in pearl-oyster fishing. (Nielson, 1958:157-160).

SEAFARING MERCHANTS

During the period of Sargon of Agade trade with Dilmun seems to have been conducted by merchants who were not Mesopotamians. Trade seems to have ceased during the confusion that prevailed at the end of Agade Dynasty. Under king Ur-Nammu (ca. 2100 B.C.), two centuries later, the coastal trade was revived and was organised by a class of private enterprising merchants of Ur called alik Tilmun. Mallowan (1965:5) terms them as "the gogetters of Tilmun". These men carried on trade with Dilmun until the Larsa period (ca. 1900 B.C.). Due to the collapse of Indus Valley Civilization the Dilmun trade ceased. After a long interruption of nearly a millennium, Dilmun reappeared in cuneiform sources. Sennacherib planted Indian cotton in his royal garden. (Oppenheim, 1964:94). Old Babylonian texts reveal that from Dilmun (Tilmun) copper was imported into Ur, the "port of entry" for Mesopotamia by these group of sea-faring merchants, alik Telmun (Oppenheim, 1954:6f). These merchants worked in cooperation and collaboration with the enterprising capitalists in Ur to take garments and other articles to Dilmun in order to buy large quantities of copper ore. Dilmun in turn acquired the copper ore ingots and copper objects from the neighbouring Magan (Oman). In an early administrative document from the site of Shuruppak (Fara), the term "gal-Dilmun" occurs; and Cornwall (144:17), on the basis of Deimel (1925), suggests that it refers to dealers or sailors engaged in the overseas trade with Dilmun.

Travels of the alik Tilmun are repeatedly mentioned in a group of tablets relating to the temple of the goddess Ningal. It seems that every time the seafaring merchants returned with goods from Dilmun, they made votive offerings as incoming tithe to the goddess. In one of the Ur excavations texts V-526 (UET), cited by Oppenheim (1954:7), we find that the "tithe of the goddess Ningal from an expedition to Telmun and (from) a single persons having gone (there on their own", comprised small amount of gold, copper, and copper utensils. Leemans (1960:31) suggests that the tithe or gift made to the goddess was according to a fix rate of a tenth part (zag-10), based on custom or regulations. From other texts (UET V, 286, 678, and 546) cited by Leemans, it is mentioned that the givers had gone to or came from Dilmun. Even Dilmunites who had gone to Ur with goods had to offer the tithe, as in the case of one Idin-Nin-Inzak, a Dilmunite. (UETV 548, cited by Leemans, 1960:29:31). These features suggests that there existed two types of trade between Dilmun and Ur; and two types of seafaring merchants: Dilmunites bringing goods in their own ships to Ur; and natives of Ur conducting trade with Dilmun in expeditions, comprising a number of people.

The texts do not indicate the manner in which Dilmun trade was conducted, except one text, which suggests that Dilmun merchants came as private traders to Ur. This is evident from the practice of the Dilmun merchants paying tithes to the temple Ningal at Ur. Had they been trading on behalf of the king of Ur or the temple, then they would not have paid the tithe. However, texts of the Ibbi-Sin period indicates, infers Leemans, (1960:35), that trade was carried an for a temple. Other texts (UET V 280, 255,286) recorded by Oppenheim (1954:7) indicates that the offering of precious objects, beads, etc., was voluntary as an expression of gratitude by the traders for the divine protection of the goddess Ningal. Dilmun generally exported raw materials to Ur and these were worked up in the local factories. One tablet (UET. V.292) found in Gipar-Ku is a bill of lading of a vessel and states: "from the expedition of Tilmun, its shipload and its tablets of account" gives an inventory of gold, copper ore, hard woods, and ivory imported in the seventh year of Sumuilum for the House of Ningal. The role of the temple in Dilmun's trade is evidenced from the eight tablets found in the ruins of the Ningal temple at Ur. (Woolley and Mallowan, 1976:10).

Dilmun merchants and messengers travelled as far as Mari is recorded in the letters (ARMI I/21, 17). On their visits they were gifted by the king Samsi-Addu by various articles : oil, sesame, boxwood and sandals. (Leemans, 1960:141). Dilmunites were also visiting Babylon and resided there. During their stay in Babylon they procured supplies and imports for Dilmun. One text (TLBI 160) mentioned by Leemans (1960:141) and dated to the twenty-one year of Sumsuiluna, originating from Lagaba, (a town between Kutba and Babylon), mentions supply of barley to the Dilmunites. One of the person was Insak-gamil, a typical Dilmunite name. The barley supplied weighted : 12 *Kur* to the value of 10 shekels of silver; and 2 *Kur* 2PI to the value of 10 shekels. He also received 2 PI *sutu* cost for shipping (?). Altogether, Insak-gamil and Ili-amtahar, persons belonging to Samas-nasir, a Dilmunite, received 14 Kur 4 PI 2 Sutu, according to the standard of Sin. A text from Susa records the delivery of 17/1/2 minas of silver by Dilmunites during the time of the sukkalmah of Elam Kuter-Nahhunte I, who reigned during ca. 1730-1700 B.C. The text is plural and as such Dilmunites are meant. This delivery by Dilmunites seems to be in the nature of gift or tribute as nothing is mentioned in return that has been given to them. (Leemans, 1968:217).

Besides the seafaring merchants, caravans were also despatched to Dilmun officially by the kings. One such case is of king of Mari who sent a caravan (*harranum*) to Dilmun. It is not known whether this carvan travelled by land to Dilmun or partly by land and partly by sea. This carvan on its return journey had some problem before reaching Babylon and was detained by one Ili-Epuh. This is attested by the letters from the archives of the palace in Mari (cited by Oppenheim, 1954:15). A Dilmunite messenger from Dilmun was also detained in Mari on his way to the king of account of an incident which occured in the house of *tamkarum*. The nature and purpose of the carvan is not known. But it is obvious that its purpose was trade. Commercial contacts of Mesopotamian cities with points outside of Mesopotamia are best documented at Umma. During Sargonic times Umma are recorded in an unpublished texts (NBC 11447, Serota 18), cited by Foster (1977:39, fn. 105)

NATURE OF BUSINESS TRANSACTIONS

The nature of business transactions carried on between Dilmun and Ur for the export of copper etc. from the former to the latter was some what peculiar. An inscription of Warad-Sin (UET.I 127) reveals the interest taken by the king Rim-Sin in Dilmun and its trade. Several texts belonging to Rim-Sin's period reveal the nature of business transactions of Dilmun's trade. The text of UET V 367 cited by Oppenheim (1954:8) and Leemans, (1960:36, 47 f) mentions a contract of partnership entered by two persons named Lu-Meslamate and Nigsianaba, who had as capital borrowed 2 minas of silver, 5 *Kur* of sesame oil and

30 garments from and Ur-Ninmar for an expedition to Dilmun to buy copper by selling the above mentioned goods. On return from Dilmun they have mutually agreed to pay to be investor Ur-Ninmar with 4 minas of copper for each shekel (of silver) as a just price of the goods they had borrowed. The partners have sworn the contract conjointly by the king in the presence of witnesses who affixed their seals. Apparently they had to pay not only for the silver received as a trading-capital but for the value in silver of the oil and garments as well. That is, for the 2 minas of silver they had to give 8 talents of copper (480 minas). The crucial clause of the contract indicates that the investors or the financiers were not responsible for the commercial losses incurred by the borrowers or partners. (Oppenheim, 1954:8). A similar type of contract for the business expedition to Dilmun for the purpose of "fish eyes" (pearls) is recorded in UET V 428. The translation and transliteration of this text is reproduced as Fig. 13a in chapter VIII *supra*. The letters or texts (UET V 22, 29, 71, 81) relating to a leading travelling merchant and importer Ea-nasir of Ur throw considerable light on the importance of Dilmun's export of copper (termed URUDU and-only in business letters - Warum, Akkadian, Wariam and Waran) and on the nature of business transactions (Oppenheim, 1954:10). The transliteration and translation of the text (UET V 796) is given by Leemans (1960:38). From the first line of the text it is evident that copper was exported by Dilmun to Ur in quite a large quantity more than 13100 minas, according to the standard of Dilmun. (see chapter VIII, *supra* for Dilmun's standard). Generally ingots of copper (termed gubarum) weighing upto 4 talents each were exported. From the text it is evident that though copper was received according to the standard of Dilmun, it was converted or equated in accordance with the standard of Ur. Thus suggesting that the Dilmun and Ur systems of measurement were different. Dilmun used mana not talents. The texts seems to refer to three persons involved in the transaction, namely, Ea- nasir, the chief, Ala, and Nauirum-ili. Several other letters reveal that Ea-nasir was a leading businessman of copper as well as leading alik Tilmun who undertook regular expedition to Dilmun to procure copper and shipped it to Ur by sailing boats. And on expedition he stayed for a considerable period of time at Dilmun. During his stay in Dilmun, he shipped copper to Ur and also received and executed fresh orders for copper from dealers of Ur. He even shipped copper to the king or palace at Ur.

Silver (money) was mainly used for buying copper from Dilmun. However, other articles, garments, oil etc., were also exported from Ur to Dilmun to procure copper in exchange as a bartar deal. The other leading business man involved with Dilmun's copper trade and Lu-Enlilla. But the difference between Ea-nasir and Lu- Enlilla was that the former carried on trade for the temple at Ur, while the latter for the private dealers of Ur. (Leemans, 1960:38-56). The basic unit for buying and selling was silver. Therefore all commodities in the text are often priced in silver for the purpose of commercial record keeping. Silver also served as a commodity as a medium of exchange. (Foster, 1977:35). In almost all the text relating to Dilmun silver is mentioned as the unit. (Leemans, 1960:22-55). Besides silver other commodities were used in exchange or in leiu of silver. Thus in one text (UET V 367) besides 2 minas of silver, two other items : 5 kur of sesame-oil and 30 garments, were advanced as a capital for an expedition to Dilmun to buy copper. (Leemans 1960:36). Another text (UET III 1507) does not mention silver; but states 10 talents of different kinds of wool put in a boat for Dilmun. (Leemans, 1960:22). Probably the wood was meant for bartar deal or otherwise. However when garments were sent to Ea-nasir at Dilmun, their value was stated in silver. One text (UET V 848) records different types of garments (totalling 50) at different values of silver. (Leemans, 1960:47, 54).

MESOPOTAMIAN CONTROL OF DILMUN TRADE

Nippur letters and archaeological evidences, such as cylindrical seals, cuneiform tablets etc., discovered during excavations in Bahrain reveal that Mesopotamian kings or government did exercise control over the Dilmun trade by deputising their officials to reside in Bahrain. A tablet discovered at Lagash of the period of Shulgi seems to suggest that a regular staff of Babylonian officials was stationed in Bahrain, probably to act as tax- collectors and port authorities. It mentions *lugir* or royal messenger to Dilmun. The translation of the text (A03474) (after Cornwall, 1944:37) reads. "2ga of Gu-meal for UrDumuzi, a messenger; 1/2 measure of Gu-meal for two invalid officials of the king, (who were) brought by Ur-Dumuzi, the messenger, from Dilmun, month of Sekintar".

Nissen (1986:338) refers to the Archaic profession list in which "Dilmun" appears (in line 85) in connection with the professional name "Zag", or enkux, for which a meaning of "tax collector" has been proposed by him. Nissen states that the text (Lines 82-85) give composites with enkux, starting with gal, enkux, perhaps 'head of the tax collector', followed by the 'harvest tax collector' and the 'tax collector of the land (?)'. Finally, in the text we find the 'tax collector of DILMUN'. Nissen says that Dilmun here stands in parallelism to things on which taxes could be levied. However, there is no evidence as to the place where the Dilmun tax collector functioned, whether it was at the port of origin Dilmun or at Ur, the port of entry for Dilmun goods, is not known. Most probably the 'tax collector of Dilmun' functioned at the port of entry at Ur and collected tax on the goods imported from Dilmun. His posting in Dilmun/Bahrain does not seems to be practical as tax may not have been collected at the port of origin before they reached the destination. By the term 'tax collector of Dilmun' we may imply special officer to collect tax on the goods or imports coming from Dilmun to Mesopotamian port of entry.

TRADE MECHANISMS

The long distance trade of Dilmun both outside Arabia and within the Arabian Peninsula involved various ways and means for safe transportation and delivery of goods at the destination. This involved various stages beginning with proper packing in suitable containers or sacks, sealing of packages for security and identification, weighing of goods to evaluate value, transshipment, and means of transport. These aspects of trade mechanisms are briefly discussed here.

CONTAINERS

In Chapter VII we have recorded a large variety of foreign pottery and soft stone vessels recovered from the archaeological excavations at Bahrain. Except in some rare cases, pottery does not seems to have been an item of trade, as every where they were manufactured locally. Thus, it appears that smaller and not heavy articles were packed in pots, sealed and transported from one place to another. Such articles could be beads, lapis lazuli, ivory pieces, carved figurines, textiles, shells, food grains, pigments, oil etc. The use of pots or jars for long distance transportation is attested by a rim sherd with capacity mark in cuneiform found in early levels at Qal'at al Bahrain and Barbar ridged jar found at Nimrud with capacity mark in cuneiform. Probably some oil or fluid were sent in them. (Bibby, 1957:158; Laessoe, 1957:164,66). Another evidence of use of pottery jars as containers for transportation of valuables from Mesopotamia to Bahrain is that of silver hoard found contained in a Neo-Babylonion pottery jar. It was discovered in levels of City IV at Qal' at al Bahrain, and is dated to 650-550 B.C. on the basis of a signet ring. (Bibby, 1964:102, fig. 1). From several cuneiform texts (Leemans, 1960 : *Passim*) it is evident that silver was used as money and that the Mesopotamians gave it to the sea-faring merchants for going to Dilmun and buying copper and other articles. Thus it is clear that one such payment-consignment of silver and silver articles was transported from Ur to Bahrain in the Neo-Babylonian jar and that the receiver retained the silver articles in the same jar. These examples account for the variety of foreign pottery jars and soft stone vessels which has been discovered in Bahrain during excavations. They are on display in the Bahrain National Museum. These in fact reached Bahrain during ancient times, as containers of goods. Bahrain/Dilmun pottery found abroad is as a result of these having been sent as containers of goods.

SEALS AND SEALINGS

At Qal'at al Bahrain, on entering the City gate from the fore shore, there was a open square on the right. (See Fig. 6 in chapter IV-A, *supra*). On either side of the square were two houses, each with two rooms. In one of them the Danish excavators found several Dilmun seals and in the other stone- weights as well as seals. Bibby (1969:345f) has suggested that these two buildings were municipal offices, where loads of goods were weighed, and either the loads themselves or the clay documents accompanying them were stamped with the seals by the persons who checked the in-coming and out-going consignments.

Dilmun seals described and illustrated in chapter VI, *supra*, were mainly meant for the purpose of foreign trade for sealing the containers and packages by way of authenticity, guarantee and identification of the sender. Two types of such seals were used in Dilmun's foreign trade : commodity seals and message seals. The former were as described in chapter VI *supra*. Seals of Indian traders resident in Dilmun and Dilmun seals found in Mesopotamia and other far of places attest this function of Dilmun's seals in international trade. Likewise cylinder seals of Mesopotamian merchants or officials found in Bahrain were meant for sealing the packages of commodities or messages dispatched by them from Bahrain. (See chapter IX for the illustration of cylinder seals of foreign origin and found in Bahrain). A cuneiform merchantile tablet found in Larsa bearing a Dilmun seal (see Fig. 1, in chapter VI, *supra*) dated to the tenth year of Gungunum of Larsa (ca. 1923 B.C.) is a commercial agreement between the travelling merchant, and his financier or the creditor. The latter has given to the former as capital investment, some items : wheat, wool and sesame oil for export to Dilmun. Obviously these were meant for sale or exchange in the market of Dilmun for the procurement of other items, may be copper etc., for export to Larsa. This example illustrates the use of Dilmun seal in commercial contract of international trade. The tablet does not mention Dilmun. But since it records the investment of wool, wheat, and sesame in a trade venture, (Bibby, 1969:326) which articles were exported by Mesopotamia to Dilmun its origin should be Dilmun or its agency in Mesopotamia who must have impressed Dilmun seal on it. Seals have been found on pottery sherds recovered from excavations at Barbar temple. (Mortensen 1970:385 Fig. 1; Beyer 1989 : 144 Fig. 259). Obviously this was meant as a mark of ownership as well as identification. The other category of sealings were message sealings attached to any container in order to convey or store some kind of information. For instance, the identity of the sender of some communication or an item of merchandise, or delegation of authority or power to some individual or agent or state to particular person who carried the seal impression.

Message sealings were also meant some times as a counter check of commodity sealings, for the purpose of checking and verifying incoming sealed containers, or packages for the goods dispatched. (Wright and Johnson, 1975:267ff; Ratnagar, 1981:188). In Bahrain several message sealings have been found, mostly from early levels of Barbar Temple III. These are all of backed clay 'bullae' and are generally hemispherical in shape with different motifs, different from those of Dilmun seals. Recently these have been illustrated by Beyer (1989:154f). Since they are altogether different from characteristic Dilmun seals, it is probable that they belonged to foreign traders visiting or residing in Bahrain. But considering the site of discovery of these clay sealing 'bullae', at the lower levels of Barbar Temple III, and recurrences of same motif on several of them, it is possible that these were meant as Temple's official authorization, for its messages and to be carried by its messengers. They could be also marks of authenticity and guarantee of consignment dispatched with these marks (Ratnagar, 1981:198). Further, the clay sealings from Barbar Temple may give rise to a speculation as to whether the Barbar temple at Bahrain played the same role as that of temple of goddess Ningal ? Did Barbar temple also advanced capital in kind for buying merchandise for export? In the absence of sufficient evidence these questions cannot be answered. One can only assume several possibilities.

WEIGHTS AND MEASURE

Weight had great significance in Dilmun's international trade. They represent one aspect of Dilmun's civilization. Dilmun being in the centre of trade between the East and the West and as emporium for their commodities had to maintain balance between their weights in order to have fair and profitable trading. The Danish found at Qal'at al Bahrain City I seven Dilmun's stone weights (see Fig. 13 in chapter VIII, *supra* for the illustration of these weights and other details of Dilmun's standard). Two of these weights are cubical, one half cube, and the remaining spherical with flattened top and bottom. (Bibby). The Dilmun weights are same as that of Harappan weights. Bibby has explained the prevalence of the Harappan rather than the Mesopotamian system of weight in Bahrain. This he has attributed on the basis that Harappans were the earliest trading partners of Bahrain. Several Mesopotamian texts mention Dilmun minas. One of them (UET 796) cited by Leemans (1960 : 38f) states that 13100 Dilmun minas are equivalent to 611 gin or talents and 6.2/3 minas of Ur standard. Bibby (1970) worked-out that Dilmun standard was 1371.5 to 1376.8 grm. and he showed that this figure corresponded exactly to the multiple of hundreds in the Harappan system of which value a weight was found at Bahrain. (See Table for these weights at P. 359, *supra*). Dilmun's adaptation of Harappan weights might have been to facilitate the weighing by a common standard the Indian commodities imported on a large scale and thus to avoid discrepancy in weighing and payment. From the above texts it is evident that Dilmun adopted the classic system known through-out the south west Asia which has the mina as its base and introduced Harappan system of weights. Thus Dilmun unified weights between the east and west. The Mesopotamian text mention only 'according to the standard of Dilmun, (Leemans, 1960:38ff). But we learn about the 'Dilmunite shekels' from the Ebla clay tablets. In Ebla texts the shekel was always written with the Sumerian term gin, and was usually accompanied by the addition of 'Dilmun'. Pettinato (1981:182) states that we may parsed here Dilmun either as a noun or as an adjective. In the first case it implies that the weight system originated in Dilmun. In the second case it means "noble shekel" or a measure of standardized by international agreements. For several reasons I would prefer to accept Dilmun as a noun as it gives sense to read the documents and thus it implies Dilmun's weight or standard. Stieglitz (1987:44) discusses Pettinato's hypothesis and in the light of the lexical evidence from Ebla, concludes that it is preferable to interpret the 'gin Dilmun' as the 'Dilmun (standard) shekel'. This could only mean that along with other systems of weight, Dilmun system was also adopted at Ebla. A lexical text (TM.75 G. 2000 VII:45-46) according D.O. Edzard (cited by Stieglitz, 1987:43) has the following entry : GIS. DILMUN=Wa-za-nu-um = sa-qi-lum. Here, says Stieglitz, an (originally wooden) object of or pertaining to Dilmun is defined by the Eblaite words : waganun - 'weight', and squlun - 'shekel' weight. These entries are evidently connected with the use of gin DILMUN in the economic texts and suggest, says Stieglitz, that we read the latter as Eblaite taqilum 'shekel'.

The use of the Dilmun shekel at Ebla not only indicates close commercial ties that existed between the two, but suggests importance and popularity of Dilmun's standard outside Dilmun. In view of the importance of the Ebla texts mentioning Dilmun weights, two specimens are given here (after Pettinato, 1981:123, 187).

(TM. 75. G. 1696)   (TM. 75 G. 357)

I.   1 Dilmunite shekel of gold   I 1)   131 minas and 53
      ornament of 1 sheet for Tubi-Sipis   Dilmunite shekels of
      the man of Asba-II   Silver.

II.   2 Dilmunite shekels of gold   2)   1 mina of gold.
      ornament of one sheet for   3)   tribute
      Ib-Malik brother of Dusigu   4)   of the governor

III. 2 Dilmunite shekels of gold   II 1)   tribute
      Ornament of one sheet for   2)   of the governor Ilzi;
      Ibbi-Sipis, son of Ebrium   3)   33 minas,
                                                   40 Dilmunite shekels
The same text records more   of silver
substantial quantities such as the   4)   -
following which refers to a donation of   5)   33 minas,
Had's temple in Halam :   30 Dilmunite shekels
                                                   of silver,
2 minas and 23 Dilmunite shekels   6)   —
of gold in the form of a "large   III 1)   4 vases of silver
sheet   2)   sum : 57 minas and
the men of the scepter   10 Dilmunite shekels
have given   of silver.

to Hada   3)   5 minas and
of Halam   50 Dilmunite shekels
in the mouth   of gold,
of Amar;   4)   tribute
the king   IV 1)   of the governor Darima :
has delivered
                                              2)   23 minas and
                                                   50 Dilmunite shekels of silver,
                                              3)   2 minas of gold,
                                              4)   tribute
                                              5)   of the governor Ladad;

From the translations of the first text (TM. 75G, 1696) it is evident that it is of commercial nature stating gold converted into sheets for three persons, and mentions Dilmun shekel. Pettinato (pp. 123, 187) has translated 'gin-dilmun' some times as 'Dilmun shekel' and some times as 'Dilmunite shekel'. The second text (TM. 75G. 1357) is not a commercial one but an administrative document stating the tribute paid by the royal governors and other persons and from cities in Dilmun shekels. This implies that the use of Dilmun shekel was not restricted to commercial transactions and trade between Ebla and Dilmun, but it was officially adopted by the Ebla government for general purpose.

So far there is no evidence of Dilmun measure. However, from level 23 at Qal'at al Bahrain excavation the Danish found a rim sherd bearing a Sumerian record of capacity. (Bibby, 1957:158). The cuneiform inscription on inside of he rim of a large clay pot according to Leassoe (1957:164-166) reads : "2(PI) 4 (ban) 7 sita". The Sumerian reading of 2 (PI) is nimina and the Akkadian reading 2 pani. The Akkadian reading of the inscription would be : "2 pani 4 sat 7 qa". That is a capacity of 167 sila (qa), or 67.468 litres. The indication of the capacity of the pot is written inverted and has to be read by tilting the pot towards one and looked down into its interior. The rim and its inscription is dated to late third or early second millennium B.C. A Bahraini pot of Barbar ridged ware discovered at Nimrud differs from the Assyrian specimens, as these were marked on the outside of the jar. Thus, we may tentatively suggest that there was a Dilmun measure system, just like the Dilmun weight standard, and its sila was probably less than 0.404 litre. Obviously the Barbar pot was dispatched from Bahrain with the capacity mark written in cuneiform by some seafaring merchant of Mesopotamia visiting or resident at Bahrain at that time. There is no evidence to support that the Bahraini's used cuneiform though of course they might have had its knowledge.

TRANS-SHIPMENT

Dilmun's role in the international trade passing through it was that of a middle man and an emporium. The trade mechanism was some what unusual with regard to the transshipment of goods not of its own origin. As it not only exported its own local products but also imported foreign goods for the purpose of export. The mechanism involved were : receiving of supply orders, placing of orders, receipt of goods, storage, despatch, payments, exchange of goods in the barter deal etc. The despatch of goods involved their packing in containers, weighing or measuring, computation of value, use of seals as authentication, etc. For the first two processes, recovering and placing of orders we have no evidence. Regarding receipt of foreign goods we have abundant archaeological evidence. Harbour activity is also attested near one of the gates in the city wall facing the sea shore at Qal'at al Bahrain. Here Bibby (1969:354f) has suggested functioning of customs house and port authority. (see Fig. 6 in chapter IV-A, *supra*). The storage system for the goods received from abroad and pending dispatch is attested by the Kassite ware house of City III period. (see Fig. 8 and details in chapter IV-A, *supra*).

TRANSPORT

The major element involved in Dilmun's foreign trade was of course, transport. The long distance trade between Mesopotomia- Dilmun on one hand Dilmun-Indus Valley on the other, was carried over the sea. The use of ships is attested in the texts of Urnanshe and Sargon the great boasting that the boats of Dilmun lay anchored at the docks of Agade (Kramer, 1964:48). Sailing boats are depicted in Dilmun's seals. (see Fig. 41a, b, in chapter VI, *supra*). The route followed within the Arabian Gulf was along the coast. This is attested by the number of coastal sites of Dilmun culture. Weather conditions, safety and supply of needs might have necessitated to follow coastal route. The use of over land route for carvans between Dilmun and the middle Euphrates river is attested by Mari texts (Oppenheim, 1954:15).

A peculiar feature of the texts relating to Dilmun's foreign trade is that all the transactions of goods for export at Ur have occured in the month of Addaru (about March). This is in agreement with the consignments of export goods, recorded in the documents (Published by Hallo, AS16, PP. 194ff; cited by Leemans 1968:219), probably somewhere in the Gulf, which occured in Ajaru (about May). Some text show that goods were imported at Ur throughout the year. This is because of the monsoon and weather conditions. Thus suggesting that ships from Ur sailed in March and reached Dilmun in May.

Finally we may conclude with the remarks of Bibby (1969:362) that merchants of Dilmun had their agencies established in Ur in the twentieth century B.C., just as in the twentieth century A.D. we have agencies and branches.

CHAPTER XII

THE DILMUNITES

Who were the Dilmunites and where did they come from ? This is one of the fundamental question which has remained inpenetrably unanswered as ever it was, observes Michael Rice (1985:276). Inspite of more than hundred years of archaeological excavations, research and writing the origin of the Dilmunites is still unknown. Mesopotamian texts and myths speak about several aspects of Dilmun: the land, holiness, cleanliness, fresh water springs, its gods and goddesses, association of Mesopotamian gods and goddesses with that of Dilmun, temple, 'apsu', trade and articles of export, its king, Mesopotamian governers over Dilmun, etc. But these texts and myths are silent about Dilmun people's origin. There is no textual evidence as to whether Dilmunites were Sumerians or vice versa.

One thing is certain from the forgoing chapters that Dilmun was inhabited through-out the priods of all Stone Ages beginning from the Lower Palaeolithic times until the present. That is, covering almost the entire period of Quaternary. This is evidenced from the stone tools of all Stone Ages recorded from Bahrain and illustrated in the Atlas. (see Chapter III, pp.70-101, *supra*). Though we have not recovered, so far, any pebbletools from Bahrain, but mid-Acheulean type of hand-axe has been recorded. Thus, Bahrain is one of the oldest and continuously inhabited geographic entity in the world. The large variety of tools of different periods suggests that different Stone Age cultures developed in Bahrain as in the case of the Arabian mainland. (see volume I in this series). Bahrain's tools have parallels with those of Arabian mainland of which Bahrain was a part until its seperation, due to geological and sea-level changes (see pp.11-18 *supra*) around 6000 B.C. That is with the seperation of geographic entity of Bahrain from the Arabian mainland, the people who were inhabiting that portion of the land during the Stone Age period were also seperated from the Arabian mainland. These people of former Arabian mainland continued to inhabit the island, the island which became famous later on as Dilmun/Bahrain and its people as Dilmunites. Thus, the origin of Dilmunites may be traced to the Arabian mainland and as such they too were Arabs. Further, the territorial extent of Dilmun comprised Bahrain and eastern part of Arabian mainland (see map at page 131 *supra*) as such it is obvious that Dilmunites inhabited eastern Arabia as well. Thus implying that the people of Bahrain and eastern Arabia were one and the same, Arabs of Arabia the original inhabitants. (For the people of Arabia readers are refered to chapter VI in volume I-"Saudi Arabia" in this series).

Cuneiform texts attest that ethnic people identified as Amorites occupied much of northern and eastern Arabia during the third millennium B.C. It is obvious that they originated from Arabia. (see Fig.4 in chapter IX, supra, for the migration of Amorites towards eastern Arabia and the Gulf). Dilmun is connected with the Amorites in two texts from Drehem cited by Buccellati (1966:249f). They record the expenditure of sheep "for Amorites (and) diviners coming (?) from Dilmun. (MAR. TU masmas NITUK-tae-ra-ne). Another text from the same place mentions an un-named "Man of Dilmun" (lUNI. TUK KI). A text from Isin records the manufacture of leather articles "for Dilmun and the Amorites". Yet another text from Drehem states a certain amount of fresh fish from Dilmun (Buccellati, 1966:249f). The coming of Amorites from Arabia is attested by a Isin-Larsa text from Diyala recorded by Gelb (1968:42f; 1980:1) which lists Amorites coming "from the sea"(a-ab-ba-ta) or as Gelb writes "from the Sea-Land or from the land across the sea, which can be only Persian Gulf". They were under the control of Akkadians. Out of the 29 Amorites cited in the list, 26 are MAR.TU e-lu-lume and 3 dhhu-me. This derivation of Amorites (s) a-ab-ba-ta "from the sea", implying from the sea land or from the land across the sea indicates that the Amorites originated not in the west but in the south eastern part of Mesopotamia near the Arabian Gulf. This evidence is further attested by a cuneiform tablet (Gelb, 1980:2) from the Qal'at al Bahrain City II dating to the Isin Larsa period, ca.1950 B.C. which lists three Amorites with patronymics. These names read by Simo Parpola and recorded by Brunswig etal (1983:108f) are: Janbi'-na`im,'Ila-milkum, and Jisi'-tambu son of Janbi'-na'im. The tablet text copies and photographs were examined by I.J.Gelb, A.W. Sjobery, E.V.Leichty and S.Parpola and have dated the script to post - Ur III or early Isin - Larsa times, ca.2050-1900 B.C. Howard-Carter (1987:63) suggests that this tablet undoubtedly came from Mesopotamia, where the Amorites/west semites introduced themselves in Ur III period and the tablet is not acceptable proof of Amorite population in Bahrain.

Several texts relating to *alik Tilmun* and their trading business with Dilmun mention persons with MAR-TU names. Few of these names from the texts are: Milku-dannum (UETV549); Zubabum (UET V 297); and Alazum (UET V 796). (Leemans, 1960:23-30).

A fragment of chlorite bowl with cuneiform inscription recovered from Qal'at al Bahrain City II or III (Middle of the second millennium B.C.) seems to have an Amorite name. (Andre, 1989:170 Fig.316). Majority of names in the Susa text, recorded by Lambert (1976:71) are MAR-TU. One of them Mi-iL-Ki-iL seems to be identical with that listed in Gelb's compendium (1980:623); with the name ILi-mi-il-kum in the Qal'at text, mentioned above, and Milik-ilija in the Ur I-L text (UETV 491). The other MAR-TU name is in the Susa text Mi-iL-Ku-ma-nu-um. Zarins finds these two names to be similar with those in the *alik Tilmun* text (UET V 549 and 491)-Mi-il-ku-da-nu-um and Mi-li-ik-i-li-a, respectively. (Zarins, 1986:246). Two of the three witnesses in this transactions, states Zarins, have MAR-TU names:A-hu-ma and Mi-nu-up-DINGER. Two factors link this text to Dilmun. Firstly the text bears the circular Dilmun seal (Persian Gulf), and secondly, Mi-il-ki-il is mentioned in the text as the son of one Te-lim-dEn-za-ag. Enzag being the titulary deity of Dilmun. This god Enzag is also mentioned in inscription of Durand's black stone found in Bahrain and in the Nippur letters emanating from Dilmun. Both these texts are cited and illustrated in chapter IX, *supra*.

Two Dilmunites are mentioned in the texts from Ur of the Larsa period. They are: Me-a-ti-a-nu-um (UET V 716) and Iddin-ilum (UET.V 548). (Leemens, 1960:29,55;Oppenheim,

1954:15). Of these two are Dilmunites, the former is of MARTU origin, and the other: anum name (Zarins, 1986:247). Discussing all the known texts Zarins (1986:231ff) finally concludes that the MAR-TU were linked to Dilmun in a political sense (rulers in the southern Mesopotamia), alik Tilmun or seafaring merchants of Mesopotamia, and inhabitants of Dilmun itself. The above cited textual evidences clearly establishes, association of Amorites or MAR-TU with Dilmun, which idea Landsberger (1954:56n,103) and Buccellati (1966:249) had originally proponded. Gelb (1968:43;1980:2) and Potts (1990:185,218,228) are also of similar opinion. However, the names of three Dilmun kings, Upri, Qana, and Hundaru are still etymologically obscure. (Haward-Carter: 1987:96).

According to Poebel's theory (1942:256ff) MAR-TU (=mar-du) is the well known name of Arab's in Sumerian Inscriptions and that these Amorites were nomads who had migrated from Arabia into Mesopotamia. However, he does not mention any specific part of Arabia. Kramer (1960:272ff) while corrborating Poebel, goes a step further and suggests that MAR-TUS and Amorites came from Arabia from a mountain district called Martu located somewhere in Arabia.

According to this theory of Kramer, a mountain area, called Martu, is to be looked for in Arabia, and from there two waves of semites started on their way to Mesopotamia. One of these groups, the Mar.TUS gave the Sumerians their word for west. Arabs have been included among the Amorites by Dhorme (1951:103f) on the ground that these are proper names which Dhorme maintained to be Arabian. The geographical name Martu/Amurru(m), suggests, Dhorme, covered the Arabian Peninsula, or atleast part of it. (Haldar, 1971:6f). Landsberger (1965:809) also suggests that their true place of origin was most likely in Arabia. Most of the Assyriologits are of the opinion that Amorites originated from Arabia. Landsberger (1944:434;1974:9) argues that in Sumerian Mythology Dilmun has been portrayed as the land of the paradise and the Dilmun possessed deities with authentic Sumerian names, such as, the chief god En-zak and his spouse Me-skil-ak, Thus the circumstances supports an overseas origin for the Sumerians. As such it is improbable that Dilmun was colonized from southern Mesopotamia. If the hypothesis of Landsberger concerning the immigration of the Sumerians is accepted then it becomes clear that they might have originated/migrated from Dilmun. McClure (1971:76) suggest that Semites lived in most part of Arabia, 'Ubaidians in east Arabian coast, Hamites in the south and Negroids in southern coast. (See chapter VI-"The 73 people", in Volume I in this series).

The question of Dilmunites and their origin and other doubtful aspects of Dilmunology can be solved only by the discovery of Dilmun's archives, in future, hopefully.

Sic Transit Gloria

BIBLIOGRAPHY

Abbreviations

A.A.	:	*Artibus Asiae*
A.A.E.	:	*Arabian Archaeology and Epigraphy*
A.J.S.L.	:	*American Journal of Sematic Languages*
Amm. Rev. Anth.	:	*American Review of Anthropology*
Arch. U.A.E.	:	*Archaeology of the United Arab Emirates*
Atlal	:	*The Journal of Saudi Arabian Archaeology*
B.A.S.O.R.	:	*Bulletin of the American School of Oriental Research.*
B.B.V.O.	:	*Berliner Beitrage Zum Vorderen Orient*, 2 (ed.D.T. POTTS), 1983
B.N.M.	:	*Bahrain National Museum*(Archaeological- Collection) Vol.I.(eds. Pierre Lombard and Monik Kervran). Directorate of Museum and Heritage. 1989.
B.T.A.	:	*Bahrain Through Ages-the Archaeology* (eds.) Shaikha Haya Ali Al Khalifa and Michael Rice. London 1986.
C.A.J.	:	*Cambridge Archaeological Journal*
D.D.	:	*Dilmun Discovered.* The Early years of Archaeology in Bahrain (ed)Michael Rice. Longmans 1983
E.W.	:	*East West*
J.A.O.S.	:	*Journal of the American Oriental Society*
J.C.S.	:	*Journal of Cuneiform Studies*
J.E.S.H.O.	:	*Journal of the Economic and Social History of the Orient.*
J.N.E.S.	:	*Journal of Near Eastern Studies*
J.O.S.	:	*Journal of Oman Studies*
J.R.Anth.	:	*Journal of the Royal Anthropological Institute of Gr. Britain & Ireland*
Kuml	:	Arbog For Jysk Arkaelogisk Selskab, Aahus
P.E.Q.	:	*Palestine Exploration Quarterly*
P. Pre. S.	:	*Proceedings of the Prehistoric Society*
P.S.A.S.	:	*Proccedings of the Siminar for Arabian Studies*
Rev. Assy.	:	*Review Assyriology Archaeology*
S.A.A.	:	*South Asian Archaeology*
W.A.	:	*World Archaeology*

Periodicals Not Abbreviated:

Ages; Antiquity; Archaeology; Atlal: Dilmun;Expedition; Iraq;, Iran; Iranica Antiqua; Paleorient; Quarternaria; Kuml; Levant;, Mesopotamia., Oriens Antiques.

Abu Daruk   H.M al Rahim, A.J. Murad
   1984   "Excavation of a Neolithic Site at Thumamma" *Atlal*(8)
Albright, W.F.
   1981   "The Mouth of the Rivers". *A.J.S.L.*
Ali, S.Al-Mughannam
   1988   "Excavation of the Dhahran Burial Mounds, Forth season, 1406". *Atlal* (11).
Allchin, Bridget and Ramond
   1982   *The Rise of Civilization in India and Pakistan.*   Cambridge.
Alster, Bendt
   1983   "Dilmun, Bahrain and the alleged paradise in Sumarian myth and literature."
          in *BBVO.*
Amiet, Pierre
   1986   "Susa and Dilmun Culture." in *B.T.A.*
Andersen, H.H.
   1986   "The Barbar Temple: Stratigraphy, Architecture and   interpretation." *B.T.A.*
Andre, Beatrice.
   1989   "The Written Documents". *B.N.M.*
Al Ansary, Abdul Rehman T.
   1982   *Qaryat al Fau-A Protrait of Pre-Islamic Civilization in Saudi Arabia,* London.
          Antiquities of Bahrain, Bahrain Historical and Archaeological Society, Manama.
Bayliss, Miranda,"The Cult of Dead Kin in Assyria and Babylonia". *Iraq*(35/2)
Belgrave, J.H.D.
   1953/1975 *Welcome to Bahrain,* Manama.
          Bahrain National Museum(Guide)1991.
Bent, J.T.
   1890   "The Bahrein Islands in the Persian Gulf,"*Proc. of the Royal Geographic Society.*
Bent, J.T. and Mrs. Bent
   1900   *Southern Arabia.* London.
Beyer, Dominique
   1989   "The Bahrain Seals". *B.N.M.*
Bibby,T.Geoffery
   1954(a) "Five among Bahrain's Hundred Thousand Grave-Mounds".   *Kuml.*
   1954(b) "The well of the Bulls". *Kuml.*
   1957 "The Hundred - Meter Section". Kuml
   1958 The"Ancient Indian Style" sealsfromBahrain, *Antiquity* (32).
   1964 "Arabiens arkaeologi". *Kuml.*
   1965 "Arabiens arkaeologi". *Kuml.*
   1966   "Arabiens arkaeologi". *Kuml.*
   1967   "Arabiens arkaeologi". *Kuml*

1969/1974 *Looking for Dilmun*, New York.

1970   "According to the Standard of Dilmun". *Kuml.*

1974   "Bahrain and the Arabian Gulf" in Hawke's *Atlas*

1986   "The origin of the Dilmun civilization". *B.T.A.*

Bordes,Francois.

1968   *The Old Stone Age.* World University Library.

Borday,Jacques

1970   *Tools of the Old and New Stone Age.*

Bowen,Robert and Jux,Ulrich.

1987 *Afro-Arabian Geology*, A Kinematic View, London.

Boucharlat R. and P. Lombard

1981   "The History and Archaeology of the Gulf From the fifth   century B.C. to
         the seventhy century A.D. A review of   Edvidence".*PSAS.*

1985   "The Oasis at Al Ain in Iron Age, Excavations at Rumilah 1981-1983, *Arch.
         U.A.E.*

Boucharlat and J.F.Salles

1984   *Arabie Oriental, Mesopotamia at Iran meridional de "Age du Fer an debnt
         de la periode islams que.* Paris.

Boucharlat Ramy and Jean-Francois, Salles,

1989   "The Tylos period" *B.N.M.*

Brunswig, R.H.Jr., Parpola,A., Potts,D.T.

1983   "New Indus and related seals from the Near East", in *BBVO*

Brown, Edwin, J., Judith Littleton and Robyn, Stocks.

1982-83 "Eighteen Mounds at the New City site "1982" (Bahrain). Australian Expedition
         Report" (Un published). Bahrain Historical and Archaeological Society.

Brunswig,R.H.,A.Parpola, and D.T.Potts.

1983   "New Indus And Related Seals from the Near East". *BBVO*

Buchanan,Briggs.

1965   'A Dated "Persian Gulf" Seals and its Implications', *Studies in Honor of Benno
         Landsberger on his Seventy- Fifth Brithday April 21, 1965,* As 16.Chicago.

Buccellati,Giorgio

1966   *The Amorites of Ur III Period.* Neples.

1967   'A Dated Seal impression Connecting Babylonia and Ancient India',*Archaeology.*

1976   "A Snake Goddess and Her companions". Paper read at the   Oriental club,
         New Haven. 1969.

1981   *Early Near Eastern Seals-in the Yale Babylonian collection*, New Haven.

Budge, E.A. Wallis

1975   *Babylonian Life and History*, London.

Burkholder, Grace,

1971   "Steatite carvings from Saudi Arabia", *A.A.*(33/4).

1972   "Ubaid Pottery sites in Saudi Arabia". *Archaeology* (25/4)

1984   *An Arabian Collection: Artifacts from the Eastern Province*, Boulder city.

Burkholder,G., Golding,M.

1971   "A Surface survey of the Ubaid sites in the eastern province of Saudi Arabia", *A.A.* (33/4).

Burrows, E.

1928   "Tilmun, Bahrain, Paradise," Rome : *Scriptura Sacraet Monumenta Orientis Antiqui*, Vol.II Rome. In *D.D.*

Bushiri, Ali Akbar,

1985/86 "The Mythology of Immortality", *Dilmun*(13)

Butz, Kilian

1983   "Dilmun in wirtschaftstexten Der Ur III-zeait", BBVO 1983 "Zwei Kleine Inschriften Zur Geschichte Dilmuns". *BBVO.*

Butzer,K.W.

1975   "Patterns of Environmental change in the Near, East during Late Pleistocine and Early Holocence time". In F.Wentorf and A.E.Marks (eds.) *Problems in prehistory: North Africa and the Levent.*

1978   "The Late Prehistoric Environmental History of the Near East", in *The Environmental History of the Near and Middle East Since the Last Ice Age* (ed.W.C.Brice),

Calvet, Yves

1989   "Failaka And the Northern Part of Dilmun *P.S.A.S.* (19).

1991   "The Dilmun culture-its Border with Mesopotamia." (Ms)

Calvet, Yves, and Jacqueline Gachet

1990   *Failaka - Fouilles Francaises - 1986-1988.* Lyon.

Caton-Thompson,G.

1953   "Same Palaeoliths from South Arabia". Proc, Pr.H.S.

Chand, Indira

1991   "4000-year-Old prints puts Jane over the Moon" *Gulf Daily News* Bahrain, X (267) dt.12.12.1991.

Chakrabarti, Dilip K.

1976   "Gujrathi Harappan connection with Asia: A reconsideration of the Evidence" *J.E.S.H.O* (18/3).

1990   *External Trade of the Indus civilization.* New Delhi.

Chapman,R.W.

1978   "General Information on the Arabian Peninsula", in S.S.Al-Sayari, and J.G.Zotl, (eds.):*Quaternary Period in Saudi Arabia.* Vienna.

Charlesworth, J.K.

1966   *The Quaterary Era.* London.

Charpin, Dominique;

1984   "Nouveaux documents du bureall del'huile a le'poque Assyrienne", *M.A.R.I.3.*

Cleuziou,Serge

1979   'The Second and Third Seasons of Excavations at Hili 8', *Arch. U.A.E.*

1980   "Three seasons at Hili : toward a chronology and cultural History of the Oman Peninsula in the 3rd millennium BC"., *P.S.A.S.,* (10).

1984   "Oman Peninsula and its relations eastward during the third millennium". *Frontiers of the Indus Civilization.* (eds.B.B.Lal, S.P.Gupta), New Delhi.

1989   "The Early Dilmun Period" and "the Middle Dilmun Period". *BNM.*

Cleuziou, MH.Pottier, J.F.Salles

1978   "Mission Archeological francaise lare compagne." *Arch.UAE.*

Cleuziou,S.,Lombard P., Salles, J.F.

1979   *Excavations at Umm Jidr,* Bahrain. Paris.

Cornwall,P.B.

1944   "Dilmun: The History of Bahrain Island Before Cyrus, (Unpublished PhD.Thesis.) Harvard University.

1946   "On the Location of Dilmun", *B.A.S.O.R.* (11).

1952   "Two Letters from Dilmun", *J.C.S.,* (VI).

Costa,P.M.

1978   "The Copper Mining settlement of `Arja:a Preliminary Survey", *J.O.S.* (4).

Crawford,Harriet

1973   "Mesopotamia's invisible exports in the third millennium B.C." *W.A.* (5/2).

1991   "Seals from the first season's excavation at Sar', Bahrain", *C.A.J.*

Crawford, H.E.W., R.G.Killick, J.Moon

1991   "London-Bahrain Archaeological Expedition-Field Report - Excavations at Saar 1990-1991". (Unpublished).

1992   "Field Report - Excavations at Saar 1991/92". (Unpublished).

Dally, Stephanie

1973   "Old Babylonian Greetings Formulae And the Iltani Archives From Rimah" *J.C.S.*

DeCardi,Beatrice

1978   (ed). *Qatar Archaeological Report-Excavation 1973.* Oxford University Press.

1983   'Ubaid Mesopotamia Reconsidered', in the *Braidwood Festschrift,* Chicago.

1985/1989 "Harappan Finds from Tomb 6 at Shimal, Ras al Khaimah, U.A.E." *S.A.A.* (ed.K.Friefelt, P.Sorensen).

1986   "Harappan Finds in a Tomb at Rasal-Khaimah, U.A.E." *P.S.A.S.* (16).

Delaparte,L.J.

1932   *Catalogue des cylinders, cachetet Pierres Gravees de style oriental.* Muse du Louvre.

Delougaz, P.

1959   "Architectural Representations on Steatite Vases", *Iraq* (21).

Deimel,.A

1928   "Remerkungen Zu P.Burrows: Tilmun, Bahrain, Paradise'. *Orient* (30).

Dhorme, E.

1951   *Recueil Edouard Dhorme* (cited in Haldar, 1951).

Doe, Brian

1986   "The Barbar Temple site in Bahrain: Conservation and preservation", *B.T.A.*

Doornkamp, J.C., Burnsden,D. and Jones,D.K.C., (eds.)
1980   *Geology, Gemorphology and Pedology of Bahrain*, Geo Abstracts.

Dougherty, Raymond Philip
1932   *The Sealand of Ancient Arabia*, New Haven.

Duckworth, J.R.
1976   "Notes on the Flint Implements from Jawa". Appendix to S.W.Helms, 1976. *Levant*..

Durand,E.L.
1880   "Extracts from Report on the Islands and Antiquities of Bahrain", *JRAS*(XII) in D.D.

During-Caspers, Elizabeth C.L.
1970   "Trucial Oman in the third millennium BC." *Ori Anti*. (4).
1971a   "The bull's head from Barbar Temple II, Bahrain: a possible contact with early Dynastic Sumer." *E.W.* 21.
1971b   "New Archaeological Evidence for maritime trade with Persian Gulf during the late Proto literature period". *E.W.* (21).
1972a   "Harappan trade in the Arabian Gulf in the third Millennium BC", *Mesopotamia*.
1972b   "The Bahrain Tumuli". PSAS (1971).
1973a   "Dilmun and the date tree". E.W. (23).
1973b   "Harappan trade in the Arabian Gulf in the third Millennium BC". *P.S.A.S.*
1973c   "Harappan" in *Journal of Archaeology & history of Bahrain*,
1976   "Cultural concepts in the Arabian Gulf and the Indian Ocean". *P.S.A.S.* (6).
1977   "A Dilmunite Seal cutter's Misfortune" *Antiquity* (41/210)
1978   "R.Thaper's Dravidian hypothesis for the locations of Meluhha, Dilmun and Makan" *J.E.S.H.O.* XXI (2).
1979   "Statuary in the Round from Dilmun".*S.A.A.*, 1975(ed. J.E. Van Louthuizen-De Leeuw).
1980   *The Bahrain tumuli: an illustrated catalogue of two important collections*. Istanbul:Nederland.
1983   "Corals pearls and prehistotic Gulf". *P.S.A.S.* (13).
1986   "Animal Design and Gulf Archaeology", *B.T.A.*
1987   "A copper Bronze Animal in Harappan Style from Bahrain: Evidence of Mercantile Interaction". *J.E.S.H.O.* (30).
1989   "Some Remarks on Oman". *PSAS* (19).

Edens,C
1986   "The Rub'al-Khali `Neolithic' revisted: the view from Naqdan 1988". *Araby the Blest*. (ed.D.T.Potts).
1982   "Protohistory : excavations on Khor lle", *Rapport d' Activite RCP* 476.
1986   "Bahrain and the Arabian Gulf during the second millennium B.C.,:Urban crisis and colonialism. *B.T.A.*

Edzard,D.O.
1981   *Verwaltungs texte verschieden Inhalts (Archivi Reali Di Ebla-II)*.

1987   *"Zeitschrift fur Assyriologie und vorderasiatische Archaologie.* (Band77). Berlin.

Eidem, Jesper

1986   "The cuneiform texts from City III, Qal'at al Bahrain". (Unpublished)

Englund,Robert

1983a   "Dilmun in the Archaic Uruk corpus" in *B.B.V.O.*

1983b   "Exotic Fruits", *B.B.V.O.*

Erlenmeyar,H,Von M.L.

1966   Uber Beziehungan des Alten Orients Zuden fruhindischen stadtkultturen". *Archivfur
          Orient forschung,* Graz.

Fairservis, W.A.

1971   *The Roots of Ancient India,* Chicago.

Falkenstein, Adam

1974   "The Sumerian Temple city". *Monographs on the Ancient Near East* (I/2).
          University of Pennylvania.

Field,Henry

1956   *Ancient and Modern Man in South West Asia,* I. Miami.

1961   *Ancient and Modern Man is South West Asia,* II. Miami

Foster, Benjamin R.

1967   "Commercial Activity in Sorgonic Mesopotamia", in *Trade in the Ancient Near
          East,* (ed) J.D. Hawkins., London., also in *Iraq* (39/1).

Frifelt, Karen

1964   "Qala'at al Bahrain", in Bibby 1964, *KUML.*

1965   "Bahrain" in Bibby 1965, *KUML.*

1970   "Jemdat Nasr Graves in the Oman", *Kuml.*

1975   "On prehistoric settlements and chronology of the Oman Peninsula" *E.W.* (25).

1986   "Burial Mounds near Ali Excavated by the Danish Expedition", *B.T.A.*

1989   "Ubaid in the Gulf Area", in *Upon this foundation-The Ubaid Reconsider* (ed.
          E.F.Henrickson and I.Thuesen).Copenhagen.

Frohlich, Buruno

1983   "The Bahrain Burial Mounds". *Dilmun* (11).

1986   "The Human Biological history of the Early Bronze Age Population in Bahrain",
          in *B.T.A.*

Gadd, C.J.

1932   "Seals of ancient Indian style found at Ur", Proceedings of the British Academy.

1979   "Seals of Ancient Indian Style found at Ur" in *Ancient cities of the Indus,*
          (ed) G.L.Posshel. New Delhi.

Garrod,Dorothy A.E.

1932   "A new Mesolithic Industry : The Natufian of Palestine", *J.R.An.I.*(XII).

Garrod, D.A.E. and D.M.A. Bate,

1937   *The Stone Age of Mount Carmel* (Oxford).

Gazder M.S., D.T.Potts, A. Livingstone.

1984   "Excavations at Thaj". *Atlal* (8).

Gelb, I.J.

1968   "An Old Babylonian list of Amorites. *J.A.O.S.* (88).   Also   in W.W. Hallo, 1968.

1980   *Computer Added analysis of Amorites.*

Glassner, Jean-Jacques

1984   "Inscription cuneiformes de Failaka", - *Failaka - Fouilles Francasis - 1983.* (ed. J.F. Salles).

Glob,P.V.

1954(a) "The flint sites of the Bahrain desert". *Kuml*

1954(b) "Bahrain-island of the Hundred thousand Burial- Mounds" *Kuml*

1954(c) "Temples at Barbar". *Kuml*

1954(D)"The Ancient Capital of Bahrain". *Kuml.*

1955   "The Danish archaeological Bahrain-expedition's second excavation campaign". *Kuml*

1956   "Reconnaissance in Qatar". *Kuml*

1957   "Prehistoric discoveries in Qatar". *Kuml*

1958   "Alabaster vases from the Bahrain temples". *Kuml*

1959   "Archaeological investigations in four Arab states".   *Kuml.*

1960   "Danish Archaeologists in the Persian Gulf" *Kuml*

Glob, PV. and T.G. Bibby

1960   "A Forgotten civilization of the Persian Gulf." *Scientific American.* (203).

Goetze,A.

1952   "The Texts Ni 615 and Ni 641, Istanbul Museum", *J.C.S.* Appendix to Cornwall, 1952.

Golding,M.

1974   "Evidence for pre-Seleucid Occupation of Eastern Arabia *P.S.A.S.* (IV).

Habgood, Phillip J.

1982   "Report for the Australian Expedition to Bahrain, 1982 the excavation of the New city Mound field". (Unpublished). (Bahrain Historical Archaeological Society Bahrain.)

Haerinck,E.

1991   "Heading for the straits of Hormuz, an `Ubaid site in the Emirate of Ajman (UAE)". *A.A.E.* (2/2).

Haldar, Alfred

1971   *Who were the Amorites ?* Leiden.

Hallo, William W.

1959   "The last years of the kings of Isin". *J.N.E.S.* (18).

1965   "A Merchantile Agreement from the Region of Gungunum of Larsa". *In Studies in Honor of Bennolandsberger.* Chicago.

1968   *Essays in Memmory of E.A.Speiser.* (ed.) New Haven.

1977/1981"Introduction and Seal Inscriptions" in Briggs Buchanan, 1981.

Hallo, W.W. and W.K. Simpson

1981   *The Ancient Near East, A History* (eds.) Harcourt,N.Y.

Hamblin,Dora Jane

1987   "Has the Garden of Eden been located ?" *Smithsonion*   (May).

Haser.J.

1990   "Soft-Stone vessels of the 2nd millennium B.C." *P.S.A.S.* (20)

Hawkes, Jacquetta (ed.)

1974   *Atlas of Ancient Archaeology.* London.

Helms S.W.

1976   "Jawa Excavations 1974-Preliminary Report", *Levant*   (VIII).

1981   *Jawa - The Lost city of the Black Desert.* Methuen.

Herzfeld, Ernst,

1968   *The Persian Empire - Studies in Geography of the Ancient Near east* (edited
        from the post thumous papers of Gerald   Walser, Wiesbaden)

Hogarth, D.G.

1920   "Discussion of a Lecture by H. Philby." Geographical   Journal.

Hojlund, Flamming

1986   "The Chronology of City II and III at Qal'at al Bahrain". In *B.T.A.*

1989   "The Formation fo Dilmun state and the Amorite Tribes". *P.S.A.S.* (19).

Hojgaard, Karen.

1983   "Dilmun's Ancient Teeth". *Dilmun* (11).

1986   "Dental anthropological investigation on Bahrain", *B.T.A.*

Hooke,S.H.

1962   *Babylonian and Assyrian Religion.* Oxford.

Howard-Carter,Theresa

1972   "The John Hopkins University Reconnaissance Expedition to the Arab Iranian-
        Gulf", *B.A.S.O.R* (202).

1981   "The Tangible Evidence for the Earliest Dilmun".*J.C.S.*   (33).

1987   'Dilmun :"At Sea or Not at Sea ?", *J.C.S.* (39).

1989   "Voyages of votive vessels in the Gulf". In DUMU-EZ-DDB-BA-A - *Studies
        in Honour of AKe W.Sjoberg.* (eds) H.Behrens, D.Loding, MT.Roth. Philadelphia.

Ibrahim,M.

1982   *Excavations of the Arab Expedition at Sar-el-Jisr, Bahrain.* Bahrain.

Jacobsen,T.

1976   *The Treasures of Darkness*, Yale University press.

Jarman, Shirley.

1977   "Bahrain island: Human skeletal material from the first millennium B.C." *Bulletin
        of the Asia Institute.* (2/4).

Kajerum,Poul

1980   "Seals of "Dilmun-type" from Failaka, Kuwait". *P.S.A.S.* (X).

1983   *Failaka/Dilmun : Second millennium Settlements 1 : the stamp and cylinder
        seals.* Vol.I Jutland Archaeological Society.

1986a   "The Dilmun Seals as evidence of Long distance relations in the early second millennium B.C." *B.T.A.*

1986b   "Architectural and Settlement Pattern in 2nd Millennium Failaka". *P.S.A.S.* (16).

Kalpan, J

1969   "Ein el Jarba' - Chalcolithic Remains in the Plains of Esdradon". *B.A.S.O.R.*

Kapel, H.

1967   *Atlas of the Stone Age Cultures of Qatar.* Aarhus.

Kassler,P.

1973   "The structural and geomorphic evolution of the Persian Gulf", in Purser,B.H.(ed.),*The Persian Gulf.* Berlin.

Kessler,Karlheinz

1983   "ZU Den Keilschriftlichen Quellen Des 2./1.Jahrtausends V. Chr. Uber Dilmun". *BBVO.*

Kervran,Monik,Arette Negre,M.P.t'Sertsevens.

1982   *Excavations of Qal' at al Bahrain.* Bahrain.

Kervran, Monik, Peder Mortensen, Fredrik Hiebert

1987   "Occupational Enigma of Bahrain between the 13th and 8th century B.C.". *Paleorient.* Also in *Dilmun* (14) 1988.

Al Khalifa, Haya

1986   "The shell seals of Bahrain". *B.T.A.*

Al Khalifa,Haya, and M.Ibrahim,

1982   "The seals" in *Excavations of the Arab Expedition at Sar elJisr Bahrain,* 1982.

Killick,R.G., H.E.W. Crawford, K.Flavin, A.Ginger, A.Lupton, C.Maclaughlin, R.Montague, J.A.Moon and M.A.Woodburn.

1991   "London-Bahrain Archaeological Expedition:1990 excavations at Saar". *A.A.E.* (II/2).

Kirkbridge, Diana

1966   "Five Seasons at the pre-pottery Neolithic village of Beidha in Jordon". *P.E.Q.*

Kohl,Philip.L.

1975   "Carved Chlorite Vessels, a Trade in Finished Commodities in the Mid-Third Millennium B.C.", *Expedition,* 18(1).

1978   "The Balance of Trade in South Western Asia in the mid- third millennium B.C." *Current Authoropology* (19/3).

Komoroczy, Vong.

1977   "Tilmun Als" Speicher deslandes" Im Epos`Enki und Ninhur sag." *Iraq* (39).

Konishi,M.A.,Gotoh,T.,Akashi,Y.

1989   *Excavations in Bahrain And Qatar,1987/8,* Tokyo.

Kramer,Samuel Noah,

1944   "Dilmun, The land of the living", *B.A.S.O.R.* (96).

1944   "The Epic of Gilgames and its Sumerian Sources". *J.A.O.S.* (64).

1947   "Gilgamesh and the land of the living". *J.C.S.* (1/1).

1955   "Sumerian Myths and Epictales", in Pirtchard, 1955.

1960   Paper read at the 9th rencontre assyriologique internationale. Genava N.S.(8). (cited in Haldar, 1971).

1961   *Sumerian Mythology*. N.Y.

1963a   *The Sumerians*, Chicago.

1963b   "Dilmun-Quest for Paradise" *Antiquity* (37)

1964   "The Indus Civilization and Dilmun, the Sumerian Paradise Land", *Expedition*.

1977   "Commerce and Trade: Gleanings From Sumerian Literature", *Iraq*. (39).

1991   *History Begins at Sumer*. (Reprint)

Laesser,J.

1957   "A Cuneiform inscription from the Island of Bahrain". *Kuml*

Lamberg-Karlovsky, C.C.

1970   *Excavations at Tepe Yahya, Iran. Progress Report I*. American School of Prehistoric Research 27, Cambridge.

1972   "Trade Mechanisms in Indus-Mesopotamian Interrelations, *J.A.O.S.* (92).

1973   *Urban Interaction on the Iranian plateau: Excavations at Tepe Yahya, 1967-73*.

1975   "Third Millennium Modes of Exchange and mode of production" in *Ancient Civilization and Trade* (eds.) J.A.Sabloff and C.C.Lamberg Karlovsky. Albuquare.

1982   "Dilmun " Gateway to Immortality", : *JNES:* (41)

1986   "Death in Dilmun". *B.T.A.*

1988   "The `Intercultural Style' carved vessels". *Iranian Antiqua* (23).

Lamberg-Karlovsky C.C. and J.A.Sabloff,

1979   *Ancient Civilizations - The Near East and Mesoamerica*, California.

Lambert,M.

1953   "Textes Commerciaux de Lagash". *Rev. Assy.* (47).

1976   "Tablette de Suse Aveccachet du Golfe," :*Rev.Assy* (70).

Landsberger, Benno

1943/45 "Three Essay on the Sumerians". :*Monographs on the Ancient Near East*: (I/2).Los Angeles, 1974 (Reprint).

1965   "Amorites". *Encyclopaedia Britanica*.

Larsen.C.E.

1983a   "The early environment and hydrology of ancient Bahrain" *BBVO*.

1983b   *Life and Land use on the Bahrain Islands: the Geoarachaeology of an Ancient Society*. Chicago.

1986   "Variation in Holocene land use patterns on the Bahrain island: construction of a land use model" *B.T.A.*

Leemans,W.F.

1960   *Foreign Trade in the Old Babylonian Period*. Leiden.

1968   "Old Babylonian letters and Economic history: a review of article with a digration on foreign trade". *J.E.S.H.O.* (11).

Legrain,L.

1929   "Gem Cutters in Ancient Ur", *The Museum Journal*, (XX/34), Pennyselvania.

Littleton, J.and B.Frohlich

1989   "An Analysis of Dental Pathology and Diet of Historic Bahrain" *Paleorient.*

Llyod, Seton.

1978   *The Archaeology of Mesopotamia - from Old Stone Age to the Persian Conquest.* (London).

Lombard,Pierre

1982   "Iron Age Stone Vessels from Oman Peninsula. A prelimi nary note. *P.S.A.S.*

1986   "Iron Age Dilmun: A reconderation of city V at Qal'at al Bahrain", in *B.T.A.*

1989   "The Late Dilmun Period" in *B.N.M.*

Lombard, P. and J.F.Salles,

1984   La Ne'cropole De Janussan (Bahrain). Lyon.

1990   "Qal'at al Bahrain" *The Arabian Gulf Gazetteer* (I/1) ed. E.C.L. During-Caspers.

Lombard,P.etal

1993   "Preliminary Report on the New French Project at Qal'at al Bahrain", in *A.A.E.* (Forthcoming)

Mackay,Earnest.

1929   "Bahrain" in *Bahrain and Hamamieh*, Publication of the British School of Archaeology in Egypt Vol.47, London.

1932   "An Important Link between Ancient India and Elam", *Antiquity* (6).

Marielle, PIC

1990   "Quelques Elements De Glyptique". *Failaka, 1986-88* (eds)   Yes Calvet and J.Gachet.Lyon.

Mallowan,M.E.L.

1965   "The Mechanism of Ancient Trade in Western Asia- Reflection on the location of Magan and Meluhha". *Iran* (III).

Masry, Abdullah Hasan

1974   *Prehistory in North Eastern Arabia* : The Problem of Interregional Interaction. Miami, Florida.

Mc Clure, Harold A.

1971   *The Arabian Peninsula and Prehistoric Populations.* Miami.

McNicoll, A and Roaf, M.

1975   "Archaeological Investigations in Bahrain, 1973-1974". (Unpublished Manu- script). Bahrain Historical And Archaeological Society.

McCown,D.E. and R.C.Haines,

1967   *Nippur I. Temple of Enlil Scribal Quarter and Soundings.* Chicago.

Meigs,Peveril.

1966   *Geography of Coastal Deserts.* Belgium, Unesco.

Miroschedji,P.de

1973   'Vases et objects en steatite susiens du Musee du Louvre', Cahiers de La Delegation *Archeologie Francaise en Iran* (3).

Mitchell,T.C.

1986   "Indus and Gulf Type seals from Ur," *B.T.A.*

Moortagart, Anton

1969   The Art of Ancient Mesopotamia.(Trs. from German by Judit Filsom.) Phaidon.

Mortensen,Peder

1956   "The Temple Oval at Barbar", *Kuml.*

1970   "On the date of the Temple at Barbar in Bahrain". *Kuml.*

1986   "The Barbar Temple: its chronology and foreign relations reconsidered". *B.T.A.*

1987   The Occupational Enigma of Bahrain between the 13th and the 8th century B.C." *Plaeorient;* also in (13/1) also in *Dilmun* (14).

Morrey,P.R.S.

1980   *Cemeteries of the First Millennium B.C. at Dave Huyak near Carchemish.* B.A.R.

Mughal, Rafique

1983   *The Dilmun Burial Complex at Sar. The 1980-82 Excavations in Bahrain.* Manama.

Nayeem,Fouzia

1992   "Social Aspects of Anatomy-The Bones Speak", *Saudi Medical Journal,* (13).

Nayeem, Mohammed Abdul

1988   "Indo-Arabian Cultural Relations During Third Millennium B.C." *Ages* (Riyadh).

1990   *Prehistory and Protohistory of the Arabian Peninsula, Vol.1 Saudi Arabia.* Hyderabad.

Nelson,Harold H.

1944   "The Egyptian Temple". *The Biblical Archaeologist.* (8/3).

Nielson,V

1958   "Famed for its many pearls'. *Kuml.*

Nissen, Hans J.

1986   "The Occurence of Dilmun in the Oldest texts of Mesopotamia", *B.T.A.*

Nutzel,W.

1974   "The climatic changes of Mesopotamia and Bordering Areas 14,000-2000 B.C. *Sumer* (32).

Oates,David

1986   "Dilmun and the Late Assyrian Empire" *B.T.A.*

Oates, Joan

1976   "Prehistory in North Eastern Arabia". *Antiquity.* (50).

1978   "Ubaid Mesopotamia and its relation to Gulf countries. In De Cardi, 1978.

1979   *Babylon,* Thames and Hudson.

1986   "The Gulf in Prehistory", *B.T.A.*

Oppenheim,A.L.

1944   "The Mesopotamian Temple." *The Bibbical Archaeologist* (8/3).

1954   "The Seafaring merchants of Ur". *J.A.O.S.* (74).

1974   *Ancient Mesopotamia* - Portrait of a Dead civilization, Chicago.

Peake,H.

1928   "The Copper Mountain of Magan". *Antiquity* (2).

Pettinato, Giovanni

1981   *The Archives of Ebla*, New York.

1983   "Dilmun nella documentazione epigrafica di Ebla",   *B.B.V.O.*

Petocz,D., and S. Hart

1981   "Report of the Australian Team working for the Bahrain Department of Antiquites, 1979-80." (Unpublished. Bahrain Historical and Archaeological Society).

Piesinger,C.Maria

1983   "Legacy of Dilmun: The Roots of Ancient Maritime Trade in Eastern coastal Arabia in the 4th 3rd Millennium B.C." (Microfilm University of Wisconsin, Madison, Michigan).   (Unpublished Ph.D.Thesis).

Piggot, Stuart

1962   *Prehistoric Societies.*

Poebel, A.

1942   "Amorites". *J.N.E.S.* (1).

Poebel, A.

1942   "The Assyrian King List from Khorsabad" *J.N.E.S.* (I/3).

Porada,Edith

1970   "Report on Seven seals from Hajar (1) Excavations", (Unpublished Manuscript). Bahrain Historical and Archaeological Society.

1971   "Introductory Remarks"-to the new Discoveries in the Persian/Arabian Gulf States and Relations with Artifacts from countries of the Ancient near East".*A.A.* (31/4).

1980 "Introduction" To Ancient Art in *Seals* (ed.) E.Paroda Princeton.

Postgate,Nicholas.N.

1972   "The role of the Temple in the Mesopotamian secular   community". In (eds) P.J.Ucko,R.Tringham & G.W.Dimleby. *Man, settlement and Urbanism.*

Potts,D.T.

1978   "Towards an Integrated History of Culture Change in the Arabian Gulf area : Notes on Dilmun, Makkan, and the Economy of Ancient Sumer". *JOS* (4).

1983a   "Dilmun:Where and When ?". *Dilmun* (11).

1983b   *Dilmun. New studies in the Archaeology and Early History of Bahrain.*

1983c   "Barbar Miscellanies". *B.B.V.O.*

1986a   "Dilmun's further relations: The syro-Anatolian evidence from the third and second millennia B.C." *B.T.A.*

1990   *The Arabian Gulf in Antiquity*. I. Oxford.

Potts, T.F.

1989   "Foreign Stone vessels of the Late Third Millennium B.C. From Southern Mesopotamia: Their Origin and Mechanics of Exchange". *Iraq.* (41).

Powell,M.A.

1983   "The standard of Dilmun". *B.B.V.O.*

Powers,R.W., R.M.Ramirez,C.D.Redmond, and E.L.Elberg.

1966   Geology of the Arabian Peninsula-Sedimentary Geology of Saudi Arabia. Washington,D.C.

Prideaux, Capt.

1912   "The Sepulchral Tumuli of Bahrain", Archaeological Survey of India, Annual Report 1908-1909. *D.D.*

Pritchard,James.B.

1955   *Ancient Near Eastern Texts.* Princeton.

Raikes,R.

1967   "Field Archaeology in Saudi Arabia". *E.W.*(17).

Rao,Nagarja,M.S.

1969   "A Bronze Mirror from the Barbar Temple, Bahrain-A fur ther link with the Kuli culture - South Baluchistan," *KUML.*

Rao,S.R.

1963   "A Persian Gulf" seal from Lothal." *Antiquity* (37).

1973   *Lothal and the Indus civilization.* Bombay.

1979   "Contact Between Lothal and Susa". *Ancient Cities of the Indus* (ed. G.L.Possels).

1986   "Trade and Cultural contact between Bahrain and India in the third and second millennia B.C." *B.T.A.*

Rashid, S.A.

1970   "Eine Fruhdynastische Statue Von der Insel Torut im Persian Golf', Gesellschaft im *Alten Zweistromland and in den angrenzenden Bebieten.* XVIII. *Rencontre assyriologique internationale* Munchen, 1970.

Ratnagar,Shereen.

1981   *Encounters - The Westerly Trade of the Harappan Civilization.* Delhi.

Rawlinson, Henry C.

1980   "Notes on Capt. Durand's Report Upon the Island of Bahrain", *JRAS* (XII). *D.D.*

Reade,Julian.

1986   "Commerce or Conquest : Variation in the Mesopotamian Dilmun Relationship". *B.T.A.*

Reade,J.E. and Burleigh,R.

1978   "The `Ali Cemetery : Old Excavations, Ivory, and Radio carbon Dating". *JOS.*

Reiner,Erica,

1974   "A Sumero-Akkadian Hymn of Nana". *JNES* (33/2).

Rice,Michael

1972   "The Grave complex at Al-Hajjar Bahrain". *PSAS* (2).

1983a   *Dilmun Discovered.* The Early Years of Archaeology in Bahrain Longman, (ed.).

1983b   *The Temple Complex at Barbar Bahrain* (ed.). Bahrain.

1985   *Search for the Paradise land - An Introduction to the Archaeology of Bahrain and the Arabian Gulf.* Longmans.

1986   'The Island on the Edge of the world. *B.T.A.*

1988   "Al Hajjar Revisited: The Grave complex at al Hajjar, Bahrain", (Revised) *P.S.A.S.*

Roaf,Michael

1974   "Excavations at al-Markh, Bahrain : a fish midden of the fourth millennium BC." *Paleorient* (2)

1976a   "Excavations at Al Markh, Bahrain", *PSAS*.

1976b   "The work of the British Archaeological Mission to Bahrain, 1976".(Unpublished.Ms, Bahrain Historical and Archaeological Society.)

1982   "Weights on the Dilmun Standard". *Iraq* (44).

Sagg,H.W.F.

1962   *The Greatness that was Babylon*, London.

1967   *Every Day Life in Babylonia and Assyria*, London.

1984   *The Might that was Assyria*, London.

Salles, J.F.,(ed)

1984   *Failaka. Fouilles Francaises 1983*. Paris.

Salles, Jean-Francois,

1990   "Funerary customs and Social Organization - A Tentative Interpretation of the Bahrain Evidence. (Unpublished). Paper read at Seminar at Lyon.

Sanlaville, Paul and Roland Paskoff

1986   "Shorelines changes in Bahrain since the beginning of Human occupation." in *B.T.A.*

Savill, Sheila

1976   Pears Encylopaedia of Myth and Legends The Ancient Near and Middle East. London.

Shaikha Haya al Khalifa,

1986   "The shell Seals of Bahrain", *B.T.A.*

Shankalia,H.D.

1974   *Prehistory and Protohistory of India and Pakistan*, Poona, Deccan College.

Shirley, Jarman

1977   "Bahrain Island:Human skeleton meterial from first Millennium B.C. *Bulletin of the Asia Institute* (2/4)

Stieglitz,R.R.

1987   "Ebla and Dilmun, in *Eblaitica:Essay on the Ebla Archives and Eblaite Language* (I)ed. C.H.Gordon etal. Indiana, 1987.

Smith, G.H.

1978   "The Stone Industries of Qatar". In De Cardi, 1978.

Smith, Sidney

1928   *Early History of Assyria*. London.

Solecki, Rose, L.

1985   "A Note on the Dating of Choppers, chopping Tools, and Related Flake Tool Industries From Southwest Asia", *Paleorient* (XI/1).

Speece,M.

1984   "The Role of Eastern Arabia in the Gulf Trade of the Third Second Millennia" In Dr. Abdul Rehman al Ansary (Chief Editor): *Studies in the History of Arabia; Pre- Islamic Arabia* (II). Riyadh.

Srivastava, K.M.

1991   *Madinat Hamad - Burial Mounds 1984-85.* Bahrain National Museum.

al-Tarawaeh,Fayes

1970   "Preliminary Report on Shakhoura Excavation - Bharain. (1969)-Unpublished Report. (Bahrain Historical and Archaeological Society Bahrain).

1971   "A Report on Al-Hajjar Excavations-Mound No.1". (1970). Unpublished Report. (Bahrain Historical and Archaeological Society. Bahrain).

Thapar, Romila.

1975   "A Possible Identification of Meluhha, Dilmun, and Makan." *J.E.S.H.O.* (18).

Thorvildsen,K.

1962   "Burial Cairns on Umm an-Nar". *Kuml.*

al-Tikriti,A.K.

1972   New Archaeological finds in Bharain". *Gulf Weekly Mirror* (9/7/1972).

1975   "The Diraz Excavation and its Chronological position," *Dilmun* (8).

Al-Tikriti, Walid Yasin

1989   "Umm An-Nar Culture in Northern Emirates: Third Millennium Tombs at Ajman" *Arch. U.A.E.* (IV).

Tosi,M.

1974   "Some data for the study of prehistorical cultural areas of the Persian Gulf", *P.S.A.S.*

1976   "The dating of the Umm an-Nar culture and a proposed sequence for Oman in the third millennium BC." *J.O.S.* (II).

1986   "The Emerging pictures of prehistoric Arabia", *Ann.Rev.Anth.,* 15(1) (Ms). 73

Vallat, Francois.

1983   "Le Dieu Enzak: Une Divinite Dilmunite Veneree A Suse". *B.B.V.O.*

Vita-Finzi,C.

1978   "Environmental History". In De Cardi 1978.

Waddell, L.A.

1976   *The Indo-Sumerian Seals Deciphered Delhi.* (Reprint of 1925 ed.)

Weisgerber,Gerd.

1978   "Evidence of ancient mining sites in Oman : a preliminary report." *P.S.A.S.*

1984/85 "Dilmun-A Trading Entrepot:Evidence from Historical and Archaeological sources". *Dilmun* (12).

Wheeler,Mortimer.

1958   "Comment". On seals from Bahrain (Bibby, 1958).

1959   Early India and Pakistan, Civilizations of the Indus Valley and Beyond (London).

Whitehouse,Ruth.

1977   *The First Cities,* Phaidon.

Willis,R.P.

1967   *Geology of the Arabian Peninsula : Bahrain*, U.S.Geological Survey Professional Paper 560-E.Washington,D.C.

Woolley, Leonard,

1982   *Ur'of the Chaldees'* Revised by P.R.S. Moorey.   The Herbert press.

Woolley, Leonard, and Max Mallawon,

1976   Ur Excavations (VIII) The Old Babylonian Period British   Museum.

Wright,G.E.W.

1944   "The significance of the Temple in the Ancient near   East". *The Biblical Archaeologist*. (8/3).

Wright,R.P and Johnsa,

1975   "Population, Exchange and Early State Formation in South Western Iran". *American* Anthropology. (77).

1989   "New perspective on the Third Millennium painted Grey Ware". *S.A.A.* 1985 (ed. Karen Friefelt and P.Sorensen)".

Wymer,John

1982   *The Palaeolithic Age*, London.

Zaccagnini,Carlo

1986   "The Dilmun standard and its relationship with Indus and Near Eastern weight systems". *Iraq* (48).

Zarins,Juris.

1978   "Steatite vessels in the Riyadh Museum". *Atlal*. (2)

1986a   "Mar-Tu And the Land of Dilmun". *B.T.A.*

1986b   Archaeological and Chronological problems within the greater southwest Asian arid Zone : 13000-1850 BC.   (*Chronologies in Old World Archaeology*, ed.R.W.Ehrich).   Chicago. (3rd ed.)

Zarins,J. and H. al Badr,

1986c   "Recent Archaeological Investigations in the Southern Tihama Plain (The Sites of Athar and Sihi, 1405/1985)". *Atlal*. (10).

Zarins, Juris, S.Mughannum and Mahmoud Kamal

1984   "Excavations at Dhahran South-The Tumuli Field",   *Atlal*.(8).

1989   "Eastern Arabia and External Relations:selected ceramic, steatite and textual evidence-3500-1900 BC". *S.A.A.* 1985   (eds.Karen Frifelt and Per Sorensen).

INDEX